A MANUAL

OF

BIBLICAL LITERATURE.

By W. P. STRICKLAND, D. D.

New York:
PUBLISHED BY CARLTON & PORTER,
200 MULBERRY-STREET.

PREFACE.

To say that the work, which is here presented, is a compilation, would be superfluous; as that will be perfectly obvious to every Biblical student, who may consult its pages. All that the author claims as original, with few exceptions, is the selection and arrangement of what he conceives to be the proper subjects belonging to the study of Biblical Literature.

In a more extensive sense, instructions in regard to the study of Church History and government, dogmatic, homiletic, and pastoral theology, might be included; but the introduction of these subjects would not, in the opinion of the compiler, be such a classification as specifically belongs to the department of Biblical Literature.

Under the head of *Theological* Literature, every subject may be embraced, which, in any way, pertains to religion—historical, theoretical, experimental, and practical; but such subjects do not, appropriately, belong to the present work. The Manual is simply designed as a guide, or hand-book, whose province it is to direct attention to the vast fields of Sacred Literature, and furnish directions, by the aid of which, the treasures therein contained may be discovered and garnered up.

The following works have been used, to a greater or less extent, in the compilation; and to them the author acknowledges himself chiefly indebted, viz.:—Ernesti, Jahn, Francké, Michaelis, Winer, Gerard, Gesenius, Marsh, Horne, Kitto, Calmet, Stuart, Lardner, Bloomfield, Robinson, Carpenter, and Gaussen. The works of modern Oriental travellers, such as Layard, Lynch, Olin, Durbin, Robinson and others, have been consulted.

In the preparation of the following work, the single aim of the author has been, to furnish an elementary treatise on those topics of Biblical Literature, a knowledge of which would enable the student to investigate the Sacred Oracles, in a thorough and systematic manner.

It will be seen that the work embraces a wide range of topics. The author has availed himself of the labours of those Biblical scholars, whose works possess the greatest merit, in the different departments of Sacred Literature embraced in this volume; and his compilation is made from their writings. In the arrangement of the topics, the order hinted at by Bishop Marsh, in his course of lectures on theology, and also by Gesenius, in his History of Introductions, has been, in a great measure, adopted.

Nothing has been omitted which the author conceived to belong to a Manual of Biblical Literature. By this he means that nothing essential has been left out so far as the outlines and general principles are concerned. In some respects he might have entered more fully into the minutiæ of the subjects treated: for example, in the part which treats of Archæology, which, according to the definition of some, embraces almost if not quite everything pertaining to the Bible, he has only made those selections which he considered most important.

The same remark will apply in a more limited sense to Biblical Analysis, History, and Geography. This would be impossible in a Manual, as each subject of itself would fill a volume.

A part might have been added entitled Biblical Biography, and such was in accordance with the author's original design; but it would have swelled the work beyond the prescribed limits, and hence it was abandoned. Such a work by itself is a desideratum, inasmuch as that completeness which is desirable in this department is not to be found in the Biblical Cyclopædias and Dictionaries which have been published.

To all who are interested in the systematic study of the Bible, it is hoped this volume may prove some help.

W. P. STRICKLAND.

CINCINNATI, MAY 1, 1853.

CONTENTS.

PART FIFTH.

PART SIXTH.

PART SEVENTH.

PART EIGHTH.

PART NINTH.

INTRODUCTION.

Such a production as this has long been a desideratum in Biblical Literature. It is true, there are many works of great merit which treat separately of the topics embraced in this volume; but they are mostly out of print, or inaccessible to the class of persons for whom this work is specially designed. Besides, these volumes are principally adapted for text-books for theological seminaries and professional theologians. Take, as specimens, the writings of Jahn, Michaelis, Eichhorn, Gesenius, Francké, Ernesti, Morus, Gaussen, Winer, Gerard, Marsh, Carpenter, Kitto, Horne, Stuart, and Robinson. Although the writings of these great authors are of untold value to the critical Biblical student, there are few who walk in the every-day path of Christian research, who have time, taste, or preliminary preparation, to read or study them with care.

A work was, therefore, needed, for private students, and literary men in general—the design of which would be to present, in one regularly-arranged view, the leading principles of all those topics which are necessary to the proper and systematic study of the Bible.

The present volume is of such a character. The author has drawn his materials from the very best sources, on the different subjects of which he treats. On inspecting the table of contents, it will be seen, that after showing the importance of the study of the Bible, the author brings to view the leading topics of Biblical Literature—such as Biblical Philology, Criticism, Interpretation, Analysis, Archæology, History, Ethnography, Geography, and Chronology.

Of course, in embracing so vast a field of Biblical research, the work must be elementary. It is, however, sufficiently copious to give a full and clear knowledge of the essential principles embraced in the various topics connected with the study of the Bible.

It is particularly adapted to all under-graduates in the ministry, and private theological students, as well as to the advanced classes in Sunday Schools, and to High Schools, Seminaries, and Colleges.

By its aid the Bible can be made the text-book, and a thorough and systematic course of study pursued in its contents. That the Bible should be a text-book in schools and colleges is now granted; but, heretofore, no systematic course of study has been struck out. This can now be done to great advantage, by the aid of Dr. Strickland's performance.

It is divided into nine parts, and each part is again subdivided into chapters, with appropriate headings, so that the student can readily find, in every department of Biblical Literature, whatever is necessary to throw light on the study of the Bible. It is a library in itself, in which the student will find the substance of what is contained in numerous large and costly works; and so arranged and divested of all unnecessary technical stiffness, as to prove a convenient thesaurus of the greatest value to all who love to search the Scriptures.

And to all the aspirants to the ministry in the Methodist Episcopal Church, how important will this volume be! It will be a great benefit to the Church to ask all the applicants for license to preach, to master this work, as a preliminary, as well as some other topics; so that when the ministry is entered on, young and inexperienced minds may not be harassed with the double task of the preparatory and the necessary principal course, at the same time. The opportunities of the times enable all, or the greater number, to obtain elementary knowledge, to some degree, whether Biblical, theological, or literary, before they enter upon the arduous work of even the first stages of the pastoral office. And, indeed, the wants of the Church demand this, and the demand must be met.

I have read the work in manuscript, and can readily recommend it to all for whom it is designed. Indeed, it is the only book extant which treats systematically of the elements of Biblical Literature, in a manner adapted for popular use.

The subjects are treated in a clear, pleasing, and forcible manner, so as to satisfy a correct taste, and to elucidate the points discussed. I hope the volume will have a wide circulation, and will therefore be eminently useful to the youth in our country, and all who engage in the study of Holy Scripture, so as to have a clear, full, and accurate knowledge of their religion.

CHARLES ELLIOTT.

CINCINNATI, O., April 12, 1852.

MANUAL

OF

BIBLICAL LITERATURE.

Preliminary Chapter.

THE IMPORTANCE OF BIBLICAL STUDIES.

ASSUMING the *authenticity* and *genuineness* of the Bible, together with its *plenary inspiration*, it is not deemed important to treat upon these subjects separately, but as they may fall within the line of observation in the discussion of the various topics embraced in this work. The discussion of these points belongs more particularly to other departments of sacred literature than those contemplated. As "all Scripture is given by inspiration of God,"—the writers of the Bible being the mere *amanuenses* of the Holy Spirit, communicating nothing more and nothing less than what was dictated,—and as every word and sentence was thus from God, it is essentially important that every man should understand their meaning.

To do this satisfactorily we must go directly to the sacred text. The practice of studying the Holy Oracles through the *media* of human expositions alone, and of obtaining a system of belief from the Writings of the Fathers, the Decrees of Councils, Synodical Conventions, Confessions of Faith, Articles of Religion, Systems of Theology, Commentaries, Compends, Digests, &c., instead of obtaining it from the great standard of faith itself, is a pernicious and prevalent evil.

The Bible is adapted to every grade of intellect, and hence all are commanded to search its pages, being assured that it will ever prove an unerring guide in all matters of faith and practice. While the profoundest mind is lost in the exploration of its boundless and fathomless ocean of truth, the most superficial can comprehend its ever luminous revelations of mercy and salvation, and a child may grow wise unto eternal life in reading its contents. In this respect it is like its emblem, the sun, whose rays are equally adapted to the eye of the *animalcula* and the mastodon. He who made the eye and the light understood perfectly the nature of both, and also what was necessary to constitute an adaptation. He who made the human mind and the Bible—for both are traceable to the same divine origin—had a like regard. If there be in divine revelation anything hard or impossible of comprehension, it is not more remarkable than that the naked eye cannot gaze upon the meridian sun, or that, in all the departments of nature and science, there are mysteries impenetrable to human vision.

We would call away the mind from all human productions, in matters of belief and duty, and bring it into immediate contact with the mind of God; and in regard to all that is difficult to understand, would recommend the sincere and humble inquirer, in his "lack of wisdom," to ask the assistance of "the Father of lights, from whom cometh down every good and perfect gift." The student, though, in the language of one, "he be the most learned, acute, and diligent, cannot, in the longest lifetime, obtain an *entire* knowledge of the Bible, because the more deeply he works the mine of sacred truth, the richer and more abundant he will find the ore." The contents of every other book may be exhausted, because they are the product of finite intellect—the contents of the Bible never. In reading a human production, mind is brought in contact with similar mind—the finite with the finite—and the one may thoroughly exhaust the other; but, in reading the Scriptures, the mind is brought into contact with God—the finite with the infinite—and hence there will be an interminable progression in Biblical knowledge. To assist in the profitable investigation of this inexhaustible storehouse of thought, the following suggestions are presented to the reader.

In the study of any science order is important, and it is none the less so in the study of sacred science. Though the contents of the Bible are not reduced to what might be denominated a scientific method, and the arrangement and classification observable in human scientific productions, still they are susceptible of such a classification in regard to all the facts and doctrines therein embraced. In this respect the Bible is like the vast field of nature spread out before us by the same Divine Author. Over all this field nowhere can be found a botanic garden of spontaneous production containing the genus and species of every tree, shrub, plant, and flower. To obtain such a classification the botanist must traverse every zone, visit every island, and gather his specimens here and there, to complete his classification. The same remark will apply to the mineral as to the vegetable world. No cabinet of minerals and fossils has ever yet been found in the earth's crust. To collect such a cabinet the geologist must travel over its mountains and through its dells—he must perforate its rocks and examine their formation—classify their fossiliferous products and analyze the ores imbedded therein. Thus it is also in the animal world. No zoological collection has ever been found instinctively or fortuitously thrown together. To find the various orders of each, the different parts of the world must be visited. All the *materials* for the above classifications have been furnished by the Creator; but it is the work of man to arrange, combine, and classify them. The same remark will apply to every science. We have first the nucleus, and then the aggregation. Facts, naked and isolated, have been gathered up here and there; their affinities have been ascertained—their bearing and relations noted; from these facts principles have been deduced, and upon these principles theories and systems have been established.

The Bible is a book of facts, which, like thė varieties we meet with in the various departments of the physical world, are more or less important, and invite our investigation. In the Bible there may be some statements which are beyond the grasp of our reason—challenging our faith alone—but there are none inconsistent with her loftiest exercise. In the language of Coleridge, with propriety it may be said, "If there be anything in all the system of revealed religion inconsistent with reason, it does not belong to the household of faith."

These facts are dispersed through sixty-six different books, written by more than forty different persons, in different ages and different parts of the world—in the deserts of Arabia, in the temple at Jerusalem, in the sumptuous palaces of Babylon, on the banks of the Euphrates and Jordan, and on the borders of the Mediterranean. A period of nearly two thousand years was occupied in its composition. Its writers were in every condition of life—kings, doctors, lawyers, vine-dressers, shepherds, and fishermen. They were of every grade of intellect and education, from the most astute and learned to the most humble and illiterate. The writer of its first five books was engaged with the pen of inspiration in chronicling the world's history ten centuries in advance of Herodotus, who is styled the father of profane history; while the topics he discusses embrace all the important facts and events of the first two thousand years of the world's history, never before chronicled by man. The truthfulness of the sacred record, in regard to the creation of the world and man, his fall and subsequent depravity, the successive judgments of Heaven upon guilty nations and cities, together with the whole scheme of human redemption, is stamped upon and attested by the physical and moral world. Its sublime and awful events are written out upon the surface of the earth, and graven deep in the everlasting rocks, as the mark of God on the brow of Cain, and echo back the faithfulness of its narratives. Its prophetic announcements, made thousands of years antecedently, have met with a literal and exact fulfilment, and now form a prominent part of the history of the world. Time, their grand expounder, has demonstrated their truth, and is vindicating it from day to day; while science, in her discoveries, has shown the writers of the sacred books gifted with an inspiration divine and infallible. Its monuments, and testimonial signs and wonders, are found to be, everywhere and in every age, accordant with the descriptions of its writers, and commemorative of its truths.

The Bible embraces every style of composition—the simple, beautiful and sublime. It contains history, chronology, geography, biography, archæology, epistles, homilies, parables, metaphors, allegories, apothegms, proverbs, dramas, dissertations, and poetry of every species—pastoral, lyrical, elegiac, and epic. Its topics are innumerable—whole libraries have been written upon its exhaustless themes. It has been the subject of criticism, verbal and written, for a period of three thousand years. It has been in every laboratory of mind, and tested in every crucible of experiment, and, having been subjected to the most thorough and searching analysis, not one of all the truths in its vast storehouse has been invalidated. In all the investigations of science, not one single physical, mental, or moral error, has been discovered. Like pure gold, the assertions of the Bible have stood every test, unimpeached and untarnished. These truths, scattered like gems and flowers over the mountains, plains and valleys of the Bible, are all consistent with every other truth, and harmonious throughout, having "God for their author, and salvation for their end."

The *facts* of the Bible are susceptible of classification, and it is the duty of the student of sacred literature to reduce them to order. Every Biblical student should collate and classify them for himself, with as much care and assiduity as though no one had gone over the field before him. The researches of another will not answer the purpose, as this work can with no more propriety be done by proxy than that of the linguist or mathematician. In studying the Bible it is of the utmost importance that attention be paid to order; otherwise much that is valuable will be lost, while that which is gained will be comparatively unsatisfactory.

The Bible should be studied under two aspects—the first has regard to the *letter*, and the second to the *spirit*—the body and the soul of the most magnificent creation of Almighty God. We should come to the study of the first as we would to the study of any other book claiming our attention, applying all those rules which govern us in literary research and criticism.

Having satisfied ourselves in regard to the external structure of the temple, and passed its outer gates, we are then prepared, under the guidance of its presiding genius—the Holy Spirit—to enter its inner courts, and gaze with unveiled eyes upon its beautiful proportions, gorgeous drapery, sublime scenery, awful mysteries, and transcendent glories, as they break upon the astonished vision, like the mysterious characters in the palace of Babylon, or the awful glory in the consecrated temple of Jerusalem.

Numerous Introductions to the study of the Bible, embracing almost every department of sacred literature, have been written, and, as the present work does not profess properly to belong to that class, a short history of these Introductions may not be out of place.

It is the province of an Introduction *critically* to examine and discuss the *historical* relations of the individual books, as well as of the whole collection. It gives, on the particular books, discussions respecting their authors, and times of composition, genuineness and integrity, contents and plan, the original language, its earliest history, the origin of the Bible collection or canon, its original language and versions, and the history of the original text. It divides itself into two parts, general and particular.

"It has been correctly observed," says Gesenius, in his Biblische Einleitung, "that this branch of learning still requires to be more accurately defined and limited—that, in particular, it often encroaches on the province of criticism and hermeneutics; and certainly the latest authors are still too discursive, especially in taking up their materials for the general introduction, and in fact the older writers (and the modern among the English) have even brought together those branches of learning which are subsidiary to interpretation, as sacred history, antiquities, geography, &c. It will not, therefore, be inconsistent with my present purpose," he adds, "to attempt, at least, to mark out this limitation, and in doing so I shall principally keep in view the general introduction, because the boundaries of the particular are more accurately settled. The leading features are the same, both with respect to the Old and New Testaments, and it may even, in many particular points, be of use to treat the general part of both in connexion. Of this I would suggest the following fourfold division:—

"1. History of the cultivation and literature of the Hebrew people in general; under which section might be digested the accounts of their language, Hebrew, Chaldee, and Hellenistic, with the history and character of each, and also of their writing.

"2. History of the canon; or of the collection, arrangement, and ecclesiastical authority of the books.

"3. History of the original text; the various fates and changes to which it has been subjected, and of the means of improving it—the latter of which belongs more particularly to the department of criticism. Here the authors of introductory works appear to have been principally in doubt respecting the extent of the points which they ought to discuss. The following principle will probably be found to mark a correct and proper division:—The criticism of the Old and

New Testaments divides itself into two parts, historical and didactic. The first of these pursues the history of the text, discovers its changes, shows the critical labours which have been expended on it, and the documents in which the text has been handed down, namely, *immediate*, as manuscripts, and *mediate*, as ancient revisions. The second communicates the rules according to which the critic must avail himself of these helps in order to recover the original text with as much probability as possible. The *historical* part of this must now necessarily be comprehended under the learning which is comprised in an introduction; but the *didactic*, which contains merely an application of the general rules of criticism to the materials here sketched out, must, by a strict limitation, be properly excluded, and preserved for criticism, as it is a science of a particular kind, or, at least, to be handled with great brevity.

"4. In the *hermeneutical* part of the general introduction; which is required to exhibit the aids for understanding the Bible, and directions for the use of those aids, and which many authors of introductory works, as Eichhorn and Bertholdt, entirely, or in part, omit. Jahn has, however, given them with considerable extent, including also the didactic part, at least as far as regards the investigation of language. To preserve consistency the last must be reserved for hermeneutics, in such a way that the author should limit himself to the historical part, which belongs to it no less than the historical part does to criticism. The helps for understanding it relate to language and things, and of course hermeneutics divides itself into an investigation of these two. For investigating the language, which is here the principal point, we have, as sources of information, the following: *First*, the interpretations of the books of Scripture which have been handed down to us from antiquity—that is, ancient versions and expositions of the Old Testament by Rabbins, and of the New by the Fathers, which it is necessary to adduce and judge of. *Second*, our knowledge arising from other sources of the eastern languages and of the Greek as existing in profane authors, which must be applied to the thorough examination, correction, and establishment of those transmitted interpretations. The investigation of things is exhibited in that branch of knowledge which is called exegetical helps. This divides itself into *historical* which includes Biblical geography, Biblical history, with chronology, and mythology; and also into *dogmatic*, which includes Biblical doctrines and morals. It is impossible, in an introduction, to treat these subjects fully; nothing more can be given than a general idea of them. In this arrangement, however, doubts may arise with respect to the ancient versions, since they must be introduced as subsidiary to criticism, as well as to hermeneutics. Hence it is probably the most advisable course to give the general information respecting them in the critical part, and their character, as far as regards interpretation, in that which is appropriated to hermeneutics. It must be remarked that the very last consideration is the identical point which is much neglected in recent works of this kind; and this is the more to be regretted as the hermeneutical value of the versions is, on the whole, much greater than the critical, since their greater or less variations from the text do but very rarely indeed contain improvements of it, but, on the contrary, are, for the most part, founded on errors in the translations. In the particular introduction to the individual books only this difference is to be observed in the plan, that some writers in this department, as Jahn, give an explanatory view of the contents of the books, which is omitted by most of the others. Besides introductions of an historical and critical character, and which are, properly speaking, *literary*, the idea of a *practical* introduction has been suggested and carried into effect—that is to say, an introduction which, setting aside discussions of a critical kind, or taking for granted the results of them, confines its attention to the books of Scripture in a practical point of view, and gives directions for the use of them in reference to the religious instruction of youth and people in general. Such works are useful when the authors, resting on the firm basis of solid learning, make the religious and moral force in the particular books, sections, and characters of the Bible stand out prominent; they will then often agree, in contents, with the view of religion and morals given in the Bible, and only vary from it in the free arrangement in which it is presented.

"The first important steps for a thorough, learned, and critical treatment of what is called the general introduction, were made in the path opened by Hottinger, a man well versed in oriental learning, and Leusden, a pupil of Buxtorf; also by Walton and Simon, the former of whom, viz. Walton, published, in his Prolegomena to the London Polyglot, very learned disquisitions on the language and writings of the Bible, the history of the text, and of the versions of the Old and New Testaments."

Part First.

BIBLICAL PHILOLOGY.

CHAPTER I.

LANGUAGES OF THE BIBLE.

BIBLICAL philology relates to the languages in which the Bible was originally written. These are the Hebrew and Chaldee of the Old Testament, and the Greek of the New. The importance of a knowledge of the original languages of the Scriptures to the critical expounder thereof cannot, with any show of consistency, be called in question at the present day. Without such a knowledge he cannot be fully qualified for his work, as one "that is approved unto God, and that needeth not to be ashamed, rightly dividing the word of truth." It is apparent to all who are acquainted with the languages that no translation, however accurate, can give a full and fair exhibition of its original. The *style* of a writer never can be translated; and as it is often the case that much depends upon the style, and as no translation ever can reach it, much is lost. The version may be better, both as to the matter and style; but it is not, and never can be, an exact representation of the original. In a translation we cannot be made fully acquainted with the original author. We can know but little of the mind of Homer by the translations of Cowper and Pope. We learn what the latter were as poets; but we are ignorant, to a great degree, of the father of profane poetry. The facts of the Iliad and Odyssey are given, but their author does not narrate them. No one can claim to be a classical scholar, though he may have devoted a lifetime to the study of translations. To attain such distinction he must read the classics of Greece and Rome, and not the translations of England or Germany. To qualify any man to speak or write critically of the merits of an author, it is conceded by all to be necessary that he have a knowledge of what the author has himself written. A version ought to be, as far as possible, an exact image of the original archetype, in which image nothing should be drawn, either greater or less, better or worse, than the original, but so composed that it might be acknowledged as another original itself. A translator should use those words, and those words only, which clearly express *all the meaning of the author*, and *in the same manner as the author*. Where the translation, however, cannot be made *ad verbum* it must be made *ad sensum*.

The English Bible corresponds to the original with sufficient exactness to impart all that is essential to salvation, and as such is "profitable for doctrine, reproof, instruction, and correction," being "able to make wise unto salvation, through faith in our Lord Jesus Christ." A man may therefore be a faithful minister of the gospel, who is qualified by "gifts, grace, and usefulness," to set forth its doctrines and to enforce its precepts, even though his knowledge of the Scriptures be confined to the English version. This, however, does not justify any who have the opportunity to acquire the original languages of Scripture for neglecting to do so.

The Old Testament having been written in the Hebrew language, with the exception of a very small portion, which was written in the Chaldee, the attention of the student should first be directed to its study. In a classical course it is usual to study the Greek language first, and then proceed to those which are more ancient. There may be good and sufficient reasons for the adoption of such method in regard to those who have an opportunity of taking a college course; but to those who have never enjoyed the advantages of a classical education, there can be no reason why they may not at once commence the study of the Hebrew. It certainly has the advantage of being the more simple and easy language.

CHAPTER II.

THE HEBREW LANGUAGE.

THE *Hebrew* is generally regarded as the most ancient of all the oriental languages. Upwards of two thousand years before Christ it was a written language, and vernacular to the inhabitants of Babylonia, Mesopotamia, Assyria, Arabia, and Ethiopia. It reached its greatest perfection in the days of David, and from that period began to decline, until the Babylonish captivity, when it became merged into the Chaldee, Syriac, Talmudic and Rabbinic dialects, and finally was lost to the literary world. After it ceased to be a living language no efforts were made to interpret the few remaining manuscripts, which scarcely comprehended two-thirds of the Hebrew language, until two hundred years after Christ. From that time to the present it has been the theme of almost endless criticism, in regard to its origin, the number and form of its letters, structure, orthoëpy, and meaning.

CHAPTER III.

THE ARAMEAN OR SYRIAN LANGUAGE.

THE Aramean or Syrian language appears from the earliest times to have been divided into two grand branches, namely, the West Aramean, or Syriac, which was the dialect spoken to the west, in Syria and Mesopotamia; and the East Aramean, generally denominated the Chaldee, which was spoken to the east, in Babylonia, Assyria, and Chaldea. There is no difference, however, between them. Michaelis has remarked that the Chaldee of Daniel becomes Syriac if read by a German or Polish Jew. One is distinguished from the other by the characters in which they are written. Down to the time of Abraham, Chaldee was identical with the Hebrew. That this was the dialect of Abraham is evident from the fact that he was a Chaldean. Isaac and his family spoke Hebrew, which was the language of Canaan; and Hebrew continued to be the language of their descendants till the time of the Babylonian captivity. During the seventy years' captivity these dialects were more or less merged. On the return of the Jews to Jerusalem the priests read the law publicly to the people, and gave an exposition of it in Chaldee. This was the commencement of those written expositions, called Targums, the most ancient of which now extant is that written by Onkelos, a disciple of Hillel, who died sixty years B. C. In purity of style Onkelos equals the Chaldaic sections of Daniel and Ezra, and his fidelity to the Hebrew text is such that he deserves to be looked upon as a translator rather than a paraphrast. Besides the exposition of Onkelos, seven others are known to be in existence; but this is by far the most important. Whether the *Hebrew language* was or was not the first language of man, and that in which the Almighty communicated his will to our first parents and the chosen depositaries of divine revelation until the days of Moses, is a question which, with our present means of knowledge, it is impossible satisfactorily to determine. It certainly bears many internal marks of a high antiquity. The majority of Hebrew words, for instance, are descriptive—that is, they specify the prominent or distinguishing quality of the person, animal, place, or thing, which they designate; and the vocabulary, though comparatively poor in abstract and metaphysical terms, is rich in words having immediate reference to those objects of sense with which a nomadic people might be supposed to be most conversant. Thus, there are no less than two hundred and fifty distinct botanical terms in the Old Testament, and synonymous forms of expression for the common actions and occurrences of life are numerous and varied. Among these synonymes have been counted no less than fourteen different words of which each signifies *to break*, there are ten words answering to the verb *to seek*, nine express the act of dying, fourteen convey the idea of trust in God, nine signify the remission of sins, and eight denote darkness; and to express the observance of the laws of God there are no less than twenty-five phrases. The language appears to have attained its utmost possible development at a very early period, and to have remained subsequently, for ages, in the same stage, without progression or retrogression. This is proven by comparing the books of the Pentateuch with those of the later prophets: the latter differ from the former only by the disuse of a few words, which, in the course of centuries, had become obsolete; and by the introduction of sundry terms which had been ingrafted on the language by intercourse with the Assyrians and Babylonians. There are, however, two hundred and sixty-eight verses of pure Chaldee in the Old Testament.

A certain stiffness of construction, joined to great energy and simplicity, appears to be the most prominent feature of Hebrew and its cognate dialects. The fundamental structure of these dialects bears the impress of premeditation and design. Unlike all other idioms, the roots, or elementary words, are dissyllable and triliteral: they are, for the most part, the third person singular, the preterite tense, active voice of the verb; and seem to have been originally framed for the express purpose of representing ideas in the simplest possible form, while the application of these ideas to denote the varied circumstances of life (such as time past, present, or future—personal agency, passion, or feeling) is effected, generally, by mere changes of the vowels, placed above, within, or below the letters of the root. Besides the vowels, a certain set of consonants set aside for this office, and hence called *serviles*, are sometimes used in modifying the meaning of the roots. With respect to the alphabetical system of the Hebrews, it has generally been the custom to attribute the introduction of the square characters to Ezra.

It has lately, however, been shown that the square characters had no existence till probably two or three centuries after the Christian era. Kopp traces the gradual formation of these characters from the inscription on the bricks of Babylon down through the Phœnician or Samaritan letters on the Maccabean coins, and thence to the Palmyrene inscriptions found among the ruins of Palmyra; and Gesenius, in his last edition of the grammar, admits that the square, or modern Hebrew character, is descended from the Palmyrene. The Rabbinical style of writing now in use among the Jews is merely a cursive modification of the square character, adopted for ease and expedition.

The Hebrew language, honoured by the Almighty as the first medium of written revelation, had, in ancient times, predominance over a far greater extent of territory than is commonly supposed. It may be inferred from various passages of sacred history that the Canaanites, or the original inhabitants of Canaan, conversed freely in Hebrew, or some closely allied dialect, with Abraham, and, many years subsequently, with the tribes of Israel, under Joshua. Thus the spies, for instance, sent by Joshua to survey the country, had no recourse to the aid of an interpreter in their interview with Rahab and others. Moreover, the Canaanitish names of places and persons, both in the time of Abraham and that of Joshua, are pure Hebrew terms. Melchizedek, Abimelech, Salem, Jericho, and, in fact, all names recorded in Scripture, of persons, cities, and towns, in Canaan, might be cited as examples. That the Canaanites formed part and portion of the people known in profane history by the name of Phœnicians, has been clearly proved by the ethnographical researches of Gesenius and other German scholars; and in the Septuagint the words Phœnicians and Canaanites, Phœnicia and Canaan, are indiscriminately used. Hence the obvious inference that Hebrew was the vernacular of the Phœnicians, and that it was, therefore, the language of Tyre, of Sidon, of Carthage, and of all the numerous colonies founded by that intelligent and enterprising people. We may thus trace the use of Hebrew, as a vernacular tongue, or as a medium of communication, all round the coast of the Mediterranean, with the exception of Italy and (in part) of Greece. When the Old Testament was written probably no language was so widely diffused as the Hebrew. It occupied just such a place as the Greek did in the days of the apostles. With the sole exception of the Jews, however, the nations by whom the Hebrew was spoken, have either passed away from the face of the earth, or have become amalgamated with other races. The number of Jews now dispersed throughout the world is generally estimated at about seven millions. Of these, there are only one hundred and seventy-five thousand in Palestine and Syria. In England there are thirty thousand Jews, of whom twenty thousand reside in London. But they are still more numerous in some parts of continental Europe. At Warsaw, for instance, they form one-fourth part of the population. Professor Gaussen says, "The restless feet of God's ancient people are pressing, at this very hour, the snows of Siberia and the burning sands of the desert." Gobat found numbers of them in the elevated plains of Abyssinia, eighteen hundred miles to the south of Cairo; and when Denham and Clapperton, the first travellers that ventured across the great Sahara, arrived on the banks of the lake Tchad, *they* also found that the wandering Jew had preceded them by many a long year. When the Portuguese settled in the Indian Peninsula they found three distinct classes of Jews; and when the English lately took possession of Aden, in the south of Arabia, the Jews were more in number than the Gentiles. By a census taken within the last year, in Russia, they amount to two million two hundred thousand; so that their population, in that immense empire, exceeds that of the island of Ceylon. Morocco contains three hundred thousand, and Tunis one hundred and fifty thousand. In the one small town of Sana, the capital of Arabia Felix, they assemble together in eighteen synagogues. Yemen counts two hundred thousand; the Turkish empire, two hundred thousand—of which Constantinople alone contains eighty thousand. At Brody, where the Christians, who are ten thousand in number, have only three churches, the Jews, twenty thousand in number, have one hundred and fifty synagogues. Hungary has three hundred thousand; Cracovic twenty-two thousand. In a word, it is supposed that, were all the Jews assembled together, they would form a population of seven millions; so that, could they be transported to the land of their fathers, this very year, they would form a nation more numerous and powerful than Switzerland.

From the first promulgation of the written word, special provision was made for its preservation. A distinct command had reference to the place where the book of the law was to be deposited. The multiplication of copies was also provided for by a divine decree. It was preserved by the Jews in their captivity in Babylon, and found in the secret vault, beneath the ruins of the temple, after their return. It was read publicly by Ezra to all the people, and, after the canon was completed, the various books were, by him, collected, and arranged in their present order. When the temple and city were destroyed by the Romans, the sacred treasure was still carefully guarded, and learned Jews opened schools for its study in Egypt and Syria. Copies were multiplied in different places, and by different persons and institutions. The Jews have, as a people, been, as it were, the life and body-guard of the Holy Book, from the earliest period of its publication until the present time.

CHAPTER IV.

THE GREEK LANGUAGE.

THE *Greek language* next claims our attention, as being the vernacular of our Saviour and his Apostles, and the medium through which they communicated the glad tidings of the new dispensation to the world. It has been asserted that the Gospel of Matthew was originally written in Hebrew, but it is now generally conceded by the most eminent Biblical critics that it was written in Greek.

The ancient Greek language was divided into four principal dialects—the Attic, the Ionic, the Doric, and the Æolic—distinguished from each other by their varieties of orthography and pronunciation. When, under Philip of Macedon, the Grecian republics lost their freedom, and became more or less united under one government, the various dialects were gradually amalgamated into one. The language which thus sprang up, from this intermixture of dialects, differed materially from that of books preserved in the writings of the early poets and philosophers. It, however, became current wherever the Greek language was spoken; it was even used by the later writers, and, on account of its wide diffusion, received the name of κοινὴ διάλεκτος, *the common dialect.*

In the flexions of nouns, in the New Testament, there are no traces of any of the ancient dialects except the Attic; but in the flexion of verbs there is more variety, the Attic furnishing the most examples, the Doric affording others, while many of the forms are exclusively to be met with in the later idiom. The influence of Hebrew characteristics is likewise to be traced in the New Testament in several passages; the phraseology being Hebrew, while the words are Greek. This is more especially observable in the frequent use of a double substantive, (arising from the paucity of adjectives in Hebrew,) and in the use of the words *of God*, as indicative of the superlative degree. The Greek alphabet is a modification of the Phœnician, and it is to the adoption of this alphabet, which is but ill-adapted to express any sounds except those of Shemitic origin, that many of the anomalies of the Greek language are to be attributed.

At the time of the first preaching of Christianity the more civilized nations of the Roman empire (however dissimilar their respective vernacular tongues) were united by the bond of a common language, which, to them, was almost the only known medium of poetry, learning, and philosophy. That language was the Greek. In certain countries, as in Greece itself, in Egypt, and, as some say, in Syria, it was used in the common affairs of life, but everywhere it was the language of literature, and, as such, held the same position that was occupied by the Latin during the middle ages. The conquests of Alexander the Great had been the primary cause, under Providence, of the wide diffusion of this language, and, although the Grecian empire was afterwards supplanted by the Roman, yet the civilization, the arts, and language of Greece, long remained predominant.

It is generally supposed that the autographs of the evangelists and apostles were not preserved beyond the commencement of the third century, even if they remained in existence so long; but, prior to that period, many copies of the sacred writings had been made and dispersed among the infant Churches. The most ancient copies appear generally to have been written on Egyptian papyrus, a very perishable material, none of which have reached our times.

Innumerable MSS. of the New Testament, from that of the Codex Alexandrinus, in the fifth century, down to those of the eighth, and on until the time of printing, have existed; and some of the more important may be found in libraries at the present day. These have been compared, from time to time, by the most eminent Biblical critics, and the integrity of the original text has thus been secured.

CHAPTER V.

HINTS IN REGARD TO THE STUDY OF THE LANGUAGES OF THE BIBLE.

PROFESSOR FRANCKE says, in his "Study of the Scriptures," that "with ministers the Greek language is not to be studied as it would be by the professed grammarian, but simply with a view to divinity and the New Testament; though certainly a student may profitably cultivate a larger acquaintance with it afterwards, provided the Hebrew and other necessary studies be not neglected. So much of it, however, as is really essential may be easily acquired by attending to the following observations:—

"The first seven chapters of Matthew's Gospel should be read with an accurate version until the learner be able to translate the Greek text, without difficulty, into his own or any other language. He ought not, however, in this his *first* attempt to be anxious to comprehend *all* the principles of grammatical construction, nor, on account of partial ignorance in this particular, should he forego the improvement which must ever attend a frequent translating of the text. Yet, in order that no delay may be occasioned through a want of some acquaintance with the grammar, it will be proper to read and review *frequently* the paradigms of the declensions and conjugations with other grammatical rudiments, and thus gradually impress them on the mind. When the study of these accompanies a perusal of the seven chapters, theory and practice mutually assist each other. It remains, notwithstanding, to devote more time to the latter than to the former—to the reading the New Testament than to studying the grammar. Practice may prove a substitute for theory, but theory can avail nothing without practice. When the seven chapters in question have been thoroughly studied, and the requisite paradigms have been familiarized, the New Testament should be read through in its natural order, with a collated and accurate version, and the signification and grammatical nature of words may be sought for in a lexicon. The student should impress the signification of words on his memory by *writing* them, or by repeatedly reading the chapters, accordingly as he may deem either method adapted to his genius. Students should remark that this reading is not to be prosecuted in an irregular and inconstant manner. Other pursuits must submit to a temporary or at least partial cessation, lest they obliterate what has been learned, and lest a distaste for this should be acquired, when long-continued labors are not accompanied with that improvement with which they would, in the course of a few weeks, be otherwise attended. Words which are continually recurring, under different forms and various combinations, are, without much difficulty, impressed on the mind. It is, therefore, a judicious distribution of time to allot a stated period to the study of a language, and remit, during that term, every other pursuit. It is proper to remark here that every one should take into consideration his time, his opportunities, his genius, &c., and not prematurely draw conclusions unfavorable to himself, from comparing his own method and progress with those of others, while he perhaps enjoys, in a higher degree, the means of acquiring other branches of this study equally useful and important.

"The New Testament being perused in this manner, and in as short a period as possible, it should undergo a *second* reading. A student of divinity could scarcely be so dull as not to gain, in this way, an acquaintance with the New Testament within *three months*. In acquiring a knowledge of the Greek tongue, as well as preserving it when attained, it will prove of considerable advantage if the learner accustom himself to carry a pocket edition of the Greek Testament about with him, and when any text is propounded, either in public or private, to search it out immediately, and collate the original with it.

"The Hebrew language next claims our attention. As it regards the order, whether the Hebrew or Greek be *first* studied, is not at all important. The method which I shall propose for acquiring the Hebrew language resembles that prescribed for the Greek. The first four chapters of Genesis should be studied and collated with an accurate version until the learner be capable of rendering the Hebrew text into his vernacular idiom without the aid of a translation. It will next be proper to commit to memory some rudiments of the grammar, so as to enable the learner to know what are prefixes and affixes, as well as the more necessary paradigms. More time, however, must be allotted to reading the text itself than to studying the grammar, which will undoubtedly be attained with greater facility and pleasure when the language is become in some measure familiarized. *Experience* has repeatedly and clearly evinced to the conviction of many besides myself, that, in the course of only *four days*, these chapters may be perfectly known—so known as that the student shall be able to translate the text into another language, to ascertain the roots and their signification, and to separate from them the prefixes and affixes with which they stand connected. The great assistance which this must afford in a second reading is evident. Surely a week so employed is calculated to improve a learner more than three months spent over the grammar, and in the practice of analyzing alone, through a dislike to which many persons have totally given up the study of the Hebrew tongue.

"The Old Testament being thus thoroughly perused, which we have known some do in the course of *three months*, it may be read a second time, and in a shorter period, remembering that it should be a chief concern with the student not to lose what was acquired in the first reading.

"In learning a language it is a practice of no small utility for two or three to *unite* in the prosecution of their studies, where it is practicable, as they will mutually assist each other.

"The following rules should be observed in the study of language:—

"1. Never be weary of *writing* the signification of words.

"2. When the root of any word is not of easy attainment, write the word in the margin, and, instead of searching it out in a lexicon, ascertain it from a tutor or friend.

"3. The Biblical student should carefully guard against reading without rule or plan; he must proceed through the books of the inspired writings in their *regular* succession.

"4. Let it be deeply impressed on the mind that all things cannot be learned at once. It is not requisite that the student should, in the first reading, make himself master of every difficulty.

"5. The text should be frequently read *aloud;* the custom of reading mentally often induces a habit of stammering.

"6. The tutor should read the text and cause his pupils carefully to imitate his pronunciation.

"7. Frequently review what has been read—at least once a week.

"8. The Book of Chronicles should follow the Book of Kings. Those parts of the *Hagiographa* which are written in Chaldee may, in the first reading, be omitted.

"9. Different teachers should not be employed.

"10. Words that seldom or but once occur may be noted on paper.

"11. Proper substantives, which are not easily distinguishable from appellatives, should be marked with a pen."

The following is Professor Tefft's plan, which has been pronounced by competent authority to be the best which has been devised. It will be seen that all plans proposing to instruct without a teacher must be deficient, more or less, especially when applied to the dead languages:—

"1. The entire grammar of the language must be presented to the *eye.*

"2. At the same time it must be represented, by a competent teacher, to the *ear.*

"3. The pupil having before him the *visible*, and listening to the *audible* representations of the language, must himself utter, in unison with his teacher, what he hears and sees.

"4. The act of seeing, hearing, and uttering the forms of the language, must be *repeated* until they are fastened on the memory, as near as may be, without the possibility of mistake, forgetfulness, or loss."

To carry out these general principles, Professor Tefft has executed a series of charts for each language, of immense size for schools, but in reduced dimensions for small classes and individuals. The smaller are perfect fac-similes of the larger charts. On these charts everything to be committed to memory is presented. The teacher standing before the large chart, points with his rod to what he utters, which the pupil sees and hears at once, and then imitates, as above explained. Each portion of the chart or lesson is repeated publicly in class, or to individual scholars, until they can easily and readily repeat it themselves, when, with the smaller or hand-chart in his room, all is reiterated at pleasure, until a perfect mastery is gained over each lesson. While this process of instruction is going forward, innumerable practical applications are made, that the pupil may, all through the course, know how to use the information he is obtaining, as well as feel the importance of absolute accuracy in what he professes to have learned. These applications, altogether too numerous and complicated to be given in detail here, are the most ingenious and valuable portion of Professor Tefft's plan. To appreciate this plan fully, the reader should procure a set of the professor's charts, together with the accompanying books, which, as we know from personal observation, will impart a knowledge of the Greek and Hebrew languages in *less than one-fourth* of the time usually employed; besides, the work done is thorough and effectual, and the knowledge, from the very nature of its reception, is scarcely, if ever, lost or forgotten. The plan has received the warm approbation of some of the greatest linguists of

America, and needs only to be known to be universally received and appreciated.

For the study of the Greek New Testament the following text-books are recommended: Bloomfield's Greek Testament, or Bagster's Critical Greek and English, in parallel columns; Robinson's Greek Lexicon, Stuart's Greek Grammar of the New Testament, Winer's Idioms of the Greek Language of the New Testament, M'Clintock's First and Second Book in Greek, and Robinson's Buttmann (late edition). For the study of the Hebrew Old Testament, Biblia Hebraica, edited by Aug. Hahn; Gesenius's Hebrew Lexicon; Gesenius's Hebrew Grammar, with Exercises and Chrestomathy, edited by Conant. The above are believed to be the most valuable of any works of the kind extant.

Part Second.

BIBLICAL CRITICISM.

CHAPTER I.

OBJECTS OF BIBLICAL CRITICISM.

THE *objects of Biblical criticism* are the several kinds of difficulties which occur in the sacred writings, and which must be removed in order to the right understanding of these writings. As all difficulties must regard either the *reading* or the *sense*, criticism is two-fold—*corrective* or *emendatory*, being employed in determining the true reading; and *explanatory* or *exegetical*, discovering the genuine sense. The latter is treated of in the chapter on Biblical Exegesis, and the object of this chapter is to treat exclusively of the former.

The first writer who directed his attention to the criticism of the Bible was Origen, who was born in Egypt, in the second century. His criticism was directed to the correction of the Septuagint, a Greek translation of the Hebrew Bible made at Alexandria for the benefit of the Greek Jews. He ascertained that in the various manuscript copies of the Septuagint which he had collected there were alterations, made either by design or carelessness of transcribers, which caused them to differ materially from each other. The name given to this work is Biblia Hexapla, or Bible in six columns. The first column was occupied by—1. The *Hebrew*, which he made the basis or standard. 2. The *Hebrew in Greek characters.* 3. The *version of Aquila.* 4. The *version of Symmachus.* 5. The *version of the LXX., or Septuagint.* 6. The *version of Theodotion.* In those books which contained likewise two anonymous versions, and occupied, therefore, eight columns, it was called *Biblia Octapla*, and in those passages where a third anonymous version was introduced, it was called *Biblia Enneapla.* Inasmuch as out of the six columns which ran through the whole work, only four were occupied with Greek translations, the work has been called by some *Tetrapla.* These, however, are only different names of one work. It is said Origen was twenty-eight years in making preparation for writing the Hexapla. It was begun at Cæsarea, and finished at Tyre. This immense work was placed in the library at Cæsarea, where it was consumed by fire on the irruption of the Saracens. Origen was followed in his labors by Lucian, a presbyter of the Church at Antioch, and Hesychius, an Egyptian bishop.

The Scriptures, as well as all other writings, being preserved and diffused by transcription, were unavoidably liable to be corrupted, and in the copies of them different readings are actually found, whence arises the necessity of criticism for determining the true reading. In order to this it will be proper to ascertain the nature of a various reading—to point out the sources of false readings—to distinguish the several kinds of them, and to lay down rules for judging of the genuine reading. This subject, which involves an inquiry respecting *fact*, namely, *what* the author wrote, may be compared to a judicial procedure, in which the critic sits on the bench, and the charge of corruption in the reading is brought against the text. The witnesses from whom evidence is to be obtained respecting what the author wrote, are manuscript copies, ancient editions, old versions, and other books of antiquity, the authors of which quoted the text from manuscripts.

CHAPTER II.

THE NATURE OF A VARIOUS READING.

However plain the meaning of a various reading may seem to be, it has been sometimes understood so as to introduce confusion or mistake. Some have allowed the name only to such readings as may possibly have proceeded from the author; but this restriction is improper. According to this definition all the differences of copies are reducible to four heads.

1. Such as are *improperly called various readings*—solecisms, absurdities, palpable blunders of transcribers, typographical errors, differences in syllabication, &c., which take in the greatest part of the variations found in copies, but are to be reckoned, some corruptions, others trifles, none various readings. To refuse these, however, the name of various readings is improper, for it is to call that no reading which is actually read in some copies; and it is useless, for the merit and the real occasion of a reading are often matters of difficult discussion.

2. Such as it is *doubtful* whether they be improperly various readings, or whether they be properly such as capable of having come down from the author—readings, for instance, in quotations which may have been taken either from a copy or from memory. Such, too, should be considered as various readings till sufficient reason appear for rejecting them on examination.

3. Such as are *real and proper* various readings, since any of them might have been the original reading, but of no importance—synonymous words, for example, or such as do not alter the sense; and of this kind there are many.

4. Such readings as are *both* real and important, as making an alteration in the sense; and these are not very numerous.

This division of various readings, when accurately defined, amounts to no more than this, that some are *genuine* and some *corruptions;* some are important and some trivial; but it does not imply that all these kinds are not truly various readings.

To speak properly, wherever, in two copies of a writing, there is a difference, that difference forms a various reading, except only when it regards the manner of syllabication. For example, ἰρήνη or εἰρήνη, ἀντεί or ἀντί, εἶρις or ἔρις, καί or κε, &c.

Every reading different from what was *originally* written by the author is a false reading, or a corruption; and every various reading shows that there is a corruption in some of the copies; for two different readings cannot *both* be the original one of the author; but every various reading is not of itself a corruption, for it may be the very one which proceeded from the author.

CHAPTER III.

SOURCES OF FALSE READINGS.

For determining between various readings it is of great use to know the sources of false readings, which are reducible to two, viz., *chance* and *design.*

To *chance* are to be ascribed all the mistakes made by a transcriber or copyist, without his intending them at the time or perceiving them afterwards. *Haste* and *carelessness* have produced many mistakes, and might introduce false readings of every possible sort, and have rendered some copies extremely inaccurate. A transcriber might become *inattentive* and *absent-minded*, and thus not write what was in his copy, but whatever he happened to be thinking about at the time. To this cause some false readings are to be attributed, and such, too, as seem most strange and unaccountable.

To ascertain more fully the occasions of false readings, it ought to be observed that as a transcriber sometimes wrote from a copy before him, so, at other times, he wrote from the mouth of a person who dictated to several at once, in both of which cases mistakes might arise from reading wrong, and, in the latter, from hearing wrong.

Many *letters*, both in Hebrew and Greek, are similar in form, and more were similar, according to the modes of writing used in some ages, than now; such letters might easily be, and have often been, put one for another; and acquaintance with the several successive modes of writing will show both the occasions of false readings thence arising, and the times of their introduction.

Many false readings have arisen from *confounding* letters or words similar in sound, especially by reason of indistinctness, either in pronouncing or in hearing, when one dictated and others wrote.

A transcriber sometimes gave a false reading by writing a word while the sound of a preceding word was still in his mind.

A transcriber having read or heard a whole clause at once, and retaining the sense, but forgetting some of the precise words, wrote a *synonymous* word in the place of what was in his copy. To this head belong very many various readings.

A reader or transcriber casting his eye on a preceding line or word, and not observing the mistake, would write over again what he had already written, which would especially happen when, in the place on which he happened to cast his eye, he found the same or similar words or letters as he had last written; or, if he cast his eye on a word or line subsequent to where he was writing, and especially if he there found a word similar to what he had written last, or to what he should have written next, he would readily write from that subsequent place, omitting all that intervened. Having written one or more words from a *wrong place*, and not observing it, or not choosing to erase it, he might return to the right line, and thus make an improper insertion of a word, or a whole sentence. Or, when a transcriber had made an *omission*, and afterwards observed it, he then subjoined what he had omitted, and thus produced a *transposition.*

From these occasions of false readings, several principles may be deduced for forming a proper decision in regard to various readings.

1. If a reading which is easily accounted for, from an ordinary blunder of a transcriber, be found only in a few manuscripts, it is, in all probability, a false reading.

2. If a reading which yields no sense, or suits not the connexion, or disagrees with other texts, can be naturally accounted for by an ordinary mistake of transcribers, it is a false reading.

3. Among different readings, that is probably the genuine one from which the others may have easily arisen, but which could not so naturally arise from them.

4. Hence the most *unusual* reading is, generally speaking, the true one: for a transcriber would not so readily write it by mistake as one to which he was more accustomed.

5. Hence, also, the *fuller* reading is generally the genuine one, whenever there is no reason to suspect an interpolation; for a letter, a word, or a sentence, may be more easily omitted than added; when there is nothing to suggest the addition.

The second source of false readings is *design.* All such as are made knowingly and wilfully are to be ascribed to this source, and also such as, having been made accidentally, are wilfully allowed to remain after being perceived. Mistakes accidentally made have often been designedly permitted to remain uncorrected, that the beauty or price of the manuscript might not be lessened by disfiguration.

Many false readings are owing to *assimilation:* when a transcriber had once found or written a word wrong he purposely altered that, or related words, in conformity to the mistake. Critical transcribers sometimes transferred what they thought a clearer or fuller expression, or added a circumstance to one place from a parallel passage—a liberty often taken, especially in the Gospels; and therefore of two readings, one of which is exactly conformable to a correspondent passage, and the other not, but yet consistent with it, the latter is preferable.

Critics sometimes *corrected* the New Testament from the *Greek* version of the Old; and therefore when one reading of a quotation agrees exactly with that version, and another not so exactly, the former, if not well supported, is suspicious, and the latter preferable. Critics sometimes altered the text of the New Testament in conformity to the *Vulgate* or Latin version, and readings plainly arising from this cause deserve no regard. They sometimes also altered their copies with a view to correct some word in them which they did not understand, or considered faulty; and, therefore, when of two readings one is perfectly clear and the other difficult or obscure, but such as may be explained by the help of antiquity or perfect knowledge of the language, the former is suspicious and the latter is probably genuine. Critical transcribers sometimes omitted words which they considered superfluous. Critics in transcribing sometimes added words for illustrating what they thought defective or improper. It was common to write alterations or additions for the sake of illustration, as glosses on the margin, from which transcribers afterwards took them sometimes into the text, and for this reason the fuller reading, whenever it could serve for illustration or connexion, is generally suspicious, and to be rejected.

Persons have sometimes made alterations in the copies of Scripture with a wilful intention of corrupting them, in order to answer some particular purpose.

It has been a question whether the Jews have, in any instance, wilfully corrupted the Old Testament? It is denied, because of their veneration for the Scriptures, their not being accused of it by Christ, the impossibility of their doing it afterwards without detection, and their having left so many predictions favourable to Christianity. But it is answered that their veneration for the Scriptures gives no absolute security—that there are good reasons why Christ did not accuse them, though guilty—that they might hope to avoid detection by the ignorance of Hebrew among the first Christians—that the earliest who understood it do charge them with wilful corruptions—that their not going all lengths is no proof that they have attempted none—that evidence of a single instance would outweigh all general arguments—and that though the charge against them has been carried too far, yet there is sufficient evidence that for the honour of their own nation, or from hatred to Christianity, they have wilfully corrupted some texts, and in others given the preference to false readings which had at first arisen from other causes.

Some false readings, though not so many as have been imputed to them by the Fathers, and by others on their authority, were introduced or attempted by the ancient heretics, purposely in favour of their errors; but such were easily detected and soon rejected.

The prevailing party in the Church, who have always called themselves the orthodox, had it much more in their power to introduce and transmit false readings, and they have sometimes introduced them, and oftener given them the preference after being accidentally made, on purpose to favour some received opinion, or to preclude an objection against it.

Mistaken zeal is forward to impute false readings to design in those whom it opposes; but we ought not to ascribe them to this principle rashly, where they might have naturally arisen from chance, or where there is no positive presumption or evidence of design.

CHAPTER IV.

KINDS OF FALSE READINGS.

FALSE readings are of *four kinds*—1. *Omissions;* 2. *Additions;* 3. *Transpositions;* and 4. *Alterations*—and each of them may be either of letters, of words, or of sentences. It will be useful to notice some of the most remarkable of each kind, especially such as are found either in several manuscripts, in received versions, or in printed editions, pointing out how they have arisen and how they are corrected.

1. *Omissions* easily happen through carelessness, and sometimes have been made by design, but always alter, pervert, or destroy the sense, which will be restored by supplying. The omission of a single letter may happen very readily, and from many different causes, and has happened very frequently, but is often of great importance. Sometimes by accident and sometimes designedly, when the introduction of the vowel-points was thought to render them unnecessary, the vowel letters, in particular, have been improperly omitted, especially *vav* and *yodh*, on account of their smallness, and the omission has produced improper and even absurd readings. The improper omission of *vav* vitiates the language, or changes the sense, by altering the persons of pronouns and the numbers of verbs, by taking away the copulative, and, when it is conversive, turning the future into the past, by suppressing the possessive pronoun. The improper omission of *yodh*, which has been very frequent, perverts the syntax or the sense, by turning plural into singular nouns, by changing the persons of verbs, by altering the future into the past, by suppressing the affixed pronoun.

Omissions of *entire words* are very frequent, and always introduce obscurity, absurdity, or a difference in sense.

There have sometimes happened omissions of *several words*

together, or of *whole sentences*, which in a variety of ways mutilate or vitiate the sense.

2. *Additions* and *interpolations* have often been made in transcribing the Scriptures, and perplex the sense, which will be cleared by removing them. The interpolation or addition of letters has been common among transcribers, but generally destroys or alters the sense.

The arbitrary and improper insertion of *vav* changes the personal pronouns, turns singulars into plurals, and gives superfluous conjunctions. The interpolation of *yodh* has in very many instances turned singular nouns into plurals, the second persons of verbs into the first, the past into the future, and gives a suffix pronoun where there should be none, and, in all these cases, introduces great impropriety or perversion of the sense. There have been interpolations of words from many causes, and particularly from taking marginal glosses into the text, which disturb or destroy the sense. Several words or whole sentences have been interpolated, to the great disturbance of the sense.

3. Other false readings are produced by *transposition*, and often create difficulties which can be removed only by correcting them. The transposition of *letters* in a word often changes its sense, or deprives it of all meaning, and, in proper names, occasions an appearance of contradiction. There are transpositions of *words* which produce confusion, obscurity, or absurdity. There are likewise transpositions of *whole sentences, or periods*, which occasion difficulties of various kinds.

4. Finally, there are many false readings, productive of difficulty or error, which consist in *change or alteration.* Not only *similar letters*, but others also have been confounded and interchanged by transcribers, and important alterations in the sense have thence arisen. Transcribers have often made a false reading by *putting one word instead of another.* There have sometimes been *substitutions of whole sentences* in place of others totally different.

CHAPTER V.

RULES OF JUDGING CONCERNING VARIOUS READINGS.

THE *evidences* by which various readings may be examined are of two kinds—*external* and *internal*—the former arising from the authority of manuscripts, versions, and quotations; the latter from the nature of the languages, the sense and connexion, and the known occasions of false readings. Parallel cases partake of the nature of both.

When the evidences of *both* kinds concur in favour of a reading, there can be no doubt that it is the genuine reading, and therefore we have full assurance of the genuineness of the great bulk of the Scriptures as contained in all the common editions.

When the evidence *for* and *against* a reading is divided, the determination must be made according to the circumstances of each particular case.

If the *external* evidence stands on the one side, and the *internal* on the other, the former ought in general to determine the question, for it is the most direct.

But the *internal* evidence may, notwithstanding, be so strong as to overbalance a great degree of external evidence, particularly where the reading supported by the latter is palpably false, or where the introduction and prevalence of it can be easily accounted for without supposing it genuine, as in copies plainly framed in conformity to the Masora.

Often both the external and internal evidence is partly for one reading and partly for another, and they are divided with so great varieties of circumstances that no rules of deciding, strictly universal, can be laid down.

But if we distinguish various readings into four classes—*certainly genuine*, *probable*, *doubtful* and *false*—it may be possible to determine with sufficient precision the circumstances which entitle a reading to be placed in one or another of these classes.

1. There are readings *certainly genuine*, and there are even different degrees of evidence which may ascertain them to be such, and all such ought to be adopted without hesitation.

Readings are certainly right, and that in the very highest sense, if at all consistent with the existence of any various reading, which are supported by several of the most ancient, or the majority of manuscripts—by all or most of the ancient versions—by quotations—by parallel places, if there be any, and by the sense; though these readings be not found in the common editions, nor perhaps in any printed edition.

Again, readings are certainly right which are supported by a few ancient manuscripts, in conjunction with the ancient versions, quotations, parallel places, and the sense, though they are not found in *most* manuscripts nor in the printed editions, especially when the rejection of them in these latter can be easily accounted for.

Readings in the Pentateuch, supported by the Samaritan copy, a few Hebrew manuscripts, the ancient versions, parallel places, and the sense, are certainly right, though they are *not* found in the generality of Hebrew manuscripts nor editions.

Readings in the Pentateuch, supported by the Samaritan, ancient versions, parallel places, and the sense, are certainly right, though they are not found in *any* Hebrew manuscripts now extant.

Ancient manuscripts, supported by some of the ancient versions and the sense, render a reading certainly right, though it is not found in the more modern.

Again, ancient manuscripts, supported by parallel passages and the sense, may show a reading to be certainly right.

The *concurrence* of the most ancient, or of a great number of *manuscripts*, along with countenance from the sense, is sufficient to show a reading to be certainly right.

The concurrence of the ancient *versions* is sufficient to establish a reading as certainly right when the sense or a parallel place shows both the propriety of that reading and the corruption of what is found in the copies of the original.

In a text evidently corrupted a parallel place may suggest a reading certainly genuine.

Readings certainly genuine ought to be restored to the text of the printed editions, though hitherto admitted into none of them, that they may henceforth be rendered as correct as possible; they ought likewise to be adopted in all versions of Scripture; and till this is done they ought to be followed in explaining it.

2. There are various readings *probably* genuine, when the evidence preponderates, but it is not absolutely decisive in their favour; of which kind—as criticism is not always susceptible of certainty—are far the greatest part of various readings, and the degrees of probability being almost infinite, according to the numberless minute alterations of circumstances, down from certainty to perfect doubtfulness, it is impossible to enumerate fully all the cases which fall under this head; but the most general cases may be distinguished.

Of two readings, neither of which is unsuitable to the sense, either of which may have naturally arisen from the other, and both of which are supported by manuscripts, versions, and quotations, the one will be more probable than the other in proportion to the preponderance of the evidence which supports it, and that preponderance admits a great variety of degrees.

Of two readings *equally* or almost equally supported by external evidence, that is probable which best suits the sense, or the nature of the language, or which could not so readily as the other have been written by mistake.

The *sense* and other external evidences may even render the reading of a few manuscripts probable, in opposition to that of the greater number, and of versions and quotations.

The *Samaritan* Pentateuch alone may render a reading

in the books of Moses highly probable, if it be supported by the sense, connexion, or parallel places, in opposition to another found in manuscripts and versions, but unsuitable to these internal circumstances.

One or a few ancient versions may render a reading probable when it is strongly supported by the sense, connexion, or parallel places, in opposition to one which suits not these, though found in other versions and in manuscripts.

The *concurrence* of all or most of the ancient versions in a reading not found in manuscripts now extant, renders it probable, if it be *agreeable* to the sense, though not absolutely necessary to it.

Conjectural readings, strongly supported by the sense, the connexion, the nature of the language, or similar texts, may sometimes have probability, especially when it can be shown that they would easily have given occasion to the present reading; and readings first suggested merely by conjecture have in several cases been afterwards found to be actually in manuscripts.

Probable readings may have so high a degree of evidence as justly entitles them to be inserted into the text in place of the received readings much less probable. Such as have not considerably higher probability than the common ones should only be put on the margin; but they and all others ought to be weighed with impartiality.

3. Readings are *doubtful* when the evidence for and against them is so equally balanced that it is difficult to determine which of them preponderates.

When manuscripts, versions, and other authorities, are equally or almost equally divided between readings which all suit the sense and connexion, it is difficult to determine which of them should be preferred.

The *sense*, and other internal evidences, may plead sc strongly for one reading, and the authority of manuscripts and versions so strongly for another, as to render it doubtful which ought to be preferred.

Both the external and the internal evidence may be so much divided between two readings as to render it doubtful which of them demands the preference.

There are passages, especially in the Old Testament, where the fewness of independent manuscripts or their discordance, the obscurity or the variations of the versions, or other defects of evidence for any one reading, render it very doubtful what is the genuine reading, and leave room for different conjectures.

No doubtful readings should be taken into the text in place of what is already there; for no alteration ought to be made in the received copies without positive reason, and such doubtful readings as are already in the text should be marked as such, and the others put on the margin; but every person is at liberty to use his own judgment in choosing which he pleases.

4. There are readings which are *obviously wrong*, and of this kind are far the greatest part of the variations from the received copies; but to it belong, likewise, several which have, by the injudiciousness, the inattention, or the prejudices of transcribers and editors, been admitted into these, and such readings are certainly wrong.

All readings are *certainly* wrong which stand in opposition to the several classes of readings certainly genuine, of which many examples might be given. Some of these have been received, though they bear plain marks of corruption, as implying barbarism, inconsistency, &c.

Readings which imply barbarism, solecism, or absurdity, may be pronounced certainly wrong, though we know of no reading certainly right to be substituted in their place.

All readings are *probably* wrong which stand in opposition to such as are probably genuine, and these, too, have been already exemplified in many instances.

Readings which imply considerable irregularity or impropriety are probably false, though it be not clear what reading should be adopted instead of them.

Readings certainly or very probably false ought to be expunged from the editions of the Scriptures, and departed from in versions of them, however long and generally they have usurped a place there, as being manifest corruptions, which impair the purity of the sacred books.

Among texts the true reading of which is controverted, the most remarkable, in several respects, is 1 John v, 7, 8, where the words *ἐν τῷ οὐρανῷ, ὁ πατὴρ, ὁ λόγος, καὶ τὸ ἅγιον πνεῦμα, καὶ οὗτοι οἱ τρεῖς ἕν εἰσι· καὶ τρεῖς εἰσιν μαρτυροῦντες ἐν τῇ γῇ*, are by some held to be genuine, and by others to be spurious; and all the kinds of evidence, both external and internal, having been urged on both sides, it is only by a fair comparison of them that it can be determined in which of the four classes this reading ought to be placed.

Part Third.

BIBLICAL EXEGESIS.

CHAPTER I.

INTERPRETATION IN GENERAL.

BIBLICAL EXEGESIS relates to the interpretation of the Scriptures, and may be defined that science which teaches the student to find not only the meaning of an author, but enables him to explain it to others. Some have made a distinction between *hermeneutics* and *exegesis*, making the former to consist in the *theory* or *science* of interpretation, while the latter relates to its *practical application*. The etymology of the words would seem to favour this idea, inasmuch as ἑρμηνεύω signifies *to interpret*, and ἐξηγέομαι *to lead out* or *teach*. The importance of both to him whose business it is to explain the sacred text, will be readily conceded by all who have correct views on this subject.

The interpretation of the sacred books is the most important and the most difficult task of the theologian. This will appear from the very nature of the work, from the experience of all who are engaged in it, and from the common consent of all periods. All correct knowledge and judicious defence of divine truth must originate from a right understanding and accurate interpretation of the Scriptures. The purity of the Christian religion has shone brighter or been obscured as the study of interpretation has flourished or decayed. Christian doctrines are preserved only in *written* records, and the interpretation of these is *essential* to a knowledge of what those doctrines are, and without this knowledge we can neither maintain their purity nor defend their principles.

The science of interpretation requires patient and diligent research and the exercise of a sound discriminating judgment; all these are necessary in enabling one to conduct an exegetical inquiry to a successful issue. The difficulties connected with this subject vanish as the student becomes familiar with the peculiar dialect, manners, customs, education, style, modes of thought and expression, location, climate, government, &c., of the authors. This only will enable the student to attach to an author's language the same meaning which the author himself attached to it, and by this he will be enabled to teach this meaning to others. We should come to the work of the interpretation of a writer with a mind unprejudiced and clear, and, having examined the grammatical construction and idiom of the language he uses, we should next examine the context and design. His meaning may be further illustrated by history, chronology, antiquities, &c.

Exegesis, considered as the science of finding the true sense of words, consists of two parts. The *first* comprises general *principles* in respect to the meaning of words, and the various kinds of words. On these *principles* the rules of interpretation, and the reasons of them, are grounded.

The *second* consists of *rules* which are to guide us in investigating the sense of an author's words.

CHAPTER II.

MEANING OF WORDS.

Every *word must have some meaning.* To every word in the Scriptures there is unquestionably assigned some meaning or sense—some idea or notion of a thing; otherwise words would be useless, and have no more signification than the inarticulate sounds of animals.

The *literal* sense of words is that which is first presented to the mind as soon as the sound is heard. It is the *sense of the letter.* It is the primitive or original sense.

Words considered simply as *sounds* have no meaning, for they are not the natural and necessary signs of things, but *conventional* ones. Usage or custom has constituted a connexion between words and ideas. The connexion between words and ideas is now rendered necessary by usage, whatever may have been the case at first. This does not mean, however, that a word may only have *one* meaning, for usage contradicts this. We must not, in interpreting or using a word, affix to it an arbitrary sense. A word cannot have a *double* sense at the *same time* and in the *same passage* or expression. An *arbitrary* sense can never, with propriety, be substituted for a *real* one.

Although a word can have but one meaning at the *same time* and in the *same place*, *usage*, which is the law of language, has gradually assigned many meanings to the same word, lest words should be indefinitely multiplied, and the difficulty of learning a language become too great. The question, then, for an interpreter is simply this: Which *one* of the significations attached to the words is connected with its use in any particular instance?

The meaning of a word in each case can be found from the general manner of speaking—*i. e.*, *common usage*, and the *words of the context.* The primary meaning is attached to the word unless the context or design requires another.

The *doubtful meaning* of words arises from various causes. 1. From the fault of writers. 2. From neglect in the construction and necessary connexion of words, care not having been taken to guard the reader against uncertainty, and to afford him the best means for finding the true sense. 3. From the manner in which common usage often forms language, which, not being guided by the philosophy of language, is frequently deficient in regard to *accuracy.*

From what has been said, we see the ground of all the certainty which attends the interpretation of language: for there can be no certainty at all in the interpretation of any passage unless a kind of necessity compel us to give a particular sense to a word, which sense must be one; and unless there are special reasons for a tropical or figurative meaning, it must be the *literal sense.* A principle of interpretation which allows many meanings to a word at the same time and in the same place, must introduce very great uncertainty into exegesis, than which nothing can be more pernicious.

The idea that the words of Scripture must be taken in every sense at the same time and place, gives a license to the introduction of allegory, prophecy, and mystery into every part of the Bible. The Rabbinic maxim is: "On every point of the Scripture hang suspended mountains of sense." The Talmud says: "God so gave the law to Moses that a thing can be shown to be clean and unclean in forty-nine different ways." A modern commentator maintains that all the possible meanings of a word in the Scripture are to be united.

The *sense* of words properly considered is not *allegorical.* Allegory is rather an *accommodation of the sense of words*, or an accommodation of *things* to the illustration of some doctrine. Moderately used and well adapted it may be of service, but in the hands of the injudicious and unskilful it may degenerate into ridiculous trifling.

Properly speaking, there is no *typical sense* of words. Types are not *words* but *things*, which God has designated as *signs* of future events. The explanation of them which the Holy Spirit himself has given makes them intelligible. Beyond *his* instructions we should be careful never to go. The Old Testament is to be no further regarded as typical than the New Testament makes it so, as that is the key which alone can discover to us what is typical in the Old Testament. A word may be tropical and yet not allegorical or mystical.

The sense of words, as we have already shown, depends upon the *usus loquendi*, or common usage. If we understand the *usage*, then, of course, we understand the sense of the words. The way to determine the *usus loquendi* is by taking into account the *religion*, *sect*, *education*, *common life*, *civil affairs*, &c., of all which have an influence on an author's language, and characterize it. The same word is employed in one sense respecting the ordinary things of life—in another respecting the things of religion—in another still in the schools of philosophy; and even these are not all alike in the use of words. To these causes, which operate upon the *usus loquendi*, must be added the *style of the writer.*

Those who make one sense the *grammatical* and another the *logical*, do not comprehend the true meaning of *grammatical sense.* Interpreters now speak of the *grammatico-historical sense*, and exegesis founded on the nature of language is called *grammatico-historical.* The grammatical sense is the only true one. If this were not the case words would have as many kinds of senses as objects are multifarious. A grammatical sense may be either *literal* or *tropical.*

The principles of interpretation are common to sacred and profane writings; hence the Scriptures are to be investigated by the same rules as other books. The Scriptures are a revelation to men, and hence they are to be read and understood by men. If the same laws of language are not observed in reading this revelation as are common to men, then they have no guide to the right understanding of the Scriptures, and an interpreter needs *inspiration* as much as the original writer, and the Scriptures would be no *revelation* at all except to those who were inspired. But God has spoken in the language of men, and he has spoken *by* men *for* men.

The interpreter is not to be guided in his work by the *analogy of faith. Things* and the *analogy of faith*, as it is called, assist an interpreter so far that when words are ambiguous, either from variety, structure, signification, or any other cause, they may help us determine the meaning. With many the analogy of faith is all the rule of interpretation they have; and this, instead of being a *Scriptural* analogy, is nothing more nor less than a *sectarian* analogy. The doctrines of the Bible are cast into this sectarian mould, be it the decrees of the Council of Trent, the articles of the Church of England, or the Saybrook platform, or any other of the many sectarian standards; and if the literal or tropical sense agree not with these, they must be tortured into a meaning correspondent thereto. With such, *vox* ECCLESIÆ *est vox Dei*, and not the voice of the living oracles. Our present standard English version of the Bible, in some points bears lamentable evidence of this fact; and every commentary, from the earliest period, is testimony to the fact. Some commentators may have been less trammelled and more independent than others, but all are more or less tinctured with the peculiarities of the standard of doctrine which they have embraced. Let the Bible speak out unfettered and free, according to the strict *usus loquendi*, and let us follow its teachings wherever they lead, according to their plain, obvious, grammatico-historical sense. *Vox Dei—et non vox ecclesiœ*—should, as all Protestant Christians concede, be the *only rule* of faith and practice. It is right and proper that we should be governed, in our searches after the true meaning of inspiration, by *Scriptural* analogy, for inspiration then becomes its own interpreter; but then it is equally important that we be certain in regard to that which is analogous.

The sense of Scripture is not arbitrary. The method of ascertaining the true meaning of words is just the same as that used in explaining or interpreting other books. We are to be governed by the laws deduced from the nature of language.

No doctrine of the Scripture contradicts reason—i. e., there is nothing contained in the Bible, when properly interpreted, that is unreasonable. The meaning which, according to grammatical principles, should be assigned to any word of Scripture is not to be rejected on account of reasons drawn from other things, or from previously-conceived opinions; for in this way interpretation would become uncertain. In books merely human, if reason and the nature of the subject are repugnant to the apparent sense of the words, we conclude there must have been either a fault in the writer or an error in the copyist. In the Scriptures, if any sentiment does not agree with our opinions, the weakness of human reason and its finite nature must be taken into the account, as many things may be in strict accordance *with* reason, though they may be far *above* it. It is remarkable that in this respect more reverence is sometimes paid to mere human productions than to the sacred books. In ancient authors, when any difficulty occurs, correction or conciliation is sought for, as if they must be rendered faultless. Multitudes of passages in sacred writ, which have been given up as unreasonable, have subsequently been elucidated by a superior criticism. Time and patient investigation will make all the dark passages of the Bible plain and satisfactory to all intelligent Christians.

In comparing reasons for the exegesis of particular passages, greater weight should be attributed to *grammatical* than *doctrinal* ones. A thing may be altogether true in doctrine which yet is not taught by some particular passage. Books of theology exhibit many doctrinal interpretations, consentaneous, indeed, with Christian principles, but not deduced from the words interpreted—*doctrinally* true, but not *grammatically*.

Real contradiction does not exist in the Scriptures. As the books of Scripture were written by men divinely inspired, it is evident there can be no real contradiction in them. God is certainly capable of seeing what is consistent and inconsistent as well as what is contradictory, and when he speaks he cannot forget what was said on former occasions. If apparent contradictions occur, a proper method of conciliation is to be pointed out which will satisfactorily remove all the difficulty.

CHAPTER III.

KINDS OF WORDS, AND THEIR VARIOUS USES.

WORDS are *proper* and also *tropical*. The first important division or distinction of words, in regard to their meaning, is into *proper* and *tropical*—i. e., literal and figurative, or, primary and secondary.

A *proper* word is a definite name given to a certain thing, and as such may be explained by adverting to the *proper names* of persons.

A *tropical* word is one used out of its *proper* or original sense. For instance, we have *rosy face*, *snowy skin*. Here *rosy* and *snowy* cannot be predicated of skin *literally* and *properly*. The names *trope* and *tropical* come from the Greek τρόπος. Tropes arise, 1. From similitude, real or supposed; for example, the vine *creeps*. This is called metaphor. 2. From *conjunction*, which is either physical or intellectual—i. e., supposed, believed. Physical or real, where a part of a thing is put to signify the whole, or the container for the thing contained; as, for instance, *to offer the cup*, is to offer what is contained in it. The conjunction is *intellectual* or supposed when the cause is put for the effect, and *vice versa;* for example, blushing for modesty—the sign for the thing signified, or the subject for the attribute. From *conjunction* arises that species of trope called *metonymy*.

Originally words were undoubtedly used in their *proper* or literal sense, because they were invented to indicate *things*, and by these things they might be easily explained, without any ambiguity. A small number of words sufficed at an early period, because there were few objects about which speech could be employed. In process of time, objects being multiplied, there arose a necessity for using words in various senses. Men began to speak concerning those things which had hitherto been neglected, and, of course, to form ideas of them in their minds, or to describe them in words. New objects, also, were invented or discovered, to describe which words became necessary. To serve this necessity men resorted to two different expedients. Either new words were coined, or old ones were applied to new objects. In those languages that were spoken by an ingenious people devoted to science, or in those which by nature or art were flexible and fitted for the coining of new words, new ones were most usually coined. This usage, however, was not without exceptions, for had new words been coined on every occasion the number of them would have been multiplied without end. In languages of a character differing from that just mentioned, there was a greater necessity of applying the same word to the designation of several things.

Tropical words sometimes become *proper* ones. The primitive or proper sense often becomes obsolete, and ceases for a long period to be used. In this case the secondary sense, which originally would have been the *tropical* one, becomes the *proper* one. This applies especially to the names of things. Hence there are many words which at present never have their original and proper sense, such as etymology would assign them, but only the *secondary* sense, which may in such cases be called the *proper* or *literal* sense—such, for instance, in English, as *tragedy*, *comedy*, *villain*, *pagan*, *knave*, &c.

Usage sometimes converts *tropical* words into *proper* ones. The tropical sense has also become so common by usage that it is better understood than the original sense. In this case, too, we call the sense *proper*, although strictly and technically speaking one might insist on its being called *tropical*. If one should by his last will give a library to another, we should not call the use of library tropical, although strictly speaking it is so, for library originally meant the *shelves* or *places* where books are deposited. Tropical names become proper by *transfer*, when they are transferred to things destitute of them: as, for instance, when we predicate *luxuriousness* of a crop; the words *perception* and *liberty*, when predicated of the human mind. Tropes are used by writers for the sake of *variety in expression*, and also to prevent tautology; hence *Heaven* is used for *God*, *sleep* for *death*, *threshold* for *house*, *uncircumcision* for *Gentiles*. Tropical words are used for ornament, by poets and orators, to give elegance to their style. Those who possess great fervour of imagination and vividness of conception, more frequently use tropes, even bold ones, and, as it often seems to others, *harsh* ones. Tropes, therefore, must not be interpreted etymologically.

Tropes used from *necessity* differ from those used for *variety* or *ornament*. In the first case a thing has a *definite* name by which it is called, and in the second case the trope is used for pleasure or ornament. The former is grammatical—the latter is rhetorical. The meaning of all words, *tropical* and *proper*, is to be deduced from the *design* of those who employed them.

From the custom of using tropical language, *synonymous* words originate. The interpreter should not seek for any definite distinction between synonymes, when they are introduced for the sake of variety, or where usage conjoins two words, or where they are used for the sake of ornament, or where excited feeling produces a repetition of the same idea, while different words are employed, or where it is the habit of an author to employ synonymes.

Emphasis.

In the use of language cases arise where the ordinary signification of a word receives *accession* or *augmentation*. This may be effected in two ways, the first of which consists in the use of a word in an honorary or in a degrading sense. For example, *εὐφημία* and *δυσφημία*—or, words of good or evil import. The second class of words are those which receive augmentation in their *extent or force of meaning.* These constitute what may with propriety be called *emphatic words.* Emphasis, then, may be defined, *an accession to the ordinary signification of a word, either as to the extent or force of its meaning.* The word comes from ἐμφαίνειν, which signifies to *show or make conspicuous.* It is to language what a nod or a sign is to looks. What action is to the orator, emphasis is to the writer.

No word is of itself emphatic. Each word has a certain power, and designates a definite idea of a thing, either small or great, in which there is no emphasis. It is not because a word designates anything which is very great or very small that it is emphatical. If this were the case, then such words as *God*, the *world*, the *sun*, would be always emphatical.

Emphasis is either *occasional* or *constant.* We call it *occasional* when it is connected with words in some particular place, or at a certain time. From the animated feelings of the speaker, or from the importance of the subject, a word is chosen to express more than its ordinary import. *Constant emphasis* is that which usage makes invariably so, by employing a word continually in an emphatic rather than in the ordinary sense. But this is a departure from the ordinary definition.

Antithesis.

Where antithesis exists, if the sense of one part can be found, the other may be easily known. As ideas are often contradistinguished from each other, so the language corresponds. When ideas are repugnant to each other, if you understand the one, of course you must understand the other, which is opposite—for what one asserts the other denies. So in antithetic *language*, whether the subject or predicate of a sentence, the rule is obvious that the interpretation of the one part must be directed by that of the other, which is understood either from the *usus loquendi*, or, where this is various, from the context. For example, when *multi* and *pauci* occur in the same sentence, and it is evident that *multi* means *all*, it is of course evident that *pauci* cannot have its ordinary sense, *non omnes*, without limiting the idea to *fewness* of number. Of a like kind are *σάρξ* and *πνεῦμα*, *γράμμα* and *πνεῦμα*, in which the interpretation of the one is to be accommodated to that of the other.

Abstract and Concrete Words.

Words are distributed into *abstract* and *concrete*. All languages, specially ancient ones, often use abstract terms for concrete ones. Abstract words are names of qualities or attributes. Concrete words are names of things or subjects. For example, *divinity* is an abstract word, meaning the quality of divine nature; *God* is a concrete term, meaning the divine agent or being. The former is, by usage, often put for the latter. The use of abstract words for concrete arose from *necessity*. Those languages which have but a few concrete terms necessarily employ abstract ones; for example, the Hebrew and its cognate dialects, in which abstracts are often used in the place of concretes. This substitution also arose from a desire to render the subject spoken of more prominent, and also to give an elevation and grandeur to the style.

CHAPTER IV.

RULES OF INTERPRETATION.

These rules define the mode by which we investigate rightly and explain clearly the sense of words in any particular author. They not only serve to assist in finding the meaning of words, but also in judging whether any particular sense put upon words be true or false. By them we may also be assisted to understand why a particular sense is erroneous, as well as why the true sense cannot be discovered. The sense of words depends on the *usus loquendi.* The *usus loquendi*, considered at large, has respect to a language generally: but, specially considered, it has respect to the language of some particular writer. To the common usage of words almost every writer adds something that is peculiar to himself, whence arise the *idioms* of particular writers.

Usus Loquendi.

By the *usus loquendi* is meant the sense which usage attaches to the words of any language. To find the sense of words in a dead language the same means precisely are to be employed which are used in finding the sense of words in a living language. The meaning of a word must always be a simple *matter of fact.* To find out that meaning recourse must *always* be had to appropriate and adequate *testimony.* This testimony is *direct* or *indirect. Direct testimony* is derived, first, from the writers to whom the language investigated was vernacular—either the same authors whom we interpret, or from their contemporaries. Secondly, from those who, though foreigners, had learned the language in question. Thirdly, from scholiasts, glossographers, and versions made while the language was spoken, and by those who were acquainted with it. Thus, the writings of Marcus Antonius, a Roman emperor, and of Philo and Josephus, who were Jews, may be used to illustrate the meaning of Greek words, because, although foreigners, they well understood the Greek language.

The testimony of contemporary writers may be drawn from three sources. *First*, from *the definition of words.* In regard to these nothing more is necessary than to take good care that the definition be well understood, and to consider how much weight the character of the writer who defines may properly give to it. *Second*, from *examples and the nature of the subject.* In regard to these it may be said that a good understanding and considerable practice is necessary to enable one to judge well and make proper distinctions. By *examples* is meant that the writer who uses a particular word, although he does not directly define it, yet gives, in some one or more passages, an example of what it means, by exhibiting its qualities or showing the operation of it. Thus Paul uses the words *στοιχεῖα τοῦ κόσμου* at first without an explanation, but gives an example of the meaning of them in Galatians iv, 9. Thus *πίστις* is illustrated by examples in Hebrews xi, and so of many other words. The *nature of the subject* helps in many instances to define which meaning the writer attaches to it in any particular passage. For example, *χάρις* is divine benevolence, pardon of sin, temporal blessings. The sense is to be determined by the nature of the subject in the passage. Third, from the *comparison of parallel passages*. Parallelism is *verbal* and *real*. The *verbal* occurs where a word is doubtful, from the fact that neither the subject nor the context affords matter of illustration, and this same word or its synonyme is repeated in a similar passage with those attributes by which it may be defined, or with some plain adjunct or intelligible comment. The sense of many words is so plain that investigation by parallelism is unnecessary. Comparison is necessary in the following instances: 1. In the illustration of words which belong to the Hellenistic or Hebrew-Greek idiom. For example, *ἐφοβοῦντο πάντες* is often said when the event to which it relates is some special favour. The language here may be compared with the synonymes *θαυμάσαι* and *θαμβῆσαι*, by which it appears that *ἐφοβοῦντο* in such cases means *admiration*, *astonishment*. 2. Words should be compared which have a kind of technical religious use. For example, *μυστήριον*. Compare Colossians i, 27; Ephesians iii, 4, 5. So *πίστις*, *δικαιοσύνη*, *μετάνοvα*, *καινὴ*, *κτίσις*, et cetera. 3. Words of unfrequent occurrence. 4. Words which are ambiguous; for words which are so in one place are frequently plain and easy to be understood in another, from the connexion in which they stand. For example, Christ is frequently called a *stone of stumbling* In 1 Peter ii, 8, those *who stumble* are said ἀπειθεῖν τῷ λόγῳ, to reject, disbelieve, or disobey the gospel of Christ. Again, 2 Corinthians i, 21, χρίσας ἡμᾶς Θεός: 1 John ii, 20, χρῖσμα is said to be *instruction in the truth.* Parallelisms *appropriately* so called are of this nature, the one often serving to explain the other. These are very numerous in the Old Testament, and considerably so in the New. Compare Matthew i, 20, with Luke i, 35. *Real parallelism* occurs when there is a parallelism of object or sentiment, although the words are not the same; or it occurs when the same object or sentiment is expressed in other words more clearly or copiously. The *real* parallelism may have respect to a *fact* or a *doctrine* related or taught in different passages, and the student can never feel too deeply the importance of a thorough comparison of all those parts of Scripture which pertain to the same subject. He should read parallel passages continuously and frequently, that he may be able readily to trace the resemblances between them. When apposite passages are compared, the rules of exegesis require that the obscure passage shall be regulated by that which is the most clear and the best sustained by the nature of the subject and the adjuncts. Parallelisms of *fact* occur frequently in the Gospels, which, in very numerous instances, relate the same facts. So also in the books of Samuel and Kings, compared with Chronicles.

Parallelism of *doctrine* is where the same principles are taught in both passages. To this head of parallelism belong repetitions of the same composition. For example, Psalms xiv and liii; Psalms xcvi and 1 Chronicles xvi; Psalms xviii and 2 Samuel xxii; some of Jude and 2 Epistle of Peter, with many other such passages.

Besides the verbal and real parallelisms, there is another which constitutes one of the principal features of Hebrew poetry, viz.: a correspondence of two parts of a verse with each other, so that words answer to words and sentiment to sentiment. This runs throughout the books of Job, Psalms, Proverbs, Canticles, and most of the Prophets. See Psalms i, ii, cxix; Isaiah i, 2–5; xl. See also Luke i, 35–46; xi, 27, and many parts of the Apocalypse, and in almost every chapter of the New Testament.

Similarity of passages should be *real* in order to be compared, and not merely *verbal.* The *same idea* should be presented by both; otherwise *real* likeness cannot exist between them, and one cannot, of course, throw any light upon the other. When this point is settled, viz., in regard to similarity of idea, which is determined by the context, then the interpreter must consider which of the two is the most clear and definite, and regulate the exegesis of the more obscure passage by that which is the more perspicuous.

Many parallel passages should be compared. To compare one passage only is not sufficient, whether you are endeavouring to find the *usus loquendi* by the aid of parallel passages, or by testimony derived from the nature of the subject and from examples. Specially is this the case if we are investigating the sense of words that have a complex or generic meaning, made up of various parts. In this case comparisons should be made from numerous passages until we perceive that what we are seeking is fully and entirely discovered. Suppose the word πίστις occurs in a particular passage, where you are doubtful what sense should be applied to it. πίστις is a generic word, having several meanings related to each other, but still diverse as species under the genus. You wish to determine how many *species* of meaning πίστις has, and in order to accomplish this *many* passages where it is used must be compared, in order that you may know whether all the species are found. This being done, you proceed to compare them with the passage under investigation, and see which will fit it. In this way all generic words must be investigated before the generic idea can be determined.

The *usus loquendi* may be found also by the testimony from *scholiasts*, either given by themselves or cited by them from others. *Scholia* means *short notes* upon any author, either of an exegetical or grammatical nature. On all the distinguished ancient Greek authors scholia have been written in more recent times. Many volumes of these scholia written upon Homer, Thucydides, Sophocles, Aristophanes, and others, are still extant. Many scholia are found on the margin of manuscripts, or interlined, or placed at the end of the book.

In a similar way is the testimony of *glossographers* to be estimated. *Glossarium* is a book or writing comprehending γλῶσσαι. Among the Greeks γλῶσσα meant either an *idiomatic word* peculiar to a certain dialect only, and unknown in others, or an *obsolete* or *obscure* word. Glossary means a book containing explanations of obscure and difficult words. It is of course not to be used as a lexicon, because it is only a comment upon particular passages.

The testimony of versions in finding the *usus loquendi* is to be estimated by their antiquity and by the knowledge of the original which the translator possessed, and this is to be determined by comparing the translation with the original; also the testimony of those writers who have explained to their readers words and obscure expressions taken from another language. Cicero explains many Greek words, and Dionysius, of Halicarnassus, many Latin ones, and writers who have inserted translations from other languages.

To qualify an interpreter fully and fairly to enter upon his work, he must make himself acquainted with *the style* of an author, *the nature of the composition*, and *the age*, *circumstances, and idiom of the author.*

First, the style of an author; and this may be known from the writer's own testimony, either expressed or implied. If an author have a manner of expression wholly *sui generis*, then his own writings are the only legitimate source of information in respect to his style. It may be known from the customs and principles of the sect to which he belongs, as every religious sect has terms used in a sense peculiar to itself. The same language will apply to a philosophical sect. Again, the interpreter must have a knowledge of the manners and customs of the age to which his author alludes, which is to be obtained by consulting those who have given information on these topics; and, lastly, the interpreter should have a general knowledge of writers of the same age.

Second, the nature of the composition, the age in which it was written, &c. History is one thing, poetry another, oratory another; and they are to be interpreted accordingly; history as history, and not as an allegory or mythic fiction; poetry as poetry, and not as prose. Particular ages have their special characteristics in each of these modes of composition, and a due regard must be had to them.

The *usus loquendi* is also to be found by *indirect testimony*. The first and best means under this head is to ascertain the *scope* or *design* of a writer. The passage to be investigated is to be compared with the general tenor of the whole. The ground of this rule is that we ought not to suppose a good and judicious writer has said what is inconsistent with his design. Difficulty may arise here from the fact that several interpretations may agree with the scope or design of the writer, and only a probability as it regards which is the true exegesis may be arrived at. We must insist upon an evident and necessary connexion with the scope of the discourse: for, 1. Where a meaning plainly contradicts the tenor of a discourse, it is to be rejected. 2. When it violates the principles of parallelism and the conclusions drawn from them as to the sense of a passage. 3. A meaning must be rejected which gives an unfit and frigid sense. By a *frigid* sense is meant one which contributes neither to argument, perspicuity, nor ornament. A meaning which infringes upon none of these negative rules will be found to harmonize with the subject of which the author is treating, unless he has violated all the rules of language and reasoning.

The *usus loquendi* is always the *best* evidence which can be had of the meaning of a passage; and nothing can be admitted which shall contradict it, where it can be established by adequate testimony. In a case where doubt arises in regard to what meaning the *usus loquendi* would assign, or at least allow, to any word or phrase, the scope of the discourse may be resorted to for the sake of obtaining the desired illustration.

The rule must have recourse to the antecedents and consequents of a passage—i. e., the *context*—in order that the meaning may be determined. This is done for two reasons. 1. That we may choose out of several meanings one which does not disagree with the *usus loquendi;* or, 2. That the meaning of an uncommon word, not explained by the *usus loquendi*, may be discovered. The evidence of the *usus loquendi* is in very many cases built upon the context, and there are few if any rules in the whole science of hermeneutics of more importance and practical utility than this.

To discover the meaning of words which are ambiguous and obscure, the comparing of subject and attribute, nouns and adjectives, words accompanied by other words that qualify them, which may consist of adverbs or of nouns, joined to the word investigated by prepositions, and constituting a kind of adverbial periphrasis, or finally of disjunctives, is of the greatest importance.

In relation to the comparison of subject with attribute it may be remarked that we are to understand as tropical all those expressions which ascribe hands, feet, eyes, ears, ascent, descent, &c., to God, who is a *spirit.* By the *adverbial periphrasis* we have an example, κατ' ὄψιν κρίσις, which serves merely as an adjective qualifying κρίσις, and showing that *judgment* from *external appearance only* is meant. By *disjunctives.* By *disjunctives* are meant words placed in antithesis. For example, *heaven* and *earth*, *flesh* and *spirit.* The rule for determining the sense in the case is obvious; for whatever meaning one term has, the other must have an opposite meaning.

Assistance in judging of the meaning of words is derived from the *analogy of languages.* Analogy means similitude. For example, from the meaning attached to the forms of words, their position and connexion, in many cases, we argue to establish a similarity of meaning where the phenomena are the same in another. This analogy is the foundation of all the rules of grammar, and of all that is established and intelligible in language. *Grammatical analogy* is not only useful in finding the *usus loquendi*, but applicable to some doubtful cases. For example, when the kind of meaning generally considered is evident, we may judge of the special force or power of the word by the aid of grammatical analogy, as 1 Peter v, 5, where many critics have attached to ἐγκομβώσασθε an emphatic sense, we must compare the other Greek phrases which relate to *clothing* or *investing*, and thus we shall see that the prepositions περί, ἀμφί, ἐν are used in composition without any accession of meaning to the verb thereby, and consequently that ἐγκομβώσασθε is no more than ἐνδύσασθε. Another analogy is that of *kindred languages*, either as derived from one common stock, as Hebrew, Syriac, Chaldee, and Arabic, or from one another, as Greek and Latin. Chaldee, Syriac, and Arabic, are ranked among the *dialects* of the Hebrew, while Greek and Latin are called *cognate* langnages. In regard to this, however, there is a difference of opinion. General usage makes the Semitic languages cognates. This analogy is of use to the interpreter, not only in assisting him by the aid of one dialect to restore roots which have perished in another that is the subject of his investigation, and thus opening a way of access to the signification of words, but still more useful as a means of illustrating and confirming that sense of words which the scope of the discourse commends. The fluctuating use of words which prevails in all languages gives rise to frequent changes in their meaning. There are but few words in any language which always retain their radical and primary meaning. Etymology often belongs rather to the history of language than to the illustration of its present meaning.

Expressions which convey a similar meaning are to be compared, although in respect to etymology they may differ. Of this nature are πεπραμένος ὑπὸ τὴν ἁμαρτίαν compared with the Latin *addictus alicui*, and ὡς διὰ πυρός compared with *ambustus*, when the Latin words are used tropically.

The foundation of analogy in all languages consists in the fact that men are affected in nearly the same way by objects of sense. Though they use language that differs in respect to etymology, yet they mean doubtless the same thing when describing the same objects.

The meaning of words in each or any language is not to be resolved into the authority of lexicons, but that of good writers. Words, phrases, tropes, &c., of any ancient languages, are to be judged of by the rules of judging among those who wrote that language, and not by those which prevail in modern times, and have originated from different habits and tastes. Conclusions as to the meaning of words in the same or different languages are not to be drawn from fanciful etymology, similarity, or metathesis of letters, &c. When the sense of words can be ascertained in any particular language by the ordinary means, other languages, even kindred ones, should not be resorted to except for the purpose of increased illustration or confirmation. Real similitude should always exist where comparison is made.

We must also resort to the *nature* of things and the analogy of the sentiment which the writer is inculcating, that we may find the true meaning of his words, and not attribute to them more nor less than he did. Every writer spontaneously, or from education, feels that his readers must understand what he is saying, so that there is no danger of misapprehension. It happens not unfrequently that on this account he uses language which is not altogether accurate, if it be judged of by the rules of logical precision. Of this nature are *catachresis*, *hyperbole*, *hypallage*,* and of those phrases which assert generally what is true of only a part, or of some particular kind. These and other like modes of speech are introduced by common custom into every language, especially the oriental ones. They abound in poetry and oratory. Nor is there any particular reason that a writer should take special pains to avoid them. It is necessary, therefore, in these cases, to have recourse, for the sake of interpretation, to the nature of things, to innate conceptions, common sense, and the plain elements of knowledge. Grammatical anomalies are not only free from fault when predominant usage sanctions them, but they become a part of the lanuguage, so that one who departs from them may be said to write inaccurately.

* *Catachresis* is the use of a word so as to attribute to a thing what cannot be predicated of it. Example: "Hear, O heavens! listen, O earth! Let the floods clap their hands and the hills skip." *Hyperbole* magnifies a thing beyond its real greatness. Example: "It is easier for a camel to go through the eye of a needle, &c." *Hypallage* is a change of appropriate for inappropriate language. Example: "His mouth and his tongue, ἀνεῴχθη.

In regard to that usage where a whole is put for a part, and a part for a whole, it is by no means unfrequent in the Scriptures. How often do we meet with πᾶς or πάντες, when only a large or considerable number is intended. A reference to the context and antithesis will determine the exegesis in all such cases. On the other hand, a part is often put for a whole. For example, Psalm viii, 7. 8; Romans viii, 38, 39. The apostle does not here mean to say that the things which he particularizes are the only things which are unable to separate us from the love of Christ. As every writer addresses himself to the common sense of his fellow-men, *common sense* must therefore be appealed to in the interpretation of parables, allegories, and all kinds of figurative language and proverbial expressions.

CHAPTER V.

USUS LOQUENDI OF THE NEW TESTAMENT.

THE language of the New Testament is the later Greek language, as spoken by foreigners of the Hebrew stock, and applied by them to subjects on which it had *never been employed* by native Greek writers. Jews who spoke Greek are called, in the New Testament, Ἑλληνισταί, and hence, in modern usage, the Greek has been termed *Hellenistic*. The language of the writers is modelled after the Hebrew not only in words, phrases, and figures of speech, but in the general texture of the language. St. Luke, who is usually thought to be the most pure in his style, has innumerable Hebraisms. The very beginning of his Gospel, after a short preface of pure Greek, immediately goes into the use of the Hebrew idiom so exactly that it seems to be translated literally from a Hebrew original.

The New Testament also contains *Latinisms*, *Syriasms*, *Chaldaisms*, and *Rabbinisms*.

Having ascertained the character of the language of the New Testament, the student is prepared to direct his attention to the rules for finding out the *usus loquendi*. The interpreter should be acquainted with the Greek and Hebrew idioms, so that he can distinguish between pure Greek and that method of writing which is derived from another language. This is necessary in order rightly to interpret either. In regard to pure Greek he must study not only the writers who have used the popular language, but those of a proximate age who have imitated in some degree the Attic diction. The basis of acquaintance with the Hebrew Greek must be the *Septuagint version;* from the fact that the origin of speaking and writing in Greek concerning sacred things took its rise from that version. Aquilia's Greek version, made not very remote from the apostles, exhibits a similar diction.

In the doctrines of religion the Hebrew idiom is to be specially regarded. In speaking of religious matters the writers of the New Testament were accustomed to use the phraseology of the Hebrew Scriptures. The interpreter will be much assisted here by the analogy of doctrine, with which he ought to be familiar, lest the words of the New Testament should be drawn to a sense alien from that which the authors desired to express, and different from the essential points of religion. The Hebrew idiom is specially to be regarded in respect to the meaning of words and phrases, and the forms and tenses of verbs, and also to the number of both nouns and verbs. In respect to these things the idiom of the New Testament not unfrequently departs from classical Greek, and follows the Hebrew. When the Hebrew idiom fails in the exposition of a word or passage, then recourse must be had to the Syriac, Chaldee, or Rabbinic.

There are many things in the New Testament which are described in a novel way, because the things themselves are *new*. Ancient doctrines are delivered in a language more perspicuous, appropriate, and distinctive—the veil of figures and allegories being removed. New words were therefore necessary in order to describe new things; among which words are many that are adapted to designate certain things on account of some similitude to them. These words were not invented by the apostles, and could not have been, for such invention is a thing that belongs to minds trained up by literary discipline, and not to unlettered men. Terms of this description were suggested by the Holy Spirit, which is an argument in favour of the inspiration of the Scriptures. Of this nature are such words as *δαιμονίζεσθαι, τάρταρος, ἀναγεννᾶν*, and others. If it is asked why the Holy Spirit did not dictate *classic* Greek instead of that which is denominated Hebrew Greek?—the answer is that those for whom it was mostly written could not have understood it without inspiration.

New words are to be explained by testimony *direct* and

indirect. They cannot be explained from the more ancient *usus loquendi*, but have an interpretation peculiar to themselves. This interpretation depends on the direct testimony of the writers, and must be gathered from the collation of similar passages. The testimony of the ancient *Greek fathers* is also to be consulted, as their writings may exhibit the interpretations of the primitive age of Christianity.

The ancient *glossaries* may be of use here, specially that of Hesychius, in which are found many things pertaining to certain passages of the New Testament that were deduced from the most ancient interpreters of it. Others are more or less important.

Glosses in some manuscripts, which have crept into the text of the New Testament in place of the true reading, may be used to assist the interpreter either to understand the true text or to find means for illustrating or confirming the true interpretation. Thus, for example, instead of *ἐρεύνησον*, in John vii, 5, Chrysostom has the reading *ἐρώτησον*, and explains it by *μάθε τοῦτο γάρ ἐστιν ἐρώτησον.* These glosses may have flowed from the ancient schools instructed by Origen, although some may have proceeded from the Latin commentaries.

When all the above means which have been described shall fail, we must then resort to the *context* and to the well-known *nature of things themselves.*

Our interpretation must be guided also by the *analogy* of *Scripture* and *Christian doctrine*, and nothing must be so explained as to contradict that analogy. Analogy of doctrine or faith does not consist in the doctrine which is approved by any particular sect; for then it would be various and inconstant, and there would be no true standard. *Grammatical analogy* is the rule of speaking or form of speech constituted by the laws of the language, which is opposed to *anomaly*, or a method of speaking in opposition to usage, or varying from it. In like manner the analogy of sacred doctrine or faith consists in the *summary* of religion and the *rules* plainly taught in the Scriptures; whence the Latin

Church called it *regula fidei.* To this analogy all things are to be referred, so that nothing may be discordant with it. When this is done the analogy of faith is said to be preserved. As to faith and practice, the analogy of Scripture does not differ from the analogy of doctrine. Examples of analogy, and of judgment agreeably to analogy, may be found in Galatians vi, 15, 16; 1 Corinthians xv, 3–11, &c. In all the departments of learning analogy of such a kind has the force of a rule, both in our judgment and interpretation of a passage. In a special manner we must betake ourselves to analogy in those passages which seem to teach what disagrees with that which is plainly taught in other parts of the Scriptures, and with common sense, concerning divine and human things.

The student should make himself familiar with the more difficult forms of speech in the sacred writers, or those forms which differ from the idioms of our own language, and are not adapted to express with simplicity and logical accuracy principles of any doctrine. For example, many things are affirmed *simply* and *without any limitation*, which, however, are to be understood as having only a *particular* and *partial application.* Specially is this the case in moral propositions. Also, active verbs do not always indicate action, and sometimes they indicate frequency of action. As there is scarcely any form of speech in the sacred writings which is not to be found in profane authors, these should be examined. Those things in the writings of Paul which appear hard to be understood, will not be wondered at by those who compare the writings of the apostle with those of Thucydides. Faults in transpositions, and want of consistency in construction, which at first sight may appear to be incompatible with the dignity and sanctity of the Scriptures, will not create alarm.

CHAPTER VI.

TROPICAL LANGUAGE.

In regard to *tropical* language the office of an interpreter is twofold. In the first place he must rightly distinguish it from language not tropical, so as not to mistake the one for the other, and so as not to pervert the *proper* sense of words by a *tropical* interpretation. Secondly, he must rightly interpret tropes, and give their true sense. It often happens that men think they have gained the *tropical* sense of words when they understand only the *literal* one, and pervert the trope by an etymological interpretation. The *literal* meaning is not to be deserted without evident reason or necessity, and, wherever there is a plain and obvious reason for such a departure, the *tropical* sense must be adopted. Some *apparent* repugnances may exist, however, in regard to things and facts, which must not readily be yielded to in the formation of a judgment in regard to a change. The older writers regard the phrase *proper sense* as of the same meaning with *literal* or *historic sense*, and rightly teach that we *should not depart from the customary signification of a word without a weighty and sufficient reason.* In respect to many words, however, the *tropical* sense is the *customary* or *usual* one.

We may generally understand at once whether a word is to be taken tropically or not, by simply examining the object spoken of, either by the external or internal senses, or by renewing the perception of the object. To judge of figurative language in such cases is very easy, because the objects spoken of are to be examined by our senses, external and internal. In the Scriptures, however, doubts have arisen in regard to the *nature* of subjects there treated, which are such as cannot be subjected to the evidences of the senses. For example: The language which respects God and his operations, and all that respects the invisible things of a future state—heaven and hell, &c. One of the things which the mind learns very slowly is to detach itself from conceptions that arise from material objects and to perceive that in *all* the descriptions of a future state words are of absolute necessity employed which originally have a literal sense, because language affords no other. Even the internal operations of our own mind we are obliged for the same reason to describe in language that of necessity must be tropically understood. It is generally conceded that most of the language employed to describe God and his operations is necessarily to be understood as tropical. So also of the language employed to describe the heavenly world; but what regards the day of judgment, or the world of woe, in the estimation of some, must be understood as strictly literal. With such the apprehension is that if the language which respects the day of judgment or the world of woe is figurative, then the *reality* of them is destroyed. But this is simply ridiculous, inasmuch as this view would also destroy the *reality* of the existence and operations of God and the heavenly world. *Reality* lies essentially at the basis of *tropical* as well as *literal* language.

Those words are not to be regarded as *tropical* which have lost their *original* and *proper* signification, and are used no longer in any but a secondary sense.

Those phrases are tropical the subject and predicate of which are *heterogeneous*, as where corporeal and incorporeal, animate and inanimate, rational and irrational, are conjoined; and also species of a different genus. For example: The *fields smile*, the *stones cry out*, the *floods clap their hands*, &c. Things that cannot possibly exist in any particular subject cannot be logically predicated of it, for the fundamental rules of logic in respect to this are inherent in the mind. If then such things *appear* to be predicated, the phrase must be tropically understood. By this rule the language of the New Testament should be interpreted which respects the person of Jesus Christ, to whom divine and human qualities are attributed. The latter are attributed to him as a man, the former as a divine person.

In regard to divine things which can only be known by revelation, and cannot be examined by the test of our own feelings and views, we can judge only from the *usus loquendi* of the sacred writers whether their language is to be understood literally or tropically. This usage can be known only from the comparison of similar passages, which is done in various ways. 1. When different words are employed in different passages respecting the same thing. For example, the phrase *to be born of water*, John iii, 5, is tropical, for the same thing is *literally* expressed in Mark xvi, 16. So the *covenant* which God made with Abraham is explained in Galatians iii, 16, as meaning a *promise*. 2. When the same word is used everywhere respecting the same thing it has a *proper* sense. For example, ἀνάστασις νεκρῶν, ἐγείρεται σῶμα, ζωοποιεῖται, are *constantly* used in respect to that which is to take place at the end of the world, and therefore are not tropical. 3. When the same method of expression is constantly used respecting divers things which are similar, or which have some special connexion, it is to be understood literally.

The *context* must also be consulted. When the whole passage is allegorical we must acknowledge a trope in particular parts that are connected with the whole allegory. For example, πῦρ, 1 Corinthians iii, 13, which relates to ξύλα and χόρτον in the context. In like manner the language is to be regarded as tropical when, although the preceding context is to be literally understood, there is a manifest transition to allegory.

In regard to *interpreting* tropical language we may observe there are two sources of aid. The one is the *subject* itself, the other the *usus loquendi*. Interpretation by the aid of the subject is easy when the nature of it affords an obvious similitude. For example, φωτισμός is easily understood as used *tropically*. In regard to the *usus loquendi*, the general usage of the Hebrew tongue in respect to tropical words must be first understood as in words corresponding to ζωή, θάνατος, τιμή, δόξα, &c.; then Greek usage in general. Passages must also be compared in which the same thing is expressed by a *proper* word, or in which such *proper* word is employed in the context, so that the sense is obvious. Here too we may use the comparison of words that are conjoined and similar, examples of which will hereafter be produced.

We must not judge of tropes merely from etymology. For example, ὀρθοτομεῖν, in 2 Timothy ii, 15, some have interpreted as implying a distinction between the law and the gospel, which is ridiculous; for λόγος ἀληθείας in the context means the gospel, and the law is not the subject of discourse here.

For the purpose of adequately understanding what tropical language is, substitute *proper* words for *tropical* ones. It is also useful to make the experiment whether when the image presented by the tropical expression is removed from the mind any idea still remains in it different from the image itself, which can be expressed by a proper word. This experiment is specially to be made when words designating sensible objects are transferred to the expression of intellectual ones. For example, θάνατος, ζωή, διαθήκη, &c., in respect to which it is easy to be deceived. The context, the nature of the subject, and parallel passages, are the most effectual means of ascertaining this.

Allegories.

The term 'Αλληγορία is derived from ἀλλὸ ἀγορεύεται; that is, *a different thing is said* from that which is meant. It differs from metaphor, which is confined to a word. Allegory extends to a whole thought, or to several thoughts. It may be expressed by *pictures*, Ezekiel iv, 1; by *actions*, Ezekiel iii, iv, v; Luke xxii, 36, or by any *significant thing*.

In interpreting allegories the first thing to be done is to

ascertain the *design*, which is readily obtained when it is connected with a context explanatory of its design. For the most part, however, the design is expressly declared. For example, the design of the parable or allegory of the good Samaritan is to illustrate *the duty and extent of beneficence*. The next thing is to find out the *primary* word, or that which designates the leading design, and all the other words are to be interpreted in conformity to it.

The design of the exhortation in form of allegory, found in 1 Corinthians v, 6, is that the Corinthians should be purified from vicious inclinations and the evil practices arising therefrom. Ζύμη, therefore, here means *vice*, and ἄζυμος, *free from vice, or without vice*. Ἑορτάζειν, consequently, is not to celebrate a feast, according to its proper signification, for a tropical meaning is required. It means *to serve God, to worship God, to be a Christian, to be free from vices, and worship him in purity*. It is altogether incongruous to understand *one part* literally and another tropically, in the same allegory, as those do who take πυρός in 1 Corinthians iii, 15 literally, when all the context is to be understood tropically. The expression ὡς διὰ πυρός makes it plain that the word is to be figuratively understood.

To explain allegory we must sometimes resort to *history*. For example, as when the kingdom of God is compared to *leaven* and a *mustard-seed*. History shows the rise and progress of the kingdom of Christ; from small beginnings it is spreading throughout the earth. In the next place, *the nature of the subject* will assist in the interpretation. For example: "*Ye are the salt of the earth*," &c., Matthew v, 13. The subject is the instructions to be given by the disciples. The *primary* or leading word (*salt*) in the allegory means *instruction*, and conveys an idea of the nature and effects of that instruction—preservative, conservative.

Not unlike the method of interpreting allegories is that of interpreting *parables*, which often contain allegory. We must guard against urging too far the meaning of all parts of a parabolical narrative, and refer the particular parts to the main design, so that all may be accommodated to it. Therefore, in Luke xv, 11, &c., we are not to seek for a doctrinal meaning in *στολή*, *μόσχος*, *δακτύλιος*, &c. Such circumstances are commonly added to complete the *form* of the narration, and to make it a more finished picture of what might be supposed to have happened.

Parable in Greek usage means *any composition introduced into a discourse.* It may be called an *example* taken from things real or fictitious, designed for special and graphical illustration. Allegory differs from parable only in the style and mode of expression. Take an allegory and express it in the historic style, and it is converted into a parable. The same rules of exegesis apply to both.

CHAPTER VII.

RULES IN REGARD TO EMPHASIS.

EMPHASIS should not be deduced from the etymology of a word, nor in tropical expressions should we recur to the proper sense of the words to deduce emphasis from it, as has been done in respect to the word *ἐρευνᾶν*. Tropically used, this word does not signify *to seek with great exertion and diligence;* for the Holy Spirit is said *ἐρευνᾶν τὰ βάθη τῆς θεότητος*, to whom this emphatic meaning surely will not apply. The ancient interpreters used *ἐρευνᾶν* in the same sense as *γινώσκειν*. In both of the above points errors are very frequent.

Prepositions compounded with Greek words do not make any accession or augmentation of signification. For example, *ἀνά*, *ἀπό*, *πρό*, *σύν*, *ἐκ*, *περί*, compounded as in *ἀνασταυροῦν*, *ἀνανήθειν*, *συμμαρτυρεῖν*, *προγινώσκειν*, &c. Many are accustomed to build arguments on such imaginary emphasis. These prepositions do not always change the meaning of simple words, but are very commonly redundant.

Emphasis must not be deduced merely from the *plural* number, supposing that where the plural is put for the singular it necessarily denotes emphasis. This is not so, either as it regards the Hebrew or Greek.

Emphasis is not to be attached to an *abstract* word when it is merely used for a concrete one. The true ground of using abstract words for concretes is either from *necessity* or *for the sake of perspicuity*, and not on account of emphasis. In the sacred books the *necessity* of it springs from the Hebrew dialect, which often employs abstract words in this manner, because it has only a few concrete ones.

In the sacred books, and especially in the Hebraisms of the New Testament, we must not seek for and recognise emphasis merely in the idiom which is so very dissimilar to our own. In the oriental languages many things, if translated literally, *appear* hyperbolical which are not so in reality. For example, in Lamentations it is said, *My trouble is great as the sea*, which is simply equivalent to the Latin expression, *mala mea sunt maxima.*

If there is no adequate testimony to show that any word has a constant emphasis, we must consult usage. We should first inquire whether, in all the passages where the word is found, emphasis would be consistent. Next, whether, in the same passage, or a similar one, another word may be substituted in the room of this, which other contains a special designation of *intensity.*

If neither of these be the case, but the word in question may be commuted for others which are plainly *unemphatic;* or, in some of the passages where the word occurs, a special designation of intensity is made by adding some other word for this purpose, then there is no emphasis to be recognised in the word in question. For example, some have attached emphasis to ἀποκαραδοκία in Romans viii, 19; but in Philippians i, 20 it would be inconsistent. There it is used as a synonyme with ἐλπίδα, and, in fact, commuted with it in verse 22. Nor is emphasis always attached to such phrases as χαρὰν χαίρειν, for such phrases are often used when another word is added to indicate *intensity;* for example, Matthew ii, 10. This would be useless if they indicated intensity themselves.

The usual or temporary emphasis arising from the *affection* of the speaker may be recognised without difficulty by the following mark, viz.: if the ordinary signification of the word is far below the manifest intensity of the affection which the speaker or writer feels.

If the usual force of the word or phrase would give a frigid meaning, when, on the other hand, an apt one would arise if some intensity were given to the word, there is a plain necessity of emphasis, which is the best guide for finding it. So in 1 Corinthians iv, 3, 4, ἀνακρίνειν is constantly emphatic; meaning either *to be tried by the judgment*, or *to take to one's self the right of trying or judging*, or *to be able rightly to judge.* If translated simply *to judge*, a frigid sense would be given to it not at all adapted to the context. In like manner πίστιν, in Colossians i, 4, is used, as the context shows, to denote the *constancy*, *greatness*, or *fruitfulness of faith.* Paul was not under the necessity of knowing by report that the Church at Colosse had simply Christian faith, inasmuch as he was himself the founder of that Church. So in Romans i, 8, that faith must have been *special* which was celebrated throughout the world. Also in Matt. iv, 2, ἐπείνασε must imply intensity, from the circumstances of the case.

The *usus loquendi* must not be neglected; and whatever rules may be devised for finding out and establishing the emphasis, the *usus loquendi* must not be contradicted, nor anything admitted implying repugnance thereto.

CHAPTER VIII.

THE AFFECTIONS OF INSPIRED WRITERS.

THAT an acquaintance with the doctrine of the affections is an essential requisite in the exposition of the Scriptures, may be proved from reason and from the authority of divines.

It may be proved from reason; for the affections of love, hatred, desire, hope, fear, joy, sorrow, &c., are frequently to be met with in Holy Writ. It is evident, therefore, that, were we ignorant of these affections, we should be inadequate to the exposition of no inconsiderable part of the sacred writings.

When no affections are *expressed* we must necessarily consider them *implied*, and that every sentence is of their dictation. In 2 Cor. ii, 4, Paul says himself that he wrote the former epistle to the Corinthians "out of much affliction and anguish of heart, with many tears." In Phil. iii, 18, he speaks of the false teachers with "weeping;" and in 1 Thess. ii, 7, &c., he describes his ardent love for the Thessalonians, in language replete with energy and pathos. Does not reason then warrant us in concluding that the affections here *expressed* are, in *similar* passages, *implied?* When Paul, addressing the converts, (1 Cor. iv, 15,) tells them, "Though ye have ten thousand instructors in Christ, yet not many fathers, for in Christ Jesus I have begotten you through the gospel," is he not influenced by the affection mentioned in 1 Thess. ii, 7, &c.? When he asserts, (2 Cor. ii, 17,) that "many corrupt the word of God," (collate iii, 2, &c.,) who but infers that he is actuated by the affection noticed Phil. iii, 18? an affection in which indignation, sorrow, pity, &c., are blended together. Hence it is evident that to neglect the affections because they are not directly expressed, would be as palpable an error as to pass them over without concern where they are plainly and fully revealed. The indications of an affection are not indeed always similar, nor uniformly perspicuous; but the judicious and spiritual reader will ever find them to be fully adequate and sufficient.

When we read the Scriptures we are bound to see that our *natural* affections be amended and corrected, and that our hearts, under the influence of the Holy Spirit, overflow with *gracious* affections. Without, however, a knowledge of these emotions, who can inspect the abyss of the human heart, and the depth of those feelings by which it is agitated? And, without forming correct ideas of the affections which it is proposed to imitate, how shall man, who is *carnal*, "put them on?"

The nature of discourse confirms the position. Christ says, (Matt. xii, 34, 35,) "How can ye, being evil, speak good things? for out of the abundance of the heart the mouth speaketh. A good man, out of the good treasure of the heart, bringeth forth good things: and an evil man, out of the evil treasure, bringeth forth evil things." These words decidedly evidence that unless some affection influenced the heart, language would not be uttered; so that a man's words are, in fact, the index of his feelings or affections. What is "the abundance of the heart," but those internal emotions which inform and actuate the human soul, and which constitute, in a holy man, holy affections, and, in an unholy man, unholy affections? So closely, indeed, are language and affections connected together—so indissoluble is the union that subsists between them—that it would be, in effect, just as unreasonable to divide soul from body as to separate these. Since, then, the affections are so intimately connected with all language, none will suppose that they are banished from the writings of the inspired penmen; and, because they are closely united with the language of inspiration, it follows that the sacred records cannot be adequately expounded by those who are satisfied with the mere shell and contemn the precious kernel of Scripture—who watch the lips, but never enter into the *feelings* of the inspired penmen.

Since different ideas and views are communicated by different affections, so that the same words pronounced under the influence of various emotions will convey various meanings, it becomes requisite to investigate and develop the affections of the sacred penmen, lest we impose on their language a sense they were not intended to deliver. Many other arguments which might be adduced we intentionally omit, because a treatise on this subject will best demonstrate its high importance.

Having shown the necessity of an acquaintance with the doctrine of the affections, on the ground of *reason*, let us proceed for a moment to enforce its claims on the *authority of divines*.

Wolfgang Franzius, in his invaluable book, "De Interpretatione Scripturæ Sacræ," discusses the question so fully, and illustrates his positions with examples so pertinent, as to render his work deserving the serious attention of the inquiring reader.

Luther also was indebted to his knowledge of the affections, and to his lively mode of representing them, for that eminent gift of exposition with which he was endowed. Of this his Comment on Genesis, and his Discourses on the Psalms, are conclusive evidences.

We next proceed to cite some observations from the letter addressed by Spener to the Philo-biblical College at Leipsic. This celebrated man observes—"No practice will prove more pleasant or beneficial, and none more suitable to the college, than after fervent, secret prayer, to discriminate and enter into the affections of the inspired writers with sacred attention and perseverance, and strive to unfold their nature and character. This being done, and the thoughts being collected and brought to bear on the subject in hand, the students will be able to mark, with the highest delight and profit, the indications of faith and of the mind of Jesus, together with the more minute circumstances, and easily awaken in their own bosoms affections of a kindred nature. That eminent divine, Luther, when speaking of this practice, says—'Whoever adopts it will, I am satisfied, learn more himself than he can gather from all commentaries united. By means of incessant and attentive reading, we should, as it were, raise the writer from the dead and consider him as alive, so as to form perfect conceptions, mentally, of what we cannot actually behold. When engaged in the study of the Scriptures the idea formed in the writer's mind should be carefully ascertained—the affections by which he was influenced—his state of life, and his office, at the time he penned the book. Much do I wish that the labour which Casaubon has bestowed upon Horace, Juvenal, and Persius, in his Prolegomena, were applied to the elucidation of the divine oracles, so as to give a just description of the genius, mind, condition, manners, and affections, peculiar to each of the sacred writers. These are desirable subjects that yet remain untouched.' Luther again remarks, 'that an expositor should, as it were, invest himself with the author's mind, in order that he may interpret him as another self.' Bernard likewise excelled in this heavenly art of correcting his own affections by those of the sacred penmen, and it was thence he derived his spiritual erudition." Thus far Spener's letter; and to these names may be added that of Flaccus Illyricus, who also recommends the study of the affections of the inspired penmen.

Let us now consider a few objections which may be made to this view of the subject. There are persons perhaps who think that the Holy Spirit is wronged when we attribute to the sacred writers affections which are in reality the fruit of his influence, and that the Scriptures are not to be referred to those holy men, but rather to the Holy Ghost who speaks by them. To this we answer that the fact of their being divinely inspired, far from militating against our position, tends itself to convince us that the Holy Spirit kindled sacred affections in the writers' souls; for it is absurd to suppose that in penning the Scriptures they viewed themselves in the light of mere machines, or that they wrote without *any* feeling or perception what we read with so great a degree of both. Doubtless their minds were illuminated by the Spirit, and their wills inflamed with pious, holy, and ardent affections, so that they wrote as they *felt*, and as they were "*moved* by the Holy Ghost." 2 Peter i, 21. Indeed, it appears that the Spirit condescended to *accommodate* himself to their peculiar genius and modes of writing, which evidently vary in the different books of Scripture. Hence we conclude that the minds of the sacred penmen were not unmoved, but on the contrary active, enlightened, and replete with holy affections.

Besides, the inspired writers sometimes *mention* the affections by which they are actuated, as has been already shown, and this must form a complete answer to the objection proposed; for who will have the temerity to affirm, when Paul expressly declares his love, joy, desire, hope, that he really is not influenced by these sacred passions?

Again, it may possibly be objected that, on the principles laid down, the language of divine truth would become ambiguous, for that any one might give it what sense he pleased by referring it to various affections. In reply to this objection, we observe that we agree in considering it a matter of high importance to develop the genuine and spiritual meaning of the written word, and then *prove* it to be so, where there is no gesture or modulation of voice to guide us in judging of the affections. To infer, however, that we must not examine into the affections of the inspired penmen, lest this ambiguity should arise, were to conceal our ignorance, and dissemble the difficulty rather than explain it. Daily experience testifies that even familiar conversation is capable of various interpretations, according to the affections that operate. Will, then, our ignorance remove these affections, which nature implanted, and which grace does not restrain? This objection is in truth a cogent argument in favour of the study of the affections; for when we have acquired ability to develop them, (which certainly is attainable,) the Scriptures will of course cease to be ambiguous.

It forms no solid objection to our view of the subject that many commentators neglect this branch of exposition and pass it over in silence. This consideration is abundantly overruled by opposing to it the high authorities that have advocated the cause of the affections. It might be added that those persons are usually but indifferent examiners of the Scriptures who, in searching into their meaning, depend partially or entirely on authority. It evidences, as Bernard has observed, that they do not read the word in the Spirit, under whose influence it was written.

Besides, a consequence deduced from the ignorance or negligence of commentators can avail nothing against the doctrine. It is indeed to be lamented that very few are solicitous to ascertain the spiritual meaning of the sacred writings, but are anxious rather to be diffuse on *critical*, *controverted*, and *difficult* points, where there is a wider field for the range of natural intellect. This inattention to the affections is a main reason why some commentaries are so meagre and unsatisfactory to spiritual readers who, with a view to personal edification, search after the mind of the Spirit and the revelations of the divine image. A comment written without adverting to the affections, is so only in name and form.

An *unrenewed* man cannot attain to a just knowledge of the affections as a help to exposition. This is evident from the following considerations:—

An unrenewed person has no *perception* of any but natural affections. He speaks of spiritual affections as a blind man does of colours; and even as it respects those which are natural his views are not just, so long as he is immured in the darkness and depravity of his corrupt nature. It is spiritual affections, however, that are chiefly to be known; for the mind of Christ best explains the mind of Christ. This is clear from 1 Cor. ii.

Again, the knowledge of the affections of which we speak is practical; whereas an unrenewed man peruses the Scriptures theoretically, and believes it sufficient if he understand them through the medium of natural reason. It likewise requires an *inward perception*, (αἴσθησις,) of which the unrenewed person is destitute, and after which, while in his unregenerate state, he never seriously aspires.

It seems indeed an objection to this statement that we daily see ungodly men not only handle the Scriptures, but also speak largely on its meaning, in books and commentaries, and indeed utter truths that cannot be controverted by pious men. This difficulty is, however, fully explained when we reflect that what is within the compass of a carnal man in profane writings, is equally so as it respects the Scriptures. He can, for instance, apprehend the terms as they are commonly received, form the affirmation and negation, understand them when formed, and perceive the necessity of a consequence, as well in Holy Writ as in profane authors. When an unrenewed person reads the precept, "Thou shalt not kill," he perfectly conceives what is meant by killing; he likewise understands what is prohibited, and, because the precept is universal, he rightly infers that *he* is forbidden to murder. But as it respects the *spiritual* meaning, which the letter does not immediately convey, and the mind of the Spirit, (τὸ φρόνημα τοῦ Πνεύματος,) how is it possible for a carnal, unrenewed man to have any perception of that from which he is so entirely alienated? In 1 Cor. ii, 11, 12, Paul affirms that "the things of God knoweth no man, but the Spirit of God, and they who have received not the spirit of the world, but the Spirit which is of God."

As an example of this we cite James iii, where the apostle, by implication, accuses the persons addressed of a breach of the fifth commandment, and (ver. 17, 18,) describes the mind of the Spirit in full, perspicuous, and energetic language—displaying that mind, as it were, before their eyes in impressive points of view. It is indubitably certain that a carnal man can apprehend the terms of the proposition here advanced, and apply the precept, by legitimate consequence, to himself; but he will not, he cannot, have any perception, or form any idea, of the *habit* of a soul that is sanctified, and endued with heavenly knowledge and divine perception. On this subject we may confidently appeal to the believer's present and past experience. Since, then, an unrenewed person has no knowledge of this *habit* of the mind, how is it possible for him to have any perception of the emotions of a holy soul?

Observation and experience have likewise evidenced most decisively, that in consequence of the incapacity already noticed, the mind of a carnal, unregenerate person is far from adequately penetrating even into the sense of the letter, because, from the very nature of things, there subsists the closest connexion between words and ideas.

The consideration of the affections is fourfold. If we examine them generally, a definition that will comport with all cannot be given; nor is it indeed necessary. Let us, however, notice them in the following points of view:—

1. As they belong to men, in common with brutes. Under this character we must class the motions of *sensitive* appetite, arising from the imagination of good or evil, whether real or only apparently so.

2. As they belong to the carnal man. In this class we may range the motions (*facultatis appetentis*) of the *desiring faculty*, sensitive or intellectual, arising from the apprehension of good or evil, whether this be of a sensitive or intellectual nature.

3. As they belong to the *spiritual* man. In this view an affection is the emotion of a soul sanctified and actuated by the Spirit.

4. As they are attributed to God himself, in the sacred writings. This the grammarians call ἀνθρωποπάθεια, (a human affection,) a word which immediately suggests that affections cannot be attributed to the Divine Being, but that

the Holy Spirit accommodates himself to human infirmity, and condescends to speak of God in a way adapted to our capacities. Luther explains the foundation of ἀνθρωποπάθεια in this way:—"Affections are attributed to God, so far as they are found in the sacred writers who were inspired by him, and also in the ministers of the word. Thus we find, Gen. vi, 6, that repentance is ascribed to God, so far as Noah, a holy man, under the sacred influences of the Spirit, felt grieved on account of the gross and universal depravity of mankind. Affections are likewise attributed to God, so far as the wicked feel them in their bosoms. Thus anger is ascribed to the Divine Being because the sinner perceives, by the disquietude of his conscience, that God is angry with him."

It will evidently be sufficient for our purpose if we consider the affections in the second and third modes; that is, as they attach to the *carnal* and to the *spiritual* man. This will suggest all that is necessary to be known respecting the other modes noticed.

As both the carnal and spiritual affections will come under consideration, it should be remarked that affections may be similar as to name, and yet, on account of their *source*, *object*, *end*, *subjects*, *adjuncts*, &c., be essentially different. By means of some definite properties or characteristics, they can, however, be readily distinguished.

Characteristics of Spiritual Affections.

1. A spiritual affection has for its source the Holy Spirit, and is the fruit of his influence.

2. A spiritual affection tends to a holy end.

3. A spiritual affection is engaged on objects that are divine, eternal, spiritual, and invisible.

4. A spiritual affection, when engaged on sensible objects, is not employed on them as such, but only so far as they have relation to those which are unseen.

5. A spiritual affection is grounded on faith and love. When these do not operate, affections cease to be spiritual.

6. A spiritual affection influences the subject of it to seek not himself nor his personal convenience as such, but God and his glory.

7. A spiritual overcomes a carnal affection, though the latter be otherwise very violent.

8. A spiritual affection is always connected with humility. The instant the mind is elated affections become carnal.

9. A spiritual affection excites no perturbation in the mind, nor does it leave behind it any bitterness. It rather assists in the regulation of the soul, receiving every dispensation with complacency, and acquiescing in God with joy.

10. A spiritual affection tends to the amelioration of nature, the increase of grace, and the edification of mankind; having no object but the glory of God.

Characteristics of Carnal Affections.

1. A carnal affection, as it is opposed to those which are spiritual, so it has nature for its source, and is destitute of grace.

2. A carnal affection has for its end the temporal preservation and amendment of nature, or it refers all things to pleasure, and *particularly* seeks such pleasure not in mental peace but personal convenience, and this often under a pretext of duty.

3. A carnal affection is engaged on objects that are corporeal, local, temporal, and sensitive.

4. A carnal affection, if engaged upon spiritual objects, does not dwell on them as such, neither with righteous views nor in a consistent manner, but only so far as they have relation to private gratification or convenience.

5. A carnal affection receives its existence and support from perverse self-love.

6. A carnal affection gives the preference to things natu-

rally pleasing, though others may approximate more nearly to real excellence.

7. A carnal affection gradually disturbs the mind when it is at all indulged, rendering it incapable of investigating truth, or of performing righteous actions, and it leaves a degree of bitterness in the mind proportioned to the strength of the affection. Cicero justly used to term them "*perturbationes animi*"—(the perturbations of the mind.)

8. A carnal affection has always a degree of pride (*αὐθάδεια*) in it, though it is often very subtile. As long as this has place in the mind, carnal affections are not put off.

9. A carnal affection often induces a visible change of the body.

The characteristics we have enumerated are by no means all, but they are the more general ones—those which are most consonant with our present object, and which may afford matter whence to derive others of a more special kind. If the reader apply himself to do this, his labor will not be unprofitable.

The object of the characteristics which have been adduced, is to develop with more facility the affections of the inspired writers.

Although the carnal affections are by these characteristics separated from the spiritual affections, we are not thence to conclude that they are so separated in the heart of a renewed person as that the former never mingle with the latter. On the contrary, the believer's daily strife is to be more and more delivered from the sinful affections of carnal nature. It is according to the *reigning* affections that a man is denominated *carnal* or *spiritual*. To suppose, however, that renewed and unrenewed men have the same perception of the affections of the sacred writers, is a radical error. It were impious to ascribe any mixture of good and bad affections to the Holy Spirit, though we cannot deny that sacred affections show themselves in a sanctified nature by external and natural indications.

1. Affections are either simple or compound. The *simple* affections are love, hatred, desire, aversion, joy, sorrow, hope, despair, fear, confidence, anger. The Cartesian philosophy not unreasonably classes with them the affections of admiration, contempt, and other emotions of the mind relating chiefly to the intellect. The *compound* are those in which many affections concur, as compassion, indignation, envy, emulation, &c. It is not enough to have a *general* knowledge of the affections, since every word may flow from a different emotion.

2. In the consideration of the sacred text, a distinction is to be made between the affections of the writer, those of the person addressed, the affections of the subject of discourse, and those which are attributed to the blessed God. Hence it is evidently necessary not only to ascertain the affection, but to determine the subject. This will have a tendency to cause the thing itself to be more accurately, distinctly, and duly weighed, and the delightful harmony that subsists between the affections of the different subjects will be likewise more fully unfolded. It will also assist us to discern the principles of holy wisdom, according to which affections may be regulated by affections. This is certainly of high importance, though as a help it has hitherto been seldom noticed or improved.

3. In examining the affections, those are to be considered first which are expressly named, and afterwards those which are not immediately declared. Thus, by proceeding from easier to more difficult points, we shall gradually enter into the affections, even in those passages that afford no direct indications of them.

4. When the affections are not expressly named, the text should be examined according to the characteristics. Every characteristic is to be so applied, both carnal and spiritual: the former class to the affections of those persons who are the subjects of the discourse, and to those of the writer; and the latter oftentimes to different subjects, but specially to the

sacred penmen. Wherever we recognise a characteristic we must conclude there is a latent affection, for dissimulation has no place in the word of God.

It is proper here not only to have the *general* characteristics of the affections ascertained, but likewise those which are *special*, and accommodated to individual affections. The reader will thus easily attain to a special as well as general knowledge of holy affections.

The characteristics may be accommodated not only to *words*, but likewise to *actions* and entire details.

The several characteristics should be separately applied to the subjects whenever an indiscriminate application would be an infringement on the Spirit speaking in the Scriptures. The reader (especially if one of the Epistles be perused) may be considered as standing in a college, where, while he listens to the person speaking, and hangs, as it were, upon *his* lips, the affections of those who are absent and those who are present are successively brought before him, and he learns from both what to imitate and what to avoid.

It would be exceedingly useful to have the several affections so practically developed, from carefully examining our own, that we might without difficulty express their characteristics in perspicuous and suitable words. To adopt the language of Franzius, "when the mind is thus engaged, the word will become ineffably sweet and inconceivably precious." He who reposes in God with placid and calm affection may contemplate the turbulent passions of the human heart, as well as the gracious emotions excited in a sanctified soul by the Holy Spirit, and by tasting of divine wisdom perceive its nature and appreciate its worth. Here, indeed, an inscrutable abyss will open to his view, and, as Luther hath remarked, "meditation, when strengthened and supported by frequent exercise, will suggest more, much more, than all our commentaries united." May the reader be encouraged to aspire after this most useful and profitable help!

It may be added that exercise will be cherished into habit, and that the characteristics can be so familiarized by patient practice and pious experience as to leave the student at liberty to draw them from "the good treasure of his heart."

5. All the circumstances which the text supplies, or which may be otherwise known, should be weighed and examined, if we aim at forming a right judgment of the latent affection. Though only one circumstance remain unknown, a very different affection may be often ascribed to the speaker, of which we have frequent examples, even in familiar conversation. The circumstances, *Who? What? Where? By what means? Why? How? When?* should be, as much as possible, applied.

The circumstance which may be more remarkable in one place than in another is to be chiefly urged, though, in particular places, the major part contribute to give weight to the affections.

All circumstances are not always necessary to be accommodated to all words. Some words have peculiar reference to particular circumstances, and, as it were, point them out. It is, however, necessary sometimes to examine all the circumstances accurately, and, indeed, the more attentive the student is, the more will he enter into the spirit of the text and the mind of the holy penmen.

6. *Love* is justly considered as the foundation, or rather source, of *every* affection in the inspired penmen.

The first fruit of the Spirit (Gal. v, 22) is love. This affection, however, sometimes receives different designations, according to the circumstances. Love to God and man was the preëminent affection in the soul of St. Paul. Hence, when he addresses penitent sinners, (as in his Second Epistle to the Corinthians,) we may plainly discover that his desire, fear, hope, piety, joy, in short, that all his affections spring from love.

7. Pronunciation, or the modulation of the voice in uttering any text, is by no means to be neglected.

This ever follows the course of the affections and the dictates of nature, and hence a discourse delivered *vivâ voce* is much more easily apprehended than one written. So facts which the eye witnesses are far more convincing than those which are related to us.

The deficiency under which every student of Scripture, in this respect, labours, may be supplied by first using every method of eliciting the true meaning of the text, and then pronouncing it according to the sense and affection previously and carefully ascertained.

It is presumed, however, that no person will raise any interpretation of Scripture on the foundation of this or any other help alone, but apply all rules of exposition in regular order. He who neglects this injunction will often deceive others and be deceived himself.

The punctuation and other distinctions which have in the course of time been introduced into the text, materially affect the pronunciation, and will often lead the reader to attribute affections which the passage, when divested of its human appendages, would by no means warrant. On this account we should lose sight of these arbitrary distinctions until the affection be ascertained. Those ancient copies in which the text is not divided into verses, are, in this view, to be preferred.

8. In examining the affections, we profit chiefly by an ardent and holy emulation of those sacred emotions which we contemplate in the inspired writers.

The more we "put on" their affections, the more deeply shall we enter into their writings and meditate on the truths which they reveal. Whenever the affections of the sacred penmen develop and unfold themselves, let us seek to possess the same amiable emotions, and, if possible, the same degree of them in our own bosoms; and let us, by the grace of God, strive to correct every irregularity of temper. The meaning of Scripture, thus laid up in the *heart* rather than the *head*, will transform our souls "from glory into glory," and we shall experience that "the word of God is quick and powerful, and sharper than any two-edged sword; piercing even to the dividing asunder of soul and spirit, and of the joints and marrow, and is a discerner of the thoughts and intents of the heart."

CHAPTER IX.

MEANS OF HARMONIZING APPARENT DISCREPANCIES.

If it could be plainly shown that two passages of Scripture *contradict* each other, and that no method of conciliation is practicable, it must necessarily follow that one of the readings in the usual copies must be faulty, and an emendation of the text must be sought. Of this nature, perhaps, is the passage in John xix, 14, compared with Matthew xxvii, 45 and Mark xv, 25; also, as many think, Luke iii, 36, compared with Genesis x, 24. Some add Matthew xxvii, 9, compared with Zechariah xi, 12, 13.

If the text of both passages plainly appears to be genuine, so that it cannot fairly be questioned, then it must be understood that there is a mere *appearance* of inconsistency, which should be removed, and the passage conciliated by a proper interpretation.

The *appearance* of inconsistencies sometimes occurs in passages of a *doctrinal*, and sometimes of a *historical* kind. The writers of the New Testament sometimes *appear* to be at variance with themselves, sometimes with each other, and occasionally with the writers of the Old Testament. As an example of variance with themselves, instance 1 Cor. viii, 1, compared with verse 7. For an example of variance with each other, Paul asserts that a man is justified by faith and not by works. James asserts that a man is justified not by faith only, but also by works. The difference is, however, only in *appearance*, not in reality.

In *doctrinal passages* an apparent contradiction, that is to be removed, arises for the most part either from the style of the authors, which is rather of the *popular* kind than that of nice refinement, or from the genius of the oriental languages, which differs so widely from that of the western ones. An apparent contradiction, in respect to doctrines plainly taught, is to be removed by theologians in the way of explaining *things* rather than words merely, and so it comes not directly within the province of the interpreter.

The method of harmonizing apparent doctrinal discrepancies may be regarded by the following rules:—1. An obscure passage should be explained in accordance with what is plain and without any ambiguity. For example, we must explain all the anthropopathical expressions in regard to God by the plain truth that his nature is spiritual. 2. A passage in which a doctrine is merely touched or adverted to, is to be explained by other passages which present plain and direct exhibitions of it. For instance, the subject of justification in Romans iii is designedly treated at large; of the resurrection, in 1 Cor. xv. Such passages are called *classic*, (*loci classici*,) and by them other expressions, which simply occur *obiter*, are to be explained.

We must, however, be careful to harmonize apparent discrepancies, if it can be done, by recourse to the *usus loquendi*, so that all occasion of doubt or cavilling may be removed; for it is very desirable that the *usus loquendi* should justify that sense which we put upon any doubtful passage, from having compared it with passages that are plain and clear.

Many things of a doctrinal nature are *simply* and *absolutely* declared, agreeably to common usage, in all languages, which still have only a *relative* sense. This may be accounted for from the fact that there are parts of religion which are commonly known and understood, therefore such parts do not need accurate limitations. For example, *that we are saved by faith* is one of the elementary principles of the Christian religion. The sacred writers, therefore, do not, on every mention of any duty, remind us of this principle, inasmuch as they expect us to keep it always in memory. When they say that *alms-giving* is acceptable to God, they expect to be understood as meaning, *if it be accompanied by faith.* In this way apparent discrepancies may be reconciled, and the reconciliation becomes the more probable as the *reason* for it can be given.

Apparent discrepancies, arising from *oriental* style or manner of expression, are quite numerous. For example, pluck out the eye that offends; cut off the hand that offends; it is easier for a camel to go through the eye of a needle, &c.; to follow Christ one must hate parents, &c., &c. The context, passages similar as to the subject, the nature of the style, the subject itself, &c., are the means of finding the true sense of such places, and then the harmony of these with other passages is obvious.

Apparent discrepancies with other writers, or between different parts of the same writer, not unfrequently occur. For example, in addition to what has been given *supra*, the advice of Paul, 1 Cor. vii, respecting matrimony, is only *pro tempore*, and dictated merely by the exigencies of the times in which he wrote. In many other places his writings contain a different sentiment. Again, in Romans iii, 20 it is said that a man cannot be justified by works; but in ii, 13 it is stated that ποιητία, *doers* of the law, shall be justified. Here one verse states the rule of *legal justification*, the other that no man can claim it on the ground of that rule. Where it is said *we are justified by faith*, the meaning is that *we receive pardon on the ground of gratuity;* but *justification* as applied to the *doers* of the law, means *reward on the ground of merit* or *perfect obedience.*

Discrepancies seem to exist at times between the writers of the Old Testament and the New, merely from the different manner in which they express themselves on the same subjects, when this is rather to be attributed to the different degrees of light which the writers had, and to the differences in the eras, manners, and habits of each. For example, the subject of war, of loving enemies, of benevolence to the Gentiles, of God's equal and paternal regard to them, of gratuitous justification, &c. A representation less perfect in the Old Testament need not be understood as contradicting one more perfect in the New.

Apparent discrepancies of an *historical* nature originate from a different *design* and *manner* in narrating the same thing, as often happens in the Gospels; for a diversity of design varies the choice of circumstances. Many circumstances differ, after all, in nothing important as to designating the ideas which the authors in common mean to designate; and oftentimes they may be either commuted for each other or omitted. It is of no importance, sometimes, whether a thing be asserted in a generic or specific form.

Far more frequently an appearance of discrepancy arises from the mere *manner of expression*, which seems at first view to imply a difference in the things described, while it is merely a difference in the *mode* of describing them. It is very evident that the best and most careful writers do not always exhibit the same precise and accurate method in respect to the *names of things*, *persons*, or *places*. For example, Matthew xvii, 14, compare Luke ix, 38; Gadarene and Gergasene; Matthew viii, 28, compare Mark v, 2; Matthew v, 1, compare Luke vi, 17. Also in regard to *numbers*. For example, Matthew xxvii, 44, compare Luke xxiii, 39; Matthew viii, 5–9, compare Luke vii, 1–10; Matt. viii, 28, compare Mark v, 2; Acts vii, 14, compare Genesis xlvi, 27; Acts vii, 6, compare Gal. iii, 17. And in regard to *dates* and *years*, see Luke ii, 2, compared with the history of the Syrian proconsuls.

Where several names of the same object exist, they sometimes exhibit one and sometimes another. In regard to the manner of expressing time, places, and numbers, sometimes they use the more common and indistinct method, and sometimes the more accurate one. In designating time, they vary. They sometimes put genus for species, and *vice versa.* Examples of such a nature occur in common histories, as well as in the Gospels. We should make ourselves acquainted with conciliations of passages in the best classic authors.

In historic discrepancies we must guard against confounding things which really differ, merely because they have some similitude; or deducing discrepancies therefrom, as has often happened in the interpretations of profane authors.

Great efforts have been made to harmonize the Gospel narrations. Several hundred *harmonies* have been written. Some have chosen one Gospel as exhibiting the regular order of time, and made the rest conform to it as a standard. Others have rejected the supposition of perfect chronological order in any. Some have made the number of facts related as small as possible, and forced the language to a harmony; others have multiplied the number of facts, so that every narration comprising a single circumstance of discrepancy from others has been supposed to contain a history of a similar, but still of a separate fact. Some have supposed the public ministry of Christ to have continued for three years; others for more than seven. Some have supposed that Paul went to Jerusalem soon after his conversion; others that he was from five to seven years in the deserts of Arabia and in the city of Damascus prior to that visit.

Among the German critics numerous and contradictory theories are found. From such a chaos of conflicting opinions the young interpreter can find refuge in the diligent, thorough, repeated study of the Gospels, with a candid mind and a prayerful, believing heart. Let him carry with him to his study a fundamental knowledge of the nature of language, that he may not be embarrassed with the mere form of words; as the *sense* of the Scriptures, and not the words, which are the mere costume of the sense, is what should govern him in his investigations. The notion which attaches absolute perfection to the *form of language*, as well as to the sense which it conveys, makes the reconciliation of them impossible. In some cases two, three, or even the four evangelists relate the same thing in different words. Now if the *form of the words* in one is *absolutely perfect*, what is to be said of the other three, who have adopted different forms? And if the form of a narration in Luke, with two or three more circumstances interwoven, is absolutely perfect, what becomes of the narrations in Matthew and Mark, where one or more of these circumstances are omitted?

It is a fact, which admits of no doubt, that the sacred writers differ from each other as much in respect to the *mode* of writing as profane authors.

In harmonizing passages, those which are doubtful should be interpreted by those which are plain. The doubtful and uncertain must always be accommodated to the plain and certain. As the subject respects occasional historical facts merely, we may add, in conclusion, that nothing endangering our salvation is connected with the discrepancies.

Part Fourth.

BIBLICAL ANALYSIS.

THE *analytical* study of the Bible is that by which we institute a *logical* analysis, and consider the structure, connexion, and order of entire books and particular texts of the Old and New Testaments; that, being thus resolved into their first principles, they may be understood with the greater facility and precision. This branch of study is not prescribed on the supposition that the sacred penmen affected to compose and arrange their subjects according to the rules of logic, for it were absurd to suppose that it were necessary for men divinely inspired thus to be obliged to a scientific arrangement but because order is so natural in the investigation of all things, that it is right and proper to apply it to language whether sacred or profane, and tends in no small degree to render it perspicuous and easy to be understood.

This is evident in all language; for, though it be of the most familiar kind, it will not please even an illiterate person unless its parts harmonize and order be observed.

The importance of obtaining an accurate knowledge of *logical analysis* is evident from the following considerations:— 1. As all helps calculated to expound the Scriptures reciprocally explain, assist, and confirm each other, so analysis has a great effect in determining the *emphasis*, *idiom*, *literal sense*, *inferences*, and *practical application*. 2. Analysis causes the several members, and even words of the text, to be considered with more accuracy and precision. 3. It affords special aid to memory. 4. When anything is to be proven, or has been proven from a text, it lays the whole connexion of the subject open to inspection. 5. It assists in meditation, and in the delivery of a sermon. 6. It develops the grounds on which the inspired writers propounded their doctrines, which is a point of much importance. 7. It conduces in no small degree to the decision of controversies.

Logical study is employed either on whole books or particular texts. The solution of particular texts, however, presupposes an acquaintance with the structure of whole books. Those who begin with *texts* are generally deficient, as they are not prepared for that branch of analysis.

In logical study the books of Scripture must evidently be considered under different points of view. First, the *doctrinal* books are to be distinguished from the *historical*, *prophetical*, and *poetical*; and these must be distinguished from each other.

The *doctrinal* books consist of *one* or *many* subjects. If they consist of many, they must be separated and analyzed apart. For example, the First Epistle to the Corinthians treats of the following subjects:—

1. The inconsiderate zeal of the Church, under the influence of which one person preferred Paul and another Apollos, to chap. 4 inclusive.

2. The incest which had been committed among them, chap. 5.

3. Their law-suits, chap. 6.

4. Their fornication, chap. 6.

5. Of marriage and divorce, chap. 7.

6. Of things offered to idols, chap. 8, 9, 10.

7. Of the external deportment of Christians in the public congregation, chap. 11.

8. Of the abuse of the Sacrament of the Lord's Supper, chap. 11.

9. Of spiritual gifts, and the harmony subsisting between such gifts in certain particulars, chap. 12.

10. Of Christian love, chap. 13.

11. Of the manner of conducting holy assemblies and teaching therein, chap. 14.

12. Of the resurrection, chap. 15.

13. Of alms, &c., chap. 16.

If they consist of but one subject, the following rules must be observed:—

1. By frequent reading, the scope or design and general subject should be well ascertained and understood.

2. All conclusions affecting the principal design and general subject of the whole book, must be sedulously compared with the design.

3. The *middle terms* must be thoroughly weighed, and compared with all the subordinate conclusions.

It may prove sufficient, to give us a proper understanding of the structure of a book, if we duly consider the design of the whole, the conclusions accommodated to the design, and the middle terms prepared to produce these conclusions all arranged in their proper order. That this may more effectually be accomplished, it will be necessary to observe the following remarks:—

1. The greater number of the books in question are of a *polemical* character, and hence, if the *opposite proposition* be examined, it will afford material service in ascertaining the design and in distinguishing it from that of other books. This is evidently the case in the Epistle to the Galatians.

Most of the epistles are divided into four parts, or rather contain *two principal parts*, of which the former is *doctrinal* and the latter *hortatory* or practical, and applicatory—as may be seen in Romans, Galatians, Ephesians, and Colossians—and the two *secondary* parts contain the *exordium* and *conclusion*. If an analysis of the *doctrinal* part be properly instituted, but little difficulty will attend the others. For instance, an analysis of Colossians will show the following:

1. The *occasion* of its writing, namely: Paul's love for the Church—the difficulties which had arisen in consequence of the errors which had been introduced by Judaizing Christians—the entreaties of Epaphras on their behalf. From these, the *design* of the whole epistle may be easily ascer-

tained, which was, that Paul, in obedience to his duty as an apostle, might confirm the Colossian converts in the doctrines of faith and holiness, and that he might heal the difficulties occasioned by Jewish errors. In regard to the *division* of the epistle, it is so plain and natural as easily to be distinguished by the careful reader. After the *inscription*, (chap. i, ver. 1, 2,) the epistle may be said to comprehend an *exordium*, (chap. i, 3–8,) a *proposition*, (ver. 9–12,) a *confirmation*, (chap. i, 13, to iv, 7,) and a *conclusion*. The exordium unfolds the *occasion* of writing the epistle—the proposition reveals the *design* of its writing—the confirmation is designed to *establish the Colossians in faith and induce holiness*. It is *doctrinal* and *elenchical*, or confutatory. The conclusion refers to the *mutual communication of their several states—the salutations of the brethren—special directions*—a *remembrance of himself*, and a *prayer for their welfare*.

Several books treat of the same, or at least of a kindred subject, and some analytical aid may be drawn from this affinity. Thus, for instance, the Epistle to the Romans and Galatians both treat of justification; and the Epistles addressed to the Ephesians, Philippians, and Colossians, touch likewise on the same subject.

The *historical books* are attended with less difficulty, because the *order* in an historical narration cannot but be obvious. The *different* histories which they contain should, however, be accurately separated, and then considered according to antecedents and consequents. It would be well to study them, not by chapters, but by distinct subjects.

The *prophetical books* are very similar in nature to the historical books, and borrow light from them. The prophetical books relate to the future, as the historical books relate to the past.

The *Psalms* must be analyzed *separately*, and being short, they will be solved with more ease than whole books, especially if the student is careful not to infringe, by any refined logical subtleties, on the *prophetic spirit*, the *affections* of the writer, and the *design* of God, the Holy Spirit. When analysis has in it anything forced, it must necessarily be defective. A warm and glowing emotion will frequently overleap the limits of *accustomed* order. We do best when we seek the *order* in the *subject*, and not the subject in an order which we may have conceived.

In analyzing a *doctrinal text*, the following rules must be observed :—

1. The text should be referred to the *proper subject* and *general design* of the whole book, for various things belong to various scopes.

2. We must examine whether the *text* has not a nearer connexion with some subordinate design, and consequently a mediate rather than an immediate reference to the design of the whole book.

3. It is proper to inquire whether the text refers to the general design as a *conclusion*, as a *middle term*, or as a *perfect syllogism ;* and also whether the argument go to *prove*, to *explain*, or to *illustrate*,—all which it will not be difficult to ascertain when we are thoroughly acquainted with the subject and structure of the whole book or section.

4. The *proposition* contained in the text must next be formed and examined, and this not in different or more simple language, (which belongs to exegesis,) but in the very words of the text.

5. The *subject* and *predicate* of the proposition must be considered.

6. The accidental matter which may attach to the subject and predicate must be separated, and it should be ascertained what part of it belongs to the former and what to the latter, as well as what relation they bear to each other.

7. If there be several *doctrines* enumerated in one text, they must be examined separately, and afterwards the *order* in which they are connected should be ascertained—a point to which the inspired writers are usually very attentive.

For instituting an analysis of any *entire doctrinal book*, the following rules are necessary :—

1. The student, by frequent reading, should make himself thoroughly acquainted with the whole book in the original. It should be read until the meaning is fully apprehended, and the subject or subjects of the whole become clear. It should be perused as we may suppose the Epistles of Paul addressed to the several Churches were perused—frequently, not with many interruptions; not by chapters, but the whole read at once, until the mind of the writer is fully understood. It would be vastly better if the Scriptures were read without any regard whatever to the arbitrary and frequently improper divisions of chapter and verse.

2. From this perusal, reperusal, and repetition, the student must be careful to derive a proper knowledge of the *design* which the author had in writing, and thus obtain an acquaintance with the general subject of the book.

The following precautions are necessary :—1. The student should observe the *words* by which the writer declares his object and design, which he frequently does in express terms. 2. He should observe the *historical incidents* noticed in the text, from which some judgment may be formed of the state of the controversy, as well as of the circumstances of the Church or person to whom the book is addressed. 3. In regard to the New Testament, when reference can be made to the Acts of the Apostles, that book should be examined and collated with the text, as it throws light on the doctrinal books. 4. Weigh *every word* attentively, and consider whether it contains anything which may lead to a more accurate judgment of the design and subject of the whole.

When all this has been done, the student should resume the book and sedulously weigh the conclusions interspersed through it. These are best ascertained by the particles *οὖν*, *ἄρα*, *διό*, &c.—*wherefore*, *therefore*, &c. With regard to these *conclusions*—1. Some knowledge must be gained of their meaning. 2. Compare them together, in order to determine in what they agree and in what they differ. 3. Compare them with the *design* and *subject* of the whole book, both of which, it is supposed, are become familiar to the student. 4. Those things should be distinguished which contain the entire *design* of the whole book, immediately in themselves; and those which are referred to it mediately, that is, are as *middle terms* to the *principal* conclusion. According to the accuracy with which the *conclusions* are understood, and the precision with which they are distinguished, will the work of *logical analysis* become more or less easy. For what is it to institute a separate reasoning or logical analysis, but to search out the truth contained in any *proposition* or *conclusion*, and the *middle terms* by which that truth is demonstrated?

The conclusions being thus examined, the student should resume the book, and ascertain the middle terms or reasons on which these conclusions are founded, whether they precede or follow them. In a logical analysis it is proper to notice that which *proves*, and to separate what is *explanatory* from that which is *illustrative.*

Having thus thoroughly examined the book, its component parts will become very perceptible. If there be an *exordium* or *conclusion*, a separation must take place between them, and each must be considered by itself. Should they prove to be twofold, partly *doctrinal* and partly *practical*, each branch must likewise be examined apart.

Since, however, this species of study is properly confined to the *letter* of the *word*, we should be more solicitous to analyze a text, than concerned about understanding and applying it.

In further illustration of this study, we shall present a full and careful analysis of the Epistle to the Ephesians.

This Epistle consists of two parts—the first being comprehended in the first three chapters, and the second in the last three. The former is *doctrinal*, and the latter *inferential* and *hortatory.*

The doctrinal division contains *one principal doctrine.* Special doctrines are interspersed; but they are incidental, and adduced to explain and enforce the principal one, or one derived from it.

The *principal doctrine* is thus stated:—"Although a Jew and Gentile convert differ, inasmuch as the former enjoyed a priority of time in point of expecting and acknowledging Christ, and through the grace of God the Jewish Church was established before the Gentile, yet now the latter are partakers of the same grace with them; and being admitted to this communion of grace, every real distinction is abolished, and Jews and Gentiles constitute one body, of whom Christ is the head. It was essentially necessary for the Ephesians, and indeed for all Gentile converts, that this doctrine should be asserted, because the contentious Jews, vain of their national prerogative, would acknowledge none to be brethren who did not submit their necks to the yoke of Judaism, observe the law, and trust in it for justification. Hence the apostle considers the subject not only in the present Epistle, but in most others as above mentioned. In his addresses, however, to the various Churches, his mode of treating the subject was accommodated to the peculiar circumstances of the persons addressed. Sometimes it was his object to prove that justification is of faith and not of the law, because false apostles maintained the contrary; at other times he exhorts the brethren to guard against such men, adding his reasons for the admonition; sometimes he only recalls them from the tenets of those persons to the true faith. In this Epistle, however, he aims at *subverting the very foundation* of the opponent's doctrine, which rested on the boasted prerogative that the Jews enjoyed over the Gentiles in point of time.

In order the more effectually to accomplish this object, he states in the first place the proper prerogative of the Jewish nation, lest, by passing in silence over these privileges, he should do an injury to himself as a Jew, and to his own nation, as well as to the truth itself, which was of infinitely greater moment. To comprehend this position, the student must examine the whole structure of the Epistle, otherwise it may not readily be discerned. Let him, in the *first* place, examine the distinction in the application of the *personal pronouns*. After using the pronouns of the *first* person, *we*, *us*, &c., as far as the 12th verse of the 1st chapter, the apostle invariable adopts the *second* person in the following verses. Hence he thus connects the 13th verse, "In whom *ye* also," &c., which clearly indicates a change in the subject; and he continues to use this pronoun until he institutes a new comparison between the subjects. When speaking in reference to the Jews, he says, "to *us*;" and when speaking in reference to the Gentiles, he says, "to *you*."

If a collation is made of chap. 2, verses 11, 12, 13, &c., it will be found that the different subjects hitherto represented by the different pronouns are expressly named—"the *uncircumcision*," viz., the Gentiles; and "the *circumcision*," viz., the Jews.

The truth of the position assumed will appear *secondly* from the circumstance that the predicate restricts the former part of the chapter to the Jews—thus they are called "those who first trusted in Christ."

The objection which lies against *predestinate*—*προορίζειν*—on the ground of its being a general word, and indicative of a priority of time and not of a priority of subjects, cannot militate against "*to trust first*"—*προελπίζειν*—because this latter word must include both, since the *trusting* here spoken of is inevitably to be referred to *man* and not to *God*.

Again, it is said in the ninth and following verses that the mystery of the divine will was revealed to them in order *that it might be dispensed*—*εἰς οἰκονομίαν*—*in the fulness of time*, and that all things, Gentiles as well as Jews, might be brought under one head, even Christ. The Jews first received this general dispensation; but the benefits of it had been conferred upon the Gentiles in common with them, priority of time only excepted. The apostle asserts, "In whom *ye*—Gentiles—*also* trusted after that *ye* heard the word of truth, the gospel of *your* salvation; in whom also after that *ye* believed, *ye* were sealed with that Holy Spirit of promise which is the earnest of OUR"—the Jews'—"inheritance." "Wherefore I, also, after I heard of *your* faith in the Lord Jesus and love unto all the saints," &c.

The apostle pursues the same subject to the 3d verse of the 2d chapter. "That *you* may know what is the exceeding greatness of his power to *us*-ward who believe, according to the working of his mighty power, which he wrought in Christ, when he raised him from the dead, and set him at his own right hand in the heavenly places, far above all principality, and power, and might, and dominion, and every name that is named, not only in this world, but also in that which is to come; and hath put all things under his feet, and gave him to be the head over all things to the Church, which is his body, the fulness of him that filleth all in all." "And YOU who were dead in trespasses and sins; wherein in time past *ye* walked," &c.

Whenever the apostle descends to the original state of the Gentiles, he institutes a comparison between it and the primeval state of the Jews, lest the latter should take occasion to assert some new prerogative. He proves, by the testimony of the consciences of each, that Jews as well as Gentiles were before Christ under sin, and that both were saved and brought to newness of life by grace alone.

The above verses, united with the subsequent as far as chap. 3d, comprehend the *principal conclusion* of the whole epistle, which fully develops its scope. The conclusion is, "Though the Gentiles were not originally possessed of the covenants of promise, or any foundation of hope, yet in Christ they, together with the Jews, were made partakers of every benefit, Christ having removed all things which opposed their union with the Jews, and forming them into one body by abolishing the law. Hence the Gentiles were not now—as was asserted by Jewish false apostles—strangers and aliens, but being reconciled to God by the blood of Christ, they were become fellow-citizens with the saints, and of the household of God."

The connexion of the 1st verse of chap. 3d with the 14th is not singular, but in perfect accordance with the design of the apostle. If the first verse is examined, it will be seen that he names the *subject*:—"For this cause, I Paul, the prisoner of Jesus Christ for you Gentiles." He then forms the *predicate*, and repeats the same words. "For this cause —I say—I bow my knees." All the words that intervene between verses 2d and 14th are insulated. The length of this parenthesis is no argument against the correctness of the position, as instances of equally copious parentheses occur in various parts of the Bible. Examples may be found, in the writings of the Fathers, of long parentheses; besides, it was a peculiarity in the writings of Paul, as may be seen by reference to 1 Timothy i, 8–17; Philippians i, 27, to ii, 16 inclusive.

The other part of this Epistle is *hortatory*, and flows from the *doctrinal* part as streams from a fountain. With the apostle, the injunctions of *practice* follow the positions of *theory*. The best example of this is in the Epistle to the Colossians, one part of which refers to *faith*, or what is to be believed, and the other to *practice*, or what is to be done.

The main exhortation that arises from the principal doctrine, is *concord and peace between the Jew and Gentile*. This is the *general scope* of the whole Epistle.

The next design is, to present before Jew and Gentile the difference between their present and former state. In order to this, he first points out the difference from ver. 17 to 24; second, he lays down some particular precepts which are universally binding, ver. 25 to chap. v, verse 21, inclusive; third, he delivers to all, according to their particular stations in life, special commandments—to wives, verse 22 to the end; to children, chap. vi, 1–3; to parents, verse 4; to servants, verses 5–8; to masters, verse 9. Here the apostle adopts the same method, always placing inferiors before superiors, and the weaker before the stronger. He likewise puts generals before specials throughout the whole epistle, which is the best mode of arrangement,—see Colossians iii, 18, &c., 1 Peter iii, 1–7, &c.,—and draws all his arguments, relative to any particular scope, from the principal doctrine proposed in the foregoing part, as plainly appears from chap. v, verse 23, &c. He also furnishes means for the attainment of the things enjoyed and for defending them against the wiles of the devil, to chap. vi, 20, inclusive.

These things being explained, and Tychicus, the bearer of the letter, being directed to give the Ephesians fuller information concerning St. Paul,—verses 21, 22,—he concludes by saluting them and invoking the divine blessing.

Part Fifth.

BIBLICAL ARCHÆOLOGY.

Biblical Archæology embraces everything in the Bible worthy of notice and remembrance, whether it be merely alluded to, or treated as something well known. It is concerned more particularly in the description of the *Domestic*, *Political*, and *Religious Antiquities* of the Bible. Its importance to the Bible student will appear from the following considerations:—

1. It enables him to go back more fully into the age, country, and situation of the sacred writers and their contemporaries, and to understand and estimate the nature and tendencies of the objects which are presented to him.

2. It places him in a better situation to detect allusions to ceremonies, customs, laws, peculiarities in the face of the country, &c., and to make himself sure of the precise import of the passages where such allusions occur.

3. It proffers him new ability in answering the objections of the opposers of Revelation, the greater part of which originate in ignorance of antiquity.

4. It presents to his view, distinctly and impressively, the adaptation of the different dispensations, the object of which was to preserve and transmit religion to the character and situation of the age.

5. It shows him where to separate moral precept and religious truth from the drapery of the figurative language in which they are clothed; since language, considered as the medium of thought, takes its character in a measure from that of the times.

6. It enables him to enter into the nature and spirit of the arguments in favour of the authenticity of the sacred books.

7. Its importance may be seen, lastly, from the fact that all who have undertaken to interpret the Scriptures while ignorant of its antiquities, have committed very great and very numerous mistakes.

In order that the student may derive real profit by the study of sacred antiquities, it is necessary that he should become acquainted with the sources from whence they are drawn. These sources are,—

1. The *Scriptures;* because they are, in fact, the testimony of the people themselves in regard to events and customs in which they were the agents.

2. *Ancient Monuments.* These are in a manner living testimonies. Such are the triumphal arch of Titus; the ruins of Persepolis; the subterranean vaults or sepulchres in Syria, Palestine, and Egypt, where pyramids, obelisks, and the ruins of temples, bear testimony both to the perfection and the antiquity of the arts; and the ruins of Babylon, Nineveh, and Palmyra. These illustrate what occurs in the Bible relative to the edifices of Herod, and the temple of Jerusalem in the time of our Saviour.

3. *Ancient Greek, Phœnician, Egyptian,* and *Roman coins;* also *Jewish coins,* with inscriptions in the old Samaritan character, and those of a few other nations.

4. *Contemporary writers.* Such, for instance, as the works of Philo the Jew and Josephus; the former of whom resided in Egypt, and the latter at first in Judea, and subsequently in Rome. Ancient Greek and Latin authors, particularly Herodotus, Xenophon, Arrian, Strabo, Plutarch, Diodorus Siculus, and almost all others of that age.

5. The *Mishna,* or the text of the Talmud, a collection of traditions made very nearly between the years 190 and 220, accompanied by the explanations of the Jerusalem and Babylonian Gemaras.

6. *Ecclesiastical writers* who lived in Syria or other oriental countries, particularly Jerome and Ephraim Syrus; also some Syriac and Arabic books, especially the most ancient. Finally, the journals of modern travellers who have visited the East, marked the appearances of the country, and given an account of the manners and customs of the inhabitants.

CHAPTER I.

DOMESTIC ARCHÆOLOGY.

Dwellings.

In the primitive condition of society men lived in plains, valleys, and on mountains, under the open sky, or under the shade of trees, or in the clefts of rocks or caves. The inhabitants of Arabia Petræa, and the Troglodytes of Palestine, and all those who are nomadic in their habits, thus dwelt without a fixed habitation, except what nature afforded.

Tabernacles.

As caves could not always be readily found, and as it was sometimes great labour to excavate one, men were compelled by the exigencies of their situation to form some other sort of residence. The shady trees, whose tops approached each other and were intertwined, suggested the idea of cutting down large branches, fixing them in the ground in parallel lines, binding them together at the top, and covering them with leaves, plants, reeds, branches, and even broad flat stones, in order to shield themselves from the cold, the heat, and the dew. Thus they built tabernacles, huts, or lodges. The Romans called them mappalia. They were small and low in the beginning, so that a person could not stand erect, but was obliged either to lie down or to sit; but afterwards were built higher. The use of these tabernacles did not cease even after the erection of more stable and convenient buildings. These rude dwellings are to this day erected by the nomades and wandering tribes of Mesopotamia.

Tents.

As tabernacles could not readily be moved from place to place, and from a want of materials could not everywhere be built, being partly made of *skins*, the design arose of erecting a shelter *wholly* of skins, extended round a pole, and so light as to be easily moved from one place to another. Jabal, it is supposed, made tents of this kind. In the progress of years they were no longer covered with skins, but with various kinds of cloth, particularly linen. The nomades of the east still use them. They pitch them in any place which appears suitable, but they give the preference to a spot near some shady tree.

The first tents which were made were undoubtedly round in their construction and small in size; afterwards they were made larger and oblong. The nomades of Arabia Petræa have two kinds, the one larger the other smaller. Genesis xxxiii, 17.

The Arabians take pleasure in pitching their tents on hills, in such a way as to form a circular encampment. When thus pitched, being of a dark hue, in consequence of being covered with a cloth made of goat's hair, they present a beautiful appearance to the distantly-approaching traveller. Cant. i, 5. The flocks and cattle are driven by night into the enclosed area, and protected by dogs. Job xxx, 1. Some one of the shepherds keeps watch during the night. This duty is performed alternately. Isaiah lvi, 9–11. The tent of the Emir or chief is placed in the centre, and is larger than the rest.

The larger kind of tents are divided by curtains into three parts, as was done also in the holy tabernacle. In the external division or apartment the servants lodge, and during the night the young animals also, to prevent their sucking the dam. In the second apartment are the males. The third or interior apartment is allotted to the women. Numbers xxv, 8. The nomades, who are less jealous than the inhabitants of the cities, watch the other sex less scrupulously. Genesis xii, 15; xviii, 6–9; xxxiv, 1, 2. The bottom of the tent is either covered with mats or carpets, and on these they are in the habit of sitting. The chiefs and more wealthy have coverlets, pillows, &c., made of costly materials, on which they repose at night. The utensils of the nomades are few; they have vessels of shell and brass, viz., pots, kettles, and cups of brass, covered elegantly with tin, also leathern bags. Their hearth is on the ground; it consists of three stones, placed so as to form a triangle. In the middle of them is a small excavation of the earth, where the fire is kindled, and the vessels placed over it upon the stones. The table consists of a round skin spread upon the floor of the tent. Clothing and military arms are hung upon nails in the poles of the tent.

Houses.

In the progress of time, as tabernacles became larger, and were defended against the injuries of the weather by broad stones and earth heaped against them, it was found that dwellings could be made of stones alone and moist earth or clay. A want of stones in some places gave occasion for the formation of tiles, which were made by reducing a body of clay to shape, and hardening it in the sun or burning it in fire. These ancient attempts are mentioned in Genesis. In Deut. viii, 12, mention is made of elegant houses; and in xxvii, 2–4, the use of limestone is spoken of as if it were common and well known.

Houses at first were small, afterwards larger, especially in extensive cities, the capitals of empires. The art of multiplying stories in a building is very ancient, as we may gather from the construction of Noah's ark and the Tower of Babel. The houses in Babylon, according to Herod., (lib. i, sec. 180,) were three and four stories high; and those in Thebes or Diospolis, in Egypt, four or five stories. Consult Diod. Sic., lib. i, chap. 45. They appear to have been low in the time of Joshua, in Palestine. Jeremiah praises houses of good form and architecture. In the time of Christ, the houses of the rich and powerful were splendid, and built according to the rules of Grecian architecture.

Many of the larger houses were tetragonal in form, and enclosed a square area. The roofs of the houses were flat, such as are still seen in the East. They were formed of earth heaped together, or, in the houses of the rich, of a firmly constructed flooring made of coals broken up, stones, ashes, chalk, and gypsum, reduced to a solid substance by application of blows. The declivity of the roof from the centre to the extremity is very small, scarcely an inch in ten feet. On these roofs, which are covered with earth, plants sometimes spring up; but they soon perish with the heat of the sun. The Orientals often ascend these roofs to enjoy a purer air, or to witness an event which happens in the neighbourhood. In the summer they sleep upon them, but not without a covering. They even erect tents and tabernacles upon them, and spread their flax and cotton there to be dried in the sun. They ascend their roofs to talk with persons privately, to witness a public solemnity, to mourn publicly, and to announce anything to the multitude, to pray to God, and to perform sacrifices. 2 Samuel xi, 2, 6, 7; Isaiah xxii, 1; Matthew xxiv, 17; Mark xiii, 15; Joshua ii, 6; 1 Samuel ix, 25; Judges xvi, 26, 27; Isaiah xv, 3; Jeremiah xix, 13; xlviii, 38; Matthew x, 27; Acts x, 9.

The roofs are surrounded by a breastwork or balustrade, to prevent one from falling. On the side next a neighbour's house it is not so high, for the purpose of allowing the occupants to pass from one to another. This railing was required by the law of Moses. Deut. xxii, 8. It was this which the men demolished, (Mark ii, 4; Luke v, 19,) that they might let down the paralytic.

The gate of the house, or door opening to the streets, is in the middle of the front side of the house. The gates, not only of houses but of cities, were usually adorned with the inscription which, according to Deut. vi, 9; xi, 20, was to be extracted from the law of Moses, a practice in which may be found the origin of the modern *mauzan*, or piece of parchment inscribed with Deut. vi, 5–9; xi, 13–20, and fastened to the door-post. The gates or doors were always shut, and one of the servants acted as porter. Acts xii, 13; John xviii, 16, 17. The space immediately inside the gate is called the porch. It is square, and on one side of it is erected a seat for the accommodation of strangers, who are not admitted into the interior of the house. Near this porch are the stairs which lead to the upper story and roof of the house. Matthew xxiv, 16, 17. From the porch we are introduced through a second door into the quadrangular area, or *court*, which is denominated the centre. 2 Samuel xvii, 18; Luke v, 19. The court is usually paved with marble of various kinds. In the centre of it sometimes there is a fountain. The court is generally surrounded on all sides with a cloister, peristyle, or covered walk, over which, if the house has more than one story, is a gallery of the same dimensions, supported by columns and protected by a balustrade. Hence occur so many allusions to columns. Psalm lxxv, 3; Proverbs ix, 1; Galatians ii, 9; 1 Timothy iii, 15. Large companies are received into the court, as at nuptials, circumcisions, &c. Esther i, 5; Luke v, 19. On such occasions a large veil of thick cloth is extended by ropes over the whole of it, forming an awning to exclude the heat of the sun. Psalm civ, 2. The veil, or curtain, of the area, is called in the New Testament στέγη. Luke vii, 6; Mark ii, 4. The back part of the house is allotted to the women, called in the Arabic the harem, and in the Hebrew, by way of eminence, *the palace.* The door is always kept locked, and is opened only when the master of the house wishes to enter. 2 Kings xv, 25; Proverbs xviii, 19. White eunuchs guard the door externally, but maids and black eunuchs only are permitted to serve within. The latter are great favourites with their masters. Isaiah xxxii, 14; Jeremiah xiii, 23; 2 Kings xv, 25. Behind the harem there is a garden, into which the women enjoy the pleasure of looking from their small but lofty apartments. The chambers are large and spacious, and so constructed as to extend round the whole of the open court. The doors of the chambers open in the first story into the cloisters, and in the second story into the gallery.

The Hebrews, at a very ancient period, had not only summer and winter rooms, but *palaces*. Judges iii, 20; 1 Kings vii, 2–6; Amos iii, 15; Jeremiah xxxvi, 32. The houses or palaces, so called, expressly made for summer, were large, and, in point of altitude, did not yield much to our churches. The lower stories were frequently under ground. The front of these buildings faced the north, so as to secure the advantage of the breezes. They were paved with marble. They were supplied with a current of fresh air by ventilators, which were perforations in the northern wall and on the top of the building, resembling turrets, which received the air and conveyed it below. One apartment worthy of notice extended from the interior of the front side into the court, sometimes a considerable distance beyond the cloisters and galleries. Its roof was supported by two columns only, and the front of it had no wall. In this apartment princes received ambassadors, transacted business, and dispensed justice. The temple of Dagon, which was destroyed by Samson, was of similar construction. It was in an apartment like this, in Herod's palace, where the Saviour seems to have been tried before Pilate. In the winter rooms and houses the windows face the south, in order to have the advantage of a southern exposure. They were not furnished with stoves and fire-places, as among us. The coals and wood are placed in a vessel which occupies a place in the center of the paved floor, and the smoke escapes through the windows. Isaiah xiv, 16; xlvii, 14. All the rooms in the upper story may be called ὑπερόων; but this applies more appropriately to the chamber over the porch, which opens by a door directly upon the roof, being generally a story higher than the other part of the house. This is a place for retirement, devotion, &c. Strangers are frequently lodged in it. 1 Kings xvii, 19; 2 Kings iv, 10; xxiii, 12; Acts ix, 37–39.

The doors were valves, suspended and moved by pivots of wood which projected from the ends of the two folds, both above and below. The upper pivots, which were the longest, were inserted in sockets sufficiently large to receive them in the lintel; the lower ones were received, in a corresponding manner, in the threshold. The doors were fastened by a lock, Prov. xxvi, 14; or by a bar. Job xxxviii, 10; Deut. iii, 5; Judges xvi, 3. These bars were commonly of wood. Those made of iron and brass were used as a security to the gates of fortified places, or of valuable repositories. Isaiah xlv, 2. The lock was nothing more than a wood slide attached to one of the folds, which entered into a hole in the door-post, and was secured there by teeth cut into it. Two strings passed through an orifice leading outside the door. A man going out, by means of one of these strings moved the slide into its place in the post, where it was fastened so among the teeth as not to be drawn back. The one coming in, who wished to unlock, had a wooden key sufficiently large and crooked, like a sickle. This was thrust through the orifice of the door or keyhole, lifted up the slide so as to extricate it from the teeth or catches, and by means of the other string the bolt was drawn back and the door opened. The rich and powerful had keys made of metal, adorned with ivory handles. The keyhole was sometimes as large as to admit a person's finger, and sometimes doors were opened in that way. Solomon's Song v, 4.

The windows look from the front chambers into the court, and from the female apartments into the garden. Occasionally a window is seen looking towards the street, but it is guarded by a trellis, and is thrown open only on public festivities. Judges v, 28; Proverbs vii, 6; 2 Kings ix, 30; Solomon's Song ii, 9. The windows are large, extending almost to the floor. They are wide, not set with glass, but latticed. In the winter they are protected by thin veils, or by valves. 2 Kings xiii, 17; 1 Kings vii, 17; Solomon's Song ii, 9. Over the windows are nails adorned with beautiful heads, and not only sustain curtains by means of a rod extending from one to the other, but are themselves great ornaments. Hence the propriety of those illustrations drawn from nails. Isaiah xxii, 23; Zechariah x, 4; Eccles. xii, 11.

Household Furniture.

In the most ancient periods these were the most few and simple. A hand-mill, and some sort of an oven to bake in, could not, of course, be dispensed with. Subsequently, domestic utensils were multiplied in the form of pots, kettles, leathern bottles, plates, cups, and pitchers. The floors were covered with mats or carpets, and supplied also, for the purposes of rest, with a sort of mattresses, of thick, coarse materials. Judges iv, 18. Bolsters, which were more valuable, were stuffed with wool, or some soft substance. Ezekiel xiii, 18–21. The poorer class made use of skins, merely for the purposes to which these mattresses and bolsters were applied. The beds were sometimes placed on a sort of gallery against the wall. The Hebrews had another sort of beds, adorned with ivory, resembling the Persian sofas, having backs and sides, six feet long, three broad, and, like the divans, nine inches high. Amos vi, 4; Psalm xli, 3; cxxxii, 3. To prevent, as much as possible, the mats and carpets from being soiled, it was not lawful to wear shoes or sandals into the room; they were left at the door. Hence it was not necessary that the room should be often swept. Matt. xii, 44. Lamps were fed with olive oil, and were kept burning all night. Job xviii, 5, 6; xxi, 17; Proverbs xiii, 9; xx, 20;

xxiv, 20; xxxi, 18. We may infer from the golden lamp of the tabernacle, that those of the opulent were splendid.

Villages, Towns, Cities.

A number of tents or cottages together were called villages. From these they increased, in progress of time, to towns and cities. The Hebrews, in the time of David, had large cities. Jerusalem must have been large, to accommodate the three millions of people who assembled there on the feast of the *Passover.* The streets were usually narrow, the design of which was to make them shady. The market-places were near the gates of a city, sometimes within and sometimes without. At these, different kinds of goods were exposed for sale. In the days of Christ, markets were held in an arched street. These streets were large, and furnished with gates. Aqueducts were common in oriental cities, ruins of which are still found. The people of the east metaphorically ascribe the character of females to cities. They represent them as *mothers* of the inhabitants; they speak of them as *wives* of the kings; and when they revolt against their sovereign they are *adulteresses.*

Shepherds.

Abraham, Isaac, Jacob, and their posterity, were shepherds until they entered Canaan. The Nomades, or shepherds of the east, possess vast flocks, large tracts of land, and numerous servants. The masters, or chief shepherds, always go armed, and spend their time in hunting, in the oversight of their affairs, and in predatory excursions. *Part* of the servants are armed, in order to keep from the flocks robbers and wild beasts. *Part* have only a staff and a pouch, which were anciently the whole property of travellers, and those who were not rich, except that instead of a pouch they carried a somewhat larger sack. 2 Kings iv, 42; 1 Samuel xvii,

40–43; Psalm xxiii, 4; Micah vii, 14; Matthew x, 10; Luke ix, 3; x, 4. In the Bible *kings* are called *shepherds*. The term was applied to God, who was the King of the Hebrews, and as a shepherd guided and protected his flock, so He guided and protected Israel. Psalm xxiii, 1–4; Isaiah xl, 11; lxiii, 11; Jeremiah x, 21; xxiii, 1; xxxi, 10; l, 6; li, 23; Micah v, 5; Nahum iii, 18; Ezekiel xxxiv, 2–18; xxxvii, 24; Zechariah xi, 15. In the New Testament it is applied to *teachers* of the Jews; those who presided in synagogues; also to *Christian* teachers. Ephesians iv, 11; Matthew ix, 36; John x, 12–14; Hebrews xiii, 20; 1 Peter ii, 25; v, 4.

Pastures.

The pastures of the *Nomades*, or shepherds, were the vast deserts or wildernesses, which could not be monopolized by any individual, but were open to all shepherds alike. After the occupation of Palestine, there was open to the Israelites not only the vast desert of Judah, but many other deserts. This accounts for what we may gather from the Scriptures in relation to the great wealth of the Hebrew Nomades. 2 Samuel xvii, 27, *et seq.;* xix, 32; 1 Samuel xxv; 1 Chron. xxvii, 29–31. Compare Isaiah lxv, 10; Jeremiah l, 19.

The shepherds occupy almost the same positions every year. In the summer they go north, or on the mountains; in the winter they go south, in the valleys. The flocks live night and day under the open sky, and this exposure renders their wool finer than if confined in sheep-cotes.

Fountains and Cisterns.

Water was scarce in the deserts; hence it was highly valued. Job xxii, 7; Numbers xx, 17–19; Deuteronomy ii, 6–28. The Nomades dug wells and cisterns, at certain distances, which they concealed to prevent others from stealing the water. They occasioned great contention. Gen. xxi, 25;

xxvi, 13–22. *Fountains* were common to all. If they flow all the year they are denominated *faithful;* if they dry up in the summer, *deceitful.* Job vi, 15–22; Isaiah xxxviii, 16; Jeremiah xv, 18. *Wells* belonged to those persons who dug them. Sometimes they were owned by a number of shepherds in common, where their flocks were admitted to drink in regular order. Genesis xxix, 3–12; xxiv, 11–15; Exodus ii, 16; Judges v, 11. The waters of wells and fountains are called *living* waters, and are much esteemed. Leviticus xiv, 5–50; Numbers xix, 17. Hence they are made a symbol of prosperity, and God himself is compared to a fountain of living waters. Isaiah xliii, 19, 20; xlix, 10; Jeremiah ii, 13; xvii, 13; Psalm lxxxvii, 7; Joel iii, 18; Ezekiel xlvii, 1, *et seq.;* Zechariah xiv, 18.

Cisterns were the property of those by whom they were made. These were sometimes made so large as to cover an acre of ground, having a small mouth. They were filled with rain-water and snow during the winter, and then closed with flat stones, over which was spread sand to prevent their discovery. Sometimes these are destroyed by earthquakes, and other casualties, and whole flocks perish in consequence. A failure of water is used in Scripture to denote a great calamity. Isaiah xli, 17, 18; xliv, 3. There is a large deposition of mud at the bottom of these cisterns; and whoever falls into them, when they are empty of water, dies a miserable death. Genesis xxxvii, 22; Jeremiah xxxviii, 6; Lam. iii, 53; Psalms xl, 2, lxix, 15. They were sometimes used as prisons. Genesis xxxix, 20; xl, 15.

Flocks of the Nomades.

These consisted of *goats* and *sheep.* The sheep are horned, and commonly *white.* Psalms cxlvii, 16; Isaiah i, 18; Daniel vii, 9. Black ones are very rare; some are spotted, others are streaked; and others, again, are distinguished by variegated hoofs. Gen. xxx, 32–34; xxxi, 10–12. The sheep mentioned in Ezekiel xxvii, 18, whose wool is of a bright brown, inclining to a gray, are found in Caramania. They are also distinguished by other varieties, such as *common*, *deformed*, *superior*, &c. The Nomades give to their sheep titles of endearment, and the ram that is called out by his master marches before the flock; hence the *rulers* of the people are called *leaders of the flock*. Jeremiah xxv, 34, 35; l, 8; Isaiah xiv, 9; Zechariah x, 3. The Arabians have certain terms by which they can call the sheep either to drink or to be milked. The sheep know the voice of the shepherd, and go at his bidding. Sometimes a lamb is brought into the tent, and trained like a dog. 2 Samuel xii, 3; Jeremiah xi, 19. Before the shearing, the sheep are collected into an uncovered enclosure. John x, 11–16. The object of this is, that the wool may be rendered finer by the sweating and evaporation which would result from their being crowded together. Numbers xxxii, 16, 24, 36; 2 Samuel vii, 8; Zephaniah ii, 6. Sheep-shearings were great festivals. 1 Samuel xxv, 2–4; xviii, 36; 2 Samuel xiii, 23. *Goats* are of a black colour; sometimes parti-coloured. They live under the open sky, with this exception only, that the kids are sometimes taken into the tent to keep them from sucking the dam. Their milk is more precious than any other. Proverbs xxvii, 27. Their flesh and hair are also valuable. *Bottles* are made of their skins. Those for holding water have the hairy side of the skin external, and those for wine the reverse.

Geese, hens, and swine were not known among the domestic animals of the Nomades. At a somewhat recent period, hens, in some places, were raised by the Hebrews. A hen that does not hatch eggs is spoken of by Jeremiah xvii, 11; and in the time of Christ, when Peter denied his Master, the cock crew in Jerusalem.

*Animals of the Ox kind.**

These animals are smaller in oriental countries than among us, and are distinguished by certain protuberances on the back, directly over the fore-feet. They were also possessed by the Nomades, though they were used chiefly for agricultural purposes. Herdsmen were held in lower estimation than keepers of flocks, but they possessed the richest pastures in Bashan, Sharon, and Achion. The oxen and bulls of Bashan, which were strong and ferocious, were used as symbols of ferocious enemies. Psalm xxii, 12; lxviii, 31; Isaiah xxxiv, 7; Deuteronomy xxxiii, 17; Proverbs xiv, 4. Heifers were symbolic of matrons. Amos iv, 1; Hosea iv, 15, 16; x, 11; Jeremiah xlvi, 20. The horns of bulls and goats and oxen were used tropically to express power. Psalm lxxv, 10; lxxxix, 17–24; xcii, 10; Amos vi, 13; Jeremiah xlviii, 25; Lam. ii, 3; Ezekiel xxix, 21; Daniel vii, 7, 8, 24; viii, 3–5; Luke i, 69. If the horns are represented as made of brass or iron, the strength and power is insuperable. 1 Kings xxii, 11; 1 Chronicles xviii, 10; Micah iv, 13–16. Hence the ancient coins represent kings with horns. Oxen were yoked together to draw carts and ploughs, and the Nomades transported goods on their backs, as they did on camels. The milk of the cows was nutritive, and of this they frequently made cheese. In the Bible there is no mention made of butter. That which in the Vulgate is rendered butter, was nothing more than a drink. Olive oil was used instead of butter.

Asses.

She-asses are considered the most valuable, on account of the colts. The Nomades possessed a great number of these animals; and in the east, if rightly trained up, they are not

*Those animals in Scripture called oxen, were bulls, as the law did not allow castration.

only patient and diligent, but active and beautiful in appearance. Their name is used tropically in the Scriptures for active and industrious men. Genesis xlix, 14. Their colour is red, inclining to a brown. Some are parti-coloured. They are sometimes used for turning mills. Matthew xviii, 6. Moses passed a law that the ox and ass should not be used together in ploughing. Anciently, princes and great men rode on asses. Genesis xxii, 3–5; 1 Samuel xxv, 20–23; 1 Kings ii, 40; xiii, 13; Zechariah ix, 9; Matthew xxi, 1–7; Luke xix, 29, 36; John xii, 12–16. Horses were used almost exclusively for war. They were saddled and bridled. Mules are spoken of in the age of David, and were probably known in the time of Moses. They were brought to the Hebrews from other nations. Wild asses are of a fine figure and rapid motion, frequenting desert places, and fleeing far from the abodes of men. They can scent waters at a great distance, and thirsty travellers often follow them.

Camels.

Camels are of two kinds. The Turkish is distinguished by having two protuberances on the back. This kind is large and strong, carrying from eight to fifteen hundred pounds, but is impatient of the heat. The other kind, called the dromedary, or Arabian camel, has but one bunch on the back, is more rapid in its movements, and endures the heat better than the other camel. Camels require but little food, and can endure thirst from sixteen to forty days. The Nomades and Arabs are esteemed of secondary rank if they do not possess them. Genesis xxiv, 10, 64; xxxi, 17; 1 Chronicles v, 19–21; Jeremiah xlix, 29. Compare 1 Samuel xxx, 17; 1 Kings x, 2; Isaiah xxx, 6; Ezekiel xxv, 4. They are used for the transportation of all kinds of merchandise. The Nomades drink the milk of camels; when it becomes sour it intoxicates. Judges iv, 19; v, 25. They also feed upon the flesh, which was interdicted to the Hebrews. Leviticus xi, 4. The hair is manufactured into cloth. Matthew iii, 4.

Horses.

We find horses in Egypt. Genesis xlvii, 17; xlix, 17; Exodus ix, 3; xiv, 6, 28; Job xxxix, 19. Joshua encountered chariots and horsemen in the north of Palestine. Anciently, horses were used exclusively for war; hence they are opposed to asses, which were used in times of peace. The Hebrews first attended to the raising of horses in the time of Solomon, who carried on a great trade in Egyptian horses. A horse was estimated at about one hundred and fifty, and a chariot at six hundred shekels. The women rarely rode on horseback; but whenever they did, it was in the same manner with the men. They were not shod with iron until the ninth century.

Dogs.

The Nomades found use for these animals, in watching and driving their flocks. Frequent as they are in oriental cities, they were universally abhorred, with the exception of the hunting dogs. Hence, to be called a dog is a cutting reproach, full of bitter contempt. Job xxx, 1; 1 Samuel xvii, 43; 2 Kings viii, 13; Proverbs xxvi, 11. Compare Luke xvi, 21; 2 Peter ii, 22. The appellation of *dead dog* indicates imbecility; that of *dumb dog*, unfaithfulness. The reward of prostitution is called dog's hire. The Jews, in the time of Christ, called the Gentiles *dogs*. Their character and habits illustrate many passages of Scripture.

Hunting.

Moses enacted laws on the subject of hunting, the object of which was to preserve the wild animals of Palestine. Exodus xxiii, 11; Leviticus xxv, 6, 7; Deuteronomy xxii, 6, 7. The implements of hunting were the same as those of war, viz., the bow and arrow, spear and lance, a javelin and sword. Hunters employed nets, in which lions were taken; likewise gins, snares, and pitfalls, which were excavated especially for lions. A pole was inserted in the centre, with a lamb attached to it, which would cause the lion to spring upon it, and, falling through the slight covering, he could be easily taken. These instruments and modes of warfare are used tropically to indicate the wiles of an adversary and great danger. Psalms ix, 16; lvii, 6; xciv, 13; cxix, 85; Proverbs xxvi, 27; Isaiah xxiv, 17; xlii, 22; Jeremiah v, 27; vi, 21; xviii, 22; xlviii, 14; Luke xxi, 35; Romans xi, 9. Death is represented as a hunter, armed with his net, javelin, or sling, with which he takes and slays men.

Agriculture—Its Value and Importance.

Agriculture, as well as the keeping of flocks and herds in the primitive ages, was a principal employment among men. Genesis ii, 15; iii, 17–19; iv, 2. Noah, after the Deluge, bestowed attention upon it. Babylon and Egypt owed their wealth and power chiefly to this source. The Hebrews learned the value of this art while in Egypt. Moses made agriculture the basis of the State. To every citizen he apportioned a certain quantity of land, and gave them the right of transmitting it to their heirs. This land could not be alienated for any longer period than the coming jubilee, and thus land monopolies were prevented. The land could be redeemed at any time by paying the amount of profits up to the year of jubilee. A tax of two-tenths of the income was to be paid annually unto God, as their king. Leviticus xxvii, 30; Deuteronomy xii, 17–19; xiv, 22–29. The custom of marking the land by stones, although it prevailed a long time before Job, was confirmed and perpetuated by Moses, and a curse was pronounced against him who, without authority, removed them. The land of Palestine was divided by Joshua, not only among the tribes, but each individual had his portion measured off to him. All who were not set apart for religious duties, such as the *priests* and

Levites, whether inhabitants of towns or the country, were considered by the law as agriculturists or husbandmen. None were so rich or noble as to disdain to put their hands to the plough. 1 Samuel xi, 7; 1 Kings xix, 19. Compare 2 Chronicles xxvi, 10.

The soil of Palestine is very fruitful if the dews and vernal and autumnal rains are not withheld. The Hebrews increased its richness in a variety of ways. They not only divested it of stones, but watered it by means of canals, and thereby imparted to their fields the richness of gardens. The soil was enriched, also, by means of ashes, to which the straw, the stubble, the husks, the brambles and grass that overspread the land during the Sabbatical year were reduced by fire, and finally the soil was manured with dung.

Different kinds of Grain.

The Hebrew word which is translated variously by the English words grain, corn, &c., is of general signification, and comprehends wheat, millet, spelt, wall-barley, beans, lentils, meadow-cumin, pepperwort, flax, and cotton. To these may be added various species of the cucumber, and perhaps rice. Barley, mixed with broken straw, affords food for beasts of burden. Wheat grew in Egypt in the time of Joseph, as it now does in Africa, on stalks, each one of which produced an ear. With us this is called corn. Cotton grows not only on trees of a large size, but on shrubs. It is enclosed in the nuts of the tree and the pods of the shrub.

Instruments of Agriculture.

At first the soil was cultivated by means of sharp sticks. These were succeeded by spades and shovels, and subsequently by ploughs. All these implements were well known in the time of Moses. The first plough was a forked limb of a tree, one of which forks was longer than the other,

The shorter piece was sharpened, which, being turned into the ground, made the furrows. At the end of the longer was a transverse beam, to which the oxen were harnessed. To this a handle was attached, by which the plough was guided. The harrow was composed of a heavy piece of wood, on which the driver sat and passed over the ploughed field. The ox beneath the yoke afforded metaphors of subjugation. Hosea x, 11; Isaiah ix, 4; x, 27; Jeremiah v, 5; xxvii, 2, 8, 12; xxx, 8; Nahum i, 13; Psa. cxxix, 3, 4; Matthew xi, 29, 30. When it was prohibited by law to sow, either in field or vineyard, seed of a mixed kind, and crops of this nature became sacred—i. e., were given to the priests—the seed-grain was carefully cleansed from all mixture of tares, so often spoken of, and which in the New Testament are called *ζιζάνιον*. The beverage formed by boiling water and tares was called poison water, because it intoxicated and was injurious to the mind. Deut. xxix, 18, 19; Psa. lxix, 21; Jer. viii, 14; xxiii, 15; Hosea x, 4. Such were their injurious qualities that they are properly said to have been sown by an enemy while the labourers were indulging in sleep at noon. Matt. xiii, 25, 40.

Harvest.

In Palestine the crops are as far advanced in the month of February as they are here in the month of May. Sometimes the crops are blasted by frost, and sometimes they are so annoyed by easterly winds as to turn yellow and never come to maturity. This is called *mildew.* Deut. xxviii, 22; Amos iv, 9; Hag. ii, 17. The crops in the *southern* part of Palestine, and in the *plains*, come to maturity about the middle of April; but in the northern and mountainous regions they are two or three weeks later. The cultivated fields were guarded by watchmen, who sat upon a seat hung in a tree or on a watch-tower made of planks, to keep off birds, quadrupeds, or thieves. It was lawful for travellers to take ears from another's field and eat, but they were not to use the sickle. Deut. xxiii, 25. The second day of the Passover, which was the sixteenth day after the new moon of April, the first handful of ripe barley was carried to the altar, and then the harvest commenced. John iv, 35. Harvest continued from the Passover to the Pentecost, a period of *seven weeks*. The reapers were masters, children, men-servants, maidens, and mercenaries. Ruth ii, 4, 8, 21, 23; John iv, 36; James v, 4. It was a time of great rejoicing. A rich harvest was attributed to the beneficence of Providence, while sterility was considered as a judgment. Sickles were used. When the wheat was cut down, it was bound and carried away to a convenient place in the field. The gleanings were left for the poor. The land yielded thirty, sixty, and a hundred-fold.

Threshing-Floor.

This was in the field, where the bundles had been carried after being bound. Here the ground was levelled and beaten down. Gen. l, 10; 2 Sam. xxiv, 16, 24; Judges vi, 37. The assemblages of bundles in the floor for threshing, was used figuratively to denote reservation for future destruction. Micah iv, 13; Isa. xxi, 10; Jer. li, 33. At first the grain was beaten out with flails; at a later period it was trodden out by oxen, or beaten out with machines, such as are used in the East at the present day. Threshing is used figuratively to denote great slaughter. The victors are represented as huge machines that thresh and crumble even the mountains; while the victims are represented by the bundles on the threshing-floor, ground to pieces by the instruments. Judges viii, 7; 2 Samuel xii, 31; Amos i, 3; Mic. iv, 12, 13. In Deut. xxv, 4, it was forbidden to muzzle the ox that was treading out the corn. Compare 1 Cor. ix, 9–12; 1 Tim. v, 18. And the cattle which drew the threshing machine were allowed to eat at pleasure.

After the grain was threshed out it was thrown into a heap in the centre of the floor, and being elevated by a fork, it was exposed to an artificial current of wind, which blew away the chaff and allowed the wheat to fall to the ground. This operation was symbolical of the dispersion of a vanquished people, and also of the separation between the righteous and the wicked. Isa. xli, 15, 16; Jer. xiii, 24; xv, 7; li, 2; Job xxi, 18; Psa. i, 4; xxxv, 5, viii, 13; Matt. iii, 12; Luke iii, 17. That part of the straw which was not used for fodder and the manufacturing of brick, was burned, and this afforded a figurative illustration of the destruction of the wicked. Isa. v, 24; xlvii, 14; Joel ii, 5; Obad. 18; Nahum i, 10; Jer. xv, 7; Mal. iv, 1; Matt. iii, 12. After it was thus cleansed, it was put away in granaries.

Vines and Vineyards.

In some parts of the East—for instance, on the southern shore of the Caspian Sea—*vines* grow spontaneously, producing grapes of a pleasant taste. Mention is made of wine at an early period. Genesis ix, 21; xiv, 18; xix, 32–35; xxvii, 25; xlix, 11, 12. The soil of Palestine yielded, in great quantities, the best of wine. The mountains of Engedi particularly, and the valleys of Eschol and Sorek, were celebrated for their grapes. In a few instances, the wine of Mount Libanus and Helbon is extolled in the Scriptures. Hosea xiv, 7; Ezek. xxvii, 18. Some of the clusters grow to the weight of twelve pounds. Num. xiii, 24, 25. The grapes of Palestine are mostly red or black, whence originated the phrase, *blood of grapes.* Gen. xlix, 11; Deut. xxxii, 14; Isa. xxvii, 2. The vine of Sodom is poisonous, and its grapes are called poisonous clusters. *Vineyards* were generally planted on the declivity of hills and mountains. They were sometimes planted in terraces. Vines were commonly propagated by *suckers*, and were of four kinds, viz., those that ran on the ground, those that grew upright of themselves, those that adhered to a single prop, and those that covered a square frame. It is not our design to treat of all these. To sit under one's own vine, tropically denotes a peaceful and prosperous life. Jer. v, 17; viii, 13; Hosea ii, 12; Micah iv, 4; Zech. iii, 10. Vineyards were defended by a hedge or wall. In the vineyards towers were erected, which, at the present time, are thirty feet square and eighty feet high. These were erected for watchmen. The passing traveller was allowed to pluck grapes by the way, though not to carry off any in a vessel.

The manner of trimming the vine, and also the singular instrument of the vine-dresser, were well known even in the time of Moses. A vintage from new vineyards was forbidden for the first three years, and the grapes of the fourth year were consecrated to sacred purposes. Pruning in March, April, and May, is mentioned by early writers. The Hebrews dug their vineyards and gathered out the stones. The young vines, unless trees were at hand, were wound around stakes; and around those vines which ran on the ground were dug narrow trenches, in a circular form, to prevent the wandering shoots from mingling with each other. In the metaphors drawn from vineyards, these practices must be duly considered. Isa. v, 1–7; xxvii, 2–6; Psa. lxxx, 9–13; Matt. xxi, 33–46.

The *vintage* in Syria commences about the middle of September and continues to the middle of November. The Hebrews were required to leave gleaning-grapes for the poor. The season of vintage was a most joyous one. With shoutings on all sides, the grapes were plucked off and carried to the wine-press, which was in the vineyard. The *presses* consisted of two receptacles, which were either built of stones and plaster, or hewn out of the solid rock. The upper receptacle is nearly eight feet square and four high. Into this the grapes are thrown, and trodden out by five men. The juice flows out into the lower receptacle, through a grated aperture made in the side, at the bottom of the larger one. *Figuratively*, vintage gleaning and treading the wine-press signified battles and great slaughters. Isa. xvii, 6; lxiii, 1–3;

Jer. xlix, 9; Lam. i, 15. The *must*, as is customary in the East, was preserved in large firkins, and buried in the earth. Formerly new wine, or must, was preserved in leathern bottles, and, lest they should be broken by fermentation, the people were careful to have the bottles new. Job xxxii, 19; Matt. ix, 17; Mark ii, 22. Sometimes the must was boiled, and made into honey. Sometimes the grapes were dried in the sun, and were afterwards soaked in wine, and pressed a second time, from which was manufactured a *sweet wine*, which was also called *new* wine—*γλεῦκος*. Acts ii, 13.

Gardens.

Gardens were very ancient, and have always been numerous. In the Scriptures, gardens are denominated from the prevalence of certain trees; as the garden of nuts, and the garden of pomegranates. The forest of palms, also, in the plain of Jericho, was only a large garden. The Hebrews frequently built sepulchres in their gardens. 2 Kings ix, 27; xxi, 18; Mark xv, 46; Matt. xxvi, 36; John xviii, 1, 2. A pleasant region is called "a garden of God." The trees which gardens constantly displayed are often figuratively used for men. Those which are flourishing and fruitful denote *good* men; the unfruitful and barren, *wicked* men. Lofty cedars, in particular, are emblems of *kings*. Job xxix, 19; Psa. i, 3; xcii, 12–14; Hosea xiv, 6, 7; Jer. xvii, 8; Dan. iv, 10–16; Luke xxiii, 31; Matt. iii, 10; vii, 17–20; xii, 33; Ezek. xvii, 3, 4; xxxi, 3–13. An assembly of men is compared to a forest, and a multitude of wicked men to briars. Isa. ix, 10; x, 19, 33, 34; xi, 1.

Trees.

The *cedar* is a large and noble evergreen tree. Its lofty height and far-extended branches afford spacious shelter and shade. The wood is very valuable; it is of a reddish colour and of an aromatic smell, and reputed incorruptible. The ark of the covenant, much of the temple of Solomon, and the temple of Diana, at Ephesus, were built of cedar. This tree is much celebrated in Scripture, and is called the glory of Lebanon. Tropically, it denotes great strength and stability of character.

The *olive* has always been a symbol of peace and prosperity among all nations. It yields an oil which is mentioned at an early period by Moses. Palestine is famous for its olives. The Mount of Olives derives its name from this tree. It is of great beauty, and remains, like the cedar, green all winter. Its multiplied branches make it the symbol of a numerous progeny. Psa. lii, 8; cxxviii, 3; Hosea xiv, 6; Jer. xi, 16, 17. It lives about two hundred years, and young olives spring up around it when it is dead. One tree will sometimes yield one thousand pounds of oil. With this article the Hebrews carried on an extensive commerce with the Syrians. The berries yielded the best kind of oil. The presses for making the oil were of a peculiar form. From these the term *Gethsemane* was derived. This oil was used, when mixed with spices, for ointment, and also for sacrifices.

Fig-trees are very common in Palestine. They flourish in a dry and sandy soil. They are not shrubs, but tall and leafy. Their shade is grateful. Micah iv, 4. They begin to sprout at the time of the vernal equinox. Luke xxi, 29, 30; Matt. xxiv, 32. The fruit makes its appearance before the leaves and flowers. The figs are of three kinds—1. The *untimely* fig, which puts forth at the vernal equinox, and before it is ripe it is called the *green* fig, but when ripe the *untimely* fig. It comes to maturity the latter part of June, and in relish surpasses the other kinds. 2. The *summer*, or *dry* fig. This appears about the middle of June, and comes to maturity in August. 3. The *winter* fig, which germinates in August, and ripens about the end of November. All figs, when ripe, but especially the untimely, fall spontaneously. Nahum iii, 12. The parable in Luke xiii, 6, *et seq.*, is founded in the oriental mode of gardening; and the method of improving the palm, whose barrenness may be improved, is transferred to the fig-tree.

Sycamore-trees, in size and figure, resemble the mulberry, and are very common, not only in Egypt, but in Judea, especially the lowlands. Its body is large, and its branches numerous, by means of which it is easy of access. Luke xix, 4, 5. It is an evergreen. Its wood, which is of a dark hue, endures a thousand years. Its fruit does not spring from the branches, but from the body of the tree itself. It resembles the fig, though it has no seeds. It is very luscious, and hence hurtful to the stomach. The fruit does not ripen until it is opened, and the milk emitted; then, when the wound grows black, it arrives at maturity. It yields its fruit seven times a year.

The *pomegranate* grows in Persia, Arabia, Egypt, and Palestine. It is not tall, and at a little distance from the ground it shoots out its branches. Its fruit is beautiful to the eye and pleasant to the palate. It is about the size of a large apple—two or three inches in diameter—and is encircled at the upper part with something resembling a crown. It is of a brownish colour, but the interior is yellow. Artificial pomegranates were made for ornament. Exodus xxviii, 33, 34; 1 Kings vii, 18.

Citron and *orange-trees* were introduced into Palestine from Persia, and hence were exotics.

The *balsam* is both a fruit and a tree. The odoriferous balsam, so salutary in some degree to health, is not gathered from the tree in Yemen, called by the Arabic name Abu Shamm, but is distilled from a fruit which is indigenous on the mountains of Mecca and Medina. It was cultivated at a very early period in Gilead, and hence called the *Balm of Gilead;* and also in the vicinity of Jericho and Engedi. Gen. xxxvii, 25; xliii, 11; Jer. viii, 22; xlvi, 11; li, 8. There are three species of the balsam: two are shrubs, the other is a tree. They yield their sap in June, July, and August, which is received into an earthen vessel. The fruit, also, when pierced by some instrument, emits a juice of the same kind, and in more abundance, but less rich. The sap extracted from the body of the tree, or shrub, is called *opobalsamum*; the juice of the fruit is called *carpobalsamum;* and the liquid extracted from the branches, when cut off, the *xylobalsamum.*

The *palm-tree* is very common in the East, and in Africa. It is not cultivated now in Palestine, and hence is rarely seen. It requires a skilful hand to make a palm-grove flourishing and productive. At a very early period they were numerous in Palestine, which we may learn from Lev. xxiii, 40; Deut. xxxiv, 3; Judg. i, 16; iii, 13; iv, 5. Also from profane writers, and Jewish and Roman coins, which exhibit the palm, a sheaf of wheat, and a cluster of grapes, as a symbol of the Jewish nation. The palm flourishes most in warm climates. It is commonly found most flourshing in valleys and plains. Exodus xv, 27. It grows very straight and lofty, and is destitute of limbs, except very near the top, where it is surmounted with a crown of foliage that is always green. The figure of a palm-tree was carved in ornamental work, 1 Kings vi, 32; and is used tropically of a beautiful person, Cant. vii, 8; and also of a religious, upright man. Psa. i, 3; xcii, 12. The dates grow on small stems, which germinate at the angles formed by the stock of the tree and the branches. Palm-trees exhibit what may be termed a sexual distinction; and in order to any fruit being produced, the seed from the flowers of the masculine palm must be borne, at the proper season, to the tree of an opposite sex. If this is not done, and at the proper time, the female palm, like the male, bears no fruit. The productions of the palm are large clusters of dates, which become ripe in August, September, and October. Some of the dates are eaten in a crude state, and the rest are strained through a press woven of osiers, and, after the juice is forced out, are reduced into solid masses and preserved. The juice pressed out is the *date wine*, and is very celebrated. At the Feast of

Tabernacles, the Hebrews bore palm branches in their hands; they also strewed them in the way before kings, as they entered their cities on public occasions. The Greeks gave a palm branch to those who conquered in the games. Compare Rev. vii, 9. This tree is regarded among the orientals as of all others the most noble. Hence the saying, *from the branch* (i. e., the *palm* branch) *to the rush or reed*, expressing and denoting the highest and lowest. Isa. ix, 14; xix, 15.

Terebinths are large trees loaded with branches and foliage, and green through the year. They live one thousand years, and, when they die, leave a scion which spreads a like luxuriance of foliage, and lives to a like number of years, so that where they once appear they will be perpetuated. On account of their perpetuity, places were named from them. Gen. xiii, 18; Judg. vi, 11; 1 Sam. x, 3; Isa. vi, 13; Ezek. vi, 13. They are used figuratively as symbols of the good, who, in Isa. lxi, 3, are called terebinths (trees) of righteousness.

The *pistacia* is a tree very much resembling the terebinth. It bears a very rich species of nuts, which hang in clusters, (Gen. xliii, 11,) and which become ripe in October. They somewhat resemble almonds in appearance, but are of a much better flavour, and are, therefore, most valued by the Orientals. Walnuts are common in Palestine, but hazel-nuts are scarce. The word which some suppose to mean hazel is the name of the almond.

Bees and Honey.

Palestine is often called the land flowing with milk and honey. This is a tropical expression, and is applied to any fruitful land. For instance, Egypt, in Num. xvi, 13. Bees were very numerous in Palestine, not only in the hives which were constructed for them of clay and straw, but frequently in the woods, in the hollow trees, and fissures of rocks. Deut. xxxii, 13; Psa. lxxxi, 17. They possess a keen animosity and an equally keen sting, with which they make an efficient attack on their enemies. Tropically they represent violent and ferocious enemies. Deut. i, 44; Psa. cxviii, 11, 12. They could be allured by anything that made a tinkling sound to any particular place. Isa. vii, 18. Honey is often mentioned in the Bible, both in a solid and liquid state. *Wild* honey is also mentioned. 1 Sam. xiv, 25–27; Matt. iii, 4. The ancients were very fond of honey, and hence it is tropically used as expressive of pleasure and happiness. Psa. cxix, 103; Prov. xxiv, 13, 14; Cant. iv, 11.

Fish.

Fish were esteemed by all Orientals, as well as Hebrews, a great delicacy. Numbers xi, 5. They were taken in great numbers from the river Jordan, and the lake of Tiberias, or sea of Galilee. Those only which were destitute of scales or fins were interdicted. Lev. xi, 10. Hence mention is made of the *fish-gate* at Jerusalem, so called from the circumstance of fish being sold there. 2 Chron. xxxiii, 14; Neh. iii, 3; xii, 39; Isa. xix, 8; Ezek. xxvi, 5, 14; xlvii, 10. Fishermen are used tropically for enemies. Isa. xix, 8; Hab. i, 15. Some of the apostles, living near the sea of Galilee, were fishermen, and this class of men were, in general, active and experienced. Luke v, 1, *et seq.* Comp. Matt. iv, 19. The instruments used in fishing were a hook, iron spear, and a net.

The Fallow Year.

Agriculture, on every seventh year, came to an end. Nothing was sown and nothing was reaped. The vines and the olives were not pruned; there was no vintage and no gathering of fruits, even of what grew wild; and whatever spontaneous productions there were, were left to the poor, the traveller, and wild beasts. This was to let the ground have rest, and recover its strength, and to teach the Hebrews to be provident of their income. Extraordinary fruitfulness was promised the sixth year. Lev. xxv, 20–24. During the seventh year the time was spent in fishing, hunting, taking care of bees, and flocks, and herds; manufacturing and the mechanic arts were also carried on. They were obliged to remain longer in the temple this year, during which the whole Mosaic law was read, and they were more largely instructed in religious and moral duties, and the history of their nation. Deut. xxxi, 10–15. The seventh year's rest, as Moses predicted, (Lev. xxvi, 34, 35,) was for a long time neglected, but after the captivity it was more scrupulously observed.

Origin of the Arts.

The arts originated partly in necessity, and partly in accident. In the fourth generation, after the creation of man, we find mention made of artificers in brass and iron, and also of musical instruments. Gen. iv, 21–23. From the construction of the ark, we learn that the antediluvians must have made considerable advancement in the mechanic arts. Not long after the Deluge, we find mention made of many things, such as utensils and ornaments, which imply a knowledge of the arts. Gen. ix, 21; xi, 1–9; xiv, 1–16; xii, 7, 8; xv, 10; xvii, 10; xviii, 4–6; xix, 32; xxi, 14; xxii, 10; xxiii, 13; &c. Soon after the death of Joshua, a place was expressly allotted to artificers. It was called the valley of craftsmen. 1 Chron. iv, 14; Neh. xi, 35. Mention is made of artificers in gold and silver. Judg. xvii, 3–5. Women spun, wove, embroidered, and made clothing for their families. Exod. xxxv, 25; 1 Sam. ii, 19; Prov. xxxi, 18–31; Acts ix, 39. Artificers among the Hebrews were men of rank. Jer. xxiv, 1; xxix, 2; 2 Kings xxiv, 14. They received instruction from the Syrians. The Talmudists taught that all parents should teach their children some art or handicraft. Joseph, the husband of Mary, was a carpenter. Matt. xiii, 55; Mark vi, 3. Simon of Joppa was a tanner. Acts ix, 43; x, 32. Alexander, a learned Jew, was a coppersmith. 2 Tim. iv, 14. Paul and Aquila were tent-makers.

The *art of alphabetical writing* is attributed to an early age. The precise time of its invention, however, is not known. Forty-five years after the death of Moses, Cadmus, of Phœnicia, introduced letters into Greece. Books and writing are spoken of in the time of Moses. Exod. xvii, 14; xxiv, 4; xxviii, 9–11; xxxii, 32; xxxiv, 27, 28; Num. xxxiii, 2; Deut. xxvii, 8. Long before his time scribes kept written genealogies. Exod. vi, 14; Deut. xx, 5–9. In the time of Jacob, *seals*, on which names were engraved, were in use. Gen. xxxviii, 18; xli, 42. *Hieroglyphics* were inscribed by Egyptians on stone. The *law* was inscribed on stones. Exod. xxxii, 16–32. The *scribes* had schools for teaching the art of writing, called schools of the prophets. 1 Sam. xix, 16; 2 Kings ii, 3–5; iv, 38; vi, 1. The *materials* for writing were *stones*, *tiles*, *brass*, *lead*, *leaves*, *bark*, *skins*, *wood*, *linen*, *paper*, *made from papyrus*, and the *sand of the earth.* The *instruments* were the *style*, made of iron, for writing on hard materials; a *small brush*, by which letters were painted on cotton, cloth, paper, skins, parchment, &c.; or a *reed* or *pen*, which was split. *Ink* was used at an early day. Num. v, 23; Jer. xxxvi, 18. *Books* are known as early as Job xix, 23; Num. xxi, 14; Exod. xvii, 14. They were written on flexible materials, and rolled round a stick; if they were very long, on two, connected with the extremities; hence is derived the name of *volume*, or thing rolled up.

Poetry had its origin in the first ages of the world. It was cultivated among the Hebrews as far back as the age of Moses. Exod. xv; Deut. xxxii; Num. xxi, 24. The book of Job is poetic. Hebrew poetry is characterized by ardent feelings, splendid thoughts, and beautiful imagery. It is distinguished from accidental poetry in several particulars, especially in its metaphors and ornaments.

Music is coeval with poetry. Musical instruments were the invention of Jubal, Gen. iv, 21; and as early as Gen.

xxxi, 27, we are introduced to a whole choir. The Hebrews insisted on having music at marriages, birth-days, inauguration of kings, public worship, and great festivals. Isa. xxx, 29. In the *tabernacle* and *temple* the Levites were the lawful musicians. The holy *silver trumpets* were only blown by the priests. Num. i, 1–10. David divided the four thousand Levites into twenty-four classes, each of which were superintended by a leader. 1 Chron. xvi, 5; xxiii, 4, 5; xxv, 1–31; 2 Chron. v, 12, 13. This arrangement for singing was transferred to the temple, and continued till the time of the overthrow of Jerusalem. The *harp* was a stringed instrument; the strings were originally swept by the hand, but subsequently with a small bow or fret. The *psaltery* was a *ten-stringed instrument;* this was played by the fingers; its form was that of a right-angled triangle. The *organ*, anciently called the shepherd's pipe, consisted at first of seven pipes, made of reeds of different length. The *horn*, or crooked trumpet, was made of the horns of oxen or rams. The *straight trumpet* was a cubit in length, hollow throughout, and bell-shaped at the mouth. The *timbrel* or *tabret* consisted of a small hoop, with a skin tensely drawn over it, and hung round with bells. The *cymbal* consisted of two thin pieces of metal of circular shape; the musician held one in his right hand and the other in his left, and smote them together. Various other instruments of music were invented from time to time, but the above are the more important mentioned in Scripture.

Dancing among the Mohammedans is esteemed an amusement unworthy the dignity of men, and hence is left to women and children. It is practised among the Orientals in a very indecorous manner; among the Hebrews it was sacredly used. Exod. xv, 20; Judg. xi, 34; 1 Sam. xviii, 6, 7; Jer. xxxi, 4–13; Psa. lxviii, 26; 2 Sam. vi, 16–23.

The art of *oratory* never flourished in the East.

Sciences.

In scientific knowledge the Egyptians and Babylonians excelled all others. The Arabians are also favourably mentioned in this respect, 1 Kings, iv, 30; also the Edomites. Jer. xlix, 7. The Hebrews became renowned for their intellectual culture in the time of David, and especially in Solomon's day. 1 Kings, v, 9–14. After this, literature declined.

The Hebrews, Babylonians, Assyrians, Egyptians, Persians, and Tyrians, had their *historical annals. Arithmetical calculations* are spoken of in Gen. xxiv, 60; Lev. xxvi, 8; Deut. xxxii, 30. *Mathematics*, *Astronomy*, and *Astrology* were cultivated at an early period. *Time* was divided into years, weeks, and days, which were divided as follows, viz.: break of day, morning or sun rise, heat of the day, mid-day, cool of the day, evening; and also into hours, the principal of which were the third, sixth, and ninth. Night was divided into four watches. In addition to the week of days, the Jews had the week of weeks, the week of years, and the week of seven Sabbatical years. The changes of the moon were employed in the measurement of time, and hence the name of month. The months were civil and sacred.

Medicine was cultivated at an early day. The Egyptians carried their sick into the temples of *Serapis*, and the Greeks carried theirs into those of Æsculapius. *Physicians* are first mentioned in Gen. l, 2; Exod. xxi, 19; Job xiii, 4. Dissections were not made till the time of Ptolemy. Among the Hebrews and Egyptians the art of healing was committed to the priests.

Natural Philosophy may be found in the book of Job, and in the thirty-seventh, thirty-ninth, and seventy-third Psalms. *Natural History* was also cultivated to some extent.

Commerce.

At a very early period traffic between different nations was carried on to a considerable extent. Frequent mention is made of public roads, fords, bridges, beasts of burden, ships, weights, measures, and coins. The Phœnicians anciently held the first rank as a commercial nation. The *ships of Tarshish* were famed for their distant voyages. The inhabitants of Arabia Felix carried on a trade with India. Goods were transported across the country on camels. Several merchants would band together and form a *caravan.* Solomon sent ships through the Red Sea to Ophir. The principal sea-port of Palestine was *Joppa.* A new port was built by Herod the Great at Cesarea.

Weights and Measures were regulated at a very early period in Asia. After the time of Solomon the models for weights and measures were deposited in the temple. A *finger*, or *digit*, was about $9\frac{1}{12}$ of an inch; a *palm*, a hand-breadth; a *span*, from the end of the thumb to that of the little finger; a *cubit*, from the elbow to the wrist; a *measure*, the length of a man's arm; a *measuring reed*, the length of the human body; a *stadium*, four feet and $6\frac{1}{10}$; a *Sabbath day's journey*, two miles; a *day's journey*, from twenty to thirty miles; an *omer*, five pints and one-tenth; an *ephah*, three pecks and three pints; and several other measures of less importance.

There is no trace of stamped silver *coin* previous to the captivity. *Gold*, even so late as the time of David, was not used as a standard of value.

A *grain of barley* was the smallest weight. The weight most in use was the *shekel.*

Clothing.

Our first parents protected themselves with the leaves of a fig-tree, and afterwards with the skins of animals. The art of manufacturing cloths by spinning and weaving is of great antiquity. Gen. xiv, 23; xxxi, 18, 19; xxxvii, 3; xxxviii, 28; Job vii, 6; xxxi, 20. The Egyptians were celebrated for such manufactures. Alexander found silks in Persia. *White* was esteemed the most appropriate colour for cotton cloth, and *purple* for the others. Kings and princes were clothed in purple. Luke xvi, 19; Rev. xviii, 12. The *scarlet colour* is first mentioned in Gen. xxxviii, 28. The *hyacinth*, or *dark blue colour*, was highly esteemed among the Assyrians. Ezek. xxiii, 6. *Black colour* was used for common wear, and particularly on occasions of mourning. *Parti-coloured* cloth was much esteemed. Gen. xxxvii, 3, 23; 2 Sam. xiii, 18. As early as the time of Moses, cloth was *embroidered*.

The *tunic* was the most simple and ancient garment; it was a piece of cloth which encircled the whole body, bound with a girdle, and extending to the knees. The *meil* was a garment which extended below the knees, open at the top, so as to be drawn over the head. The *ephod* consisted of two parts, united by a clasp or buckle on the shoulder. The *hat* or *turban*, worn on the head, was early used. The *toga* was a Roman garment, and the *cloak* a Greek garment. *Sandals* were small pieces of wood, or leather, bound to the bottom of the feet. To loose and bind on sandals was the lowest office of a servant. In contracts, the seller gave his sandal to the buyer in confirmation of the bargain.

The *beard* was considered among the Hebrews a great ornament. No one was allowed to touch it, except for the purpose of kissing it. To cut, or shave, or mar it in any way, was considered a great disgrace. 1 Chron. xix, 3–5; 2 Sam. x, 4–10. The beard was used tropically for distinguished men of any nation. The shaving of it denoted servitude. Isa. vii, 20. The Egyptians and Arabians were in the habit of shaving the beard; sometimes the Hebrews applied the razor. Shaving was absolutely interdicted to the Nazarites. Num. vi, 5; Judg. xiii, 7; xvi, 17. Baldness was a source of contempt. The head was combed, set in order, and the hair anointed, especially on festive occasions.

Females allowed the hair to grow long. They braided it, and sometimes interwove gems and gold. Anciently the hair was the only covering for the head. Afterwards, mitres made of cloth were used. Those worn by the priests were higher.

The difference between the dress of the men and women was small, and consisted chiefly in the fineness of the material and the length. The women wore a veil, which was customary with all, except maid-servants, and those in low condition, and prostitutes. Veils were of different kinds.

The Hebrews carried a *staff*, to assist in a journey, as well as for an ornament. Exod. xii, 11; Gen. xxxviii, 18, 25. They also, in imitation of the Egyptians, wore a *seal* suspended from the neck, over the breast. Gen. xxxviii, 18. Frequently a ring, with some inscription on it, was used as a seal, by a delivery or transfer of which, from a monarch, the highest offices of the kingdom were created. Gen. xli, 42; Esth. iii, 10–12; viii, 2; Jer. xxii, 24; Dan. vi, 10; xiii, 7. They were worn as an ornament of the finger on the right hand. The ladies wore a number of rings on their fingers, and also in their ears, and sometimes in their nose. Gen. xxiv, 22; Exod. xxxii, 2, 3; xxxv, 22. They also wore rings of silver and gold around their ancles: they also wore necklaces, bracelets, &c. Hebrew women carried amulets for ornament, and to keep off incantations.

Mirrors were made of polished brass. In Job xxxvii, 18, the heavens are compared to a molten mirror. The ladies carried their mirrors in their hands.

A man's girdle fulfilled for him all the purposes of a purse. The purse of a lady, which was made of solid metal, sometimes of gold, and fashioned like a cone, with a border of rich cloth at the top, was suspended from the girdle which she wore. Both sexes either wore napkins attached to their girdle, or bore them upon their hand or left arm. The dress used on festival occasions was very splendid, and perfumed with myrrh, cassia, and aloes. Gen. xxvii, 27;

Psa. xlv, 8; Cant. iv, 11. Vast expense was bestowed on these garments, both as respected their quality and number. 2 Kings v, 5; Matt. x, 10; James v, 2. The *mourning-dress* or *sackcloth* extended down to the knees. It is a coarse dark cloth of goat's hair.

Food and Feasts.

At first men lived on the fruit of trees, upon herbs, roots, and seeds, and whatever else they could find nutritive in the vegetable kingdom. Gen. i, 29; ii, 16. Afterwards, a method was invented to bruise grain, and to reduce it to a mass; with this water, milk, and honey were sometimes mixed. Before the Deluge the flesh of animals was used for food. Gen. vii, 2, 8. Originally food of every kind was eaten without being cooked, because there was no fire; and even if there had been, its use in the preparation of food was unknown. Corn was eaten at first without any preparation at all, and this custom had not gone into total desuetude in the time of Christ. Matt. xii, 1. Some, who found a difficulty in mastication, broke the kernels with stones, which suggested the idea of mortars and mills. Meal is spoken of as far back as the time of Abraham. As there were no public bakers except the king's, each family owned a hand-mill, consisting of two stones. One person could not take another's mill as a pledge. Deut. xxiv, 6. Enemies taken in war were condemned to turn the mill. Judg. xvi, 21; Lam. v, 13. The business of baking was performed by women, no matter how high their station in life; cooking was also done by the matron of the family. The use of salt is very ancient. Num. xviii, 19; 2 Chron. xiii, 5. It is a symbol of inviolable friendship. A covenant of salt means an everlasting covenant. It is also used tropically for wisdom and for preservation, Mark ix, 49, 50; Col. iv, 6; and salt that lost its savour or saltness, on the contrary, folly and corruption. Matt. v. 13. Some sorts of food were interdicted:—1st, Quadrupeds which do not ruminate, or have cloven feet;

2d, Serpents and creeping insects; 3d, Certain species of birds; 4th, Fishes without scales or fins; 5th, All food, all liquids standing in a vessel, and all wet seed into which the dead body of any unclean insect had fallen—water in cisterns, wells, and fountains, could not be contaminated in this way; 6th, All food and liquids which stood in the tent or chamber of a dying or dead man, remaining uncovered; 7th, Everything which was consecrated by any one to idols or gods. 1 Cor. viii, 10. Blood was interdicted; also, an animal that died of itself, or was torn to pieces by wild beasts; and the fat covering the intestines, the large lobe of the liver, the kidneys, and the fat on them.

The Mohammedans drink water commonly, but the rich a beverage called sherbet. The Orientals frequently use wine, and sometimes it was used to excess, from which circumstance many tropes are drawn. Isa. v, 11–22; xxviii, 1–11; xlix, 26; Jer. viii, 14; ix, 14; xvi, 48; Deut. xxxii, 42; Psa. lxxviii, 65. Wines were sometimes mixed or adulterated, and sometimes diluted. Their drinking vessels were a cup of brass covered with tin, in form resembling a lily; the bowl was also of the same form; they were sometimes of silver and gold. The larger vessels were urns and bottles.

The time of taking refreshments was about eleven o'clock of our time. Their principal meal was about six o'clock in the afternoon; hence their feasts were always at supper-time. The table was a piece of round leather, spread on the floor, around which they sat in a circle. They had neither knife, fork, nor spoon. In the time of Christ the Persian custom prevailed of reclining at the table. The guests reclined upon the left side. Luke vii, 36–38; xvi, 22, 23; John ii, 8; xiii, 23. Anciently females were excluded from the table, with the exception of Babylon and Persia. After supper they usually drank. The cup is used tropically to represent a man's lot. Psa. xi, 6; lxxv, 8; Isa. li, 22; Jer. xxv, 15–27; xxxv, 5; xlix, 12; Ezek. xxiii, 31–34; Matt. xxvi, 39.

Feasts are mentioned at an early period. Gen. xxi, 8;

xxix, 22; xxxi, 27–54; xl, 20. In respect to the second tithes, which originated from the vow of Jacob, (Gen. xxviii, 22,) Moses was very particular in his laws. At the feast of the second sort of first-fruits, servants, widows, orphans, and Levites should be made free partakers. Deut. xvi, 11–14. Jesus alludes to this festival, which was designed for the poor. Luke xiv, 13. The guests appeared in white robes. These feasts sometimes continued from evening till morning. Feasts are symbolical of a state of prosperity and happiness; and exclusion from them, of destitution and misery. The kingdom of Christ is compared to a feast.

There being no public inns in the East, great hospitality characterized the inhabitants. This extended to all classes; even the wandering Arabs receive and treat strangers with hospitality to this day.

State of Domestic Society.

Polygamy and fornication were condemned by that primeval institution which joined in marriage *one* man and *one* woman. Gen. i, 27, 28. Before the time of Moses, morals had become very much corrupted, and not only the prostitution of females, but of boys, was very common among many nations, and even made a part of the divine worship. To prevent these evils, Moses made the following regulations: 1. Among the Israelites no prostitute, male or female, was tolerated. 2. That the price of whoredom, though presented in return for a vow, should not be received at the sanctuary. Deut. xxiii, 19. 3. A man who had seduced a female should marry her, and, in case the father would not consent, should pay thirty shekels; and, if violence had been offered, fifty. 4. That a person who, when married, was not found to be a virgin, as she professed, was to be stoned. Notwithstanding the severity of these laws, prostitutes of both sexes were set apart in the time of the kings for the service of idols. Prov. ii, 16–19; v, 3–6; vii, 5–27; Amos ii, 7; vii, 17; Jer. iii, 2; v, 7; 1 Kings xiv, 24; xv, 12.

Lamech is the first mentioned having two wives. After the Deluge the example of Noah and his sons was a good one, but it was not followed. Polygamy prevailed very much in the time of Moses. Deut. xvii, 17. Moses regulated polygamy by requiring the husband to bestow his attention on each one at certain times. Exod. xxi, 10, 11; Gen. xxx, 14–16. Intercourse was prohibited during the *menses* on pain of death. Uncleanness contracted by sexual connexion continued through a whole day. The father of a family selected wives for his sons and husbands for his daughters. Intermarriage with foreigners was prohibited, lest the Hebrews should be seduced to idolatry. A priest was not allowed to marry a prostitute, or a divorced or profane woman. A marriage covenant was a vow between the father and brothers of the bride, and the father of the bridegroom. Wives were sometimes purchased. The honour which is now rendered to the female sex originated from the instructions of the apostles. An interval of ten or twelve months elasped between the agreement to marry and the consummation, during which time there was no intercourse. If the bridegroom, from any cause, was unwilling to fulfil his engagements by marriage, he was obliged to give her a bill of divorcement, the same as if she had been his wife. On the occasion of the marriage the bridegroom prepared a feast. Judg. xiv, 17. In the evening the bridegroom, with his company, came, and conducted the bride from the house of her father to the place where the nuptials were celebrated, with great feasting and rejoicings. After this the nuptial blessing was pronounced, and the spouse, who up to this time is veiled from head to foot, is led to the bed-chamber.

Concubines were sometimes associated with individuals of the other sex, and were entitled to claim the privileges of a wife; they were obtained in various ways. Exod. xxi, 9–12; Deut. xx, 10–14. A large number of offspring was considered an instance of the divine favour, while *sterility* was looked upon as a reproach and punishment. 1 Sam. i, 6, 7;

Psa. cxxvii, 3–5. The state of *celibacy* was also considered a great reproach. If the husband died, leaving a widow without issue, the brother of the deceased, or nearest male relation, was bound to marry her.

If a married man has criminal intercourse with a married woman, or one promised in marriage, or a widow expecting to be married with a brother-in-law, it is accounted *adultery.* If the woman is unmarried it is *fornication.* Before the time of Moses this was reckoned a crime, and was punished. Gen. xxxviii, 24. In Egypt the nose, and in Persia the nose and ears of an adultress were cut off. In the penal code of Moses it was punished by death. Lev. xx, 10. The *suspected* wife was subjected to the ordeal oath. To this oath dreadful penalties were attached. This was abrogated forty years before the destruction of Jerusalem. In the latter periods of the Jewish Church adultery and licentiousness in every form abounded, so that few could be found innocent. John viii, 1–8.

Though the power of the husband over the wife was great, the law did not permit him to repudiate his wife without a bill of divorce. Deut. xxiv, 1–4 ; xxiii, 14, 15. The wife, under certain circumstances, could obtain a divorce. Exod. xxi, 10.

Mothers were generally the only assistants of their daughters at child-birth. In cases of difficulty, midwives were called in. The birth of a son was a time of rejoicing. The mother, after the birth of a son, was unclean for seven days, and remained at home thirty-three days. If a daughter was born, the number of unclean days was doubled. After the expiration of this period she went into the tabernacle, or temple, and offered a lamb, or doves and pigeons, for a sacrifice of purification. Lev. xii, 1–8 ; Luke ii, 22.

On the eighth day the son was circumcised, and by this rite was consecrated to God. *Circumcision* was a preventive of the disease called the *anthrax*, or carbuncle, originating from the impurities which collect under the foreskin. Gen. xxxiv, 25. This rite was known previous to the time of

Abraham. It was practised in Egypt. Gen. xii, 10–15. A *name* was given to the male child at the time of circumcision. Gen. xvi, 11; xix, 37; xxv, 25; Exod. ii, 10; xviii, 3, 4. Names were given from the circumstances of birth, from peculiarities in the history of the family, &c. They were sometimes compound, one part being the name of the Deity, and, among idolatrous nations, the name of an idol. Sometimes the Orientals had two names. A new name is tropically used to denote distinction. The *first-born* inherited peculiar rights and privileges; he received a double portion of the estate. Gen. xlviii, 5–8; Deut. xxi, 17. The first-born was the priest of the whole family. Num. iii, 12–18; viii, 18. They had an authority over those who were younger. Gen. xxv, 23.

In the first ages of the world mothers nursed their children themselves. The day when the child was weaned, which was thirty months, was made a festival. If the mother died, nurses were employed. The sons remained in the care of the mother until they were five years old, when they were taken by the father and instructed in the arts and duties of life, in the Mosaic law, and all parts of their religion. Deut. vi, 20–25; vii, 19; xi, 19. Some were sent to the schools of the prophets. The daughters were always in the care of their mothers, and spent their time in learning domestic duties. Implicit obedience was required and enforced by the father of his children. Gen. xxi, 14; xxxviii, 24.

At the death of the father his estate was divided among his sons, the first receiving two, and the rest equal shares. Presents were made by *will* to the sons of concubines, and sometimes they were made equal. The *daughters* not only had no portion in the estate, but, if unmarried, were considered as making part of it, and could be sold by their brothers into matrimony. If there were no brothers the estate fell to them. *Slaves* were sometimes made heirs. The *widow* of the deceased had no right to any part of the estate. Widows were often neglected. Isa. i, 17; x, 2; Jer. vii, 6.

Slavery existed and prevailed before the Deluge. Gen. ix, 25. Some of the patriarchs had thousands of slaves. The laws of Moses permitted the Hebrews to own slaves, male and female, but they were bound to circumcise them, and instruct them in the worship of the true God. Gen. xvii, 13–17. Though the Hebrews were permitted to hold foreigners in slavery, yet they were prohibited from making slaves of the Canaanites, and also the Gibeonites, the Kephirites, the Berothites, and the inhabitants of Kirjath-jearim. Among the many ways by which men were reduced to slavery, we notice the following:—1st. *Captivity in war.* Deut. xx, 14; xxi, 10, 11; Gen. xiv. 2d. *Debts.* 2 Kings iv, 1; Isa. l, 1; Matt. xviii, 25. 3d. *Theft.* Exod. xxii, 2; Neh. v, 4, 5. 4th. *Man-stealing.* Exod. xxi, 16; Deut. xxiv, 7. 5th. The *children of slaves*—those born in one's house—children of maid-servants. Gen. xiv, 14; xv, 3; xvii, 23; xxi, 10. 6th. *By purchase.* (See Jahn's Archæology, p. 180—Andover, 1832.) The medium *price* of a slave was thirty shekels. Lev. xxvii, 1–8. The food and clothing of slaves were of the poorest description. All their earnings went to their master. Deut. xv, 18. They had the consent of their master to marry, or live with a woman. The children addressed their owners as lord or master. Gal. iv, 6; Rom. viii, 15. The servant most discreet and faithful was placed over the rest, and made steward of the house. Some of the servants instructed the children of their masters, while some waited upon their masters and others on their mistresses. The law required the masters to treat their slaves with humanity. Lev. xxv, 39–53. The master who slew a servant was held responsible. Exod. xxi, 20, 21. An injury inflicted by the master secured the freedom of the slave. Exod. xxi, 26, 27. On the Sabbath and festivals they had a cessation from labour. Exod. xx, 10; Deut. v, 14. They were invited to those feasts made of second tithes. Deut. xii, 17, 18. They were to receive an adequate subsistence from their masters. Deut. xxv, 4; 1 Tim. v, 18; 1 Cor. ix, 9. The master was bound to provide for the marriage of maid-servants, unless he took them as concubines or gave them to his sons. Exod. xxi, 8. A servant of Hebrew origin was not obliged to serve over six years. Exod. xxi, 2. He could, however, give himself up to perpetual servitude. Exod. xxi, 5, 6; Deut. xv, 16. The master, however, could not sell such to any out of Hebrew territories. Ibid. Servants might redeem themselves, or be redeemed by the purchase of their time. Lev. xxv, 47–55. All Hebrew servants were emancipated in the year of jubilee. Lev. xxxix, 25–41. Finally, a slave who had fled from another nation was to be treated kindly, and not forcibly returned back. Deut. xxiii, 15, 16.

In other countries there was no Sabbath or rest of any kind for slaves. Runaway slaves were branded in the forehead. Gal. vi, 17; Rev. xiv, 9; xxii, 4. They were debarred from a participation in all civil festivals and religious exercises. Christianity ameliorated their condition in this respect. Gal. iii, 28; Col. iii, 10, 11; Philemon 10; 1 Cor. xii, 13; Eph. vi, 8.

Social condition of the Hebrews.

The forms of *salutation* which prevailed among the ancient Hebrews were as follows:—1. Be thou blessed of Jehovah. 2. The blessing of Jehovah be upon thee. 3. May God be with thee. 4. May peace and prosperity attend thee. 5. Sir, be your life preserved. The gestures and inflexions of the body, made on an occasion of salutation, were varied, according to the dignity and station of the person saluted. The ceremony of advancing and receding, kissing the hand and the beard, is sometimes as often repeated as ten times. Hence it was anciently inculcated upon messengers whose business required haste, to salute no man by the way. 2 Kings iv, 29; Luke x, 4. Prostration was made before kings. 1 Kings ii, 19.

In *visiting*, a person would stand at the gate and knock, or call with a loud voice, till the master came out. If the visitor were a proper person, the females were required to repair to their respective apartments, and he was introduced into the house. 2 Kings v, 9–12; Acts x, 17. Presents were carried by visitors. Gen. xxvii, 27; Exodus xxx, 37, 38. Kings were in the habit of making and receiving presents.

Kings, princes, and national ambassadors, whenever on a public occasion they enter cities, receive great attention and honour. The windows are opened, and the flat roofs crowded with spectators. The path is strewed with flowers and branches, and sometimes spread with carpets, while shouts are echoed on every side. 2 Sam. xvi, 16; 1 Kings i, 40; 2 Kings ix, 13; Isa. lxii, 11; Zech. ix, 9; Matt. xxi, 7, 8. The musicians first walk in the procession. 1 Kings xviii, 46; 1 Chron. xv, 27–29. The persons who sustain offices in the government, and are attached to the palace, are the next in the procession. Then follows the king. All are carried on noble coursers. Anciently, on such occasions, kings rode in chariots. Gen. xli, 43; 2 Sam. xv, 1; 1 Kings i, 5.

Conversation was usually held in the gate of the city, where there was an open space fitted up with seats for the accommodation of the people. Gen. xix, 1; Psa. lxix, 12. Judicial trials were commonly investigated at the gate. Gen. xix, 1; xxxiv, 20; Psa. xxvi, 4, 5; lxix, 12; cxxvii, 5; Ruth iv, 11; Isa. xiv, 31. The ancient Asiatics were also delighted with singing and dancing, and instruments of music. *Promenading* was wearisome in the warm climates of the East, and hence the people sought retired places, beneath the shade of vines and fig-trees. 1 Samuel xxii, 6; Micah iv, 4.

The *bath* was also very agreeable to the Orientals, not only on account of its cool and refreshing nature, but the necessity of cleanliness, in order to health. Baths were frequented by the ladies, and formed an agreeable resort. The Egyptians, at the earliest period, were in the habit of bathing in the waters of the Nile. Exod. ii, 5; vii, 13–25. It was one of the civil laws of the Hebrews that the bath should be used. Lev. xiv, 2; xv, 1–8; xvii, 15, 16; xxii, 6; Num. xix, 6.

In conversation, the Orientals are candid and mild, very rarely using any terms of reproach. The severest terms are *adversary*, *raca*, or *fool*. Job ii, 10; Psa. xiv, 1; Isa. xxxii, 6; Matt. v, 22; xvi, 23. The formula of assent or affirmation was σὺ εἶπας, *thou hast said*, or *thou hast rightly said*. This explains the answer of Christ to Caiaphas, in Matt. xxvi, 64. To *spit*, in company, in a carpeted room, was an indication of great rusticity of manners. To spit in one's face was an indication of great indignity. Matt. xxvi, 67; Mark xiv, 65.

The Jews were instructed, by the laws of Moses, to treat *strangers* with hospitality. Of this class were all *foreigners*, whether Hebrews or others destitute of a home, as well as all who resided in Palestine, but were not natives; the latter were strangers or foreigners, in the strict sense of the term. Both these were to be treated as citizens, and enjoy the same rights. Lev. xix, 33, 34; xxiv, 16–22; Num. ix, 14; xv, 14; Deut. x, 18; xxiii, 8; xxiv, 17; xxvii, 19. At a later period, foreigners were compelled to labour on the public edifices. 1 Chron. xxii, 2; 2 Chron. ii, 16, 17. In the time of Christ, the Jews had degenerated in hospitality.

Although Moses made abundant provision for the *poor*, he does not say anything in respect to *beggars*. The first notice of mendicants is in Psa. cix, 10. In the time of Christ, they were found sitting in the streets, at the doors and gates of the rich, and also at the entrance of the temple and synagogues. Mark x, 46; Luke xvi, 20; Acts iii, 2. Sometimes food and money were given to them. Matt. xxvi, 9; Luke xvi, 21. Oriental beggars do not appeal to the *pity* of those they solicit, but to their *justice*. Job xxii, 7; xxxi, 16; Prov. iii, 27, 28; xxi, 21; Psalm xxiv, 5; Eccles. iv, 1; xiv, 13, 14; Matt. vi, 1.

Persons *defiled* from disease, or any other cause, were excluded from the intercourse of society, and the tabernacle and temple; but they might, by ceremonial purification, be restored. Lev. xiii, 3. The Levitical law regarded the following persons as *unclean*:—

1. Those who had the *leprosy*. They were excluded from cities and villages, and were compelled to cry out, to all they met, *unclean! unclean!* Lev. xiii, 45; Num. v, 2, *et seq.*

2. Those who had the *gonorrhœa*, whether in a mild or virulent form. Lev. xv, 3.

3. Those who had *emissio seminis*, even in legitimate intercourse, were to be unclean till evening. Lev. xv, 16–22.

4. Women after the birth of a son were unclean for seven days, and after the birth of a daughter twice as long. In the former case they were excluded from the temple for thirty, and in the latter, for sixty days. Lev. xii, 1–6; xv, 16–28.

5. Women during the period of the *menses* were unclean Lev. xv, 19–21; Matt. ix, 20.

6. A person who touched the corpse of a man, or the dead body of an animal, or a sepulchre, or had been in the tent or room of a dying or dead person. Priests wearing badges of mourning were made thereby unclean; and hence they never wore them, except in case of the death of their relatives. Lev. v, 2; xi, 8–11; xxiv, 31; xxi, 1–5, 10, 11; Num. xix, 11–15.

Diseases.

The disease which is mentioned in 1 Sam. v, 6–12; vi, 18, was the *dysentery*, according to some, and by others it is supposed to have been an inflammation and swelling of the fundament, produced by the bite of a venomous animal belonging to the spider class, but much larger. The bite of these animals was fatal in its consequences.

The disease of King Jehoram, mentioned in 2 Chron. xxi, 12–15, 18, 19, was the dysentery.

The *leprosy* was regarded by the ancients as a marked exhibition of the justice and wrath of God. It was denominated by the Hebrews the *stroke* or *wound of the Lord.* Num. xii, 1–10; 2 Kings v, 1; xv, 5; 2 Chron. xxvi, 20. The disease commences internally, and finally develops itself until it appears on the surface of the body. The first appearance is small red spots about the nose and eyes; and they increase in size for a number of years, until they become as large as a pea or bean, and cover the whole body. There are four kinds of leprosy. The first kind is of so virulent and powerful a nature that it separates the joints, and mutilates the body in the most shocking manner. The second is *white* leprosy, the third is *black* leprosy, and the fourth is *red* leprosy. The disease is almost always fatal, however long it may be in passing through the various stages. To a certain extent it is hereditary, and passes down to the third and fourth generation. There was a species of leprosy termed *Bohak*, which was not infectious. Lev. xiii, 38, 39. The peculiarities belonging to *real* leprosy are—1. It is *incurable;* 2. It is *infectious;* and, 3. It is *hereditary.*

The *pestilence* was any sudden calamity which, in the form of disease, fell upon the people, and speedily put an end to their existence; as, for instance, the destruction of Sennacherib's army.

Demoniacal possession is frequently mentioned in the New Testament. Some have supposed that there was no such thing as demoniacal possession, or, what is the same thing, that those said to be possessed were either madmen, epileptics, or persons subject to melancholy. That demoniacs were really possessed with devils, will appear from the following considerations:—

1. They expressed themselves in a way different from epileptic, melancholy, or insane persons. Matt. viii, 28; Luke viii, 27; Mark v, 7. They possessed the supernatural power of sundering all sorts of cords and chains. They requested Jesus not to torment them. They answered, with propriety, questions proposed to them. Demons departed from them, and entered into swine.

2. No symptoms of disease are mentioned in the case of the dumb demoniac in Matt. ix, 32, Luke xi, 14, and Matt. xii, 22.

3. The damsel of Philippi (Acts xvi, 16) practised *divination*, which evidently could not have been done by an insane person.

4. The demoniacs themselves say they were possessed with a devil. The Jews themselves assert the same thing. The apostles and evangelists allege that persons possessed with devils were brought to Christ, and that they departed at his command; and, finally, Jesus asserts himself that he cast out devils.

5. The sacred writers make an express distinction between the demoniacs and the sick, and likewise between the exorcism of demons and the healing of the sick. Mark i, 32; Luke vi, 17, 18; vii, 21; viii, 2; xiii, 32.

6. Demoniacs knew what madmen, deranged, epileptic, and melancholy persons could not of themselves know, viz., that *Jesus was the Son of God, the Messiah, the son of David*, &c. Mark i, 24; v, 7; Matt. viii, 29; Luke iv, 34.

7. Jesus speaks to demons and asks their name, and they answer him. He also threatens them—commands them to be silent—to depart and not return. Mark i, 25; v, 8; ix, 25; Matt. viii, 29–31; Luke iv, 35; viii, 30–32.

8. When the seventy returned from their labours, they reported that the devils were subject unto them, through the name of Christ; and Jesus replied, "I saw *Satan* as lightning fall from heaven."

9. When Jesus was accused of casting out devils by Beelzebub, he replied that a house divided against itself could not stand.

10. Jesus makes remarks in Matt. xii, 43 and in Luke xi, 24 which could not apply to persons diseased.

11. The woman in Luke xiii, 11 was bound by Satan. Peter says, Acts x, 38, that all who had been oppressed with the devil were healed.

12. The Church Fathers, without one dissenting voice, embraced the opinions expressed above, in regard to demoniacal possessions.

The *paralysis*, or *palsy*, of the New Testament, had a wide import. Many infirmities were thus denominated.

1. *Apoplexy*, a paralytic shock which affected the whole body.

2. The *hemiplegy*, which paralyzes one half of the body.

3. The *paraplegy*, which paralyzes all parts of the body but the neck.

4. The *catalepsy*, which is caused by a contraction of the muscles in the whole or part of the body, and is very dangerous.

5. The *cramp*, which originates from the chills of the night.

Death, Burials, and Mourning.

Reception into the *presence of God* at death, is asserted in only two passages of the Old Testament, viz., Haggai ii, 23 and Eccles. xii, 7. The opinion that life is a journey, and death its terminus, where the traveller mingles with the hosts that have gone before, originated the following phrases: *To be gathered to one's people; to go to one's fathers.* Gen. xv, 15; xxxvii, 35. *The visiting of the fathers* has reference to the immortal part, and is clearly distinguished from the burial of the body. Gen. xxxvii, 35.

Sometimes the Hebrews regarded death as a friendly messenger, but more frequently as a formidable enemy. He was figuratively represented as a hunter, armed with a *dart* or *javelin*, and having a *net* and a *snare*, and when he made captive the children of men he slew them. 2 Sam. xxvi, 6; Psa. xviii, 5, 6; cxvi, 3; 1 Cor. xv, 55, 56. Some represented death as the king of the lower world, and had him occupying a subterranean place called *Sheol* and *Hades*, in which he exercised sovereignty over all men, even kings and warriors, who had departed from this existence. This place occurs also under the phrases, *the gates of death, or Hades.* Job xxxviii, 17; Psa. ix, 13; xlix, 15; cvii, 18; Isa. xxxviii, 10–18; Matt. xvi, 18. Mention is made in Psa. xviii, 4–5 of the rivers of Hades.

When a man died, the friends or sons of the deceased closed his eyes. Gen. xlvi, 4. The corpse was washed with water, and, except when buried immediately, was laid out in an upper room or chamber. 2 Kings iv, 21; Acts ix, 37. *The Egyptians embalmed* the body. There were three methods of embalming, and these were determined by the condition and circumstances of the person deceased. The first method was adopted in embalming the bodies of Jacob and Joseph, which was very costly. Gen. l, 2–26. Herodotus says that the process consisted in removing the intestines, and washing the internal portion of the body with the wine of the palm-tree, and then anointing it with a composition of myrrh, cassia, salt of nitre, &c. The brain was also removed, and the cavity filled with aromatic substances. The whole body was then wrapped around with linen, and each member was also bound separately, in the same manner. The process of embalming occupied thirty days. Genesis l, 2–26. The other two modes took a much less time. After the embalming, the body was placed in a sarcophagus of sycamore-wood, resembling, in shape, the human form, and was in this way preserved in the house, sometimes for ages, leaning against the wall. Exod. xiii, 19; Josh. xxiv, 32.

The Hebrews were accustomed to wrap linen round the body, and place the head in a napkin. John xi, 44. They also placed, in the folds of the linen, aromatic substances. Matt. xxvi, 6–14; xxvii, 59; John xix, 39, 40; xx, 7; xi, 44; Mark xiv, 8; Acts ix, 37.

Funeral ceremonies were different in different countries. Not to inter the corpse, was considered a mark of great indignity. The patriarchs buried their dead in a few days after death. Gen. xxiii, 2–4; xxv, 9; xxxv, 29. Their posterity in Egypt deferred burial. In a subsequent age, the

Jews imitated the Persians, and buried the body soon after death. Acts v, 6–10. The interment of Tabitha was delayed on account of sending for Peter. A box or coffin was not used for the dead, except in Egypt and Babylon. The corpse was wrapped in folds of linen, and placed upon a bier, which was carried by four persons. In the time of Christ, the bearers travelled very rapidly. Luke vii, 14.

Sepulchres, otherwise called the *everlasting houses*, were situated beyond the limits of cities and villages. Isa. xiv, 18; Eccles. xii, 5; Luke vii, 12; Matt. viii, 28. Kings were allowed to repose within cities. 1 Sam. xxviii, 3; 2 Kings xxi, 18; 2 Chron. xvi, 14; xxiv, 16. The sepulchres of the Hebrew kings were on Mount Zion. With the exception of the burial of kings, the Hebrews chose gardens. Gen. xxiii, 17; xxxv, 8. Sepulchres were the property of a single person, or a number of families united together. Gen. xxiii, 4–20; l, 13. To be buried in the sepulchre of one's fathers was a distinguished honor, and to be excluded therefrom as signal a disgrace. Kings who had incurred the hatred of the people were not permitted to be buried in the royal tombs. To be buried like an ass, without mourning or lamentation, was considered a very great disgrace. Jer. xxii, 16–19; xxxv, 30.

Sepulchres of the common class of people were mere excavations in the earth. Persons of rank and wealth had vaults or *crypts*. Gen. xxiii, 6; Matt. xxiii, 27–29; xxvii, 52, 53. The entrance to these tombs was by a descent down a number of steps. The interior contained niches or cells for the bodies. The entrance was closed by a stone, door, or slab. Psa. v, 9; John xi, 38; xx, 5–11; Matt. xxviii, 2; Mark xvi, 3, 4. The doors of sepulchres were painted white on the last month (Adar) of every year. The object of the practice was to warn all who came to the Feast of the Passover not to approach, lest they should be contaminated. Matt. xxiii, 27; Luke xi, 14.

Mention is made of *sepulchral monuments*—*μνημεῖον*—

from the time of Abraham down to the time of Christ. Gen. xxiii, 6; xxxv, 20; 2 Kings xxiii, 16, 17; Matt. xxiii, 27. These consisted of stones, hewn and ornamented with an inscription. Sometimes heaps of stones were piled up, and these were constantly added to. The *pyramids* of Egypt are supposed to be monuments of kings.

The ancient Hebrews considered the *burning of the body* as a matter of great reproach, and rarely did so, unless they wished to inflict the greatest ignominy. Gen. xxxviii, 24. The body of Saul was burnt by the inhabitants of Jabesh Gilead, to preserve it from *further* disgrace. 1 Sam. xxxi, 12. The sentiment in regard to the burning of bodies was changed at a later period. One hundred and forty years after Saul, King Asa was burnt with many aromatic substances, as a mark of honour. After this, *not* to be burnt was more a mark of disgrace than honour. 2 Chron. xvi, 14; xxi, 19; Amos vi, 10; Jer. xxxiv, 5. After the captivity the Jews conceived a great hatred to this rite.

The *mourning* of the Orientals, on account of the dead, was extreme. As soon as a person dies, all the females of the family, with a loud voice, set up a sorrowful cry. They continue it as long as they can, without taking breath. This they continue for eight days. Until the corpse is carried away, the women who are related to the deceased sit on the ground, in a circle. The wife, or daughter, or other nearest relation of the deceased, occupies the centre, and each one holds in her hand a napkin. *Eulogists* are present, to chant, in mournful strains, the virtues of the dead. When the one who sat in the centre gave the sign with her napkin, the persons who recalled the memory of the departed remained silent; the rest of the females rose, and, wrapping together their napkins, ran like mad persons. The nearest relative remained in her position, tearing her hair, and wounding her breast, arms, and face, with her nails. Gen. l, 3; Numbers xx, 29; Deut. xxxiv, 8; 1 Sam. xxxi, 13. The lamentations began, *Alas! alas! my brother!* or, *Alas! alas! my sister!*

If the king were dead, it was, *Alas! alas! the king!* 1 Kings xiii, 29, 30; 2 Chron. xxxv, 25; 2 Sam. i, 12. It was customary for the women to go to the tomb, and pour out their lamentations there. John xi, 31. Another indication of grief consisted in rending the garment. Gen. xxxvii, 34; Judges xi, 35; 2 Sam. i, 2; iii, 31; 2 Kings v, 7, 8; vi, 30. The Hebrews, when in mourning, sometimes walked with their shoes off and their heads uncovered. They refused to bathe, anoint themselves, or converse with people; they scattered dust and ashes into the air, or placed them on their heads, or lay down in them. Job i, 20; ii, 12; Lev. x, 6; xiii, 45; xxi, 10; 2 Sam. i, 2–4; xiv, 2; xv, 30; Jer. vi, 26. They struck their hands together, threw them up towards the sky, smote their breast and thigh, and stamped with the foot. 2 Sam. xiii, 19; Jer. xxxi, 19; Ezek. vi, 11; xxi, 12; Esth. iv, 1–3. They fasted, abstained from wine, and avoided mingling in festivals. 2 Sam. i, 11, 12; iii, 35; xii, 16; Jer. xxv, 34. Elegies were composed on the death of distinguished individuals. 2 Sam. iii, 33. Refreshments were furnished, after the burial, for mourners, which was denominated the bread of bitterness and the cup of consolation. 2 Sam. iii, 35; Jer. xvi, 4–7; Hosea ix, 4; Ezek. xxiv, 16, 17. Public calamities, such as famines, pestilences, incursions of enemies, defeat in war, &c., were occasions of mourning. Ezek. xxvi, 1–18; xxvii, 1–36; xxx, 2, *et seq.;* xxxii, 2–32; Amos v, 1, *et seq.* Fast days were days of grief. Jonah iii, 5–7. It was customary for a person to rend his clothes when he heard blasphemy.

CHAPTER II.

POLITICAL ARCHÆOLOGY.

THE posterity of Jacob, while remaining in Egypt, maintained the patriarchal form of government. Every father of a family exercised a father's authority over those of his own household. Every tribe obeyed its own prince, who was originally the first-born of the *founder* of the tribe, but, in progress of time, appears to have been elected. As the people increased in numbers, various heads of families united, in order to form a compact, and selected some individual from their own body as a *leader*. Num. iii, 24, 30, 35. The number thus associated was sometimes more and sometimes less than a thousand. 1 Sam. x, 19; xxiii, 23; Judg. vi, 15; Num. xxvi, 5–50. Princes and heads of families are mentioned under the common names of *seniors*, or *senators*, and *heads of tribes*. The princes of the tribes at first kept the genealogical tables, but subsequently they employed scribes, who, in the end, took part in the government of the nation. Exod. v, 14, 15, 19. It was by magistrates of this description that the Hebrews were governed in Egypt, and the Egyptian kings made no objection to it. Exod. iii, 16; v, 1, 14, 15, 19.

The posterity of Abraham, Isaac, and Jacob were set apart for the great object of preserving the true religion. Gen. xii, 3; xvii, 9, 14; xviii, 18; xxii, 18; xxviii, 14. They were separated from idolatrous nations, and confined to a small extent of country. Those of them who had been tainted with Egyptian idolatry, were to be brought back again to the knowledge of the true God. The fundamental principle of the Mosaic institutions was to develop the great truth, *that the one living and true God, the Creator and Governor of the universe, should alone be worshipped.* To secure this, God, through the instrumentality of Moses, offered himself as a king to the Hebrews, and was accepted by the united voice of their community, and the land of Canaan was hence declared to be the land of Jehovah. In consideration of their acknowledgment of God as their Ruler, they were bound, like the Egyptians, to pay a twofold tithe. Exod. xix, 4–8; Lev. xxvii, 20–34; Num. xviii, 21, 22; Deut. xii, 17–19; xiv, 22–29; xxvi, 12–15. God was their lawgiver. Exod. xx. The people were taught that the tabernacle was not only the temple of Jehovah, but the palace of their king—that the table supplied with wine and shew-bread was the *royal* table—that the altar was the place where the provisions of the *monarch* were prepared—that the priests were the *royal* servants, and were bound to attend not only to sacred but secular affairs, and were to receive as their salary the *first tithes*, which the people, as subjects, were led to consider a part of that revenue which was due to God, their immediate sovereign. The commission of idolatry, by any inhabitant of Palestine, was regarded as a defection from the true king. It was, in fact, *treason*, and was considered a crime equal in aggravation to that of murder, and was, consequently, attended with the severest punishment. Incantation, necromancy, and similar practices, were looked upon as arts of a kindred aspect with idolatry itself, and were punished in the same way. The law, with the penalty attached to it, had reference only to the *overt* acts of idolatry. Deut. xiii, 2–19; xvii, 2–5. It was not so much a *religious* as a *civil* law.

The Mosaic ceremonies were instituted to preserve the Hebrews from being seduced by idolatrous nations around them, and to preserve their integrity to their God and king. Though debarred by their rites from any close intimacy with these nations, they were obliged to extend to them the rites of hospitality, and, under certain restrictions, were allowed to form friendly treaties. The following nations were excepted:

1. The *Canaanites*, including the *Philistines*, not of Canaanitish origin. They were neither to be admitted to treaty nor to servitude, but to be destroyed by war or driven from

12

the country. This was not only to be done because they unjustly retained the pasture-grounds of the patriarchs, but because they were idolaters, and hence traitors to God. Exodus xxiii, 32, 33; xxxiv, 12–16; Deut. vii, 1–11; xx, 1–18. The Phœnicians were not included in this hostility, as they dwelt on the northern shore of their country, and were shut up within their own limits.

2. The *Amalekites* or *Canaanites of Arabia Petræa* were in like manner to be destroyed with universal slaughter. This was to be done because they had attacked the weak and weary Hebrews in their journey through Arabia, and because the robberies which were committed by them on the southern borders of Palestine could not be restrained in any other way. Exodus xvii, 8–14; Deuteronomy xxv, 17; Judges vi, 3–5; 1 Sam. xv, 1; xxvii, 8, 9, and the 30th chapter.

3. The *Moabites and Ammonites* were to be excluded forever from the right of treaty or citizenship with the Hebrews, but were not to be attacked in war. Deut. ii, 9–19; xxiii, 7. The reason given that this middle course should be preserved was, that they had granted a passage through their country, though they refused to supply them with provisions. Deut. ii, 29; xxiii, 5. They afterwards invited Balaam to curse the Hebrews, and finally they allured them to idolatry. Deut. xxiii, 3–8. They ultimately crushed the Midianites, who had conspired with the Moabites in their plans, in a war of dreadful severity. Num. xxv, 16, 17; xxxi, 1–24. War was carried into the country of the *Ammonites* in consequence of the kings Og and Sihon refusing a free passage to the Hebrews, and they were subdued.

Moses, by the advice of Jethro, his father-in-law, increased the number of rulers by the appointment of an additional number of *judges*. Some were to judge over ten, some over fifty, some over a hundred, and some over a thousand. Exodus xviii, 13–26. These judges were elected by the people from among the rulers and princes. They occupied a subordinate rank to Moses and the high-priest, who constituted the ultimate appeal.

The various civil officers, such as *heads of families*, *judges*, *genealogists*, *elders* or *senators*, *princes of the tribes*, &c., were dispersed, as a matter of course, in different parts of the country. Those who dwelt in the same city or neighbourhood formed the *comitia*, *senate*, or *legislative assembly* of their immediate vicinity. Deut. xix, 12; xxv, 8, 9; Judg. viii, 14; ix, 3–46; xi, 5; 1 Sam. viii, 4; xvi, 4. When all of those who dwelt in any particular tribe were assembled, they constituted the *legislative assembly* of the tribe; and when they were convened in one body from *all* the tribes, they constituted the general assembly of the nation, and were the representatives of all the people. Judg. i, 1–11; xi, 5; xx, 12–24; Josh. xxiii, 1, 2; xxiv, 1. The *priests*, who were a learned class in the community, and, besides, were hereditary officers in the state—being set apart for civil as well as religious purposes—had, by the divine command, a right to sit in this assembly. Exod. xxxii, 29; Num. xxxvi, 13; viii, 5–26.

Each tribe was governed by its own rulers, and, to a certain extent, constituted a civil community, independent of the other tribes. Judg. i, 21, 27, 33; xx, 11–46; 2 Sam. ii, 4. Any affair concerning the whole or many of the tribes was determined in the legislative assembly of the nation. Judg. xi, 1–11; 1 Chron. v, 10, 18, 19; 2 Sam. iii, 17; 1 Kings xii, 1–24. All the tribes were bound together by reciprocal ties. Rivalries sometimes existed among the tribes, especially between Judah, to which belonged the right of *primogeniture*, and the rest; and also the tribe of Joseph, which had *a double portion*. Gen. xlix, 8–10; xlviii, 5, 6. From these rivalries a schism arose, in progress of time, which finally sundered the nation. 1 Kings xii.

The *Legislative Assembly*, or *Congress* of the nation, was convened by the judge or ruler for the time being, or, in his absence, the high-priest. Num. x, 2–4; Judg. xx, 1, 27, 28;

Josh. xxiii, 1, 2. The *place* of assembling was the door of the tabernacle; sometimes other places were selected. Josh. xxiv, 1; 1 Sam. xi, 14, 15; 1 Kings xii, 1. While the Hebrews were in the desert of Arabia, the assembly was convened by the blowing of trumpets. After they were settled in Palestine, the members were notified of the meeting by messengers.

To these assemblies Moses, from time to time, announced the commands of God, which were afterwards communicated to the people by the genealogists or scribes. In these assemblies the rights of sovereignty were exercised, wars were declared, peace was concluded, treaties were ratified, civil rulers and generals, and eventually kings, were chosen. The oath of office was administered to its members by the judge, or the king of the state; and the latter, in turn, received their oath from the assembly acting in the name of the people. Exod. xix, 7; xxiv, 2–8; Josh. ix, 15–21; Judg. xx, 1, 11, 14; xxi, 13–20; 1 Sam. x, 24; xi, 14; 2 Sam. xi, 14; ii, 4; iii, 17–19; v, 1–3; 1 Kings xii. The assembly acted without instructions from the people, on their own authority, and according to their own views, and the people did not exhibit any disposition to interfere with their deliberations; still the assembly referred their decisions to them for ratification. 1 Sam. xi, 14, 15; Josh. viii, 33; xxiii, 2, *et seq.;* xxiv, 1, *et seq.* When God was chosen as king, it was not done by the assembly, but by the people themselves, all of whom, as well as their rulers, took the oath of obedience, even to the women and children. Exod. xxiv, 3–8; Deut. xxix, 9–14.

God, as the chosen king of the Hebrews, enacted laws, decided litigated points of importance, answered and solved questions, threatened punishment, and actually inflicted it, in some instances, on the hardened and impenitent. Num. xvii, 1–11; xxvii, 1–11; xxxvi, 1–10; xv, 32; xi, 33–35; xii, 1–15; xvi, 1–50; Josh. vii, 16–22; Judg. i, 1, 2,; xx, 18, 27, 28; 1 Sam. xiv, 37; xxiii, 9–12; xxx, 8; Lev.

xxvi, 3–46; Deut. xxvi and xxx. The form of government, which is denominated theocratical, was of a nature well suited to the character of that age. Although the form was a theocracy, it was nevertheless not destitute of the usual forms of civil government. The political affairs were conducted by the elders and princes. It was to them Moses gave the divine commands, determined expressly their powers, and submitted their requests to the decision of God. Num. xiv, 5; xvi, 4, *et seq.;* xxvii, 5; xxxvi, 5, 6. The influence possessed by the people was such, that the Hebrew government may properly be denominated a *democracy.* Exod. xix, 7–8; xxiv, 3–8; Deut. xxix, 9–14; Josh. ix, 18, 19; xxiii, 1; xxiv, 2; 1 Sam. x, 24; xi, 14, 15; Num. xxvii, 1–8; xxxvi, 1–9. In some respects, however, it assumed the aristocratical form.

The part sustained by Moses in the government was that of a mediator, or internuncio between God and the people; he was also in a distinguished sense their leader. Joshua became the successor of Moses in leading the Israelites into Canaan. After this office ceased, by the death of Joshua, *judges* or governors were appointed. 1 Sam. viii, 20; Isa. xi, 4; 1 Kings iii, 9. In the time of Samuel the government, in point of form, was changed into a monarchy; the election of king, however, was committed to God, who chose one by lot, so that God was still the ruler, and the king the vicegerent. The terms of government, as respected God, were the same as before, and the same duties and principles were inculcated. 1 Sam. viii, 7; x, 17–23; xii, 14, 15, 20, 22, 24, 25. When Saul did not obey the commands of God, the kingdom was taken from him and given to another. 1 Sam. xiii, 5–14; xv, 1–31. Under this form of government the true religion was preserved, and propagated to other nations, as was promised.

Kings, Officers of State, &c.

When we hear of the anointing of Jewish kings, we are to understand by it the same as their *inauguration*. 2 Sam. ii, 4; v, 3. As far as we are informed, however, *unction*, as a sign of investiture with the royal authority, was bestowed only upon the first two kings who ruled the Hebrews, viz., Saul and David, and subsequently upon Solomon and Joash, whose right to the succession was in danger of being disputed. 1 Sam. x, 24; 2 Sam. ii, 4; v, 1–3; 1 Chron. xi, 1, 2; 2 Kings xi, 12–20; 2 Chron. xxiii, 1–21. The ceremonies of inauguration were as follows:—

1. The king, surrounded with soldiers, was conducted into some public place—latterly the temple—and was there anointed with sacred oil by the high-priest. The kings of Israel were not anointed because they could not obtain the sacred oil, and no other would answer the purpose.

2. It appears from 2 Sam. i, 10, Ezek. xxi, 26, and Psa. xlv, 6, that a sceptre was placed in the hand of the monarch at his inauguration, and a diadem was placed on his head.

3. The covenant which defined and fixed the principles according to which the government was to be conducted, and likewise the laws of Moses, were presented to him, and he accordingly took an oath that he would rule according to the principles of that covenant and the Mosaic Law. 1 Sam. x, 25; 2 Sam. v, 3; 1 Chron. xi, 3; 2 Kings xi, 2; 2 Chron. xxiii, 11; Deut. xvii, 18. The principal men of the kingdom, princes, elders, &c., promised obedience, and, in proof of their pledge, they kissed either the feet or knees of the person inaugurated. Psa. ii, 13.

4. After the ceremonies were completed, the king was conducted into the city with great pomp, amid the acclamations of the people and the cries of *Long live the King!* Sacrifices, and subsequently feasts, were observed, as a confirmation of the oath which had been taken. 1 Kings i, 1, 11,

19, 24, 34, 39, 40; 2 Kings xi, 12–19; 2 Chron. xxiii, 11; Matt. xxi, 1–11; John xii, 3.

5. Finally, the king is seated upon the throne, and receives the congratulations usually presented. 1 Kings i, 35–48; 2 Kings ix, 13; xi, 19.

The *robe* which was worn by kings was costly and gorgeous, and the retinue was large and splendid. Ezek. xxviii, 13–20; 1 Kings iv. The materials of which the robe was made was fine white linen or cotton, though the usual colour was purple, *πορφύρα καὶ βύσσος*. The *diadem* was costly and splendid, and among the Persians was decorated with gems and pearls. It was composed of a band two inches broad, bound around the head and tied behind. *Crowns* were likewise in use. 2 Sam. xii, 30; Zech. vi, 11–14; Psa. xxi, 3. In form they somewhat resemble the mitre.

The *throne* was a seat with a back and arms, and of so great a height as to render a footstool necessary. Gen. xli, 40; Psa. cx, 1. The throne of Solomon, which consisted wholly of gold, ornamented with ivory, was a little curved in the back, and near each arm was placed the figure of a lion. 1 Kings x, 18–20; 2 Chron. ix, 17. This throne was elevated six steps, on which were twelve lions. It was customary for the high priest, previous to the time of the monarchy, to occupy an elevated seat. 1 Sam. i, 9; iv, 18. Both the *throne* itself, and *sitting upon the throne*, are used tropically to denote power and government. 2 Sam. iii, 10; Psa. ix, 7; lxxxix, 44; Isa. xlvii, 1. In some passages a throne is assigned to God, not only as the king of the Hebrews, but as the sovereign of the universe. Job xxiii, 3; Exod. xvii, 16; Isa. vi, 1; 1 Kings xxii, 19; Isa. lxvi, 1; Matt. v, 34.

The *sceptre* of King Saul was a *spear*. 1 Sam. xviii, 10; xxii, 6. A sceptre is used tropically for royal dignity and authority; and a just or righteous sceptre for a just government. Gen. xlix, 10; Num. xxiv, 7; Amos i, 5–8; Jer. xlviii, 17; Psa. xlv, 6.

The *tables* of Hebrew kings indicated exorbitant luxury and immense quantities of provisions were consumed. 1 Kings iv, 22, 23. They were set with numerous articles of gold; musicians and dancing ladies were present to enliven the feast. Gen. xl, 20; Dan. v, 1; Matt. xxii, 1; Mark vi, 21. The Hebrews were in the habit, at the season of their great national festivals, of preparing a feast, either at the tabernacle or in Jerusalem, of the thank-offerings, and thus participated in a season of joy, in which God might be considered as the author. The blood of the sacrifices thus appropriated was shed at the foot of the altar.

The kings of the East are very rarely seen in public. Among the Persians a person could not gain a sight of the monarch only by special invitation. Esther iv, 11. There was a free access, however, to the monarchs of the Jews. 2 Sam. xviii, 4; xix, 7; 2 Kings xxii, 10; Jer. xxxviii, 7. It was considered a good omen to see the face of the king. The tropical expression, therefore, "*to see God*," signifies to experience his favour. When the kings of Asia make long journeys, they send before them *forerunners*, or heralds, to prepare their way. These are called, in Persia, joyful messengers. Mal. iii, 1; Isa. lxii, 10–12. The Talmudists contend that God has a forerunner, whom they call *metatron*. His existence and character they derive from the following passages. Zech. iii, 1, 3, 4, 5; Gen. xvi, 10–14; xxii, 15; Exod. iii, 4–20; xx, 2, 3; xxiii, 20–23; Isa. xlviii, 16; xliii, 14. They regard him as uncreated, and in his character approaches nearest to God himself. That he is the same being who anciently appeared to the patriarchs, and is expressly called God. *Vide Buxtorf's Chal. Talmudic and Rab. Lex., col.* 1192. Also *Appendix to Jahn's Hermeneutics, Fasc.* 1, pp. 58–63.

The eastern monarchs sought for glory by building magnificent temples and palaces, and by planting gardens and erecting fortifications. The palace of the kings occurs in the most ancient times, as well as at the present day, under the name of *the gate.* 2 Sam. xv, 2; Dan. ii, 49; Esther ii, 19–21; iii, 2, 3; Matt. xvi, 18. Kings were objects of the greatest veneration. 1 Sam. xxiv, 4–15; xxvi, 6–20. Want of respect and veneration was punished with death. Magistrates were sometimes called *gods*, both in *poetry*, Psa. lxxxii, 1, 6, 7; cxxxviii, 1; and also in *prose.* Exod. iv, 16; vii, 1. This term is never applied to kings, except, perhaps, in Psa. xlv, 7, 8. Kings were called the Lord's anointed. Isa. xlv, 1. In poetry, the king is sometimes called *the son of God*, 2 Sam. vii, 14; 1 Chron. xvii, 13; hence the inauguration of a king is called his *birth.* Psa. ii, 6, 8, 12.

Appellatives for monarchs:—1. *Cesar*, a general name for king or emperor among the Romans; 2. *Ptolemy*, used in the same way among the more recent Egyptians; 3. *Agag*, a common name for the kings of the Amalekites; 4. *Hadad*, *Adad*, or *Ben Hadad*, the name of the kings of Syria; 5. *Abimelech*, the same among the Philistines; 6. *Candace*, the usual appellation of Ethiopian queens. The proper names *Pharaoh* and *Darius*, monarchs of Egypt and Persia, signify king or monarch.

In poetry, kings are sometimes denominated *shepherds*, and sometimes the *husbands* of the state. The state is sometimes called the *wife* of the king, sometimes a *virgin*, and sometimes the *mother* of the citizens. It is likewise represented as a *widow*, and in some instances as *childless.* God is represented as the *husband* of the Hebrew state, and the state as his *spouse;* and hence, whenever she became idolatrous, she was denominated an adulteress or a fornicatress.

The Hebrews were accustomed to expect of their kings the fulfilment of two offices—those of judge and chieftain. 1 Sam. viii, 5; xii, 12; 2 Chron. xxvi, 21; Isa. xvi, 5. Kings tried appeals from judges. 2 Sam. xv, 2; 1 Sam. xvii, 9–19. The powers and prerogatives of kings were regulated by the institutes of Moses. Laws, prophecies, and instructions were usually promulgated in the temple. Jer. vii, 2, 3;

xi, 6; xvii, 19, 20; xxxvi, 9–19; John x, 3; Luke ii, 46; Matt. xxvi, 55; Mark xii, 35; Acts iii, 11; v, 12. Kings could not arbitrarily tax their subjects or require any service, unless legally prescribed. 1 Sam. x, 25; 2 Sam. v, 3.

The sources of royal revenue were derived as follows:—

1. Voluntary presents. 1 Sam. x, 27; xvi, 20.

2. The products of the royal flocks. 1 Sam. xxi, 7, 8; 2 Sam. xiii, 23; 2 Chron. xxvi, 10; xxxii, 28, 29; Gen. xlvii, 6.

3. The royal mansion, vineyards, and olive gardens, which had been taken from a state of nature, or were the confiscated possessions of criminals, and which were cultivated either by slaves or conquered nations. 1 Kings xxi, 9–16; Ezek. xlvi, 16–18; 1 Chron. xxvii, 28; 2 Chron. xxvi, 10.

4. A tenth part of the income of the Hebrews; imposts and tributes, and the customary taxes. 1 Sam. xvii, 25; 1 Kings iv, 4, 6, 9, 12, 13; 1 Chron. xxvii, 25.

5. The spoils of conquered nations. These nations were also required to pay tribute of money, flocks, and grain. 1 Kings iv, 21; Psa. lxxii, 10; 2 Chron. xxvii, 5.

6. Tribute imposed upon merchants passing through the territories of the Hebrews. 1 Kings x, 15. There was also a tax on articles of consumption, called the *excise* and the *toll.* Ezek. iv, 14, 19, 20.

Judges maintained their authority after the introduction of the monarchy, and acted the part of a legislative assembly to respective cities in or near which they resided. These, together with the genealogists, were appointed by the king, as were also other royal officers, the principal of whom were the following:—

1. The royal *counsellors.* 2. The *prophets.* 3. The *secretary* or *scribe.* 4. The *high-priest.* The officers of the king's palace consisted of, 1. The *governor* of the palace; 2. The *keeper of the wardrobe;* 3. The *king's friend*, or *intimate;* 4. The *king's life-guard.* These officers, with their attendants, were immediately attached to the palace.

Though Moses had interdicted the multiplication of wives and concubines, yet the Hebrew kings, especially Solomon, devoted much time and attention to the harem. No expense was spared in decorating the persons of the women. These harems were kept by eunuchs, brought from foreign countries, as the laws of Moses forbade castration. Lev. xxii, 24; Deut. xxiii, 1. That they were employed at the Hebrew court, see 1 Kings xxii, 9; 2 Kings viii, 6; ix, 32, 33; xx, 18; xxiii, 11; Jer. xiii, 23; xxxviii, 7; xxxix, 16; xli, 16.

After the subjugation of the Jews by the Romans, certain provinces of Judea were governed by that class of Roman magistrates denominated *Tetrarchs*. The tetrarch was, of course, subordinate to the king. Matt. xiv, 1; Luke ix, 7; Acts xiii, 1. They were inferior in point of rank to *ethnarchs*, who were sometimes addressed as king. Matt. ii, 22. *Procurators* were sometimes Roman knights, and sometimes the freedmen of the emperor. *Felix* was one of the latter class. Acts xxiii, 24, 26; xxiv, 3, 22, 27. *Festus* also belonged to this class. The business of a procurator was to exact tribute, administer justice, and repress seditions. They possessed the power of life and death. The military force granted to the procurators of Judea consisted of six cohorts, five of which were stationed at Cesarea, and one at Jerusalem, in the castle of Antonia.

Revenues were collected by *publicans* or Roman knights, who took their stations at the gates of cities and public ways, and at the place called for that purpose the *receipt of custom*, where they examined the goods that passed in, and received the duty that was to be paid. Matt. ix, 9; Mark ii, 14; Luke v, 27–29. In consequence of their extortion, they were regarded as great sinners. Luke iii, 13; Mark ii, 15, 16. The Pharisees would have no communication with them; and one ground of their reproaches against the Saviour was, that he associated with them. Matt. v, 46, 47; ix, 10, 11; xi, 19; xviii, 17; xxi, 31, 32.

The *half-shekel tax* was required to be paid annually by every Jew in the temple. This tax must be paid in Jewish coin. Matt. xxii, 17–19. It was this that led money-changers to take their places in the temple, for the purpose of exchanging Roman and Greek coins for Jewish half-shekels. The acquisition of property in this way was contrary to the law, (Deut. xxiii, 20, 21,) and hence Jesus drove them from the temple. Jews were appointed in Judea to collect the taxes, and also among foreign nations from their brethren, which they sent up yearly to Jerusalem.

Trials and Punishments.

The judicial establishment was reorganized after the captivity, and two classes of judges, inferior and superior, were appointed. Ezra vii, 25. The more difficult cases, however, and the appeals, were brought before the ruler of the state or the high priest.

The *Sanhedrim* was instituted in the time of the Maccabees, and was composed of seventy-two members. The high priest generally sustained the office of *president* in this tribunal. He was assisted by two *vice-presidents*, one of whom sat on the right and the other on the left. It was composed of the following members:—viz., *chief priests*, *elders*, and *scribes*, or learned men. These latter were elected, as also the elders, from the classes to which they belonged. The Sanhedrim had also secretaries. The assembly met in a rotunda, half of which was within, and the other half without the temple. The members were seated in a semi-circular form, and the president, vice-president, and secretaries occupied the centre. Appeals and other weighty matters were brought before this tribunal. Its power was limited by the Romans in the time of Christ; but still it was in the habit of sending its legates to the synagogues in foreign countries, (Acts ix, 2,) and retained the right of passing sentence of condemnation, though the power of *executing* the sentence was taken from it and lodged with the Roman procurator. John xviii, 31. This

Sanhedrim is not to be confounded with the seventy-two counsellors appointed to assist Moses in the wilderness.

There was also in every city a tribunal of seven judges, denominated in the New Testament κρίσις, or *the judgment.* Matt. v, 22. There were courts, also, of twenty-three judges, which merely tried questions of a religious nature, and sentenced to no other punishment than "*forty stripes save one.*" 2 Cor. xi, 24.

The time at which courts were held, and cases heard, was in the *morning.* Jer. xxi, 12; Psa. ci, 8. It was not lawful to try causes of a capital nature in the night, or to execute the sentence on the same day on which the trial was had. This law was, however, set at defiance in the crucifixion of Christ. Matt. xxvi, 57; John xviii, 13–18.

The *place* for judicial trials, in ancient times, was the gate of the city. Gen. xxiii, 10, *et seq.;* Deut. xxi, 19; xxv, 6, 7; Ruth iv, 1, *et seq.;* Psa. cxxvii, 5. The Greek *forum*, ἀγορά, was also a place for trial. The *"Areopagus*, ἄρειος πάγος, i. e., the *hill of Mars*, was so called because justice was said to have been pronounced there against Mars. Acts xvii, 19.

Originally trials were everywhere very summary, except in Egypt, where the accuser committed the charge to writing, and the accused replied in writing, which was again repeated before decision. Job xiv, 17. Moses pursued the summary course, and made God a witness to the judicial transaction. He interdicted, in the most express terms, gifts or *bribes* intended to corrupt the judges. Exod. xxii, 20, 21; xxiii, 1–9; Lev. xix, 15; Deut. xxiv, 14, 15. A trial was conducted in the following manner:—1st. The accuser and accused were brought face to face. Deut. xxv, 1. A secretary was present, who wrote down the proceedings. Isa. x, 1, 2; Jeremiah xxxii, 1–14. 2d. The accuser was denominated *Satan*, or *the adversary.* Zech. iii, 1–3; Psa. cix, 6. The judge, or judges, were seated, and the accuser and accused stood before him, the one on the right and the other on the left. 3d. The witnesses were sworn, and in capital cases the parties concerned. 1 Sam. xiv, 37–40; Matt. xxvi, 63. To establish the charges alleged, two witnesses were necessary besides the accuser. The witnesses were examined separately, and the person accused had a right to be present when their testimony was given in. Num. xxxv, 30; Deut xvii, 1–15; Matt. xxvi, 59. 4th. Parties made use of the *lot* in determining points of difficulty between them. The sacred lot of Urim and Thummim was anciently resorted to to detect the guilty. Josh. vii, 14–24; 1 Sam. xiv. 5th. Very soon after the completion of the trial the sentence was pronounced. Josh. vii, 22, *et seq.;* 1 Sam. xxii, 19; 1 Kings ii, 23.

As the execution so soon followed, there was no need of prisons. They are not to be found in Persia at the present day. It was customary to confine prisoners in the house of the judge. Gen. xl, 3, 4. The instrument of punishment mentioned in Job xiii, 27; xxxiii, 11, the *stocks*, was probably of Egyptian origin. There were a great variety of prisons, employed both for the detention and punishment of criminals. Jer. xxxvii, 15–20. The Jews imprisoned for *debt.* They sometimes inflicted *tortures* and *stripes.* Matt. xviii, 34; Acts xvi, 23. The Romans sometimes fastened their criminals by *one* or *both* hands to a soldier; such remained in their own houses. Acts xxviii, 16. Keepers, or jailors, who allowed prisoners to escape, were subjected to the same punishment which had been intended for the prisoners. Acts xii, 19; xvi, 27.

Those who had property due them might secure it by mortgage or pledge, or by a bondsman. The creditor who took a pledge was not allowed to make his own selection. Deut. xxiv, 10, 11; Job xxii, 6; xxiv, 3, 7, 9. When a mill, or a mill-stone, or an upper garment, was given as a pledge, it was not to be kept over night. A debt which remained till the Sabbatic year was not to be exacted during that period, and at that time lands which had been taken for debt were restored to the original owner or his heirs. Prov. xxxi, 16.

For debt, the man and his wife and children were liable to be sold into slavery. Prov. xxii, 27; Micah ii, 9.

The laws of Moses prohibited the taking of usury from a poor person, either for *borrowed money* or articles of consumption. A difficulty arose in determining who was a *poor person*, and hence the law was altered, (Deut. xxiii, 20, 21,) and was made to apply to all but foreigners. Deut. xv, 7–11; xxiv, 13; Psa. xv, 15; xxxvii, 21, 26; cxii, 5.

Transgression of the ceremonial law, without *malice prepense*, could be atoned for by voluntarily offering a sacrifice. Num. xv, 27–31. A *sin-offering* means the *sin* itself, and the same of a *trespass-offering*. Both are expressly defined in Leviticus, fourth and fifth chapters. *Sins* are violations of prohibitory statutes; *trespasses* are violations of *imperative* statutes. The guilty person incurred the expense of the victim. *Restitution* was required. Lev. vi, 1–5; Num. v, 5–10.

The amount of *fine* or *indemnification* was to be determined by the injured person. Exod. xxi, 30.

The amount to be paid to secure a *commutation* of punishment, was to be determined by the avenger of blood. Exod. xxi, 28–31.

If two men, contending with each other, injured a woman with child, so as to produce premature birth, the fine was to be determined by the husband and the judge.

If a servant was slain by an unruly bull, known to be such by the owner, he was obliged to pay thirty shekels. Exod. xxi, 32; Deut. xxii, 19. These fines were all paid to the person injured, and not to the State.

The restitution required in case of *theft* was double the amount taken. Exod. xxii, 3, 6, 8. In case of a sheep it was *fourfold*, and of an ox *fivefold*. Exod. xxii, 1. If the thief were unable to make restitution, he and his wife and children were sold into slavery. Exod. xxii, 2; 2 Kings iv, 1; Gen. xliii, 19; xliv, 17.

Capital punishment was decreed only against a thief who had stolen anything that was *accursed*. Josh. vii, 25. Whoever slew a thief who was attempting to break open a house at night, went unpunished. Exod. xxii, 1.

Corporal punishment was inflicted with the *rod*, or *scourging*. Lev. xix, 20; Deut. xxii, 18; xxv, 2, 3. The dignity or high standing of a person liable to this punishment could not avert it. Prov. x, 13; xvii, 26; Jeremiah xxxvii, 15–20; Psa. lxxxix, 32. *Scorpions*, or thongs set with sharp iron spikes, called by the Romans *horribilia*, were applied as a torture only by those who had no relentings of heart, especially by cruel masters in the punishment of slaves. 1 Kings xii, 11. *Scourging* was a punishment inflicted by the lash upon the bare back. This kind of punishment could not be inflicted on a Roman citizen. Acts xvi, 22, 25, 30, 37. The eyes of rebellious kings were sometimes put out. Jer. lii, 11; 2 Kings xxv, 7.

If a man in a fight wounded another, so as to disable him, he was bound to make indemnification. Exod. xxi, 18, 19. If injury was intentionally done to any member of the body, or life was taken away, life was rendered for life, eye for eye, tooth for tooth, burning for burning, wound for wound, hand for hand, foot for foot. Exod. xxi, 23–25; Lev. xxiv, 19–22. A false witness, according to the law of retaliation, was to receive the same punishment which was decreed against the crime concerning which he had falsely testified. Deut. xix, 16–21.

At a very early period criminals who had committed *homicide* were punished with *death*. Gen. ix, 6. The mode of execution, however, is not stated.

Decapitation was early practised among the Egyptians, Gen. xl, 17–19. From the following passages, it would appear that this mode of punishment existed among the Hebrews. 2 Sam. iv, 8; xx, 21, 22; 2 Kings x, 6–8; Matt. xiv, 8–12; Acts xii, 2. Beheading was not, however, sanctioned by the laws of Moses. The mode corresponding to it was slaying by the *sword*. Judges viii, 21; 1 Sam. xxii, 18; 2 Sam. i, 15; 1 Kings ii, 25, 29, 31, 34.

Lapidation or *stoning* was a mode of punishment authorized by the laws of Moses. The witnesses were ordered to throw the first stone, and afterwards the people. Deut. xiii, 10; xvii, 7; Josh. vii, 25; John viii, 7. The punishment of *stoning* is to be understood whenever the mode of putting to death is not mentioned. Lev. xx, 10; Ezek. xvi, 38–40; John viii, 5; Exod. xxxi, 14; xxxv, 2; Num. xv, 35, 36.

To cut off from the people, means some event in divine providence which shall eventually terminate the life of that person's family. 1 Kings xiv, 10; xxi, 21; 2 Kings ix, 8. This *excision*, or excommunication, as Jewish interpreters have explained it, consists of three kinds:—

1. Separation from the synagogue, and suspension of all intercourse with the Jews, and even with one's wife and domestics. This separation lasted thirty days.

2. A *curse* was pronounced with imprecations in the presence of ten persons; such were excluded from all communion whatever with their countrymen.

3. A solemn and absolute exclusion from all intercourse with any other individual of the nation, and the criminal was handed over to the justice of God. 1 Cor. v, 5; 1 Tim. i, 20.

Punishments which consist of *posthumous insults* were as follows:—1. The body of the criminal who had been stoned was burnt. Gen. xxxviii, 24; Lev. xx, 14; xxi, 9; Joshua vii, 15–25. 2. The suspension of the dead body on a tree. Gen. xl, 17–19; Num. xxv, 4, 5; Deut. xxi, 22, 23. The body was taken down and buried on the same day. 3. Heaps of stones were raised, either on the dead body, or the place where it was buried. Josh. vii, 25, 26; 2 Sam. xviii, 17.

Other punishments were introduced among the Hebrews at a later period from other nations. 1. *Decapitation*. 2. *Strangulation*. 1 Kings xx, 31. 3. *Burning alive in a furnace*. Dan. iii; Jer. xxix, 22. 4. *The lions' den*. Dan. vi. 5. *Dichotomy*, or *cutting asunder*. Dan. ii, 5; Luke xii, 46; Matt. xxiv, 51; 2 Sam. iv, 12. 6. *Beating to death*. This was a punishment among the Greeks, and designed for slaves. Heb. xi, 35. 7. *Sawing asunder*. This punishment was practised in Persia. *Isaiah* was put to death in this manner. David inflicted this punishment on the inhabitants of Rabbath Ammon. 1 Chron. xx, 3. 8. The Romans compelled their criminals, and those taken captive in war, to fight with wild beasts in the amphitheatre. They were also compelled to contend with one another, in the manner of gladiators. 2 Tim. iv, 17; 1 Cor. xv, 32. 9. The Greeks and Romans threw their criminals into the sea or river. They were placed in a sack, and a stone tied around their necks. Matt. xviii, 6; Mark ix, 42. 10. *Crucifixion* was a common mode of punishment among the Persians, Carthaginians, and Romans. Servants, assassins, robbers, and rebels, were sentenced to the *cross*. Luke xxiii, 1, 5, 13, 15. The person sentenced was deprived of all his clothes, except something about his loins. In this state they were scourged. Matt. xxvii, 29; Mark xv, 17; John xix, 2–5. The criminal was obliged to carry his own cross. The crime for which the person suffered was inscribed on the transverse piece, near the top of the perpendicular one. The victim, perfectly naked, was bound to the cross, and spikes were driven through the hands and feet. In this position he remained until life was extinct. The corpse was not buried except by express permission, which was sometimes granted by the emperor on his birth-day; but only to a very few. An exception was made in favour of the Jews on account of Deut. xxi, 22, 23, and hence, in Judea, crucified persons were buried on the same day. To hasten their death for burial, sometimes a fire was kindled beneath the cross, to suffocate the victim; or their bones were broken, or a spear thrust into the heart. An intoxicating potion was given, to render the sufferer insensible to the pains. This Jesus refused. Matt. xxvii, 34; Mark xv, 23.

The execution of those guilty of *homicide* devolved upon the brother, or next nearest relative of the deceased. If he did not slay the guilty person he was considered infamous. To prevent abuses growing out of this custom, Moses appointed *cities of refuge.* Any one who had slain a person without *malice prepense*, fled to one of these cities of refuge, where he was to remain until the death of the high priest. If, upon examination, after gaining the city of refuge, a person should be found guilty of murder, he was delivered up to the avenger of blood—the altar itself could not afford a refuge for such. Exod. xxi, 12; Num. xxxv, 9–35; Deut. xix, 1–13; 1 Kings ii, 28–34.

If one is found slain, and it is not known who killed him, the laws of Moses ordained that the elders of the nearest city should take a heifer that had never been yoked, and, in an uncultivated valley, it shall have its head struck off, and the elders shall wash their hands over it, as a declaration of the innocence of the judges and elders, and also of the horrid nature of murder.

Military Affairs.

Various implements of war are mentioned in the Pentateuch. Subsequent to Solomon military arms were improved in their construction, the science of fortification made advancement, and large armies were mustered. In the second year after the exodus from Egypt, there was a general enrolment of all who were able to bear arms. A second enrolment was made forty years after the exodus. Num. xxvi, 2; Judg. xx; 1 Sam. xi, 7; Exod. xvii; Num. xxxi; Josh. vii, 7, 11, 12.

Whenever there was an immediate prospect of war, a levy was made by the *genealogists.* Deut. xx, 5–9; 2 Chron. xxvi, 11; 2 Sam. viii, 17; xx, 25.

The following persons were excused from military service. Deut. xx, 5–8. 1. Those who had built a house, and had not yet inhabited it. 2. Those who had planted an *olive* or *vine-garden*, and had not tasted the fruit thereof. 3. Those who had bargained for a wife, but had not celebrated the nuptials; and also those who had not lived with their wife a year. 4. Those who were faint-hearted.

The army was divided into three bands, viz., the *centre*, *right* and *left* wings. Gen. xiv, 14, 15; Job i, 17; Judg. vii, 16–20; 1 Sam. xi, 11; Exod. xiv, 7; xv, 4. When the Hebrews left Egypt, they marched in military order, in ranks of fifty deep. Over each rank or file was a captain. Other divisions consisted of a hundred, a thousand, and ten thousand, each of which was headed by a commander. Num. xxxi, 48; Deut. i, 15; Judges xx, 10; 1 Sam. viii, 12; xviii, 13; xxix, 2. The leader of the whole army was denominated *the captain of the host.* There was also a *muster-roll* officer and an *engineer.* The army of David consisted of two hundred and eighty thousand men. Every twenty-four thousand had a commander. These divisions served alternately, a month at a time. 1 Chron. xvii, 14–17. The *genealogists* had the right of appointing officers of the army. This practice ceased under the kings, and, when they were not chosen by them, the office became hereditary in the heads of families. Kings and generals had *armour-bearers*, chosen from the bravest of the soldiery, who bore the arms of their masters and carried their messages. The *infantry*, the *cavalry*, and *chariots of war*, were so arranged as to make separate divisions of the army. Exod. xiv, 6, 7. The infantry were divided into *light-armed* troops and *spearmen.* Gen. xlix, 19; 1 Sam. xxx, 8, 15, 23; 2 Sam. iii, 22; iv, 2; xxii, 30; Psa. xviii, 30; 2 Kings v, 2. The light-armed infantry were furnished with a sling and javelin, with a bow, arrows, and quiver, and also a buckler. They fought the enemy at a distance. The spearmen were armed with spears, swords, and shields, and fought hand to hand. 1 Chron. xii, 24–34; 2 Chron. xiv, 8; xvii, 17.

The Roman soldiers were divided into *legions*, and each legion into ten *cohorts*, and each cohort into three *bands*, and each band into two *centurions;* so that a legion consisted of thirty bands of six thousand men, and a cohort of six hundred. Matt. xxvii, 27, 28; Mark xv, 16; Acts x, 1; xxi, 31; xxvii, 1.

It is necessary to distinguish the Roman soldiers mentioned in the New Testament, not only from the soldiers of Herod, but from the band of Levites who guarded the temple, and had a priest of high standing for their captain. Luke xxii, 4, 52; Acts iv, 1; v, 24.

The *shield* is first mentioned in Gen. xv, 1. The word frequently occurs tropically as denoting *defence* or *protection.* 2 Sam. xxii, 31–36; Prov. xxx, 5; Psa. xlvii, 9; cxiv, 2. Some shields were so large as to cover the whole body. They were of different forms, and constructed of different materials; sometimes of light wood or osiers woven together and covered with bull's hide. The hide was oiled, to render it smooth and slippery, and prevent its being injured by wet. Shields made wholly of brass were very uncommon. They were sometimes covered with plates of brass, and also of silver and gold. 1 Kings x, 16, 17; xiv, 25–28; 2 Chron. xiii, 13–16. When an attack was made, the shield was held in the left hand; and an army was able, by joining their shields, to oppose a wall, as it were, against the assaults of their foes. The phrases *to seize the shield*, &c., are used tropically to denote preparation for war. 2 Chron. xxv, 5; Job xli, 7; Ezek. xxxviii, 45; Jer. xlvi, 9; li, 11.

The *helmet* was a piece of armour which covered the head, and was surmounted, for ornament, with a plume and a horse-tail. Anciently, the spearmen alone wore the helmet. Uzziah furnished an armory with helmets for the use of his soldiers. 2 Chron. xxvi, 14. The helmet was made from an ox-hide, but usually covered with brass. It denoted tropically defence and protection. Eph. vi, 16.

The *breast-plate* or *coat-of-mail* consisted of two parts, one of which covered the fore-part of the body, and the other the back—both pieces being united at the sides with clasps or buttons. The breast-plate worn by Goliath was made of brass. 1 Sam. xvii, 5, 38. It was very common among the Hebrews after the days of David. It is also used tropically for defence. Isa. lix, 17; Eph. vi, 14; 1 Thess. v, 8; Rev. ix, 17.

The *girdle*, from which the sword was suspended, is frequently mentioned among the articles of military dress. Isa. v, 27; Eph. vi, 14.

Military fortifications were at first nothing more than a trench or ditch dug around a few cottages, on a hill or mountain, together with the mound which was formed by the sand dug out of it. A city of this kind was built and fortified by Cain; for to *build* a city and *fortify* it are the same thing. The art of fortification was encouraged and patronized by the Hebrew kings, and Jerusalem was always well defended—especially Mount Zion. The principal parts of a fortification were as follows:—1. The *wall*. This was erected round cities, and was sometimes double and triple. 2 Chron. xxxii, 5; Jer. li, 58. The main wall terminated at the top in a parapet. 2. *Towers*, which were erected at certain distances from each other, on the top of walls. Towers were also erected over the gates of cities. These were occupied by watchmen, who, on the approach of an enemy, blew the trumpet. 2 Sam. xiii, 34; xviii, 26, 27; 2 Kings ix, 17–19; Nahum ii, 1; 2 Chron. xvii, 2. Large towers were also erected in different sections of the country, on elevated places. They were guarded by a military force. Judg. viii, 9–17; ix, 46, 49, 51; Isa. xxi, 6; Hab. ii, 1; Hosea v, 8; Jer. xxxi, 6. Prophets are frequently compared to guards stationed in towers. Ezek. iii, 17; xxvii, 11; xxxiii, 1–9; Hosea xii, 13. 3. *Bastions*, or protections to walls. 4. The *fosse*, or an excavation by which the elevation of the walls was increased. 2 Sam. xx, 15. This was filled with water. 5. The *gates*. These were constructed in the manner of valve-doors, and were secured by means of wooden bars. Sometimes they were covered with plates of brass or iron. The bars were secured by a sort of lock. Psa. cvii, 16; Isa. xlv, 2.

The *arms* used in fighting hand to hand were a *club* and a *battle-hammer*. The *sword* was used among the Hebrews. 2 Sam. xx, 8; 1 Sam. xvii, 39. The phrase *to gird one's self with a sword*, tropically denoted to commence war; and *to loose the sword*, to finish it. Some swords had two edges. Psa. cxlix, 6; Isa. xli, 15; Judg. iii, 16. From its being kept highly polished, it was compared to lightning. Gen. iii, 24; Psa. vii, 12. A sword is also attributed to God. Wicked persons are represented as the sword of God. Magistrates, also, in the execution of justice, are represented as the sword of the Lord. The *spear* was a wooden staff, surmounted with an iron point. It was about eleven cubits long. *Javelins* were of two kinds, one larger and the other smaller. They were missiles to be thrown by the hand. The *bow* and *arrows* are weapons of a very ancient origin. Gen. xlviii, 22; xlix, 24. Archers were very numerous in the tribes of Ephraim and Benjamin. The bows were made of wood, sometimes of brass. The strings were made of thongs of leather, horse-hair, and the sinews of oxen. Arrows were made of reeds, and surmounted with an iron point. They are sometimes used tropically for lightning. Psa. vii, 13; Deut. xxxii, 23. *Quivers* were pyramidal in form, and suspended from the back, so that the soldier could easily take therefrom his arrows. The *sling* was perhaps the most ancient weapon of warfare. Job xli, 28. The Benjamites were expert slingers. Judg. xx, 6; 1 Chron. xii, 2. *Engines of war* were erected by King Uzziah on the towers and angles of the walls. They were of two kinds—*catapults* and *ballistæ*. The former were immense bows, bent by means of a machine, which threw with great force large arrows, javelins, and beams of wood. The latter threw stones and balls of lead. *Battering-rams* are first mentioned by Ezek. iv, 1, 2; xxi, 22; xxvi, 9. They were long and large beams of wood, the ends of which were brass, shaped like the head of a ram. They were suspended, by means of a chain, in equilibrium, and thus, by means of soldiers, were driven against the wall. Those engaged in the battery were protected from the missiles of the enemy by a roof erected over them. *Elephants* were used in war, and sometimes carried a tower on their backs, armed with thirty soldiers. The elephants also fought with their proboscis. *Chariots* were also early used in war. Exod. xiv, 6, 23, 28. They could only be used, however, in the level country. Deut. xx, 1; Josh. xvii, 16–18; Judg. i, 19; ii, 7; iv, 3–7. They were used tropically for protection and defence of the highest kind. 2 Kings ii, 12; xiii, 14. They were supported on two wheels, and drawn by two horses, and sometimes by four abreast. The end of the tongue and axles were armed with iron scythes, which were very destructive.

Hunting and *gymnastic sports* were used as preparatory exercises, to teach the youth skill in the use of arms, and thus fit them for war. The *gymnasia* were large edifices of an oblong square, with a portico. The eastern part of one of these piles of buildings was separated by a wall from the rest, and occupied more than half of the area allotted for the erection of the whole. A range of porticos extended round three sides of the interior of this part of the gymnasium, but the *fourth* side was lined with a flight of chambers—some for bathing, some for anointing the body, and some to serve as wardrobes. The middle of these chambers was denominated *ephebium*, where the *ephebi*, or youth, exercised. The area, or the open court, including the porticos just mentioned, one range of which—that on the north side—was double, was denominated the *palæstra*, in which were witnessed games and exercises—dancing, wrestling, throwing the quoit, and the combat with the cæstus. The western part of the gymnasium was an oblong, and was surrounded by a portico, in which the *athletæ* exercised in unpleasant weather. The porticos for this purpose are called *xysti*, from which the other parts of the building, denominated *xysta*, differed in the following particulars, viz.: they were surrounded with rows of trees, were not covered with a roof at the top, and were used as places for promenading. At the end of the western part of the *gymnasium* was the *stadium*. It was a large semi-circle, a hundred and twenty-five geometrical paces long, and was furnished with seats, which ran around it in a circuitous manner, and ascended gradually one above another, for the accommodation of the spectators. The games which were more particularly witnessed in the *stadium*, were races on foot, on horseback, and with chariots.

The athletæ, after the fourth century before Christ, went wholly naked, with the exception of those who threw the quoit, or rode in the chariot. Heb. xii, 1. The *cæstus*, to which an allusion is made in 1 Cor. ix, 26, was a leather strap, bound, by the athletæ, round the right hand and fingers. This strap was wide enough to receive a piece of iron or lead, which was rolled upon it, and was discharged, with all the strength of the combatant, against his adversary. It became the one against whom it was discharged to be on the look-out, and avoid, if possible, the intended blow.

The *chariot race*, which was run in the *stadium*, and from which Paul, in 1 Cor. ix, 24–27; 2 Tim. iv, 7, 8; Phil. iii, 11–14, borrows certain illustrations, was as follows:—Four chariots started at the same time for the goal, which was at the farther extremity of the stadium. The one who reached it first was the conqueror. Other competitors presented themselves, and the course was run again, by four at a time, as in the first instance. The one who successively gained the victory over all, won the crown. This was woven of branches of evergreen. A crown of this description was given to all who were victorious in any contests. 1 Cor. ix, 54; Phil. iii, 14; Col. iii, 15; 2 Tim. iv, 8. Wherever the victor went he received a branch of palm, (Rev. vii, 9,) was robed in a splendid dress, and conducted home with honour. The athletæ were obliged to abstain from enervating food and wine, and prohibited all intercourse with the other sex—not allowed even so much as to look upon them. If any of the laws regulating the contests were violated, no award of honour could be given, though the person was victor. He must strive lawfully. 2 Tim. ii, 5; iv, 8.

The Jews had a game of lifting a stone. The one who could raise it the highest from the ground was the victor.

The theatre, which was introduced by Herod and his sons into Palestine, was an edifice constructed in such a manner as to describe the larger half of a circle. The games were exhibited in that part where a line would have passed to enclose precisely a semi-circle.

Amphitheatres may be described by saying that they were two theatres united. They were, of course, oblong in point of form, and games were exhibited in the centre of them. The seats extended round the interior, one above another. In theatres of this kind comedies and tragedies were acted. Assemblies were also held in them, and ambassadors received. Acts xii, 20; xix, 29.

Encampments.

The art of laying out an *encampment* was well understood in Egypt before the departure of the Israelites. Moses copied after the Egyptians in forming encampments in the wilderness. Num. i, 53; iii, 21–38. The camps were guarded by sentinels. Judg. vii, 19; 1 Sam. xiv, 16; xxvi, 14–17. Moses gives the following regulations in regard to encampments: 1. Every unclean person shall live out of it. 2. They were to bury all their evacuations without the camp, that there might be no filth.

The following was the order of marching:—As soon as the cloud ascended over the tabernacle, the priests sounded the silver trumpets. Then immediately the tribes of Judah, Issachar, and Zebulun, on the east, set forward. At the second sound, Reuben, Simeon, and Gad, on the south, followed. The march was next commenced by the Levites, who bore the parts of the tabernacle and the ark of the covenant. Then, at the third sound of the trumpet, followed Ephraim, Manasseh, and Benjamin, from the west; and, at the fourth sound, Dan, Asher, and Naphtali, from the north, who brought up the rear. Each one followed the particular standard of his corps and family. When the cloud descended again, the encampment was formed as before.

Military Standards.

1. The *standard* denominated *degel* was of four kinds. They were large, and ornamented with colours, in white, purple, crimson, and dark blue. 2. The standard called *oth* belonged to the separate classes of families. 3. The standard called *nes* was not, like the others, borne from place to place. It was a long pole fixed in the earth. A flag was fastened to the top, which, floating in the wind, could be seen at a great distance. In order to render it visible as far as possible, it was erected on the tops of the highest mountains, and thus was a signal to assemble soldiers. Whenever it was hoisted the war-cry was uttered and trumpets were blown. Isa v, 26; xiii, 2; xviii, 3.

War.

The heathen nations consulted oracles, soothsayers, necromancers, and the lot which was ascertained by shooting arrows of different colours. 1 Sam. xxviii, 1–10; Isa. xli, 21–24; Ezek. xxv, 11. The Hebrews, to whom things of this kind were interdicted, in the early part of their history were in the habit of inquiring of God by means of the *Urim* and *Thummim.* Judg. i, 1; xx, 27, 28; 1 Sam. xxiii, 2; xxviii, 6; xxx, 8. After the times of David, the kings of Palestine, according to the different characters which they sustained, consulted *true* prophets, and sometimes *false* prophets, in respect to the issues of war. 1 Kings xxii, 6–13; 2 Kings xix, 2, *et seq.;* 20, *et seq.* Sacrifices were offered, in which the soldiers were said *to consecrate themselves to war.* Isa. xiii, 3; Jer. vi, 4; li, 27; Joel iii, 9; Obad i. There are instances of formal *declarations of war*, and sometimes of previous negotiations. 2 Kings xiv, 8; 2 Chron. xxv, 17;

Judg. xi, 22–28; 2 Sam. x, 1–12. Military expeditions commonly commenced in the spring, (2 Sam. xi, 1,) and continued in the summer. War is considered by the Orientals as a judgment sent from heaven. They considered that God granted victory only to those whose cause was just. 2 Chron. xx, 12; Isa. lxvi, 15, 16.

Before battle the various kinds of arms were put in the best order; the shields were anointed, and the soldiers refreshed themselves by taking food. Jer. xlvi, 3, 4; Isa. xxi, 5. The generals and kings were clothed in splendid habiliments, denominated the *sacred dress.* Psa. cx, 3. The army was drawn up so as to form a phalanx. It was the duty of the priests, before battle, to exhort the Hebrews to exhibit that courage which the occasion required. Deut. xx. 2, *et seq.* This, in more recent times, was done by generals and kings. The last ceremony previous to engagement, after the offering of sacrifices, was the sounding of the silver trumpets by the priests.

The Greeks commenced the war-song when within about a half of a mile of the enemy. 2 Chron. xx, 21. They then raised a shout, *ἀλαλάζειν*, which was also done among the Hebrews. 1 Sam. xvii, 52; Josh. vi, 6; Isa. v, 29, 30; xvii, 12; Jer. iv, 19; xxv, 30. The war-shout in Judg. vii, 20, was, "*The sword of the Lord and of Gideon.*" A common stratagem among the Hebrews was that of dividing the army and placing one part of it in ambush. Gen. xiv, 14–16; Josh. viii, 12; Judg. xx, 39. There is only one instance of deception in war used by the Hebrews, and that was not approved of. Gen. xxxiv; 25–31. It was the practice of the Roman armies to stand still and receive the shock of their opposers. There is an allusion to this in the following passages: 1 Cor. xvi, 13; Gal. v, 1; Eph. vi, 14; Phil. i, 27; 1 Thess. iii, 8; 2 Thess. ii, 15.

Sieges.

When a city was threatened with a *siege*, it was first invited to surrender. Deut. xx, 10; Isa. xxxvi, 1–20; xxxvii, 8–20.

Circumvallation was known in the time of Moses; also the *mound*. Deut. xx, 19, 20; 2 Sam. xx, 15. The besiegers dug a ditch between them and the city for their own security, and another parallel to it, outside, so as to enclose their camp on both sides, and to prevent their being attacked on the rear as well as front. The earth thrown out of the ditch formed a wall, on which towers were erected. The inhabitants of a city shut up in this way perished by famine, pestilence, and missile weapons. 2 Kings xxv, 1; Jer. lii, 4; Ezek. iv, 10–12; xvii, 17; 2 Kings vi, 28–31.

The besiegers cast up a mound near the wall of the city, and strengthened it on both sides with beams of timber. 2 Sam. xx, 15; 2 Kings xix, 32; Jer. vi, 6; xxxii, 24; xxxiii, 4; Ezek. iv, 2; xvii, 17–23; xxvi, 8. From this the besiegers threw their weapons into the city.

Conquered Nations.

The power of the conquerers owned no limitations. The flocks, cattle, fruits of the earth, fields, gardens, houses, idol gods, and all, fell into their possession. The wives and children of those who had been subdued were sold for slaves, and their cities were razed to the ground. 2 Sam. v, 21; 2 Chron. xxv, 14; Hosea x, 5, 6; Jer. xlvi, 25; xlviii, 7. Soldiers, artificers, engineers, and principal men, were sent into foreign countries. Kings were sometimes allowed to remain in authority, by promise of good faith and payment of tribute. If they rebelled they were treated with great severity. Gen. xiv, 4; 2 Kings xxiii, 34; xxiv, 1, 14; Isa. xxiv, 2; Jer. xx, 5, 6. Soldiers who were taken were deprived of all their property, and sold naked into servitude. When the city was taken by assault, all the men were slain, and the women and children were carried away as prisoners, and sold for a very low price. Micah i, 11; Isa. xlvii, 3; xx, 3, 4; 2 Chron. xxviii, 9–15; Psa. xliv, 12. When a city was taken, all who could escape fled and sought for safety in the tops of mountains, in caves and rocks; hence God, on account of the protection he affords, is called a *rock.* Judg. xx, 47; Jer. iv, 29; xvi, 16; xxii, 20; Ezek. vii, 7, 17; Isa. xxvi, 4.

Captive kings and nobles were bound, their eyes were put out, their bodies mutilated, and they thrown on the ground and trodden under foot until they died. Judg. i, 6, 7; 2 Kings xxv, 7; Josh. x, 24. They were sometimes thrown down upon thorns, sawn asunder, or beaten to pieces with threshing instruments. 2 Sam. xii, 31; 1 Chron. xx, 3; Judg. viii, 7. Frequently, old men, women, and children were slaughtered and thrown into heaps. 2 Kings viii, 12; Hosea x, 14; Isa. xiii, 17, 18. Even the women with child were ripped up. Isa. xiii, 16–18; 2 Kings viii, 12; Amos i, 13. Everything was devoted to death, and the very land desolated. Lev. xxvii, 21, 28, 29; Num. xviii, 14; Deut. xiii, 17. In some cases the conquered nations were only made tributary. 2 Sam. viii, 6; 2 Kings xiv, 4.

The people all went out, not excepting the women, to meet the conquerors, with singing and dancing. Judg. xi, 34–37; 1 Sam. xviii, 6, 7. Triumphant songs were uttered for the living, and elegies for the dead. Monuments, in honour of victories, were erected, (2 Sam. viii, 13,) and the arms of the enemy were hung up in the temples, as trophies of victory. 1 Sam. xxxi, 10; 2 Kings xi, 10.

David instituted separate corps of military men, composed of those most renowned for warlike deeds. 2 Sam. xxiii, 8, 39.

Character of Ancient Wars.

Ancient warfare was characterized by great cruelty among all nations, and the Hebrews must be judged by the times in which they lived. The same clemency could not be extended to enemies then as now, without exposure to all sorts of injury. Num. xxxi, 14, 15; 2 Sam. xii, 31; Amos i, 13; ii, 1; 2 Kings iii, 27.

In regard to the Canaanites, God selected the Israelites as his agents to punish them for their great wickedness, (Gen. xv, 16,) and hence their utter extirpation was but the carrying out of the divine will, as in the case of the inhabitants of Sodom and Gomorrah. That they had a *right* to the possession of the land, however, did not arise from the consideration that they had conquered it in war, though *might*, in such instances, has given the right, but arose from a very different and less questionable consideration. Canaan originally belonged to Abraham; and he virtually declared, by the wells which he dug and the altars he erected, his right to the land, and his determination to hold it. Gen. xii, 5, 6, 8, 9; xxi, 25–30; xiii, 4, 14, 18; xv, 7, 13, 21; xvii, 8. The *patriarch* left the soil, after his death, to *Isaac*, not to Ishmael, who in turn transmitted it to *Jacob*, to the exclusion of Esau. It had been occupied by the patriarchs for a period of two hundred and fifty years; and when Jacob and his descendants emigrated to Egypt, they intended to return. Gen. xlviii, 4, 21, 22; xlix, 1, 26; 1 Chron. vii, 21, 24. During the abode of the Israelites in Egypt, the Canaanites, who had increased in numbers, occupied the whole territory, and the Hebrews, thus excluded from their own soil, had the right to repossess it; and if the Canaanites would not acknowledge that right, a resort to arms was perfectly justifiable on their part. Josh. xi, 19; ix, 3, 36.

Spoils.

The spoils of the enemy's army were divided among the victorious soldiers, as the reward of the toils they endured. Gen. xlix, 27; Exod. xv, 9; Judg. v, 30; Isa. ix, 2, 3; Ezek. xxix, 18–20; Psa. cxix, 162. There was a propriety in this, inasmuch as common soldiers paid their own expenses, or were supported by their parents. Judg. xx, 10; 2 Sam. xvii, 17–20. Hebrew kings, however, in a subsequent age, made provision for soldiers, in what was called *store cities.* 2 Chron. xvii, 12; xxxii, 28. Soldiers were sometimes *hired;* and hence we find, in the New Testament, mention of the wages of a soldier. Luke iii, 14; Rom. vi, 23; 1 Cor. ix, 7; 2 Cor. xi, 8; 2 Tim. ii, 4. Men, women, and children were regarded as spoils. Things of great value were the property of the leader or commander. 2 Sam. viii, 11, 12; xii, 30; 2 Chron. xxviii, 14–19. Cities devoted to the *curse* were destroyed with all their spoils. Deut. ii, 34; iii, 7; Num. xxxi, 9; Lev. xxvii, 28; Josh. vi, 24–26; viii, 26, 28, 30.

After the commencement of war, the people could make plunder of the property which had been deposited with them, or what they had borrowed. Exod. iii, 22; xi, 2. The word literally to *plunder*, or rob, which in Exod. iii, 22 is used in reference to this subject, appears to be employed *tropically*, and out of its usual signification.

Four months of the year were regarded as *sacred*, and during this time the Hebrews abstained from the use of arms. The same custom prevailed among the surrounding nations, and this accounts for the fact that the Hebrew territories were not invaded at such times. God had promised them security from invasion during their solemn festivals, and no instance occurs of their country being invaded at such times.

CHAPTER III.

SACRED ARCHÆOLOGY.

Historical View of Religion.

IT is not unreasonable to suppose that when Adam was created he was made a perfect man, not only in his form, but also in the accomplishments of his mind; for to imagine that he came from the divine hand in a state of stupidity and ignorance, would not only be doubting the wisdom and goodness of God, but the truth of the Bible. Created in the very image of God, he was endowed with full capacity of knowing him, and he was also perfectly adapted to appreciate and enjoy the Eden of happiness over which he presided as lord of the lower world. When, in the full and unrestrained exercise of his emotions and volitions, he violated the divine prohibition, he fell from his perfect and happy estate into one of sin and misery, and involved his whole posterity in the lamentable consequences of his defection. His knowledge of evil was purchased at the terrible price of his happiness for time and eternity, and that of his race. By his act the bitter fountain of death and sorrow was unsealed in the very bowers of life, and the dark, deadly streams were made to flow, blasting the joys of Eden, and spreading lamentation, mourning, and woe over all the earth.

The curse which was pronounced upon Adam for his transgression, and the punishment inflicted upon Cain for murder, were clear indications of the odiousness of sin in the mind of the Creator, and were designed to remain as perpetual monitions that misery and wretchedness are inseparable concomitants of transgression. These visible punishments, however, did not deter the race from sin. As the human family increased in numbers it increased in crimes, until the whole earth was filled with violence and slaughter. About the year of the world 235, wickedness was carried to such an extent that the religious portion of it thought it necessary to take to themselves the name of the *sons*, or *worshippers of God*, in contradistinction from the sons of *men*, or those who had forgotten God, and were hurried, by the impulse of corrupt passions, to every species of wickedness. These evils were increased from the circumstance that the *sons* or *worshippers of God* married the daughters of *men*, or the irreligious. Wives of this description neglected the right instruction of their children; and as this devolved on them rather than on their fathers, the children followed the former rather than the latter. Gen. iv, 26; vi, 1. In this way corruption increased and prevailed to such a degree that the warnings of God were of no avail. Gen. vi, 3. The destruction of the entire race, with the exception of the righteous, which consisted of but one family, was determined by the Almighty, and a deluge swept the guilty world of mankind from existence.

This terrible destruction of every living thing was predicted one hundred and twenty years before its consummation, (Gen. vi, 3,) so that the family of Noah might know that it was sent from God, and that the object of it was to leave, by such a signal event, a long-to-be-remembered impression that God is the governor of all things, to whom the vices of men are abhorrent; and that, however long-suffering, he will at last punish the guilty. A command was given by the Almighty, after the Deluge, that every homicide should be punished with death, and a promise, also, that the Deluge should no more return. The rainbow was made a visible sign of this promise, as well as a confirmation of it. The posterity of Noah laid up in their minds the principles and instructions which had been communicated; and when, afterwards, they attempted to build a tower, and were confounded and scattered from each other, they easily learned from that event that their conduct was displeasing to God. They reproved Nimrod for a similar attempt, and, in allusion to his conduct, called him *the rebel*, and made his memory a proverb, saying, "*Even as Nimrod the mighty hunter.*" At a later period, as men degenerated, and were unable to direct themselves, and forgetting God, or not liking to retain a knowledge of him, they turned aside and looked for help from surrounding inanimate objects, and rocks, trees, rivers, winds, the sun, moon, stars, and dead men, and finally, also, living animals, became deities. Then followed sculptured images and temples. At first, as we have seen, they worshipped God as the ruler and governor of all things; but, finally, the creature usurped the place of the Creator, and as their dumb idols uttered no commands, they gave loose rein to their evil imaginations, and the greatest crimes were committed, and made a part of the religious worship offered to their idols.

This corruption continued to spread itself wider and wider, until God gave a peculiar call to Abraham, whose ancestors had, from the beginning, sustained a religious character, (Gen. v, 1–31; xi, 10–32,) but who at length became involved in the general idolatry. Josh. xxiv, 3. It was designed, in the providence of God, that Abraham the Chaldean, and his posterity, should preserve and transmit his religion to other nations. As the descendant of Shem, God promised to Abraham a large posterity, possession of the land of Canaan, and also that, through his seed, all nations should be blessed and receive the true religion. Gen. xii, 13; xviii, 18; xxii, 18. With these promises were connected the rite of circumcision. Gen. xviii, 19. God afterwards repeated the same promises to Isaac and Jacob, (Gen. xxvi, 4; xxviii, 14,) who faithfully performed their various duties, taught the true worship of God to their domestics, and left it to their posterity. Gen. xxviii, 20–22; xxxv, 2, 7, 9, 13; xxxix, 9; l, 17–20. These promises, and the fulfilment of their corresponding duties, form the fundamental principle of the *ancient covenant*, and with them the *new covenant* is very intimately connected.

The knowledge of the true God, which was coeval with

the existence of the human race, was originally communicated by *revelation.* The worship of God was simple and unconstrained, such as was prompted by conscience and approved by reason, and consisted chiefly in tithes, vows, and prayers, and in the erection of altars and the offering of sacrifices. Gen. iv, 3, 4; viii, 20; xii, 7, 8; xiii, 4–18; xiv, 20; xv, 18–20; &c.

The *Sabbath* was consecrated from the beginning, as may be inferred from Gen. ii, 2; vii, 4–10; viii, 10–12; xxix, 27. Many traces of *moral discipline* occur. Gen. iv, 6–16; vi, 3–8; xi, 4–6; xiii, 8; xiv, 14–24; xviii, 19.

When Moses was sent as a divine messenger to break the chains of Hebrew servitude, many of them were addicted to the worship of Egyptian gods. Exod. iii, 13. To rescue the Hebrews from bondage, who were destined to be the defenders of the true religion, and to bring them back to that worship which they had lost while in Egypt, gave occasion for the most surprising miracles—*miracles* which not only compelled Pharaoh to dismiss the Hebrews, and brought destruction upon his army when he pursued them, but were also a new and overwhelming proof to the Hebrews themselves that there is indeed a *God all-powerful and omniscient,* and that Moses, by whom these wonderful works had been predicted and performed, was his messenger. Exod. vi, 7; vii, 5; ix, 14, 16, 29; x, 2; xiv, 4, 17, 18, 31; xvi, 12; xix, 4–9; Deut. iv, 35–39. It was also shown, at the same time, that the Egyptian gods were destitute of power, and altogether unable to protect their votaries. Exod. xii, 12. Nothing but this wonderful manifestation, from time to time, of their miracle-working God, could have preserved the whole nation from being seduced into idolatry.

To preserve the true religion, and keep constantly before the mind of the nation the true nature and character of God, the *Sabbath* was rigidly observed, and the *Pentecost,* the *Jubilee,* the *Passover,* and the *Feast of Tabernacles,* were sacredly observed. The *book of the law* was publicly read, every seven years, in the tabernacle, and every Hebrew was commanded to commit to memory the thirty-second chapter of Deuteronomy, as a perpetual monitor of their duty.

The laws of Moses enjoined a supreme love to God, as the creator and governor of the universe; a love to the neighbour; prohibited hatred and revenge, cruelty and inhumanity to servants; and enjoined benevolence and beneficence to the poor, especially widows and orphans; and the whole institution was a system of moral discipline, designed to secure uprightness and integrity of heart.

The laws of Moses contained *historical* and *moral types.* This is evident from the passover and feast of tabernacles; (Exod. xii, 1, 13, 16; Lev. xxiii, 4–8; Deut. xvi, 1–8;) also from the rite of circumcision, and the gold mitre of the high priest; for a typical import is expressly assigned to the last of these by Moses himself. Exod. xxviii, 38; Deut. x, 16; xxx, 6.

The influence of the institutions of Moses was retained through many ages of trial. Whenever religion was endangered by neglect or by idolatry, the invariable consequence was that there were calamities and evils which admonished the people of the necessity of choosing rulers who would restore their religion. Sometimes God sent public calamities, and he also sent his prophets, who reproved kings and princes, and threw great obstacles in the way of their wicked attempts to introduce idolatry. When at length admonitions ceased to be of any avail, and everything was growing worse and worse, the *Israelitish* commonwealth was overthrown, two hundred and fifty-three years after their separation from Judah, and seven hundred and twenty-two before Christ. The people were carried away into Assyria, and Gozan, and Chalacene, cities of Media. The kingdom of Judah was overthrown three hundred and eighty-seven years after the separation, and five hundred and eighty-eight before Christ, by the Chaldeans, and the people were carried captive to the banks of the river Chebar, in Babylonia.

The *return* of the Jews from captivity witnessed a return

to true religion, and in this revival an utter extinction was given to idolatry among them as a nation. Synagogues were built, sacrifices offered, and the law of Moses read in those synagogues every Sabbath day; while schools were established for the education of the rising generation.

True religion was not restored, as some suppose, by the example of the Magian worship, or by philosophic development, but by a recurrence to their ancient history, their ancient miracles, and the fulfilment of prophecy.

A Future State.

The ancient Hebrews had some idea of a future life, and this we learn from the sacred record. Their views, however, were limited and obscure, as will be seen by a reference to the distinction which they made between the subterranean residence denominated *sheol*, and the *grave*, or place of interment for the body. Gen. xxv, 8; xxxvii, 35; xlix, 33; l, 2–10; Num. xx, 24–26; Deut. xxxiv, 7; xxxi, 16; 1 Kings xi, 43.

That they believed in the existence of the soul after the death of the body is evident from the credit they gave to *necromancy*, by means of which the Jews believed that the *spirits of the dead* were summoned back to the present scene of existence. Lev. xix, 31; xx, 6, 7, 26, 27; Deut. xviii, 11; 1 Sam. xxviii, 3-10; 2 Kings xxiii, 24; 1 Chron. x, 13; Isa. xix, 3; xxix, 4; lvii, 9; Zech. xiii, 2–6.

The ancient Hebrews believed that the *spirits* of the dead were received into *sheol*, a large subterranean abode. Gen. xxxvii, 35; Num. xvi, 30–33; Deut. xxxii, 22. Into this abode the wicked were driven suddenly, but the good descended into it tranquilly. This spacious dwelling-place is described as dark, sorrowful, and inactive. Job x, 21; Psa. vi, 5; lxxxviii, 11, 12; cxv, 17; Isa. xxxviii, 18. In other places—such as Isa. xiv, 9, Job xxvi, 5, 6, and 1 Sam. xxviii, 7—it is represented as full of activity. A superhuman knowledge is ascribed to its inhabitants. In this abode *departed spirits* rest, Job iii, 13; and there the living hope again to behold their ancestors and children. Gen. xxxvii, 35; xxv, 10; xxxv, 28; xlix, 29; Num. xx, 24–26; 1 Kings ii, 10, 11.

It is supposed by some that the passages in Dan. xii, 2, 3, 13 were a confirmation of the *resurrection of the dead*, and also Haggai ii, 23; Zech. iii, 7. This doctrine was at length adopted by the Jews, with the exception of the Sadducees. It remained for the gospel to bring *life and immortality to light.*

Propagation of Judaism.

During the four centuries preceding the destruction of Jerusalem, the Jews were scattered abroad extensively among the nations. This dispersion enabled the Jews to propagate their religion, and such was their zeal and success that they won whole nations. The Idumeans, Itureans, and Moabites made profession of the Jewish faith, and underwent the rite of circumcision. The King of Yemen, in Arabia Felix, became a Jew more than one hundred years before Christ, and his successors defended and propagated the Jewish religion. The Jews in Asia Minor, in Greece, and, in the progress of time, at Rome also, were the means of drawing numbers within the pale of their country's religion. In Rome they became so numerous as to have a majority at the elections. Proselytes, especially from the female sex, who were not subjected to the inconvenience of circumcision, were perpetually multiplied. See Acts ii, 11; vi, 1; xiii, 43–50; xvi, 14; xvii, 4; xviii, 7–13; xix, 29. Providence thus prepared the way for the introduction of the Christian religion into all parts of the world, and the apostles found everywhere in their travels those who had embraced the Jewish religion; and they not only had liberty to preach in their synagogues, but they were essentially aided by Jewish proselytes in announcing Jesus Christ to the heathen. Acts ii, 5–11; xi, 19; xiii, 4, 6, 13, 52; xiv, 1–28; xvi, 1–40; xii, 1–17.

The Jews preserved great harmony among themselves, and those who lived in foreign countries maintained a connexion with each other by means of the temple at Jerusalem. The Jews of Egypt, who inhabited Leontopolis, in the district of Heliopolis, from the year 149 before Christ to Anno Domini 73, hád a temple of their own, though they still kept up a connexion with the Jews at Jerusalem.

Though the Jews were divided into three prominent sects, the *Pharisees*, *Sadducees*, and *Essenes*, yet their harmony or unity was not affected thereby.

Doctrines of the Pharisees.

The Pharisees boasted that they were peculiarly acceptable to God, on account of their accurate knowledge of the Jewish law and religion. The following were the opinions entertained by them:—

1. They agreed with the Stoics in teaching the doctrine of *fate*, or an immutable order of things fixed by the decree of God.

2. They taught that the souls of men were immortal, and dwelt after the present life in *sheol.* They further taught that the spirits of the *wicked* were tormented with everlasting punishments, and that they at times made their reappearance upon the earth to vex men with epilepsy, mental derangement, madness, and melancholy; and that the *good*, on the other hand, received rewards, and at length passed into other human bodies. Matt. xiv, 2; xvi, 14; John ix, 2–34.

It is nowhere remarked by Josephus that they believed in the *resurrection of the dead*, though it is evident, from several passages, they held such belief. Matt. xxii, 24–34; Mark xii, 18–23; Luke xx, 27–36; John xi, 24.

3. They believed in, and taught the existence of *angels*, both good and bad. They believed that angels were the ministers of God on earth, and that some one of them was assigned to every kingdom, and also to every individual, and at times made his appearance. Matt. xviii, 10; Luke iv, 10; Heb. ii, 5; Acts xii, 15; xxiii, 8, 9.

4. They believed, furthermore, that God was under obligation, and bound in justice, to bestow favours upon the Jews, to render them partakers of the kingdom of the Messiah, to justify and to render them eternally happy, and that he could not condemn any of them. With them the ground of *justification* was Abraham's faith and works, the knowledge of God which existed among them, together with circumcision and the offering of sacrifices. Rom. ii–xii, Heb. x, 1–18.

They put a very lax construction upon the laws of Moses in regard to the *law of retaliation*, the *divorce of a wife*, and *the loving one's neighbour*. They maintained that the oath in which God was not expressly named was not binding. They forbade the gathering a few ears of corn, and healing the sick on the Sabbath. They gave the preference to *ceremonial* laws; and they esteemed anger, and the exercise of impure affections, of little consequence. They manifested great anxiety in making proselytes, and were avaricious, fond of pleasure, vain glory, uttered their prayers publicly, and took pride in ornamenting their tombs.

They observed a multitude of *traditions*, and placed these unwritten ordinances of the ancients on an equality with the divine laws themselves. These they collected, and formed out of them the Talmud. Various other observances, not above enumerated, were regarded by them, such as the *washing of hands* before meals, *not eating with Gentiles* or tax-gatherers, *fasting twice a week*, *enlarging their phylacteries* and the borders of their garments, &c., &c. Phylacteries were pieces of parchment, on which were written four passages of Scripture. Exod. xiii, 1, 10, 11, 16; Deut. v, 4–9; xi, 13–21.

Doctrines of the Sadducees.

Their opinions were peculiar. They believed—

1. That besides God there was no other spiritual being, whether good or bad. They believed that the soul and

body died together; and that there neither was, nor ever could be, a resurrection. Matt. xxii, 23; Acts xxiii, 8.

2. They rejected the doctrine of fate, and maintained, on the contrary, that the events which happened depended upon the free, unconstrained actions of men. They held that the traditions received by the Pharisees were not binding. It is supposed by some that in progress of time they admitted the existence of angels and the immortality of the soul.

Doctrines of the Essenes.

The principal ground of difference between the *Essenes* and the *Therapeutæ* consisted in *this*:—The former were *Jews*, who spoke the Aramean; the latter were *Greek Jews*. The Essenes lived chiefly in Palestine; the Therapeutæ lived in Egypt. The Therapeutæ were more rigid than the Essenes, since the latter, although they made it a practice to keep at a distance from large cities, lived, nevertheless, in towns and villages, and practised agriculture and the arts, with the exception of those which were subservient to war. The Therapeutæ, on the contrary, fled from all inhabited places, dwelt in fields, and deserts, and gardens, and gave themselves up to contemplation. They both held their property in common. Candidates for admission among the Essenes gave their property to the society, but those among the Therapeutæ left *theirs* to their friends. After a number of years of probation they made a profession, which bound both of them to the exercise of the strictest uprightness.

The Essenes offered prayers before sunrise, after which each one was sent, by the person who was placed over them, to his respective employment. About eleven o'clock they left their work, and assembled to partake of their bread and pottage. In the evening, also, their supper was in common. Before and after meals the priest offered up prayers. On the Sabbath the Essenes listened to the reading of the law in their synagogues, which was attended with an allegorical explanation; they also read books by themselves in private on that day. They pretended to possess the secret names of angels, which it would have been an act of impiety to have communicated to profane persons. They never took an oath, except when joining the order. They asserted slavery was repugnant to nature. Some of them made pretensions to the gift of prophecy. They avoided matrimony, except among a particular class of them. The rest lived in celibacy, because they had no confidence in the virtue of women. In point of *doctrine* they very nearly resembled the Pharisees.

The Therapeutæ agreed in most things with the Essenes, but they *all* lived unmarried. They received females into their sect; but they remained virgins, and followed the same mode of life with the men. They kept vigils on the night of the Sabbath, sung hymns, and led sacred dances.

Hellenists.

This name was given to the Jews who are mentioned in Acts vi, 1; ix, 29; xi, 20; and who, not only in Egypt, Asia Minor, and Greece, but in all places, spoke the Greek language as their vernacular tongue. They do not appear to be the same as those mentioned in John vii, 35, James i, 1, and 1 Peter i, 1, and are called the *dispersed among the Gentiles;* for it appears that the Hellenists were found at Jerusalem, (Acts vi, 1,) and they were likewise found among the dispersed Jews who spoke the Aramean; as, for instance, Paul, who was born at Tarsus. 2 Cor. xi, 22; Phil. iii, 5.

Proselytes.

Proselytes, *προσήλυτοι*, i. e., *those who have come in*, are mentioned at a very ancient period in connexion with the journey through Arabia, and in the history of David and Solomon.

In the time of Christ and the Apostles they were found everywhere in great numbers, some *circumcised* and some *uncircumcised*. The former were called *just* or *righteous proselytes*, and the latter *the proselytes of the gate.* These worshipped the one true God, but refused to obey the laws of Moses: such were the Kenites and the Rechabites. They observed the precepts of Noah, viz.:—1. That men should abstain from idolatry. 2. That they should worship the true God. 3. That they should hold incest in abhorrence. 4. That they should not commit homicide. 5. That they should not steal or rob. 6. That they should punish a murderer with death. 7. That they should not eat blood, nor anything strangled.

They frequented the synagogues in company with the Jews; and although they were at liberty to offer sacrifices to God in any place where they chose, they preferred visiting the temple of Jerusalem, and offered sacrifices through the priests.

The other class of *proselytes*, denominated the *just*, were united with the great body of the Jewish people not only by circumcision, but by baptism also, which was a symbol of regeneration. Exod. xix, 10–14; xxiv, 8; Gen. xxxv, 2. Christ speaks of this baptism in such a way as to imply that it was well known. John iii, 10.

Samaritans.

The people who were sent by Shalmaneser and Esarhaddon from Cuthah, Ara, Hamath, and Sepharvaim into that portion of country which formerly belonged to the tribes of Ephraim and Manasseh, united with one another, and with the Israelites who were left there, and formed one people. They were called Samaritans, from their principal city, Samaria.

At first these people worshipped the respective gods of their own nation, but, being harassed by lions, they attributed their sufferings from this source to the circumstance of their not worshipping the *God of the country* where they now lived. They therefore received back from the King of Assyria an exiled Hebrew priest, who took up his residence in Bethel, where the *golden calf* had formerly been. This priest taught them the worship of Jehovah, from the books of Moses, but mingled with it the idolatry of the calf, and represented that animal as the embodied form of the Deity, and thus the people were led into the worship of idols and Jehovah at the same time. 2 Kings xvii, 26–34; 2 Chron. xxx, 1–10.

They proposed to assist the Hebrews in rebuilding the temple after their return from exile, but their proposals were finally rejected, which occasioned an implacable hatred on their part, and they impeded the work as much as possible. Manasses, the son of the high priest, who had married the daughter of Sanballat, the ruler of the Samaritans, refusing to comply with the order of Nehemiah, in regard to putting away his wife, on account of her foreign extraction, went over to the Samaritans, and his father-in-law built a temple on Mount Gerizim, and placed him over its sacred observances. While Manasses fulfilled the office of high priest among them, they appeared to have dismissed their idols. Jews, who had transgressed the laws to evade punishment, fled to Samaria, and thus the hatred increased on both sides. One hundred and sixty-seven years before Christ, Antiochus Epiphanes, king of the Syrians, consecrated their temple to Jupiter, but they returned afterwards to the religion of Moses. About thirty-eight years after this, John Hyrcanus destroyed their temple. At the time of Christ there was no intercourse whatever between the Jews and Samaritans. Luke xvii, 16; John iv, 9. The Jews, out of hatred, changed the name of the city of *Sichem* to *Sychar*, which means *drunken*. John iv, 5. The Samaritans only received the Pentateuch as of divine authority; they nevertheless expected the advent of the *Messiah*, (John iv, 25,) and grounded their expectations on Gen. xii, 3; xviii, 18; xxii, 18; xxvi, 4; xxviii, 14. They contended that the proper place of worship was Mount Gerizim, and not Jerusalem. John iv, 20.

SACRED PLACES.

In the earliest ages of the world there was no distinction in regard to the time or place where God was worshipped.

The earliest *altar* of which we have any account, was that erected by Noah on Mount Ararat. Gen. viii, 20. Abraham, Isaac, and Jacob erected a number of *altars* in the land of Canaan, particularly in places where they had been favoured with the divine communications. Gen. xii, 7; xiii, 4–18; xxvi, 25; xxxiii, 20; xxxv, 1, 3, 7. Moses, and the author of the Book of Joshua, both speak of idols, altars, and groves, but are silent respecting *temples*. The first temple of which we have any account was the one at Shechem, which was dedicated to the god *Baal-berith;* but, as it was furnished with a tower, there had probably been others before it. Judg. ix, 4. Moses constructed a *tabernacle*, while marching through Arabia, which could easily be transferred from place to place. This was not the first of its kind. Amos v, 26. With respect to the temple, which was subsequently erected in Palestine, Moses gave no command on the subject.

The Tabernacle.

The *place* where public worship was held, from the time of Moses till Solomon, was the tabernacle, variously denominated *a tent*, *a habitation*, *a sanctuary*, *a house*, *the dwelling-place of Jehovah's glory*, *Jehovah's tent*, and *palace*, and *the tent of the congregation*. It was divided into three parts. The *first* part was the *area* or court of the tabernacle, a hundred and fifty feet long and seventy-five feet broad. It was surrounded on all sides with *curtains*, to the height of seven or eight feet. They were suspended from rods of silver, which reached from one column to another, and rested on them. The *columns* on the east and west were ten, and on the north and south twenty, in number, and were made of *acacia*, (shittim-wood.) The columns, in order to prevent their being injured by the moisture of the earth, were supported on *bases of brass*. Near the top of the columns were *silver hooks*, in which the rods that sustained the curtains were inserted. That part of the court cf the tabernacle which formed the *entrance* was on the east side, and thirty feet in extent. The entrance was closed by letting fall a sort of tapestry, which hung from rods or poles, resting on four columns, and which was adorned with figures in blue, purple, and scarlet. When the entrance was opened the tapestry was drawn up. The curtains in the entrance were different from those that were suspended around other parts of the court of the tabernacle. Exod. xxvii, 9–19; xxxix, 9–20.

The *tabernacle*, strictly so called, was situated in the middle of the western side of the *court*. It was covered on every part, and, in point of form, was an oblong square, being thirty cubits, or forty-five feet long, from east to west, and ten cubits, or fifteen feet broad, from north to south. The walls were composed of forty-eight boards, or planks, viz., twenty on the north side, and twenty on the south side, and six on the west. The two at the angles were doubled, making forty-eight. Exod. xxvi, 15–30. The eastern side was not boarded. The *boards* were of *acacia*, fifteen feet long and twenty-seven inches broad, and overlaid with plates of gold. They rested on bases of silver, and were united together by bars or poles, also of gold. The tabernacle thus constructed was shielded by four coverings. The first, or interior or lower covering, was made of fine *twined linen*, extending down within eighteen inches of the earth, and displaying pictures of cherubim, wrought into it with the various colours of blue, purple, and scarlet. The second was a fabric woven of goats' hair, and extended very nearly to the ground. Exod. xxvi, 7–13. The third was of rams' skins, dyed red; the fourth of the skins of some sea animal of a sky-blue colour. The *eastern* side, or *entrance*, was closed by means of a curtain made of cotton, which was suspended from silver rods that were sustained by five columns, covered with gold.

The interior of the tabernacle was divided into two parts, the first thirty feet long and fifteen broad and high, and was separated from the second, or inner apartment, by a curtain or veil, which hung down from four columns overlaid with gold, and was denominated *the inner veil.* Exod. xxvi, 36, 37. The first apartment was called *the holy*, and the inner apartment *the most holy*, and, sometimes, *the inner tabernacle.*

Altar and Brazen Laver.

Nearly in the centre of the outer court was the *altar*. Exod. xl, 29. It was a kind of coffer, four and a half feet high, and seven and a half feet long and broad, made of acacia. The lower part rested on four short columns, or feet, the sides of which were gates of brass, through which the blood of the victim flowed out. The sides of the upper part of the altar were covered with brass, and the interior space was filled with earth, upon which the fire was kindled. The four corners of the altar projected upwards, so as to resemble horns. At the four corners were rings, through which poles were placed, for the purpose of carrying it from place to place. On the south side there was an ascent to it, made of earth heaped up. Exod. xx, 24; xxiv, 4; xxvii, 1–8; xxxviii, 1–7; Lev. ix, 22.

The appurtenances, or furniture of the altar, were the *urns* for carrying away the ashes, the *shovels* for collecting them together, the *skins* for receiving and sprinkling the blood of the victims, a sort of *tongs* for turning the parts of the victim in the fire, the *censers* for burning incense, and *other instruments of brass.* Exod. xxvii, 3; xxxviii, 3.

Between the altar and the tabernacle, a little to the south, stood a circular *laver*, which, together with its base, was made of brazen ornaments which the women had presented for the use of the tabernacle. Exod. xxx, 18; xl, 7. The priests, when about to perform their duty, washed their hands in this laver.

Golden Candlestick.

The *golden candlestick* was placed in the first apartment of the tabernacle, on the south side. It stood on a *base*, from which the principal *stem* arose perpendicularly. From this stem three *branches* on each side projected upwards, describing parallel curves. They arose from the main stem at equal distances, and to the same height with it. The height of the whole was five feet, and the distance between the exterior branches three and a half feet. The stem and branches were adorned with knops, flowers, and other ornaments of gold. The seven extremities of the main stem and branches were employed as so many separate lamps, all of which were kept burning in the night, but *three* only in the day. Exod. xxx, 8; Lev. xxiv, 4. In the morning the priest put the lamps in order with his golden snuffers, and carried away the filth that might have gathered upon them, in golden vessels made for that purpose. The weight of the whole candlestick was one hundred and twenty-five pounds. Exod. xxv, 31–40; xxvii, 20; xxxvii, 17–24; Lev. xxiv, 1–4; Num. iv, 9.

Table of Shew-Bread.

In the first apartment of the tabernacle, on the north side, was a *table*, made of acacia wood, three feet long, one and a half broad, and two and a quarter high, covered over with leaves of gold. The top of the leaf of this table was encircled with a rim or border of gold. The frame of the table, immediately below the leaf, was encircled with a piece of wood about four inches broad, around the edge of which there was a rim, the same as around the leaf. A little lower down, but at equal distances from the top of the table, there were four rings of gold fastened to the legs of it, through which staves or poles, covered with gold, were placed, for the purpose of carrying it. Exod. xxv, 23–28; xxxvii, 10–16.

The *rings* were not found in the table of shew-bread which was afterwards made for the temple, nor, indeed, in any of the sacred furniture where they had previously been, except in the *ark of the covenant*. Twelve unleavened loaves were placed upon this table, which were sprinkled over with frankincense, and, it is stated in the Alexandrine version, with salt likewise. They were placed in two piles, one above another, were changed every Sabbath day by the priests, and were called the *bread of the face*, because it was exhibited before the face or throne of Jehovah. Lev. xxiv, 6, 7; 1 Chron. xxiii, 29.

Wine was placed upon the tables in *bowls*, some larger and some smaller; also in a sort of vessels that were covered, and in *cups* which were employed in pouring in and taking out the wine from the other vessels. Exod. xxv, 29, 30; xxxvii, 10–16; xl, 4, 24; Lev. xxiv, 5–9; Num. iv, 7.

Altar of Incense.

The altar of incense was placed between the table of shew-bread and the golden candlestick, towards the veil which enclosed the interior apartment of the tabernacle, or *holy of holies*. It was constructed of acacia wood, eighteen inches square and three feet high. It was ornamented at the four corners, and overlaid with leaves of gold; hence it was called the *golden altar*, also the interior altar, in contradistinction from the altar for the victims, which was in the large court.

The *upper surface* of this altar was encircled by a *border*, and on each of the two sides, at equal distances, were fastened two rings, for the admission of the rods of gold, by which it was carried. Incense was offered on this altar daily, morning and evening, a description of which is given in Exodus xxx, 1–10, 34–37; xxxvii, 25–29; xl, 5–26.

Ark of the Covenant in the Holy of Holies.

The ark of the covenant was deposited in that part of the tabernacle called the *holy of holies*, a place so secluded that the light of day never found an entrance within it. It was a chest of an oblong shape, made of acacia wood, twenty-seven inches broad and high and three feet long, and covered on all sides with the purest gold. It was ornamented on its upper surface with a border or rim of gold, and at equal distances, on each of the two sides, from the top, were two gold rings, in which were placed, to remain there perpetually, the rods of gold by which the ark was carried, and which continued with it after it was deposited in the temple. It was so situated in the *holy of holies* that the ends of the rods touched the *veil* which separated the two apartments of the tabernacle. Exod. xxv, 10–15 ; xxxvii, 1–9 ; 1 Kings viii, 8.

The *lid* or *cover* of the ark, *ἱλαστήριον ἐπίθημα*, was of the same length and breadth, and made of the purest gold. Over it, at the two extremities, were two cherubim, with their faces turned toward each other, and inclined a little to the lid, otherwise called the *mercy-seat*. Their wings, which were spread over the top of the ark, formed the throne of God the king, while the ark itself was his footstool. There was nothing within the ark excepting the two tables of stone, on which were inscribed the *ten fundamental laws* of the Jewish religion and commonwealth. A quantity of *manna* was laid up beside the ark in a *vase of gold*. Exod. xvii, 32–36 ; also the *rod of Aaron*, Num. xvii, 10 ; and a copy of the *Books of Moses*. Deut. xxxi, 26.

Temple of Solomon.

The temple was erected on the summit of Mount Moriah, encircled by a wall of hewn stone, rising up from the valleys around it, from four to six hundred feet in height. The area of the temple was about the eighth of a mile square. This area was divided into the *exterior* and *interior* courts, the latter of which was called the *court before the temple*, or the *court of the priests*. 1 Kings vi, 36 ; vii, 12 ; 2 Kings xxiii, 12 ; 2 Chron. iv, 9 ; xx, 5 ; Ezek. xl, 28.

Whether these two *courts* were separated from each other by a wall, or merely a lattice or *trellis*, does not clearly appear. 1 Kings vi, 1–38 ; vii, 13–51 ; 2 Chron. iii, 1, 4, 22.

There were various buildings and *apartments* in which provisions were kept, also the vases and other utensils which belonged to the temple, and some of which were occupied by the priests and Levites, while they were employed there in the fulfilment of their sacred duties. 1 Chron. ix, 26–33; xxiii, 28; xxviii, 12; 2 Chron. xxxi, 12; Jer. xxxv, 2–4; xxxvi, 10.

The *altar* in the interior court was built of *unhewn* stones. It was thirty feet long and fifteen high and broad, and covered with brass. 2 Chron. iv, 1–10.

The *vases*, and other utensils belonging to the altar, were much more numerous than in the tabernacle. 1 Kings vii, 40–47. The very large brazen *laver* called the *molten sea* was in the form of a half globe, forty-five feet in circumference, fifteen in diameter, and seven and a half in depth. It could contain three thousand baths, and was adorned, in its upper edge, with figures that resembled lilies in bloom. It was also enriched with various ornamental figures, and rested on the backs of twelve oxen, three facing each of the cardinal points. There were, in addition to the brazen sea, ten *smaller brazen lavers*, which were also set off with various ornaments, five on the north and five on the south side of the *court*. They rested on bases and wheels of brass, were each six feet in circumference, and held forty baths. The flesh of the victims that were sacrificed was washed in these lavers. 1 Kings vii, 27–39; 2 Chron. iv, 6.

The *sanctuary* was ninety feet long, thirty broad, and forty-five high, with the exception of the part called the *sanctissimum* or *most holy*, the height of which was only thirty feet, so that there remained above it a room fifteen feet high. The windows were latticed.

In front of the sanctuary was the *porch*, one hundred and eighty feet high, thirty broad from north to south, and fifteen long from east to west. 1 Kings vi, 3; 2 Chron. iii, 4. Two *columns of brass* were erected near the entrance of this *porch*, each eighteen feet in circumference. The one to the north was called *Jachin;* the other, to the south, was called *Boaz.* The height of the *shafts* of these columns was twenty-seven feet, the *capitals* seven and a half, and the *base* nineteen and a half, making in all forty-five feet. These pillars were profusely ornamented with carved representations of leaves, pomegranates, net, and lily work. They were hollow within, and the brass of which they were made was four inches thick. 1 Kings vii, 15–20; 2 Chron. iii, 15–17.

A *gallery* extended along the sides of the sanctuary, with the exception of the eastern, which was three stories high. It was constructed of beams and planks, and there was an ascent to it on the south by means of a flight of winding-stairs. 1 Kings vi, 5, 6–8. The sanctuary itself was constructed of square stones, covered with boards of cedar within and without, in which a variety of ornamental figures were cut, and which was overlaid with leaves of gold. The passage into the porch was very lofty and broad; but it was merely an open entrance, without any door. The entrance into the *sanctuary*, on the contrary, was closed by a valve or folding-door, made of the *oleaster* or wild olive, which was ornamented with specimens of carved work, in the shape of cherubim, palms, and flowers. It was covered with gold, and turned on golden hinges. 1 Kings vi, 33–35.

The door that opened into the *sanctissimum* or *holy of holies*, which was pentagonal in form, was adorned and enriched in the same way with that of the sanctuary. Both doors were covered with a veil of linen, wrought with embroidery.'

Within the sanctuary was the *altar of incense*, overlaid with gold, *ten tables*, also overlaid with gold, and ten *golden candlesticks*, five on the north and five on the south side. On these tables were placed twelve loaves and a hundred golden cups. The other vessels of the sanctuary were likewise more numerous than those in the tabernacle.

The *ark of the covenant* was placed in the *holy of holies*. Its position was such that the rods touched the veil, from which circumstance it may be inferred that the door of this apartment stood open. 1 Kings viii, 8; 2 Chron. v, 9.

Near the ark were two *cherubim*, made of the wood of

the wild olive and covered with gold, each of which was fifteen feet high, and each extended one of its wings over the ark to the middle of it, and the other to the wall. 1 Kings vi, 23–28; 2 Chron. iii, 10–13.

The *temple of Zerubbabel*, which was completed B. C. 515, was, in height and breadth, ninety feet. Its length is not known. It differed from Solomon's Temple in several respects, the more important of which were that there was only one candlestick and one golden table. The ark of the covenant, the sacred oil, the Urim and Thummim, and the sacred fire were gone, and also that singular cloud, the *Shekinah*, which anciently was seen over the tabernacle, and afterwards filled the temple. 2 Chron. v, 13, 14; vi, 1; vii, 1–3; 1 Kings viii, 10–12.

Herod rendered the temple, by repairs and additions, exceedingly magnificent. As improved by Herod, it had three *courts*, or open *areas*, each one of which was situated above the other. The first *court* was enclosed by that outer wall which has been described, and which was raised from the base of the mount. In the middle of this court was an ascent of four steps, which led to an enclosure of stone. On the gates that opened through this enclosure, and on the columns contiguous, were inscriptions in Hebrew, Greek and Latin, which interdicted, under penalty of death, any further entrance to the unclean and the Gentiles. Immediately back of this wall succeeded an ascent of fourteen steps, into a level space fifteen feet broad, which was succeeded by another ascent of five steps, to the gate of the second wall, which was sixty feet high outside, and thirty-seven within. This wall enclosed the *court of the Israelites*, while the *first* court, where the inscriptions were, was that of the *Gentiles.*

Between the courts of the Israelites and the Gentiles, on the east side, was the *court of the Hebrew women*, which was separated from the court of the Israelites by a wall so low as to permit them to see the men, while they themselves remained unseen. The entrance to the court of the women was through two gates, one on the north and the other on the south side.

The *quadrangular area*, immediately around the altar and the sanctuary, was called the *court of the priests*. It was surrounded by a low but elegant enclosure, so that the people had an opportunity of looking into it, while, at the same time, they were not permitted to enter.

The largest *gate* was situated in the outer wall, on the east side. It was called *The Beautiful*, *θύρα ὡραία*, and was splendidly ornamented with Corinthian brass, which was reckoned preferable to silver or gold. This gate equalled the sanctuary in height, which, in the highest place, was more than a hundred and fifty feet. The folds of this gate were seventy-five feet high and sixty broad, and were covered with plates of gold and silver. The ascent to it was from the valley of Kedron, over many steps. To the *south* of the temple there was a valley six hundred feet deep. There was a gate, nevertheless, in that direction, leading from the wall into the lower part of the city. On the west side two gates led, by numerous steps, into the valley below, which ran in a southern direction, and was filled with houses. On the western side there were also two other gates besides these, one of which connected the temple with Mount Zion, by means of a bridge over the valley, and the other conducted into the lower part of the city. On the *north* there was no gate, but the tower or castle of Antonia was connected with the temple by means of a subterranean passage. On the north and south sides of the *inner* wall there were six gates, three on each side, which faced each other. On the eastern side there was a gate which corresponded to The Beautiful Gate, and led into the court of the women. The western side of the inner wall, which was contiguous to the sanctuary, had no gate. All these gates had folds. They were forty-five feet high and twenty-two broad. The thresholds and the posts, as well as the gates, were covered with silver and gold. They were all surmounted with a sort of turret, which increased the height to sixty feet. Around the gates were vacant spaces, where the people were in the habit of assembling.

A *triple porch* extended around the southern wall of the *court* of the Gentiles; but the porches that were contiguous to the northern, eastern, and western sides or walls of this court, were merely *double*. The porches in the court of the Israelites were double likewise. Each double porch rested on a triple, and each triple porch on a *quadruple* row of columns, the last row being contiguous to the wall. The columns, which were Corinthian, were hewn out of white marble, and were thirty-seven feet high; but the entire altitude, including pedestals, capitals, cornice, and roof, was nearly sixty-five. The columns were so large that three men could scarcely extend their arms round them. The roof, which was flat, was constructed of cedar-wood. Each of these porches was forty-five feet broad and seventy-five feet high, with this exception, that the middle one, on the south side, was sixty-two feet broad and one hundred and fifty high, from the roof of which to the valley below was seven hundred and fifty feet. It was this porch, without doubt, that St. Matthew (iv, 5) called πτερύγιον τõν ἱεροῦ, the *pinnacle of the temple.* The eastern porch of the court of the Gentiles was called Solomon's.

All the porches were paved with marble of various colours. Those in the court of the Gentiles were resorted to by money-changers and those who sold animals destined for the altar.

The altar for the victims was constructed of unhewn stones, twenty-two feet high and seventy-five in length and breadth, the corners of which projected upwards like horns. The ascent to it was on the south side.

The *sanctuary*, or *temple* proper, was constructed of white marble, and higher than the *court* of the priests. It was approached by an ascent of twelve steps. The *porch* of the sanctuary, πρόναος, was a hundred and fifty feet high and as many broad. The open space which served as an entrance into it, and which was destitute of folds or door of any sort, was one hundred and five feet high and thirty-seven broad.

The *interior* of the porch was one hundred and thirty-five feet high, seventy-five from north to south, and thirty from east to west; so that on the north and south there was room for recesses or chambers, of thirty feet in extent.

The entrance, which opened into the sanctuary, was seventy-seven feet high and twenty-four broad. Over it was the figure of a *vine*, in gold, of the size of a man, and loaded with golden clusters. This entrance was closed with an embroidered veil. It was in the porch of the temple that Judas cast down the thirty pieces of silver. Matt. xxvii, 5.

The *sanctuary* itself was thirty feet broad, ninety long, and ninety high. It was surrounded on three sides with a structure three stories high, making an altitude of sixty feet. It equalled the porch in breadth, into the two chambers of which there was an entrance from it. On the flat roof of the sanctuary were erected long, sharp rods of iron, covered with gold.

From the sanctuary we enter the *sanctissimum*, or *holy of holies*, which was thirty feet long, thirty broad, and thirty high, so that there were two stories above, each of thirty cubits. In the sanctuary were the golden candlestick, the golden table, and the altar of incense; but in the *most holy* place nothing was deposited. The walls within and without were covered with gold, and it was separated from the sanctuary by an embroidered veil.

Synagogues.

Although the sacrifices could not be offered, except in the tabernacle or temple, all the other exercises of religion were restricted to no particular place. Accordingly we find that the praises of God were sung, at a very ancient period, in the schools of the prophets; and those who felt any particular interest in religion, were assembled by the seers on the Sabbath and the new moons, for prayers and religious instruction. 1 Sam. x, 5–11; xix, 18–24; 2 Kings iv, 23.

During the Babylonish captivity the Jews, who were then deprived of their customary religious privileges, were wont to collect around some prophet, or other pious man, who taught them and their children in religion, exhorted to good conduct, and read one of the sacred books. Ezek. xiv, 1; xx, 1; Dan. vi, 11; Neh. viii, 18. These assemblies or meetings became, in progress of time, fixed to certain places, and a regular order was observed in them. This was the origin of synagogues.

In speaking of synagogues it is worthy of notice that they were first established in the reign of the Maccabean princes. In *foreign* countries it is supposed they existed at an earlier day, inasmuch as the apostles found them wherever they travelled among the Jews. They were built in imitation of the temple, with a *court* and *porches*. In the centre of the court is a chapel, supported by four columns, in which is placed, on an elevation, a roll of the Book of the Law, which is publicly read on appointed days. The seats nearest the chapel were called the *uppermost*, and esteemed the most honourable. Matt. xxiii, 6; James ii, 3.

The *proseuchæ*, *προσευχαί*, are supposed to have been smaller synagogues, where the Jews assembled for religious exercises. They were distinguished from the synagogue proper in not being set apart especially for divine worship. Acts xvi, 13–16. When the Jews had no synagogues they held their religious meetings in dwelling-houses. The apostles imitated them in this; hence we hear of *Churches* in houses. Rom. xvi, 5; 1 Cor. xvi, 19; Col. iv, 15; Philem. 2; Acts ii, 46; v, 42.

Συναγωγή means *literally* a convention or assembly; *tropically*, it is used as the *place* of meeting. In the same way *ἐκκλησία* means literally a calling together; tropically, the *place* of convocation.

SACRED SEASONS.

Sabbath.

In speaking of *sacred seasons*, the *Sabbath*, *σάββατον*, is particularly worthy of notice. The practice of consecrating the Sabbath, or *seventh day of the week*, originated from what is stated in Gen. ii, 1–3. That it was observed from the creation is evident from the form of the commandment, (Exod. xx, 8,) *Remember the Sabbath*, &c. It was no *new* thing, and it had been previously spoken of in Exod. xvi, 22–30.

The Sabbath was *designed* to exhibit a symbolic representation that God was the creator of the universe, and ought to be worshipped; hence the same punishment, viz., death, was attached to a violation of this institution, that there was to an open defection from the true God. Exod. xxxv, 2; Num. xv, 32–36.

The more recent Jews distinguished certain Sabbaths by particular names. The Sabbath, for instance, immediately preceding the Passover, was denominated the *Great Sabbath*. John xix, 31. Another kind of Sabbath is called the *second first*, *σάββατον δευτερόπρωτον*. Luke vi, 1. It is difficult to tell what this meant.

The name of Sabbath, which signifies *rest*, is an intimation that all ordinary labour is to be suspended on that day. There were exceptions to this in the following things:—The healing of the sick was not forbidden; nor a walk or journey of a thousand geometrical paces; nor the plucking a few ears of corn to appease hunger; nor the performing any act of necessity, such as feeding cattle, plucking them from the ditch, &c. Matt. xii, 1–15; Luke vi, 1–5; xiii, 10–17; Mark iii, 2; John v, 2–18; ix, 1–34.

Certain duties of a religious nature were not prohibited, such as circumcision on the eighth day, the slaughter and burning of victims, and the labours in general connected with the observances practised in the tabernacle. Lev. vi, 8; Num. xxviii, 3; Matt. xii, 2; John vii, 23.

Sorrow on the Sabbath day was an indication of great calamity. Hosea ii, 11; Lam. ii, 6. The Hebrews spent the day in dancing, singing songs, and playing on instruments. These, however, were religious exercises. Exod. xv, 20, 21; xxxii, 6, 7; 2 Sam. vi, 14; Psa. lxviii, 25–27; cxlix, 3; cl, 4.

Sabbatic Year.

As the period of seven days was completed by the Sabbath, so a period of seven years was completed by the *Sabbatic year.* It was the design of this year to afford a longer opportunity for impressing on the mind the great truth that God was the *creator and governor of the world, and alone ought to be worshipped.* During the feast of tabernacles this year the law was to be publicly read for eight days together, either in the tabernacle or temple. Deut. xxxi, 10–13. Debts were not collected, (Deut. xv, 1, 2,) though they were not *cancelled.*

Year of Jubilee.

The Jubilee followed seven Sabbatic years, i. e., it was on the fiftieth year. Lev. xxv, 8–11. The return of the year of jubilee was announced on the tenth day of the seventh month, or *Tishni*—October—being the day of propitiation or atonement, by the *sound of the trumpet.* Lev. xxv, 8–13; xxvii, 24; Num. xxxvi, 4; Isa. lxi, 1, 2.

All the servants of Hebrew origin, on the year of jubilee, obtained their freedom. Lev. xxv, 39–46; Jer. xxxiv, 7, *et seq.*

All the fields throughout the country, and the houses in the cities and villages of the Levites and priests, which had been sold on the preceding years, were returned on the year of jubilee to the sellers, with the exception of those which had been consecrated to God, and had not been redeemed before the return of said year. Lev. xxv, 10, 13, 17, 24, 28; xxvii, 16–21.

Debtors, for the most part, pledged or mortgaged their land to a creditor, or left it to his use till the time of payment; so that it was in effect *sold* to the creditor, and was accordingly restored to the debtor on the year of jubilee. At this time there was a general cancelling of debts.

New Moons.

The return of the new moons was announced by the sounding of the silver trumpets. It was commanded that, on the new moons, in addition to the daily sacrifices, two bullocks, a ram, and seven sheep, should be offered to God, together with a meal-offering and a libation. These were to constitute the burnt-offering, and a goat the sin-offering.

Passover.

The festival of the Passover was instituted for the purpose of preserving the memory of the deliverance of the Hebrews from Egyptian servitude, and of the safety of their first-born on the night in which the first-born of the Egyptians perished. Exod. xii. It was celebrated for seven days, viz., from the 15th to the 21st of April. Exod. xii, 1–28; xxiii, 15; Lev. xxiii, 4–8; Num. xxviii, 16–25; Deut. xvi, 1–8. During the whole of this period the people ate unleavened bread, and hence it was called the feast of unleavened bread. Exod. xii, 18; xiii, 6, 7; xxiii, 15; Lev. xxiii, 6; Num. xxviii, 17. On the 10th day of the month the master, or head of a family, separated a ram or a goat of a year old, which he slew on the 14th, between the *two evenings*, before the altar. Deut. xvi, 2, 5, 6. The priest sprinkled the blood upon the bottom of the altar. In Egypt it was sprinkled on the lintels and door-posts. Exod. xii, 7. The ram or kid was roasted whole, with two spits thrust through it, the one lengthwise, and the other transversely crossing, near the fore legs, so that the animal was in a manner *crucified*. Thus roasted, it was served up with a salad of wild and bitter herbs, and with the flesh of other sacrifices. Not fewer than ten, nor more than twenty persons, were admitted to these sacred feasts. The command not to break a bone was observed ever after the original foundation of this feast.

The master of the family, after the paschal supper is prepared, blesses the bread, and breaks it, and divides it among the rest, who are seated around him, so that each one may receive a part, and has liberty, if he chooses, to dip it, before eating, into a vessel of sauce.

The *third* cup of wine which is drunk on this occasion is properly termed the *cup of benediction*. Matt. xxvi, 27; 1 Cor. x, 16. After this, songs of praise are sung, and another cup is drank, (Mark xiv, 26,) and another Psalm sung. The wine is mingled with water.

On the second day of the Passover, i. e., the 16th, a sheaf of barley was offered up; also a lamb of a year old, for a burnt-offering; also a meal-offering and a libation. On every day of the Paschal week there were offerings more than usual, and victims were immolated for sin. Num. xxviii, 16–25.

Pentecost.

Forty-nine days after the 16th of April introduced the *Pentecost*, πεντηκοστή, i. e., the *fiftieth*. It was also called the *feast of weeks*, from the circumstance that it followed a succession of seven weeks. Exod. xxxiv, 22; Lev. xxiii, 15, 16; Num. xxviii, 26; Deut. xvi, 10; Acts ii, 1. It was a festival of thanks for the harvest, and was accordingly called the *feast of the harvest*. And it was for the same reason that two loaves, made of new meal, and the tenth part of an ephah of grain, were offered as the first-fruits. Lev. xxiii, 17; Num. xxviii, 26. Hence the Pentecost is sometimes called the *day of the first-fruits*. On this day many Jews from foreign countries assembled at Jerusalem.

Feast of Tabernacles.

The feast of tabernacles was celebrated from the 15th to the 23d of October. The last day was the one most particularly distinguished as a festival. Leviticus xxiii, 34–42; Num. xxix, 12–35; Deut. xvi, 12–15; Neh. viii, 18; John vii, 2–37.

It was instituted in memory of the journey through the Arabian wilderness. During its continuance the Jews dwelt in booths or tents, as they did in their journey from Egypt. Lev. xxiii, 42, 43. It was also called the *feast of the gathering*, in honour of the vintage. It was a season of great joy among the Jews.

More public sacrifices were directed to be offered on this occasion than on the other festivals. Num. xxix, 12–39; Deut. xvi, 14, 15; Lev. xxiii, 38–40.

The *fifth* day before the feast of tabernacles, viz., the 10th of October, was the day of *propitiation* or *atonement*. Lev. xvi, 1–34; Exod. xxiii, 26–30; Num. xxix, 1–11. It was a day of fasting, and the only one during the whole of the year when food was interdicted from evening to evening. Lev. xxiii, 27–29; xxv, 9.

The high priest himself conducted the sacred services of this day, and the ceremonies now to be mentioned, which differed from those on other occasions, were performed by him alone. When he had washed himself in water, put on his white linen, hose, and coat, and adjusted his girdle, he conducted to the altar, with a sacerdotal mitre on his head, a bullock, destined to be slain for the sins of himself and his family; also two goats, for the sins of the people; the one of which was selected by lot, to be sacrificed to God, the other was permitted to make an unmolested escape. Lev. xvi, 6–19. Presently he slew the bullock for his own sins, and the goat which had been selected by lot for that purpose for the sins of the people. He then filled a censer with burning coals from the altar, and putting two handfuls of incense into a vase, he bore the incense into the *sanctissimum*, or *holy of holies.* Having here poured the incense, he returned, took the blood of the bullock and the goat, and went again into the *most* holy place. With his finger he first sprinkled the blood of the bullock, and afterwards the blood of the goat, upon the lid of the ark of the covenant; and seven times, also, he sprinkled it upon the floor before the ark. He then returned from the *most* holy, to the *holy* place or sanctuary, and sprinkled the horns of the golden altar, which was there placed, with the blood of the bullock and the goat, and scattered the blood seven times over the surface of the *altar*. This was done as an expiation for the uncleanness and sins of the children of Israel. Lev. xvi, 11–19. The high priest, then going into the *court* of the tabernacle, placed both hands, with great solemnity, on the head of the *scape-goat*, as a symbolic representation that the animal was loaded with the sins of the people. It was then delivered to a man, who led it away into the wilderness, and let it go free, to signify the liberation of the Israelites from the punishment due to their sins. The goat which was *slain* for the sins of the people, and the bullock slain for those of the high priest, were designed to signify that they were guilty, and that they merited punishment; and were to be burnt whole beyond the limits of the camp or the city. Lev. xvi, 20, 22, 26, 28. The high priest then took off his white vestments, and assuming the splendid robes of his office, offered a holocaust for himself and the people, and then offered another sin-offering. Lev. xvi, 23–25; Num. xxix, 7–11.

Fasts.

The Hebrews were in the habit of fasting whenever any calamity came upon them. Judg. xx, 26; 1 Sam. vii, 6; xxxi, 13; 2 Sam. iii, 35; Isa. lviii, 3–12. About the time of the captivity they instituted anniversary fast days, as follows:—

1. The seventeenth of July, in memory of the capture of Jerusalem. Jer. lii, 6, 7; Zech. viii, 19.

2. The ninth day of August, in memory of the burning of the temple. Zech. vii, 3; viii, 19.

3. The third day of October, in memory of the death of Gedaliah. Jer. xl, 4; Zech. vii, 5; viii, 19.

4. The tenth day of January, in memory of the commencement of the attack on Jerusalem. Zech. viii, 19.

Feasts or Festivals.

The feast of *purim*, or lot, was held on the fifteenth day of March, in commemoration of the deliverance of the Jews from the cruel designs of Haman. Esther iii, 7; ix, 26.

The *festival of encœnia, or the purification of the temple.* The temple was profaned by Antiochus Epiphanes in the year 167, and was purified in the year 164 before Christ. Its dedication, at the time of its being purified, was celebrated eight days with many sacrifices, beginning on the twenty-fifth of December. This dedication was converted into an anniversary. 1 Mac. iv, 52, 59; 2 Mac. x, 1–8; John x, 22.

SACRED THINGS.

Sacrifices.

A *sacrifice* is that which is offered directly to God, and is in some way destroyed or changed, which is done, as far as respects the flesh employed in the sacrifice, by *burning it*, and as far as concerns the *libation*, in this: in a *sacrifice*, there must be a real change or destruction of the thing offered; whereas an oblation is but a simple offering or gift. It is accordingly to be understood, that neither the wood necessary for cherishing the fire of the altar, nor any presents which might at any time be offered for the use of the temple or sanctuary, are properly called sacrifices.

Sacrifices were coeval with the existence of the human race. Gen. iv, 3–5; viii, 20; xii, 7; xiii, 4; xv, 9–21;

xxii, 13. Some of the sacrifices that were authorized by Moses were *bloody*, (slain victims,) others were *not;* the latter consisted of cakes, wafers, meal, and libations of wine. The bloody sacrifices were some of them *expiatory* and some of them *thank-offerings*. The expiatory offerings were either holocausts, sacrifices for sin, or trespass-offerings. The holocausts were offered for the whole people. The expiatory secured expiation in a *civil* point of view. Sacrifices of this kind were slain to the north of the altar, and were regarded as *most holy*. The *thank-offering* was slain to the south of the altar, parts of which were burnt, parts were given to the priests, and parts to the person who brought the sacrifice.

The victims to be offered were only of the *ox kind*, and *sheep*, and *goats*—no wild beasts being permitted; also, *turtle-doves* and *young pigeons*. They must all be perfect, having no defect.

The person who offered the victim presented it before God, i e., led it before the altar in the *court*, with its head turned towards the door of the sanctuary. The offerer placed his hand upon the head of the victim, and by this imposition the victim was *substituted* in the place of the person who brought it to the altar.

Holocausts were sacrifices in which the victims were *wholly* consumed. The victims were bullocks of three years old, goats and lambs of a year old, turtle-doves and young pigeons.

The victims selected for *sin-offerings* were as follows, viz., a *bullock* for the high priest, a *goat* for the civil magistrate, a *kid* or *lamb* for private persons, a *turtle-dove* and a *young pigeon* also a *lamb* for mothers at childbirth, a *goat*, *dove*, or *pigeon* for a leper, and a dove or pigeon for a contaminated Nazarite.

Trespass-offerings were not required of the people as a body. They were offered by persons who, through ignorance, mistake, or want of reflection, had committed trespasses, and were subsequently made conscious of their error. Lev. iv, 1–16; v, 1–19.

Peace or *thank-offerings* were sacrifices offered as an indication of gratitude, and were accompanied with unleavened cakes and oil. Lev. iii, 1–17; vii, 11, 23, 27, 28, 35.

First-Born.

The *first-born*, both of men and animals, was to be consecrated to God. The first-born children were to be presented before the Lord, and were to be redeemed according to the estimation of the priest; but the amount of the sum paid in this redemption could not exceed five shekels. They could not be redeemed before the age of a month, and for the most part were not so till the ceremony of purification for childbirth. Num. xviii, 14–16; Exod. xiii, 13; Luke ii, 22.

The first-born cattle of sheep and goats, from eight days to a year old, were to be offered in sacrifice, and the parts designated being burnt, the remainder was left to the priests. Num. xviii, 17, 18; Lev. xxvii, 26. It was in this way that the Hebrews exhibited their gratitude to God, who preserved their first-born in Egypt from the impending destruction. Exod. xiii, 2, 11, 16; Num. iii, 12, 13. The first-born sons were by birth *priests*, and were to be redeemed from serving at the altar. Num. iii, 20–51.

First-Fruits.

The first sheaf of barley, on the second day of the Passover, and the first loaves on the feast of Pentecost, were offered in the name of the *people*. *Individuals* were obliged to offer the first-fruits of the vine, of fruit-trees, of their grain, honey, and wool, by means of which offerings they exhibited that gratitude which was due to God for the country he had given them. Exod. xxiii, 19; Lev. ii, 12; Num. xv, 17–21; xviii, 11–13; Deut. xxvi, 1–11. The offerings thus made became the property of the priests. Num. xviii, 11–13; Deut. xviii, 4.

Second first-fruits were appropriated to the eucharistical sacrifices.

Tithes.

Tithes are very ancient, and were exacted in the earliest times among almost all nations. Abraham offered the tithes of his spoils to Melchizedec, priest of the most high God. Gen. xiv, 20. Jacob vowed unto God the tenth of all his income. This vow was observed by himself and all his posterity. Gen. xxviii, 22. Tithing is mentioned as a practice well known. Deut. xii, 11, 17, 19; xiv, 22, 23. Tithes were presented every year at the tabernacle, with one exception. Every third year they were permitted to make a feast of them at their own houses, for servants, widows, orphans, the poor, and the Levites. Deut. xiv, 28, 29; xxvi, 12–15. Tithes were of the *first* and *second* kind. Lev. xxvii, 30; Num. xviii, 20–24; Deut. xiv, 22, 23; Neh. xiii, 5–12.

Sacred Oil.

The *sacred oil* with which the tabernacle, the ark of the covenant, the golden candlestick, the table, the altar of incense, the altar of burnt-offerings, the laver, and all the sacred utensils, and, indeed, the priests themselves were anointed, was composed of the oil of olives, the richest myrrh, cassia, cinnamon, and sweet calamus. Exod. xxx, 20–23.

Oaths.

The person who confirmed his assertion by a voluntary oath pronounced the same with his right hand elevated. Sometimes the swearer omitted the imprecation, as if he were afraid to utter it. Gen. xiv, 22, 23; Psa. cvi, 26; lxxx, 18; Ezek. xvii, 18.

When the oath was *exacted* by a judge it was put in form, and the person responded, "*So let it be*," or, "*Thou hast said.*" Num. v, 19–22; Lev. v, 1; 1 Kings xxii, 16; Deut. xxvii, 15–26.

As an oath was an appeal to God, the taking a false oath was considered a heinous crime, and perjury was accordingly forbidden in those words, "*Thou shalt not take the name of the Lord thy God in vain.*" Exod. xx, 6. It was common in Egypt to swear by the life of the king. The Hebrews also swore by cities and consecrated places, such as Hebron, Shilo, and Jerusalem.

The Jews, in the time of Christ, were in the habit of swearing by the *altar*, by *Jerusalem*, by *heaven*, by the *earth*, by *themselves*, by their *heads*, by the *gold of the temple*, by *sacrifices*, &c., &c. Because the name of God was not in these oaths they considered them as imposing but small obligation. Matt. v, 33–37; xxiii, 16–22.

Vows.

Vows were solemn promises made by persons to consecrate themselves to God, or *something* which they intended to set apart for his service. The earliest vow is that of Jacob. Gen. xxviii, 22. The father and husband had power of annulling the vows of a daughter or a wife. Num. xxx, 2–17.

Vows were of two kinds, *affirmative* or *negative*. *Affirmative* vows consisted in the consecration of money, lands, houses, animals, servants, sons, and the person himself to God. *Negative* vows consisted in abstaining from anything lawful, and were denominated a restraint on the appetite. The principal among this class of vows was that of the Nazarites.

Prayers.

It was at first an unspoken emotion of reverence and gratitude to God that constituted prayer. *Supplications* were subsequently added. Gen. xii, 8; xxi, 33; xxiv, 26–48; xxvi, 25; xxxii, 9–12; Deut. xxvi, 3, 10, 13, 15.

Our Lord's prayer (Matt. vi, 9–13) is a selection of the most devotional and appropriate sentiments from the Jewish formularies extant in his time.

Hymns were sung on particular occasions, accompanied with sacred dances and instruments of music. Exod. xv; Judg. v; 1 Kings viii, 14, 21, 23, 53; Psa. lxxii, 20; Neh. viii, 6.

Private prayer was uttered *aloud*. 1 Sam. i, 12–15; Luke xviii, 10–14. The Hebrews prayed in various attitudes, such as standing, kneeling, and prostration on the ground. They raised their hands, and sometimes smote upon their breasts. Anciently there were no fixed hours for prayer. Daniel, at a more recent period, prayed three times a day.

Worship was held in the synagogues on the Sabbath day. The exercises consisted in reading from the Mosaic law, singing the doxology, and reading from the prophets. The apostles gathered the first Churches. After they were excluded from them they assembled at evening, at the house of some friend, which was lighted for the purpose with lamps. Acts xx, 7–11. The reader or speaker stood—the others sat. All arose in time of prayer. Whatever was stated in a foreign tongue was immediately interpreted. 1 Cor. xiv, 1–33.

NOTE.—The above part was compiled from the following authors, viz.:—Jahn, Michaelis, and Kitto. Should the reader wish to extend his researches, he may consult the writings of the above authors with great profit. It is modestly conceived, however, that all essential to Biblical archæology will be found in the above pages.

Part Sixth.

BIBLICAL ETHNOGRAPHY.

CHAPTER I.

THE FIRST RACES OF MANKIND.

In treating of the nations of the Bible, as we have of the times, manners, and customs, events, countries, and languages of the Bible, it shall be our object to confine ourselves strictly to those mentioned in its history, and in doing so shall call attention to them, as far as practicable, in the order in which they occur in the sacred record. The nations of the Bible may be divided into the *ante* and *post* diluvian. In regard to the former we know but little. The period from the Creation to the Deluge embraced ten generations, and it is supposed, by one of the ablest writers on the patriarchal age, that the population of the earth was as great at that time as it is at the present. Whether the inhabitants before the Deluge were united in one or divided into many nations, we have no means of knowing. One thing is certain: the race had become numerous and powerful, as well as wicked and revengeful; and, in the days of Enoch and Noah, their extraordinary crimes involved the whole race, with the exception of one family, in destruction. We shall not stop here to discuss the question in regard to the unity of the human race, touching their oneness of origin. These questions are now undergoing an investigation, in the hands of naturalists and historians, and they do not, in the least, affect the verity of the sacred record. Whether mankind proceeded from one or a dozen pairs is a matter of no consequence, as it does not involve the Bible account of our common origin.

It is enough for us to show *what nations* took their origin in Adam, and the several relations they sustained to the events of the Bible. It is the subject of *Biblical ethnography* we propose to discuss in this chapter, and hence we shall nowhere run across, nor even so much as touch the lines of controversy, in relation to the primitive races of the earth.

The generations of the Bible are given in clear historical narrative, unmixed with fable, and present an unbroken stream from Adam to Noah, embracing a period of near two thousand years. From the sons of Noah, Europe, Asia, and Africa were peopled by the different races which originally inhabited them. From Japheth descended the Germans, Turks, Hungarians, Fins, Medes, Spaniards, Greeks, Romans, Tartars, Muscovites, and Thracians. This is denominated the Caucasian, or white race. From Shem proceeded the Persians, Assyrians, Jews, Arabians, Lydians, and Syrians. This is denominated the olive, or Mongolian race. From Ham descended the Babylonians, Egyptians, Libyans, and Phœnicians. Ham was the father of the black race.

These sons, and their descendants, went out from the valley of the Euphrates, to build cities and found nations. As population increased, they conceived the idea of building a tower of immense size and height, that would prove a bond of union, and form a great central point for all the families and tribes. Up to this time there was but one language, and Jehovah, to break up this arrangement, evidently with the design of scattering them abroad, that all parts of the earth might be peopled, confounded their language, or, what was equivalent, gave them different forms of speech. From this confusion of tongues the tower was afterwards named Babel, as significant of the miracle which had been wrought by the Almighty.

CHAPTER II.

THE ASSYRIANS AND BABYLONIANS.

From this date the Assyrian empire took its rise, about one hundred and twenty-seven years after the Deluge. The Assyrians derive their name from Ashur, who, according to the Mosaic account, left the land of Shinar after the confusion of Babel, and built Nineveh and other cities. The city of Nineveh was rich in magnificence beyond any city of antiquity. The history of the Assyrians is involved in the greatest obscurity, and all the satisfactory information we have respecting them is drawn from the sacred annals. The Babylonian empire, which was founded about the same time, by Nimrod, "the mighty hunter" of Scripture, lay on both sides of the Euphrates, near its mouth, and also bore the name of Chaldea. It is thought by some that before the confusion of tongues Babylonia was founded. The city of Babylon, built upon the site of Babel, was made, in after years, to excel, if possible, in magnificence, the proud city of Nineveh. The Assyrians and Babylonians were governed by monarchs whose will was supreme. They were at once the heads of Church as well as State, and claimed divine honours. Their religion was a species of *Sabeanism.* They were considerably advanced in the mechanic and fine arts. They were among the earliest nations that possessed the art of alphabetical writing. Their language was the Semitic, of which the Hebrew, Arabic, and Syriac are branches, the characters of which are to this day undecipherable. Should a key to this long-lost language be discovered, the characters which have recently been found engraven on brick and tile, and alabaster slabs, as brought to light by the excavations of Layard, will throw much valuable light upon the history of these once vast and flourishing empires. The nations have passed away like their mighty cities, and the descendants of Ishmael have taken their places, only, however, to wander in wildness over their plains and guard their ruins. The destruction of Babylon and Nineveh were of divine appointment, and serve as melancholy memorials of the fate of all nations that forget God. Belshazzar having taken, with impious hands, the holy vessels of the temple of the Lord, and prostituted them to the vile purposes of his midnight bacchanal, the handwriting of God, interpreted by Daniel, revealed the fate of his kingdom, and, on the same night, Cyrus having diverted the course of the river, his army entered the city and slew the king, and the empire passed under the dominion of the Persians.

CHAPTER III.

THE EGYPTIANS.

We shall next call attention to the Egyptian nation. This nation, founded by Menes in the year of the world 2188, is remarkably identified with the Bible. Its history, is interwoven with some of the most interesting events of the sacred narrative, and hence must be deeply interesting to the Biblical scholar. According to the commonly-received standard of chronology, the Egyptian empire was founded about one hundred and three years after the Assyrian; though in regard to this there is no certain knowledge. Egypt is still, though in ruins, a land of wonders. Obelisks, sphinxes, tombs, temples, and pyramids, many of which are standing almost as perfect as when they were finished by the artist two thousand years ago, meet the eye of the traveller whereever he goes. The "land of Ham" was early peopled with the dispersed from Babel, and the rich and fertile valley of the Nile presented even greater attractions to the adventurer than those of the Euphrates and Tigris. Here were the magnificent cities of Thebes and Memphis. In an early day Egypt was invaded by shepherd kings from Arabia, who possessed themselves of a part of the country. Abraham visited the city of Memphis, and was received at the court of the reigning Pharaoh with great hospitality. About two hundred years subsequent to the departure of Abraham from Egypt, a melancholy affair arose in the house and family of Jacob. The peculiar partiality shown by this patriarch for one of his sons, elicited the envy and consequent enmity of the rest, and they made the beloved of their father a victim of that enmity. They determined on putting him to death, but commuted it to bondage and expatriation. Arabian merchants, on their way to Egypt, purchased Joseph, and sold him to a captain of Pharaoh's guard, named Potiphar. While serving in the house of his master, he was charged by his mistress with a crime of which he was not guilty, and thrust into prison. While there he interpreted Pharaoh's dreams, in relation to the years of plenty and famine, was restored to liberty, and made vice-regent over all Egypt. During the prevalence of the famine the brethren of Joseph came into Egypt to purchase corn. A recognition and reconciliation took place, and the whole family, on the invitation of Pharaoh and Joseph, consisting of seventy persons, removed from Canaan to Egypt, and settled in Goshen. Here they led a pastoral life, and multiplied exceedingly, under the blessing of God. The days of Jacob were numbered, and, obtaining a promise of burial in his native land, he departed this life, was embalmed, and borne to Machpelah, by a procession of Egyptian magnificence which peculiarly impressed the Canaanites, where he was entombed beside those whom living he loved, and from whom in death he desired not to be separated.

After living in Egypt nearly a hundred years, Joseph also finished his day and slept with his fathers. He was also embalmed, and placed in a sarcophagus in Egypt. After Joseph's death, with that of all his brethren and his generation, there arose another king who "knew not Joseph"—

supposed to be one of the shepherd kings—who, envying the prosperity of the Israelites, and fearing their power, devised means for their destruction. A decree was passed that all the male children should be cast into the river. While this decree was in force Moses was born. When he was three months old his mother made an ark of bulrushes, and, placing the child therein, deposited it among the flags, near the bank of the river. Little did that fond mother know that the fate of Egypt and Israel was contained in that frail vessel. He who guided Joseph into Egypt, and preserved him there, watched over Moses, and, by a wonderful train of providences, he was, like Joseph, introduced to royalty, and made an heir to the crown. When he arrived at maturity he espoused the cause of his oppressed and down-trodden people, and was obliged to flee from the country and take refuge in the mountains of Media. While there the Lord Jehovah appeared to him on Horeb, and, investing him with power, commissioned him to return to Egypt and deliver his brethren from bondage. On the refusal of Pharaoh to let the people go, the Almighty, by the hand of Moses, sent upon the whole land the most wonderful judgments. After a residence in Egypt of four hundred and thirty years, during which the children of Israel suffered many cruel hardships from their oppressors, upwards of six hundred thousand men, besides women and children, entered upon their journey to the land which the Lord had promised to their fathers. This happened during the reign of Thothmes the Third. This monarch succeeded in expelling the Hyk-sos from the country, who had kept possession of Lower Egypt for two hundred and fifty-nine years.

It will be interesting to consider the condition of Egypt at this period. It was the most celebrated for its learning, opulence, and magnificent monuments, of any country in the world. It had reached a high state of cultivation in the arts. The mysterious rites of its worship, the grandeur of its morality, and, above all, the perplexing enigma of its written monuments, threw an impenetrable veil over its history. The learned approached this shadowy land as if, in the most obvious facts, they had to decipher a hieroglyphic legend, and inclined to look upon the Egyptians as a people that, even in the more modern periods of their history, retained the faint tints and ill-defined traits of remote antiquity, and which, consequently, might boast an antiquity beyond computation. By the persevering study of numerous scholars, at the head of whom stand Young and Champollion, the mysteries hidden beneath their hieroglyphics have been brought to light, and the lost history of this people, thus revived, takes its stand by the side of other empires. The paintings and sculptures found upon existing monuments reveal all the processes of the arts and of domestic life, the manners and customs of the earliest ages, with a definiteness and minute accuracy surpassing the most lucid and truthful narrative. The whole public and private life—from the bloody arena of mailed warriors to the puppet-show, from the dignified monarch to the nursery sports of children—is engraved and painted on these enduring monuments—fixed and changeless as eternity—ever ready to reveal to the student the events of ages gone by.

From this time on to the close of their history as a nation, the Egyptians were almost constantly engaged in offensive or defensive wars with contiguous nations. Five hundred years after the departure of the Israelites, Shishak, king of Egypt, with an immense army, aided by the Ethiopians, invaded Judea, and plundered Jerusalem.

Two hundred years later, An′y-sis the Blind was expelled by Sab′a-co, an Ethiopian conqueror, and a dynasty of three kings reigned in succession on the united thrones of Egypt and Ethiopia. After another period of one hundred years, Psammeticus obtained supreme power, and with him terminated all historical uncertainty. A few years subsequently, Pharaoh Necho subdued all Asia, as far as the Euphrates. He was finally defeated by Nebuchadnezzar. Pharaoh Necho was succeeded by Psammis, and Pharaoh Hophra, and Amasis, and, finally, by Psammenitus, the last of Egyptian kings. Cambyses, the Persian monarch, invaded Egypt; the Egyptian army was entirely overthrown, the nobles all put to death, with their king, and their wives and children reduced to slavery. Cambyses slew all the sacred animals of the Egyptians, destroyed their altars and idols, scourged their priests as slaves, and pillaged their temples. They made many ineffectual efforts to regain their independence, but prophecy had sealed the fate of the nation, and it was made desolate, and dispersed among the countries around them.

CHAPTER IV.

THE JEWS.

THE nation which now claims our attention as the most prominent and eventful nation of the Bible, has been designated by several names, as *Hebrews*, *Israelites*, and *Jews;* these having been given to them in the successive periods of their history. The last is the name by which they have been called from the days of Judah, and is the cognomen by which they are called to the present day.

Without any reference to its religious history, this nation is perhaps the most remarkable in the annals of mankind. It sprang from one definite parent stock, in the year of the world 2000, and has ever since retained its individual, isolated character, amid an almost infinite variety of character. The Jews were called to be a "peculiar people," and they have ever been known as such, whether united in national sovereignty, under varying forms of government, or expelled from their native land and dispersed among other nations. They constitute, perhaps, the only unmingled race which can boast very remote antiquity, and, though hated, scorned, and oppressed in all countries, they subsist, a numerous and thriving people. In all the changes of manners and opinions around them, they rigidly preserve their divinely-appointed and time-hallowed institutions, their national spirit, and their deathless hope of restoration to grandeur and happiness in the home of their fathers. In the language of one, "If we speak of pedigrees, the Talbots, Percys, and Howards are like mushrooms of yesterday. Show me a Jew, and you show me a man whose genealogical tree springs from Abraham's bosom—whose family is older than the decalogue—and who bears incontrovertible evidence, in every line of his oriental countenance, of the authenticity of his descent through hundreds of successive generations. You see him a living argument of the truth of the Bible. In him you behold the literal fulfilment of its prophecies. With him you ascend the stream of time, not voyaging by the dim, uncertain, and fallacious light of tradition, but guided by an emanation of the same light which to his nation was 'a pillar of cloud by day and a pillar of fire by night.' In him you see the representative of the once chosen and favoured people of God—to whom he revealed himself as legislator, protector, and king—who brought them out of the land of Egypt, and out of the house of bondage. You behold him established, as it were, forever, in the pleasant places allotted him. You trace him, by the peculiar mercy of his God, in his transition state from bondage to freedom, and, by the innate depravity of his human nature, from prosperity to insolence, ingratitude, and rebellion. Following him on, you find him the serf of Rome. You trace him from the smouldering ashes of Jerusalem, an outcast and a wanderer in all lands; the persecutor of Christ, you find him the persecutor of Christians—bearing all things—suffering all things—strong in the pride of human knowledge—stiff-necked and gainsaying—hoping all things. 'For the Lord will have mercy upon Jacob, and will yet choose Israel and set them in their own lands, and the strangers shall be joined with them, and they shall cleave to the house of Jacob.'"

There is no religious history of any people so peculiar and extraordinary. It informs us in regard to opinions and ceremonies, events and transactions of a kind widely different from any others, and instructs mankind in a mode unknown to other narratives, because it brings directly into view the supernatural operations of God. Throughout the whole history the divine design seems to be kept in view, in setting apart one family from the rest of the nations; that is, to preserve the true religion in the world, and to prepare the way for the establishment of Christianity in after ages. The national faith, amid all its exposures and temporary suspensions, is identified with the history of the nation. To a Jew the State and Church were ever identical; his government was his religion, and his religion his government.

The father of the Jewish nation was *Abraham*, or, as it was originally called, *Abram*. The place of his nativity was Ur, a district of Chaldea, now known as Orfa, in Mesopotamia, where the Mohammedans have erected a splendid mosque to his memory. His father's name was Terah, and his brethren Nahor and Haran. The country was open, dry, and barren, and the inhabitants were idolaters. A change of location, so common to the nomadic tribes of the East, at length took place, and the family of Terah removed to Charræ, or Haran. They had not remained here long when the command of God came to Abraham to leave his country and kindred, for the purpose of establishing an independent tribe, in a distant, and, to him, unknown country. Abraham was now in his seventy-fifth year, and Lot, his nephew, chose to accompany him in his journey. Starting with his family, which consisted of several persons, with all their servants and flocks, he travelled a distance of three hundred miles, taking the desert of Syria in his route, and finally settled in Palestine, in the fertile valley of Sichem, between the mountains of Ebal and Gerizim. After this he removed to a mountain on the east of Bethel, and from thence journeyed south. When he first came to the country, "the Canaanite was in the land," and hence he knew that Canaan was the country to which he was called, and which had been promised as his inheritance, and that of his descendants. The Canaanites were descended from the son of Ham and his brethren, which were eleven in number. Trade and war was their chief occupation, and they flourished exceedingly in all their undertakings. They also engaged in manufactures, and became opulent. They settled colonies over almost all the islands and maritime provinces of the Mediterranean. Including the Phœnicians, they must be considered as among the more early civilized communities. Among them were different classes of merchants, artificers, soldiers, shepherds, and farmers. Their religion seems to have been that of their fathers, and they had kept it pure and uncontaminated to the days of Abraham. Melchizedek was one of their priests, and divinely accredited of God. The Phœnicians early devoted themselves to learning. The sciences of arithmetic and astronomy were invented, or, at least, greatly improved by them, and it is a matter of certain history that they introduced letters into Greece. The arts and sciences of the Phœnicians were widely diffused among the Canaanites. The occurrence of a famine induced Abraham to remove into Egypt, one of the greatest corn countries of antiquity. We have already alluded to his visit to Egypt, and his hospitable reception there. Having, while there, acquired great possessions, he returned again to Canaan, and re-occupied his former dwelling-place, between Bethel and Hai. The district of country he possessed, however, could not well support the large flocks owned by Abraham and Lot. This created a difficulty between the herdsmen of the two patriarchs, and, to settle it, they agreed to separate. Lot, going eastward into the rich and populous valley of the Jordan, settled in Sodom, and Abraham pitched his tents in the "plain of Mamre that was in Hebron." Near this time the first wars, the details of which are recorded in history, occurred. Sodom and all the adjacent country was ravaged and subdued by the arms of Chedorlaomer, king of Elam. Thirteen years before, this king, in confederacy with predatory tribes on the Euphrates and Tigris, attacked the princes of the valley, and, subduing them, subjected them to the payment of a tribute, which, on their refusal, involved them in a second war. Lot, with others, was taken captive. One who had escaped communicated the intelligence to Abraham, who, taking with him three hundred and eighteen of his own servants, and some confederates, pursued the enemy to the sources of the Jordan, where, attacking them in the night, he vanquished them, and brought back Lot and the other captives in safety. He also recovered the booty which they had taken away. He was greeted, on his return, as a victorious leader. One extraordinary personage paid him peculiar honour. Melchizedek, the king of Salem, Jerusalem, who united in his person the offices of king and priest, and worshipped the one true God, brought forth bread and wine, and blessed the deliverer of his country. Prosperous in external circumstances, still the pious patriarch had no heir. His anxiety on this subject, however, was relieved by an audible voice from heaven, which assured him not only of an immense progeny, but of a territory for their possession, extending from the Euphrates to the Mediterranean. By his maid-servant, Hagar, he had a child born to him, whom he named *Ishmael.* To this child he was strongly attached. About this time the rite of circumcision was instituted—a rite which was to distinguish the chosen seed. A short time subsequent to these transactions, Abraham was visited by angels, who tarried with him on their mission to destroy Sodom and the surrounding cities. After partaking of his hospitalities, and assuring him of the birth of the promised seed, and promising, upon his intercessions, if there were ten righteous persons in Sodom, to spare it, they journeyed on. But, alas, these licentious cities had fitted themselves for destruction. Their guilt was universal, and their ruin was inevitable. Lot, with his family, his wife excepted—being, by her dalliance, involved in the ruin—having made their escape, a fiery inundation swallowed them up. Present appearances of the valley covered by the Dead Sea, as well as the records of history, attest the nature of the judgment described in the Bible. All who visit this region unite in their testimony in regard to its peculiarities. These cities occupied the most fruitful and beautiful valley in the world. Inspiration compared it, in Lot's time, to the garden of Eden. It is a sad and melancholy fact, connected with the history of our race, that the most lovely and beautiful spots on our earth have been the most defiled by sin, and for this have been blasted of God forever. A dark and sullen sea of bitter waters, deserts of desolation, interspersed with heaps of decaying ruins, all over the eastern world, mark localities which once smiled with beauty, and charmed the eye with their magnificence and grandeur. They are to us solemn warnings from the dead, speaking to us in tones of sadness from the grave of buried joys.

Resuming our narrative, we come to a period in the history of Abraham when he found it necessary to remove from the plains of Mamre to the country of the Philistines. Here, when he had attained the age of a hundred years, *Isaac*, the child of promise, was born. This event was hailed with every demonstration of joy. But life is a state of trial, and often clouds of gloom are permitted to cast their shadows over the brightest scenes. The free-born child occasioned jealousy to Hagar and her son; for the former had scarcely attained his tenth year, when his mother, perceiving that Ishmael treated him with disrespect, resolved to part them forever. Sarah's request, enforced by the divine sanction, induced the patriarch to send Hagar and her son away. Though the son of the bond-woman might have no part in the inheritance, yet, according to divine promise, Ishmael was to become the father of a great nation. And such, in fact, he became. The Arabians are a vast nation, and, like the Jews, have been kept separate and distinct from all others.

It is said in Scripture that "Ishmael shall be a wild man; his hand shall be against every man, and every man's hand against him;" and this has been literally fulfilled, to the present day, by his descendants, the Arabs. "God has sent them out free, loosed from all political restraint. The wilderness is their habitation, and, in the parched land, where no other human beings could live, they have their habitation. They scorn the city, and, therefore, have no fixed dwellings. *For their multitude they are not afraid*, and, when they make depredations on cities, they retire with such precipitancy that all pursuit is eluded. In this respect, the *crying of the driver is disregarded.* They may be said to have no lands, their soil not being portioned out to them in fee-simple; yet *the range of the mountains is their pasture.* They pitch their tents and feed their flocks where they please. They *search after every green thing.* Every kind of property they meet with is their prey."

About twenty-five years after Hagar and her son were sent into the wilderness, the faith of Abraham, in being commanded by the Almighty to take Isaac upon Mount Moriah and offer him up in sacrifice, was put to a severe test. Notwithstanding the alarming nature of the divine requirement, Abraham bowed in obedience, and, just as he was going to slay the youth, having bound him to the altar for that purpose, an angel stayed his hand, and he was directed to take a ram, caught in the thicket by his horns, and perfect the sacrifice. He named the place where his faith was so severely tried, *Jehovah-Jireh*—the Lord will provide. Soon after this Sarah died, and Abraham procured for her a place of interment in the territory of a neighbouring prince. The place of sepulture which he purchased was named Machpelah. As the Jews were to live alone, their burial-places were also to be kept separate and distinct from all others; hence he refused the offers of the chiefs of the tribe of Heth to deposit her remains in the national cemetery. Not long subsequent to the death of his mother, Isaac was married to

Rebekah, of his own kindred. The descendants of Abraham, by his second marriage, were settled in Arabia, apart from the inheritance of Isaac, where it is supposed traces of them are to be found at the present day. Nothing more is recorded of this distinguished patriarch, except that at the age of one hundred and seventy-five he died, and was buried in Machpelah. No personage of antiquity is more renowned than Abraham. The Arabs boast their descent from "the father of the faithful"—the "friend of God," and he is equally venerated by Jew, Christian, and Mohammedan. He was selected from that nomadic race which stretches from the north-eastern extremity of Asia to the north-western shores of Africa. His simple, unadulterated mind, had become impregnated with the central truth, the one idea of the existence of one God, and he became the proper witness of it to the chief nations of the earth, with which he was respectively brought into contact, especially if Ur was, as some maintain, on the borders of Northern India. He was in fact a princely missionary from country to country, between nation and nation. In the year of the world 2167 two sons were born to Isaac, Esau and Jacob. In temper, and disposition they were opposite. Esau was fierce, restless, and sensual; Jacob was gentle, cautious, quiet, and calculating. The red-haired, rough Esau, was occupied and delighted in rude scenes and exercises. The smooth Jacob sought the pastoral occupation, and cherished the peaceful, practical thoughts which it inspired, and was, of course, far better fitted to become the father of a united, settled people, than his brother. Their natures indicated their destinies. Esau became the father of the Edomites, or Idumeans, and, though they reached a higher civilization and were farther removed from barbarism than the Bedouins, who sprung from Ishmael, yet in their scattered condition and continual wars, either among themselves or with others, they could not but be regarded as antagonistic to the purposes that were sought in the isolation of the Abrahamic race. According to the declarations of the Bible, they were to live as their father, by the sword and the bow.

Jacob was destined to inherit the blessing or privileges of the first-born. After a day of unsuccessful hunting, and consequent hunger and exhaustion, Esau sold his right of primogeniture to his brother for a mess of herbs. In addition to this, Jacob obtained, through the counsel of his mother, by craft, the solemn blessing of his father, confirming the right of primogeniture, in the following words: "Be thou lord over thy brethren, and let thy mother's sons bow down before thee."

This act aroused all the vindictiveness of Esau, and he determined on having revenge. Fearing his wrath, Jacob fled to Mesopotamia, where he subsequently married two wives, for whom and his cattle he served twenty years. Taking his family and servants, he set out on his return to the land of his nativity. When he arrived at the neighborhood of Seir, he learned, by his messenger, that Esau, being apprised of his approach, set out with four hundred men to meet him as an enemy. Finding himself involved in the greatest danger, he made all the arrangements that prudence would dictate, and betook himself to prayer. During the night, while engaged in supplication, the Scriptures inform us he wrestled with an angel, and at day-light prevailed, receiving an assurance of victory over his brother. It was not to be achieved by might or power, but by the Spirit of the Lord, which holds and guides the hearts of all men. Consequently, Esau met his brother with every token of kindness and affection, and, after many solicitations, accepted the gifts presented by Jacob. The brothers separated in peace, and Jacob took up his residence in Shechem, a short distance west of his former position, and nearly central in Palestine. A melancholy event happening to his only daughter, and avenged by her brothers, induced him to leave this part of the country. He tarried awhile at Luz, where he raised an altar, and called the place El-Bethel.

From Bethel he proceeded to Ephrath, and, having survived Rachel and erected a monument to her memory, he sought a new settlement beyond the tower of Edar, supposed to have been near Jerusalem. Family affliction again induced him to move his residence to Hebron, where Isaac, his father, who was still alive, resided. Soon after this, however, Isaac, having attained the age of one hundred and eighty years, died, and both Esau and Jacob paid filial respect to his venerable remains. From this period an entire separation in the family of Isaac ensued; Jacob remained in Canaan, and Esau took his possessions in Mount Seir or Arabia Petræa. Ten years after the death of Isaac, circumstances which we have already detailed caused the migration of Jacob and his family into Egypt, where they passed through various fortunes, during a period of four hundred years, and were finally led out into the wilderness of Arabia by the hand of Moses, and, after wandering forty years, they entered Canaan—the land promised to their fathers. Canaan and the adjacent country, as we have already intimated, was inhabited by many powerful native tribes, and it is important to our purpose to give a brief description of them. In the south part of Syria the earliest inhabitants known seem to have been a race of giants, or a people of large stature, which distinguished them from the Canaanites. The Avites in the south-west were partly exterminated and partly driven south, by the Philistines, a colony from Crete. The Horites, "cave-dwellers" or Troglodytes, seem to have been invaded by and to have mingled with the Canaanites. They inhabited Mount Seir also, whence they were exterminated by the Edomites.

The Rephaim were a very ancient people of East Canaan, tall of stature, divided into several families, and having many cities which were in the sequel destroyed, founded anew or occupied by the later Canaanites. Connected with them were the Emims, or Terribles, so called by the Moabites, and a wealthy people, of high stature, whose territory was afterwards called the land of Moab. The Zamzummim also, as the Ammonites called them, were a rich people, of extraordinary stature. Their territory was called the land of Rephaim, and, after their extirpation, the land of the Ammonites. A plain and valley contiguous to Jerusalem on the south-west bore the name of these giants. The Rephaim of the kingdom of Bashan, called the land of Rephaim; probably the only remnants of this people were exterminated by Moses. The *Anakim*, that is, giants, were a mountain race, very formidable to the Israelites. Like the Rephaim, they were divided into several families, as the Nephilim about Hebron, of whom were probably Arba, Ahiman, Sheshai, and Talmai; the Anakim of the mountains, not only of Hebron, but of Debir, Anah, and most of the mountains of Judah and Israel, both in the north and south of Canaan, these were all destroyed by Joshua. The Anakim of Gaza, and Ashdod, and Gath, were alone left. Of the last-named was Goliath. The *Kenites* dwelt in the land in Abraham's time, and were probably driven southward by the Canaanites and settled among the Midianites, as Hobab is said to have been their father. In the time of Moses they resided in the mountains near Moab and Amalek. Saul, when about to invade Amalek, warns the Kenites to depart from among them, lest they be destroyed with them. The Kenizzites are thought to have dwelt in Edom. The Kadmonites, that is, "Easterns" or "Orientals," resided about Mount Hermon, and were probably Hivites. The Perizzites, that is, "dwellers in the plain," were between Bethel and Ai, and about Shechem also, in the lot of Ephraim and Manasseh, and in South Judah.

CHAPTER V.

THE CANAANITES AND NEIGHBOURING NATIONS.

THE *Canaanites* were descended from the eleven sons of Canaan, the son of Ham. The descendants of five of these sons, named respectively Sidon, Arki, Arvadi, Hamathi, and Sini, settled in Syria and Phœnicia, and their history will be given with that of the Syrians and Phœnicians. The descendants of the other six sons of Canaan, namely, Heth, Jebusi, Amori, Gergashi, Zemari, and Hivi, settled in Canaan proper. We shall now endeavour to give an account of these Canaanites proper.

The children of Heth, or Hittites, dwelt among the Amorites, in the mountains of Judah : they possessed Hebron in Abraham's time, and he bought of them Machpelah, which was made the family tomb of the patriarchs. It is still shown, beneath the mosque of Abraham at Hebron. Esau married two Hittites, while his father resided at Beersheba. Sculptures on Egyptian monuments show that in patriarchal times they were waging a continual war with the Egyptians. Uriah, the Hittite, was one of David's officers. Solomon was the first to render them tributary, and Hittites were found in his harem. The last we hear of them is on the return of the Jews from their captivity in Babylon, where they are mentioned as one of the heathen tribes from which the Jews unlawfully took wives.

The *Jebusites* dwelt in the city and mountains of Jerusalem, and, after David took the place, they remained there still under his laws. He purchased the temple area on Mount Moriah of a Jebusite. Egyptian monuments show that this people, also, warred with the Egyptians.

The *Amorites* are found in Abraham's time about Engedi, a fertile spot, with a tropical climate, lying on the western coast of the Dead Sea, improved afterwards by Solomon as a botanic garden. Spreading thence over the mountainous country which forms the south part of Canaan, they gave their name to it. Jacob speaks of a piece of ground he obtained from them by force of arms, as far north as Shechem. Before the time of Moses they had founded two kingdoms, Bashan on the north and another south to Arnon, driving out the Ammonites and Moabites from between that river and the Jabbok. This latter territory Israel took from the Amorite king, Sihon.

The *Gergashites* dwelt between the Canaanites and Jebusites, and a region east of the sea of Galilee is called the "*country of the Gergesenes.*" This is the only tribe we miss in subsequent history except the Zemarites, who are mentioned but once, though a city Zemaraim is spoken of in Joshua.

The *Hivites* were in the northern part of the land, at the foot of Anti-Lebanon or Hermon, in the land of Mizpeh. Some yet remained in David's time, and they, with the Amorites, Perizzites, Hittites, and Jebusites, were taxed for bond service by Solomon. The Gibeonites and Shechemites were of this race.

The *Amalekites* sprang from Esau's grandson, a duke of Edom: there seems, however, to have been a mutual aversion between the Edomites and Amalekites. They occupied the country from South Canaan to the very angle of the Sinaitic peninsula. They attacked the rear of the Israelites, on their march from Rephidim to Horeb, but were put to flight after a hard-fought battle. In conjunction with the Canaanites, they repulsed the Israelites from the southern slope of Judea. They also allied themselves with the king of Moab, Eglon, and the Ammonites, and afterwards with the Midianites under Zeba and Zalmunna, to root out the Israelites, but by a stratagem of Gideon were made to destroy each other. Nothing more is heard of them until the time of Saul. The sentence of extermination pronounced on them by Joshua, when their deadly hostility to Israel first manifested itself, was partially executed by Saul, more completely by David, and finally consummated by the Simeonites, in the reign of Hezekiah. Saul invaded them with an immense army, and all that could be taken, men, women, and children, were put to death. Their king, Agag, a very graceful person, of noble bearing and address, was spared on that account; but Samuel afterwards, in obedience to the divine command, hewed him in pieces.

Lot's posterity, the *Moabites* and *Ammonites*, destroying the gigantic Emims, spread themselves to the eastward of the Dead Sea, which still bears the name among the Arabs of Lot's Sea. The country of the Moabites—forty miles square—was bounded south by the brook Zered, Midian, and Edom; east by the Arabian Desert; north by the Ammonites; and west by the Dead Sea and Jordan. The Israelites were forbidden to disturb them, notwithstanding great provocations. When the Israelites under Moses had subdued Sihon, they pitched their camp in that part of their new possessions called the plains of Moab. The king of Moab, dismayed at their presence and unable to resist them, assembled the most eminent men of his nation, and also the sheikhs of the Midianites, and, on consultation with them, it was thought best to send for Balaam, a distinguished prophet, to curse Israel. Balaam, after receiving two messages and a liberal promise of reward, undertook to curse them, but was forbidden by the Lord. He however gave them advice of the most wicked character, which proved infinitely worse than any verbal curse. His advice was, that the Israelites should be seduced to heathenism by the charms of Moabitish and Midianitish women. The very chief men of the nation did not hesitate to send their daughters on this infamous errand. The scheme succeeded but too well; the enamoured Israelites found the blandishments of the beautiful idolatresses more formidable than the mightiest engines of war. Their debaucheries infected them with a deadly disease, which carried off twenty-four thousand, besides those whom Moses ordered to be put to death. The Moabites became subject to David and Solomon, and remained so until the revolt of the ten tribes. The kings of Judah, Israel, and Edom, leaguing together, defeated the Moabites, demolished their cities, except Kir-haraseth, in which the king of Moab shut himself up; after several other unsuccessful wars, passing through a variety of fortunes until Nebuchadnezzar's time, when they partook of the fate of the other people of Syria. In the time of Josephus they were a populous nation; but in the third century they lost their name, and became included under the general designation of Arabians.

The *Ammonites*—descendants of Lot—destroyed the gigantic Zamzummim, and occupied their territory, which fell into the possession of Moses, who divided it to Gad and Reuben. It is described by travellers as a charming country of hills, groves, valleys, and streams, presenting lovely images of pastoral beauty, and the Arab proverb extols it as incomparable.

Ammon joined Moab, under Eglon, in opposing Israel, as already alluded to. About two hundred years later, we find them as principals in a war against the Israelites, under an unknown leader. This prince attempted to recover the ancient country of the Ammonites, which had passed through the hands of the Amorites to Israel. He invaded this land, and held it in subjection many years. Encouraged by success, he crossed the Jordan, and pillaged Judah, Benjamin, and Ephraim. Returning, he aimed to make a complete conquest of the whole country, at the same time. Jephthah attacked him, near Aroer, and defeated him with great slaughter, which put an end to Ammonitish tyranny. The next of the kings of the Ammonites was Nahash, who lived in Saul's time. He revived the old claim, and fought with great success. At last he besieged Jabesh Gilead, and it was just at the point of falling into his hands, on the condition that each of its inhabitants should lose an eye, when

Saul made an assault upon the camp, and a terrible battle ensued, in which they were completely routed, so that no two of them could be seen together. About sixty years after, they treated David's messengers with the most shameful indignity, which brought on a war. Their king, Hanun, allied himself with a vast host of Syrians, Moabites, and Ammonites, but was defeated by Joab, and again by David, in person. Joab laid siege to Rabbah, their capital, and David took it by storm, wreaking terrible vengeance. About one hundred and forty years after, they allied themselves again with Moab, and invaded Judah; but the allied armies quarrelled, and destroyed each other. Uzziah defeated them and made them tributary, but they rebelled against his son Jotham. Again defeated, they were compelled to pay one hundred talents of silver, ten thousand measures of wheat, and as many of barley—that is, one hundred and sixty thousand bushels—for three successive years. When Reuben and Gad were carried away captive, the Ammonites occupied their empty cities.

In Zedekiah's attempt to throw off the yoke of Nebuchadnezzar, Baalis, the last king of Ammon, seems to have joined him; but when Jerusalem was destroyed, the Ammonites exulted over its ruin. Baalis advised Ishmael to assassinate Gedaliah, appointed by the king of Babylon to govern the poor remnant of Jews. A long time after, we find them united with the Arabians, Moabites, and Samaritans, in attempting to prevent the rebuilding of the city of Jerusalem. Probably Cyrus had restored them, as we find them, even previous to this, subject to Egypt, and then to Syria. Under the leadership of Timotheus, their governor, they fought with Judas Maccabeus, who at last burnt their city, murdered its inhabitants, and extinguished them as a nation. Their name was finally merged in the general appellation of *Arabs*.

The *Midianites* dwelt south and east of Edom. Moses found them about Sinai, and one of their chief cities, Midian, was in the north, towards Rabbath-Moab, and another of the same name, in the south, by the Red Sea, on the eastern shore of the Gulf of Akaba. They are thought to have sprung from Abraham's fourth son. We find them early confounded with the Ishmaelites; later with the Nabatheans; and, in the time of Moses, the Midianites and Moabites appear to have been almost one people, alike in religion and interests. This numerous people were early known as rovers, divided into two classes, the shepherds and the merchants; the latter, as early as the time of Joseph, were engaged in the trade from Gilead to Egypt. The merchants moved in caravans, and carried on a trade between the Mediterranean, India, Assyria, and Egypt. They left the care of their cattle to women, and hence Jethro's daughters were found tending the flocks of their father. Jethro, the "prince-priest," a Kenite, lived in the city of Midian. His seven daughters were insulted by shepherds, and Moses defended them. For this vindication he was admitted to the hospitalities of their father's house, and subsequently became the husband of Zipporah.

From this period the Midianites are lost to history for a half century. They had grown rich in trade, which consisted mostly of costly jewelry. They were early familiar with letters. Traces of the worship of the crescent planet Venus, or the crescent moon, are found among them, indicating their attachment to Islamism. The Midianites had no reason to exult over the success of Baalam's wicked advice, in which they heartily coöperated; for Moses sent twelve thousand men against them, under Phineas, and, notwithstanding their stout resistance, they were defeated and put to the sword, including the wicked prophet; and all their towns and castles were burnt. Every person was destroyed, except thirty-two thousand virgins, who were made prisoners. The whole country was laid waste, and the cattle driven off, amounting to the number of two hundred and eight thousand, of different kinds; besides, the spoil of gold, silver, and iron, was immense.

A century and a half later, by the stratagem of Gideon, with the trumpet and lamps at midnight, one hundred and twenty thousand were slain in this battle and one subsequent; so that *doomsday* had come to Midian. Many ages after, the tribe was distinguished for its wealth and the magnificence of its tents; but, in the course of time, its distinctive name shared the fate of its contemporaries, and was merged in that of the Arabs.

The most vigorous, highly civilized, and respectable of all these nations remains yet to be noticed. The *Philistines* were only inferior in attainments to the Phœnicians and Egyptians. The Philistines were Misraimites, supposed to have migrated from India. They drove out the Avites, and settled upon the southern half of one of the most fertile and beautiful plains in the world. It is bounded on the north by Carmel, south by the desert, west by the Mediterranean, and east by the mountains of Judah. This energetic race was under five lordships, each with its head city, namely, Gaza, Askelon, Ashdod, Gath, and Ekron. They were not destined to extermination, but Joshua attacked them. Until David's time they had their kings, and some of them oppressed Israel for many years.

David subdued them, as also Jehoram and Uzziah; but, in the reign of Ahaz, they annoyed Judah. They were again subdued, but they became free. They were partially conquered by Esarhaddon and Psammeticus; afterwards by the Persians and by Alexander, who destroyed Gaza. After this they fell under the Asmonean government, which is the last we hear of them in history. Two of their towns sustained famous sieges. Ashdod, afterwards called Azotus, withstood the whole force of Egypt, under Psammeticus, for the space of twenty-nine years. This is the longest siege recorded in history.

Their country having become the theatre of war between the mighty nations of Assyria and Egypt, they finally lost their independence, and became tributary to the succeeding empires. From the hieroglyphics upon the contemporary monuments of Egypt, we learn that their personal appearance resembled the Egyptians, except that they were whiter, and shaved both beard and whiskers, and differed in arms and equipments from all other nations east of Egypt.

We now return to the journeyings of the Israelites, who were on their way to the occupancy of the country inhabited by the nations we have described. During their forty years' wanderings they passed through many remarkable scenes. The giving of the law on Sinai—constant miraculous supplies—the death of Moses—the passage of the Jordan—the destruction of Jericho—the capture and occupancy of Canaan—all were marked by the most signal interposition of divine power in their behalf, and should have forever impressed them with a sense of grateful dependence, and prompted them to the most cheerful obedience.

After the termination of the wars in Canaan the Israelites proceeded to attend to the instructions given to them by Moses, which were the solemn recognition of the Lord as king, and swearing allegiance to the constitution. They next proceeded to the survey and partition of the land, with the location of the several tribes.

Joshua, after having gathered together all the people, exhorted them to obedience, and renewing the oath of fealty and allegiance, died, aged one hundred and ten years, B. C. 1426. After his decease, and that of the elders, there succeeded a generation of men who disregarded the pious customs of their fathers, and mingled with the Canaanites in marriages and idolatrous worship. During the period of the judges, personal activity, courage, and craft were qualities which gave distinction; and hence this was called the heroic age, contrasting with the Homeric and Grecian contemporaries. Samson is compared with Hercules; Shamgar with Achilles; Jephthah with Agamemnon; Saul with Hector, &c., &c. Also the domestic life of the Homeric age, as described by Homer, was contrasted with the pleasant picture of Hebrew rural life given in the Book of Ruth.

Voltaire says: "These times and manners have nothing in common with our own, whether good or bad; their spirit is not ours; their good sense is not ours." On this very account, the five books of Moses, Joshua, and the Judges, are a thousand times more instructive than Homer and Herodotus.

During this period, the nation was involved in numerous wars, and exhibited scenes of capture and deliverances. Becoming tired of the theocratic form of government, the people desired a monarchy, and, accordingly, Samuel, the prophet, anointed Saul as king over Israel.

This kingdom, under the successive reigns of David and Solomon, became rich and powerful, and extended its territory from the Euphrates to the Mediterranean, and from Phœnicia to Edom.

Solomon, the wisest of kings, erected a most magnificent temple for the worship of God. He also erected sumptuous palaces in and around Jerusalem, and, during his reign, the kingdom embraced the largest extent of territory it ever did, extending from the Mediterranean to the Persian Gulf, and from the borders of Tyre and Sidon to the Elanitic Gulf of the Red Sea. The population of the empire was estimated at eight millions. Commerce and the arts of life were promoted, and literature and science more highly cultivated than at any former period.

During the reign of *Rehoboam*, the successor of Solomon, ten of the twelve tribes rebelled against the government, which was regarded by the people as tyrannical. These tribes renounced their allegiance, and made Jeroboam their king. The separate kingdoms of Judah and Israel were soon embroiled in wars, which proved disastrous to both. The kingdom of Israel fell into the most grievous idolatry, from which, however, it was restored in the days of the prophet Elijah, and the ancient religion revered. Under the reign of Ahaziah, the kingdoms were joined in a confederacy, which lasted two years. After several successive reigns of various fortunes, the kingdom at last fell into anarchy, and, being besieged by the king of Assyria, its independence was destroyed, and the ten tribes were scattered abroad, none knows whither.

The contemporaneous history of Judah is involved, more or less, with that of Israel. Her kings were, many of them, devoted to the religion and institutions of the country. A few of them, however, imitated the profligate kings of Israel; but a reign of misrule and irreligion was almost invariably succeeded by a return to order and the national faith.

The Jewish kingdom, in the year 610 B. C., was subdued by Nebuchadnezzar, and the temple was plundered, and the people were carried as captives to Babylon. This captivity lasted seventy years, after which they were permitted by Cyrus, king of Persia, to return and rebuild their temple, which had been destroyed. The king of Persia sent Ezra, the priest and scribe, to officiate as governor, and appoint superior and inferior judges, rectify abuses, enforce the observance of the laws, and various means were allowed him for the use of the temple. He read the books of the law to the assembled people, and collected all the manuscripts of the prophets and sacred writers, and placed them in their present form. Nehemiah was sent as governor in 444 B. C., and under his direction the walls of the city were built.

One hundred years afterwards, the country was invaded by Alexander, and he removed one hundred thousand of the Jews to Egypt. Subsequently, Ptolemy, king of Egypt, attacked Jerusalem on the Sabbath-day, and, meeting with no resistance, in consequence of the regard of the Jews for the Sabbath, it was taken. It was twice wrested from his hands by Antigonus. Ptolemy, however, had it made part of his share as one of the successors of Alexander. He carried away one hundred thousand captives, whom he settled chiefly in Alexandria and Cyrene. Under the first three Ptolemies, the Alexandrine and native Jews enjoyed many marks of royal favour.

Antiochus Epiphanes, the king of Syria, in the year 176 B. C., marched against Jerusalem, sacked and pillaged the temple, destroyed forty thousand of the inhabitants, and seized as many more, to be sold as slaves. These outrages were followed by attempts to abolish the worship of God, and force the Jews to forsake their religion. The Samaritans disowned their relation to the Jews, to whom, in prosperity, they pretended alliance, and they consecrated their temple on Mount Gerizim to Jupiter. In the midst of the most fierce and bitter persecutions, to induce the Jews to renounce their religion, they were firm.

Mattathias resisted the officer of Antiochus, who came to execute the edict against the Jewish religion, in the place of the priests' residence. He was supported in this by his five sons, who fell upon the king's commissioner and put him to death. Mattathias then summoned all the citizens who were zealous for the law, to follow him to the mountains. One thousand of them perished in their caves, as they would not defend themselves on the Sabbath, when attacked by the Syrians. After this, Mattathias and his followers discarded that view of the Sabbath. After the death of Mattathias, Judas Maccabeus, one of his sons, assumed the leadership in the glorious enterprise. Apollonius, the governor of Samaria, who came against him, was slain, and his army totally defeated. Seron, governor of Lower Syria, advanced to avenge the defeat of Apollonius, but met a similar fate, and lost eight hundred men. The next year Antiochus sent an army of forty-seven thousand men against him, but he defeated them with an immense slaughter. Then followed Lysias, with a still larger force; but he was overcome by Judas, and lost five thousand men. The Maccabean then triumphantly entered Jerusalem, purified the temple, and placed a wall around Mount Zion. From thence, he carried his victorious arms into the territories of the Idumeans and the Ammonites, and enlarged his boundaries.

In the meantime Antiochus died in Persia, and was succeeded by his son Antiochus Eupator, 162 B. C. He made peace with the Jews, but soon violated it by putting Menelaüs, the high-priest, to death, and conferring the priesthood on Alcimus. In the meantime Demetrius Soter, lineal heir to the throne of Antioch, had escaped from Rome and came to Syria, where he caused himself to be crowned king, and, after some struggle, overpowered Lysias and Antiochus, and put them to death.

At the instance of Alcimus, the high-priest Demetrius sent Nicanor, with a great army, against Judas; but his army was routed, and he was slain. After this, to secure the independence of the country, Judas entered into a formal treaty of alliance with Rome; but, before its consummation, the heroic Maccabean had terminated his brilliant career. Demetrius sent Alcimus and Bacchides, with a new army of twenty thousand men, against him. Judas was abandoned by all his troops, except eight hundred, yet he would not be prevailed upon to retreat. He fell, nobly fighting to the last, 161 B. C.

His brother Jonathan was chosen general in his stead. He consummated the alliance with Rome, and obliged Bacchides to make a league, and withdraw his army from Judea.

Alexander Balas, who announced himself as the son of Antiochus Epiphanes, came with an army into Syria; the garrison of Ptolemais opened their gates to him, on account of their hatred to Demetrius, and the latter prepared himself for war. Alexander courted an alliance with the Jewish general, and conferred on Jonathan the high-priesthood, who immediately assumed the pontifical robes, and, in his person, commenced the reign of the *Asmonean princes*, 152 B. C.

Demetrius and Alexander, having come to a battle, the former was defeated and slain. His eldest son, Demetrius Nicanor, entered Cilicia with an army, 148 B. C. Apollonius, his general, receiving the command of Syria, attacked Jonathan, the high-priest, who overcame him, took Joppa and Azotus, and burnt the temple of Dagon.

In the year 144 B. C., Tryphon took Jonathan by stratagem, and subsequently put him to death. His brother Simon was chosen in his stead. The Romans renewed their leagues with Simon, and wrote them in tables of brass. Soon after this, Simon intrusted the command to his sons, Judas and John Hyrcanus. In 107 B. C., Aristobulus, the eldest son of Hyrcanus, succeeded his father. He was the first, after the captivity, who set a crown upon his head, and changed the State into a monarchy.

There were several successors of the Asmonean race in the kingdom,—Alexander, Jannæus, Alexandra, Aristobulus II., Hyrcanus II., and Antigonus,—whose rule, including that of the founder of the dynasty, continued about one hundred and twenty-six years. In the year 63 B. C., Pompey came to Jerusalem to settle the affairs of Judea. He restored Hyrcanus, between whom and his brother, Aristobulus, there had been a contest for the crown, with the title of "Prince of the Jews," and conferred the government of the country on Antipater, an Idumean proselyte. He made the Jews tributary to the Romans.

Herod, afterwards named the Great, was a younger son of Antipater, the Idumean. His father had appointed him to the government of Galilee, in the year 47 B. C. In the year 38 B. C., he took Jerusalem, married the beautiful Mariame, the daughter of Hyrcanus, of the Asmonean family, and was made king of Judea by the Roman power. He was the last independent sovereign of Palestine, and began his reign 37 B. C. His reign was one of unmitigated cruelty. The last year of his life he ordered the murder of the children of Bethlehem, for the purpose of securing the death of Christ, who was born at that time; and the last act of his life was the execution of his own son, Antipater. He had married ten wives, and his family was numerous. To his two sons by Malthace, a Samaritan, *Herod Antipas* and *Archelaüs*, he divided his dominions. Antipas had Galilee and Perea; and Archelaüs, Idumea, Samaria, and Judea. The Roman government gave Philip a share in the government of Judea. Archelaüs received only the title of Ethnarch, and, under this name, he assumed the government of Judea, three years before Christ. After a reign of nine years of great cruelty, he was deposed and banished by the Roman emperor, and *Judea was reduced to a Roman province.*

Augustus, the emperor of Rome, appointed a number of successors to the government of Judea, none of whom remained in office for any length of time. Tiberius adopted a different policy, and, during his reign of twenty-three years, Judea had only two rulers—Valerius Gratus, A. D. 16; and Pontius Pilate, A. D. 29. It was before Pontius Pilate that Jesus Christ was led by the Jews. After having declared him innocent, he, nevertheless, sentenced him to crucifixion, A. D. 33.

During this period, the other two sons of Herod reigned in peace—Herod Antipas, tetrarch of Galilee; and Philip in Perea. After the death of Philip, his territory was annexed to the province of Syria, and subsequently his vacant tetrarchate was given by Caligula to Agrippa, the son of Aristobulus, who also received the title of king. On the accession of Claudius his territories were enlarged. He endeavoured to gain the favour of the Jews by observing the Mosaic law with great exactness. In this spirit he also commenced the persecution of the Christians. He put to death James, and threw Peter in prison. Having reigned over the whole of Palestine for three years, he died in extreme agony at Cesarea Palestina, A. D. 44.

He left one son, who succeeded his father, but was too young to bear the burdens of royalty, and Judea relapsed into a Roman province. Cassius Longinus was appointed to the presidency of Syria, and Fadus was sent as governor of Judea. Tiberius Alexander succeeded Fadus, but his government was short and eventful. He in turn was followed by Ventidius Cumanus, and the latter by Claudius Felix, who was born a slave and addicted to all manner of crimes.

Porcius Festus next was appointed governor. His administration was rigid, but upright. He was succeeded by Albinus, and he in turn by Gessius Florus, in whose time the most fearful calamities befell the Jews. Difficulties arose in Cesarea among the Jews and the Greek magistrates. The spirit of insubordination extended to Jerusalem; and Florus, for the purpose of suppressing an insurrection, to which he had driven the people, had thirty-six hundred men, women, and children, butchered in the streets. He also had twenty thousand Jews slain in Cesarea. The Jews were driven to madness, and went out through the land destroying city after city, and being in turn themselves destroyed by the Romans. The Jews offered such a deadly resistance to Roman power that Nero selected his most valiant military commander, Vespasian, to conduct the war. Vespasian sent his son Titus to Alexandria, to conduct the fifth and tenth legions, while he himself travelled with all speed by land to Syria, gathering armed forces in his train. Vespasian desolated every city he visited, and continued his war of extermination until he received intelligence that he was elected emperor, when he repaired to Rome, and his son Titus became commander-in-chief. Titus determined on taking the city of Jerusalem, and marched his army up to its walls. After a desperate and long-continued effort, in which thousands died from starvation within the walls and tens of thousands in defending the city, an entrance was made, and a scene of slaughter and destruction ensued which beggars all description. The whole city was laid waste; temple, palace, tower, all alike fell beneath the stroke of the ruthless invader. During the wars of Vespasian and Titus, it is computed that one million five hundred thousand were slain, including one hundred thousand who perished in gladiatorial fights and by wild beasts in the amphitheatre at Rome. Josephus, King Agrippa, and his sister Berenice, escaped the general wreck of the country, and, while Josephus became a favourite and wrote his histories in Rome, vouched for by Titus, Berenice would have been taken to the throne by Titus, who became enamoured of her beauty, but for the prejudices of his subjects—she being an Idumean.

The political existence of the Jewish nation was now at an end, and from that time to the present they have been scattered and oppressed among the nations of the earth. Here Biblical Ethnography closes in regard to this nation, and their subsequent history belongs to another department.

Part Seventh.

BIBLICAL HISTORY.

History in general is an authentic narrative of facts and events in the order in which they occured. *Biblical History* is a narration of the facts and events of the Bible, and differs widely from a history *of* the Bible. These are often confounded by Bible historians, when they should be kept entirely separate and distinct.

Bible history, according to the above definition, is simply a narrative of the contents of the Bible; whereas *a history of the Bible* is confined as specifically to an account of its origin, structure, and character, together with the times in which and the authors by whom it was written, as well as the languages in which they wrote. It also embraces an account of the manuscripts, their transcription and preservation, and the various translations which have been made from time to time, and the extent of their circulation. This department gives the historian the widest field of observation, inasmuch as it pertains to everything connected with the origin, progress, and fate of the Scriptures.

Biblical history confines the writer to the simple text. It is only with the *contents* of the books of the Old and New Testaments that he has to do; and hence the design of this part will be to give a succinct analysis of the subjects embraced in each particular book of the four divisions of the Old, namely, the Pentateuch, the Historical, Poetical, and Prophetical; and the three of the New Testament, namely, the Historical, Doctrinal, and Epistolary.

CHAPTER I.

HISTORICAL BOOKS OF THE OLD TESTAMENT.

Genesis.

A. M. 1. The first book of the Pentateuch, which is called Genesis, derives its appellation from the title it bears in the Greek Septuagint version, ΒΙΒΛΟΣ ΓΕΝΕΣΕΩΣ, (*Biblos Geneseos,*) which signifies the Book of the Generation or Production, because it commences with the history of the generation or production of all things.

Different opinions have been entertained in regard to the time when Moses, its author, wrote it; but the most probable conjecture is that which places it after the departure of the Israelites from Egypt, and the giving of the law on Sinai. It comprises the history of about two thousand three hundred and sixty-nine years, according to the common computation of time.

This book is divided into four parts. The first part contains *the origin of the world*, chapter first and second. The second part contains *the history of the former world*, chapter third to seventh. The third part contains *the general histors of mankind, after the Deluge*, chapter eighth to the eleventh. The fourth part contains *the particular history of the patriarchs*, chapter twelfth to the fiftieth.

SUMMARY OF SUBJECTS.

The Creation—The Fall of Man from his Innocency—His Expulsion from Eden—The History of Adam and his Posterity—Translation of Enoch—Noah and his Preaching—The Increase of Wickedness in the World—Its Destruction by a Deluge—The Preservation of Noah and his Family—The Division of the Earth among the Sons of Noah—The Building of Babel—The Confusion of Tongues—The Dispersion of Mankind—The Particular History of the Patriarchs—Destruction of Sodom—The History of Abraham and his Family—Birth of Isaac—The Trial of Abraham—The Death of Sarah—Marriage of Isaac—Death of Abraham—History of the Church, under the Patriarchs Isaac, Jacob, and Joseph, containing Remarkable Instances of Particular Providences.

Exodus.

A. M. 2299. The title of this book is also derived from the Septuagint version, and is significant of the principal transaction it records, namely, the ΕΞΟΔΟΣ, (*Exodos,*) Exodus, or departure of the Israelites from Egypt. It comprises a history of the events that took place during the period of one hundred and forty-five years—from the year of the world 2369 to 2514, inclusive—from the death of Joseph to the erection of the tabernacle. This book shows the accomplishment of the divine promises made to Abraham of the increase of his posterity; and their departure from Egypt, after suffering great affliction. It contains—

1. An account of the oppression of the Israelites, and the transactions previously to their departure out of Egypt, chapter first to the eleventh.

2. The narrative of the Exodus, or departure of the Israelites, chapter twelfth and thirteenth.

3. Transactions subsequent to the Exodus, chapter fourteenth to the eighteenth.

4. The promulgation of the law on Mount Sinai, chapter nineteenth to the fortieth.

SUMMARY OF SUBJECTS.

The design of this book was evidently to preserve the memorial of the departure of the children of Israel out of Egypt, and the wonderful providence of God in their deliverance and preservation as a nation. It records events which are the fulfilment of promises and prophecies made to Abraham. The contents of the book may thus be summed up:—The Affliction of the Israelites under Egyptian Task-masters—The Destruction of all the Male Children at Birth—The Birth of Moses—His Preservation—His Adoption into the Family of Pharaoh—His Flight to Midian—The Burning Bush—His Commission to deliver Israel—A Sign given him—His Return to Egypt, and Message to Pharaoh—Miracles wrought by him—Magicians of Egypt imitate them—The Ten Plagues—The First-born slain—The Departure of the Israelites—Sanctification of the First-born—Pillar of Cloud and Fire—Passage of the Red Sea—Destruction of the Egyptian Army—Marah sweetened—Manna given—

The Covenant of Sinai—Ten Commandments given—Law concerning Altars—Judicial Laws—Moral and Ceremonial Laws—Sabbatical Year—Israel's Covenant with God—Moses converses with God, in the Mount, Forty Days—Directions for making the Ark, and the Furniture of the Tabernacle—The Veil and the Altar of Burnt-offering—Aaron set apart for the Priesthood—The Urim and Thummim—Patterns of the Priestly Robes—Consecration of the Priests—Altar of Incense—Ransom of Souls—Sacred Perfume—Sabbath, a Perpetual Covenant—The Tables broken by Moses—He intercedes for the People—God talks with him—Tables renewed—God's Instruction to Moses—Comes down from the Mount—Contributions for the Tabernacle—Construction of the Tabernacle, and Making of its Furniture—The Altar of Burnt-offering, and the Offerings made thereon—Holy Garments, and Dress of the Priests—The Tabernacle completed, and filled with Glory—Burnt-offerings of the Flocks.

Leviticus.

A. M. 2514.

Leviticus, called in the Septuagint ΛΕΥΙΤΙΚΟΝ, (*Levitikon*,) derives its name from the circumstance of its containing the laws concerning the religion of the Israelites. It is of great use in explaining many passages of the New Testament, especially the Epistle to the Hebrews, which, otherwise, would be inexplicable. The book may be divided as follows:—

1. The laws concerning *sacrifices*, in which the different kinds of sacrifices are enumerated, together with their concomitant rites, chapter first to the seventh.

2. The institution of the priesthood, in which the consecration of Aaron and his sons to the sacred office is related, together with the punishment of Nadab and Abihu, chapter eighth to the tenth.

3. The laws concerning purifications, both of the people and the priests, chapter eleventh to the twenty-second.

4. The laws concerning the sacred festivals, vows, things devoted, and tithes.

SUMMARY OF SUBJECTS.

The Ceremonial Law of the Israelites, such as Burnt-offerings of the Flocks—Law of Peace-offering and Sin-offering for the People—Law in Relation to Unclean Things—Trespass-offering—Meat-offering—Peace-offering—Portion of the Priests—Aaron and his Sons consecrated—The Ram of Consecration—High Priest's Offering—Aaron enters on the Priestly Office—Death of Nadab and Abihu—Clean and Unclean Animals—Casualties making Meats unclean—Ceremonial Purification—Law concerning Leprosy—Cleansing the Leper—Rites and Sacrifices—Ceremonial Purifications—High Priest's Sin-offering—The Live Goat—Directions concerning Sacrifices—Blood forbidden to be eaten—Incest defined and forbidden—Ceremonial and Moral Laws and Ordinances repeated—Laws against Iniquity—Moral Laws—Laws concerning the Priests and Sacrifices—Divers Feasts and Offerings—Yearly Sacrifices and Solemn Feasts—Blasphemy punished with Death—Sabbatical Year and Jubilee—Redemption of Servants—Promises and Threatenings—Mercy promised to the Repentant—Law concerning Vows.

Numbers.

A. M. 2514. This book was entitled ΑΡΙΘΜΟΙ, (*Arithmoi,*) and, by the Latin translators, it was termed *Numeri*, *Numbers*, from whence the English title is derived, because it contains an account of the numbering of the children of Israel. Besides the numeration and marshalling of the Israelites for their journey, several laws, in addition to those delivered in Exodus and Leviticus, and likewise several remarkable events, are recorded in this book. It contains a history of the Israelites, from the beginning of the second month of the second year after their departure from Egypt to the beginning of the eleventh month of the fortieth year of their journeyings; that is, a period of thirty years and nine months. This book may be divided into four parts:—

1. The census of the Israelites, and the marshalling of them into a regular camp, each tribe by itself, under its own captain or chief, distinguished by his own peculiar standard, and occupying an assigned place with reference to the tabernacle. The sacred census of the Levites, the designation of them to the sacred office, and the appointment of them to various services in the tabernacle, are related in chapters third and fourth.

2. The institution of various legal ceremonies, chapter fifth to the tenth.

3. The history of their journey from Mount Sinai to the land of Moab, which may be described and distinguished by their eight remarkable murmurings in the way, every one of which was visited with severe chastisements, chapter eleventh to the twenty-first.

4. A history of the transactions which took place in the plains of Moab, chapter twenty-second to thirty-sixth.

SUMMARY OF SUBJECTS.

The Numbering of the Men of War, and all the Israelites—The Levites are exempted—Stations of the Several Tribes—Separation of the Israelites—Levites numbered—Office of the Levites—Unclean put out of the Camp—The Bitter Waters of Jealousy—The Law concerning Nazarites—A Form of Benediction appointed—The Offerings of the Princes upon dedicating the Altar—The Light of the Sanctuary—Law of the Passover—Pillar of Cloud and Fire—Use of Silver Trumpets—Moving of the Camp—Murmurings of the Israelites—Manna loathed—Prophecy of the Seventy Elders—Miriam smitten with Leprosy—Mission of the Twelve Spies—Murmurings—Intercession of Moses—Death of the Evil Spies—Laws concerning Sacrifices—Sabbath-breaker stoned—Rebellion of Korah, Dathan, and Abiram—Their Destruction—Blossoming of Aaron's Rod—Maintenance of the Priests—Ashes of Purification—The People murmur for Water—Miraculous Supply from the Rock—Death of Aaron—The Brazen Serpent—Balak and Balaam—Balaam's Journey to Balak—Balaam's Ass speaketh—Balak's Sacrifice—Balaam's Parables of Israel's Prosperity—The Zeal of Phineas—Numbering of the People in the Plains of Moab—The Land divided—Moses warned of his Death—Joshua named as his Successor—Laws concerning Sacrifices—Solemnities of the Seventh Month—Concerning Vows—Slaughter of the Midianites—Spoil of the Midianites, and the Distribution thereof—Request of the Reubenites respecting their Inheritance—Encampment of the Israelites—Canaanites doomed—Boundaries of Canaan—The Law of Murder.

Deuteronomy.

A. M. 2553. The fifth book of Moses derives its name from the title ΔΕΥΤΕΡΟΝΟΜΙΟΝ, (*Deuteronomion*,) prefixed to it by the translators of the Septuagint, which is a compound term, signifying the *second law*, or *the law repeated*, because it contains a repetition of the law of God, given by Moses to the Israelites. The period of time comprised in this book is about two months. It has four parts, as follows:—

1. A repetition of the history related in the preceding books, chapter first to the fourth.

2. A repetition of the moral, ceremonial, and judicial law, chapter fifth to the twenty-sixth.

3. The confirmation of the law, chapter twenty-seventh to the thirtieth.

4. The personal history of Moses, chapter thirty-first to the thirty-third.

The thirty-fourth chapter was, in all probability, written by Joshua.

SUMMARY OF SUBJECTS.

Cities of Refuge—Law of Inheritance—Moses rehearseth the Story of God's Promises—Seed of Esau and Lot spared—History of the Moabites—Sihon and Og subdued—Allotment of the Conquered Land—Moses exhorts to Obedience—Cities of Refuge—The Decalogue repeated—Canaanites to be destroyed—Conditions of God's Mercy—Idolatry to be avoided — Moses's Charge continued —Israel's Rebellion rehearsed—Renewing the Two Tables—Obedience recommended—Charge continued —Place of Burnt-offering—Blood forbidden—Cautions against Idolatry —Meats Clean and Unclean—Concerning Tithes—The Year of Release—Yearly Feasts—Authority of the Judges—Idolaters must be slain—Duties of a King—The Great Prophet—Cities of Refuge—Laws to be observed in War—Hittites to be destroyed—Of Uncertain Murder—The Wicked Son—Punishment of Fornication—Punishment of Rape—Cleanliness enjoined—Law of Divorce—Justice and Generosity—Amalek to be destroyed—First-fruits and Tithes—The Curse from Ebal—Promises —Threatenings in Case of Disobedience—The Covenant renewed—Mercies to the Penitent—Advantages of Revelation—Solemn Warnings—Apostasy foretold—The Song of Moses—Moses's Blessing on the Twelve Tribes—Moses's View from Pisgah—His Death and Burial.

Joshua.

A. M. 2553. The book of Joshua, which, in all the copies of the Old Testament, immediately follows the Pentateuch, is thus denominated because it contains a narration of the achievements of Joshua, the son of Nun, who had been the minister of Moses, and succeeded him in the command of the children of Israel. It has always been received by the Jews as part of their canon of Scripture. This book comprises the history of about seventeen years, and, some chronologers think, thirty. It contains—

1. The history of the occupation of Canaan by the Israelites, chapter first to twelfth.

2. The division of the conquered land, chapter thirteenth to the twenty-second.

3. The assembling of the people, by the dying address and counsels of Joshua—his death and burial, chapter twenty-third to the twenty-fourth.

SUMMARY OF SUBJECTS.

Joshua succeeds Moses—The Two Spies and Rahab—Joshua's Approach to Jordan—Passage over Jordan—God magnifies Joshua—The Manna ceases—Siege of Jericho—Jericho destroyed—Israelites smitten at Ai—The Sin of Achan—Destruction of Ai—Reading of the Law—The Gibeonites' Craft—Sun and Moon stand still—Five Kings slain—Joshua's Victories—Opposition of Jabin—Hazor taken and burned—Distribution of Canaan—Caleb's Inheritance—The Borders of Judah—Othniel's Valour and Reward—Cities of Judah—Borders of the Sons of Joseph—Tabernacle at Shiloh—Inheritance of Benjamin—Simeon's Inheritance—Lots of Several Tribes—Joshua's Inheritance—Six Cities of Refuge—Forty-eight Cities given by Lot to the Levites—Two Tribes and a half dismissed—Altar of the Reubenites—Joshua's Farewell and Exhortation—His Death and Burial.

Judges.

A. M. 2579. The book of Judges derives its name from its containing the history of the Israelites, from the death of Joshua to the time of Eli, under the administration of thirteen judges, and, consequently, before the establishment of the regal government. It was supposed to have been written by the prophet Samuel, and contains the following parts:—

1. The state of the Israelites after the death of Joshua until they began to turn aside from serving the Lord, chapter first to the third.

2. The history of the oppressions of the Israelites, and their deliverances by the judges, chapter fourth to the sixteenth.

3. An account of the introduction of idolatry among the Israelites, and the consequent corruption of religion and manners among them, for which God gave them up into the hands of their enemies, chapter seventeenth to the twenty-first.

SUMMARY OF SUBJECTS.

Judah's Commission to fight the Canaanites—An Angel rebukes the Israelites—Idolatry of the Israelites—Eglon slain by Ehud—Israel enslaved by Jabin—Defeat and Death of Sisera—Song of Deborah and Barak—Call of Gideon—Gideon's Deliverance—Gideon's Fleece—Gideon's Stratagem—His Victory—Succoth and Penuel punished—Gideon's Ephod—The Cruelty of Abimelech—Gaal's Insurrection—Abimelech's Vengeance—His Death—Israel oppressed by the Ammonites—Jephthah's Expedition to Ammon—Jephthah's Rash Vow—The Ephraimites quarrel—An Angel appears to Manoah—Manoah's Sacrifice—The Birth of Samson—Samson's Riddle—Slaughter of the Philistines—Delilah's Treachery—Death of Samson—Micah and his Gods—Expedition of the Danites—The Levite and his Concubine—The Wickedness of Gibeah—The Israelites roused to Revenge—War with the Benjamites—Their Defeat—Lamentation for them—The Virgins of Shiloh surprised.

Ruth.

A. M. 2682. The book of Ruth is generally considered as an appendix to that of Judges, and an introduction to that of Samuel. It is, therefore, with great propriety, placed between the books of Judges and Samuel. It relates, with great beauty and simplicity, the history of a Moabitish damsel, who renounced idolatry, and, by marriage, was engrafted among the Israelites. David descended from her. The adoption of Ruth, a heathen convert to Judaism, into the line of Christ, has generally been considered as a pre-intimation of the admission of the Gentiles into the Church. A further design of this book is to evince the care of Divine Providence over those who sincerely fear God, in raising the pious Ruth from a state of the deepest adversity to that of the highest prosperity.

SUMMARY OF SUBJECTS.

The History of Elimelech and Naomi—Ruth's Constancy to Naomi—Kindness of Boaz to Ruth—Ruth's Visit to Boaz—Her Marriage to Boaz—The Birth of Obed.

Books of Samuel.

A. M. 2833. In the Jewish canon of Scripture these two books form but one, termed, in the Hebrew, the book of Samuel, probably because the greater part of the first book was written by that prophet, whose history and transactions it relates. According to the Talmudical writers, the first twenty-four chapters of the first book of Samuel were written by the prophet whose name they bear, and the remainder of that book, together with the whole of the second book, was committed to writing by the prophets Gad and Nathan, agreeably to the practice of the prophets, who wrote memoirs of the transactions of their respective times.

The *first book* of Samuel contains the history of the Jewish Church and polity, from the birth of Samuel, during the judicature of Eli, to the death of Saul, the first king of Israel, a period of nearly eighty years. It comprises—

1. The transactions under the judicature of Eli, chapter first to the fourth.

2. The history of the Israelites during the judicature of Samuel, chapter fifth to the thirteenth.

3. The history of Saul, and the events of his reign, chapter fourteenth to the thirty-first.

The *second book* of Samuel contains the history of David, the second king of Israel, during a period of nearly forty years. This book consists of three principal divisions, relating the triumphs and troubles of David, as follows:—

1. The triumphs of David, chapter first to the tenth.

2. The troubles of David, and their cause, together with

his repentance and recovery of the divine favour, chapter eleventh to the twenty-fourth.

3. David's restoration to the throne, and subsequent transactions, chapter twentieth to the twenty-fourth. The two books of Samuel are generally regarded as a key to the book of Psalms.

SUMMARY OF SUBJECTS.

The History of Elkanah and Hannah—Hannah's Prayer—Wickedness of Eli's Sons—Eli and his House threatened—The Call of Samuel—The Israelites overcome by their Enemies—Death of Eli—The Ark among the Philistines—Restoration of the Ark—The Philistines smitten—Request for a King—Saul seeks his Father's Asses—His Interview with Samuel—Samuel anoints him—Saul among the Prophets—The Election of a King—Samuel's Discourse to Israel—He calls for Thunder—The Philistines war against Israel—Jonathan's Miraculous Success—Saul's Harsh Oath—Jonathan condemned—The Amalekites destroyed—Saul's Dethronement foretold —Samuel kills Agag—David anointed by Samuel—Goliath's challenge to Israel—David comes to the Camp and slays Goliath—Jonathan's Love to David—Saul seeks to kill him—David marries Saul's Daughter—Saul's Jealousy of David—Saul prophesies before Samuel—Jonathan's Covenant with David—David at Nob with Abimelech—David in the Cave of Adullam—Saul destroys the Lord's Priests—David in the Wilderness of Ziph—David spares Saul in a Cave—Death of Samuel—Nabal's Provocation of David—David threatens to kill Nabal—Abigail pacifies David —David spares Saul's Life—Saul acknowledges his Fault and ceases his Persecution—He consults the Witch of Endor, who raiseth Samuel —Saul's Ruin foretold—The Amalekites burn Ziklag—David recovers the Spoil—Death of Saul and Jonathan—David laments for Saul.

A. M. 2948. The second book of *Samuel* contains the following:—The Ascension of David to the Throne of Israel—Asahel slain by Abner—Abner's Desertion to David—Joab's Murder of Abner—Death of Ishbosheth by his Servants—David reigns over all Israel—The Bringing of the Ark from Kirjath-jearim—Joy on the Restoration of the Ark—God's Covenant with David—David's Conquests—His Kindness to Jonathan's Son—Hanun's Usage of David's Servants—David's Sin with Bathsheba—Nathan's Parable—Death of David's Child—Solomon's Birth—Amnon's Incest—Absalom causes Amnon's Death—Joab's Art in Absalom's Favour—Absalom's Return—Absalom's Rebellion—David's Flight —He is cheated by Ziba, and cursed by Shimei—Ahithophel's Counsel—Hushai's Counsel accepted—Ahithophel hangs himself—Death of Absalom—David's Lamentation over him—Shimei pardoned—David returns to Jerusalem—Sheba's Rebellion—Amasa slain—The Gibeonites avenged—The Giants subdued—David's Song of Praise—David's Last Words—His Mighty Men—Solomon proclaimed—David's Dying Charge—The People numbered—The Numbering punished.

Books of Kings.

A. M. 2989. The two books of Kings are closely connected with those of Samuel. The origin and gradual increase of the united kingdom of Israel, under Saul and David, having been described in the latter, the books now under consideration relate its advancement and glory under Solomon—its division into two kingdoms, under Rehoboam—the causes of that division, and the consequent decline of the two kingdoms of Israel and Judah, until their final subversion—the ten tribes being carried captive into Assyria, and Judah and Benjamin to Babylon.

In the Jewish canon these books constitute but one, termed Kings, having been divided, at some unknown period, into two parts, for the convenience of reading. In the Septuagint and Vulgate they are termed the third and fourth book of Kings. They are generally ascribed to Ezra.

The *first book* of Kings embraces a period of one hundred and twenty-six years, from the anointing of Solomon and his admission as a partner in the throne, to the death of Jehoshaphat. It may be divided into two principal parts, containing—

1. The history of Solomon's reign, embracing the latter days of David. The reign of Solomon to the dedication of the temple, and subsequent transactions, chapter first to the eleventh, and second to the forty-sixth, and chapter third to the eighth.

2. The history of the two kingdoms of Judah and Israel, including the accession of Rehoboam and the division of the two kingdoms. The reigns of Rehoboam and Jeroboam. The reigns of Abijam and Asa, kings of Judah, and the contemporary reigns of Nadab, Baasha, Elah, Zimri, Omri,

and the reigns of Jehoshaphat, and Ahab, and Ahaziah, chapter eleventh to the twenty-second.

The *second book* of Kings continues the contemporary history of the two kingdoms of Israel and Judah, from the death of Jehoshaphat to the destruction of the city and temple, a period of three hundred years. The history contained in the book may be divided into two parts—

1. The contemporary history of the kingdoms of Israel and Judah to the end of the former, chapter first to the seventeenth.

2. The history of the decline and fall of the kingdom of Judah, chapter eighteenth to the twenty-fifth.

SUMMARY OF SUBJECTS.

Adonijah's Invasion of the Throne—Solomon proclaimed—David's Dying Charge—Adonijah's and Joab's Death—Destruction of Shimei—God's Appearance to Solomon—The Wisdom of Solomon—Solomon's Princes and Officers—His Distinguished Reputation—His Agreement with Hiram—Building of the Temple—Ornaments and Sacred Vessels—Dedication of the Temple—Solomon's Prayer—He blesses the Congregation—God's Answer to Solomon—Solomon's Buildings—Visit of the Queen of Sheba—Solomon's Degeneracy—God's Anger against Solomon—Death of Solomon—Revolt of the Ten Tribes—Jeroboam's Idolatry—Jeroboam's Hand withered—The Deceived Prophet slain—Jeroboam threatened—Rehoboam's Disgrace and Death—Asa's Excellencies and Defects—Baasha's Wicked Reign—Zimri's Treason and Death—Ahab's Wickedness—Elijah fed by the Ravens—Elijah's Interview with Obadiah—Trial of the False Prophets—Elijah's Flight from Jezebel—The Call of Elisha—Benhadad's Siege of Samaria—Death of Benhadad—Ahab's Folly reproved—Naboth murdered by Jezebel—Ahab's Humility—Jehoshaphat's League with Ahab—Micaiah's Prediction—Ahab's Death—Jehoshaphat's Death.

A. M. 3208. The Second Book of *Kings* contains:—The Rebellion of Moab—Elijah brings Fire from Heaven—His Translation to Heaven—Elisha heals the Waters of the Jordan—Defeat of the Moabites—Increase of the Widow's Oil—The Restoration of the Shunemite's Son—The Healing of the Deadly Pottage—Miracles by Elisha—Cure of Naaman's Leprosy—Gehazi's Sin and Punishment—The Syrian ensnared—Famine in Samaria—Samaria plentifully supplied—The Shunemite's Land restored—Hazael's Barbarity predicted—Jehu anointed King—Joram and Ahaziah slain—Death of Jezebel—Baal's Worshippers slain—Jehu's Inconsistency—Death of Athaliah—Wicked Reign of Jehoash—Death of Elisha—Jehoash defeats Amaziah—Reign of Azariah—Reigns of Shallum, Pekahiah, Pekah, &c.—Reign of Ahaz—The Israelites carried Captive—The Samaritans' Idolatry—Hezekiah's Good Reign—Sennacherib invades Judea—Rabshakeh's Blasphemous Speech—Hezekiah sends to Isaiah—Sennacherib's Fall predicted—Hezekiah's Sickness and Recovery—Manasseh's Impious Reign—His Ruin foretold—Josiah's Pious Reign—Destroys Idolatry and reforms Judea—His Zeal—Death of Josiah—Jehoiachin carried into Captivity—Nebuchadnezzar takes Jerusalem—The High-priest and Nobles slain.

Books of Chronicles.

A. M. 1-3381. The Jews comprise the two books of Chronicles into one, which they call *The Words of Days*, because they were compiled out of *diaries* or *annals*. In the Septuagint they are called *Paraleipomena*, or *things omitted*, because many things omitted in the former part of sacred history are here recorded. The appellation of Chronicles was given by Jerome, because they contain an abstract, in the order of time, of the whole of sacred history, to the time in which they were written. They are a compilation from other books. The period of time embraced in them is about three thousand four hundred and sixty-eight years. They may be divided into four parts—

1. Genealogical tables, from Adam to the time of Ezra, 1 Chronicles, chapter first to the ninth.
2. The histories of Saul and David, chapter tenth to the twenty-ninth.
3. The history of the united kingdom of Israel and Judah, under Solomon, chapter twenty-ninth, verses twenty-third to thirtieth; 2 Chronicles, first to the ninth.
4. The history of the kingdom of Judah, from the revolt of the ten tribes to its termination, 2 Chronicles, tenth to the thirty-sixth.

As the books of Samuel, Kings, and Chronicles, relate to the same histories, they should each be read and collated together, as they give a comprehensive history of the Jewish nation, and serve to illustrate each other.

SUMMARY OF SUBJECTS.

Genealogies—The Sons of Israel—The Family of David—Genealogies—Defeat of the Hagarites—Posterity of Judah—The Line of Reuben—The Sons of Levi—The Sons of Issachar—The Sons of Benjamin—Genealogies of Israel and Judah—Saul's Overthrow and Death—David made King of Israel—The Armies that helped David—David removeth the Ark—Hiram's Kindness to David—David's Psalm of Thanksgiving—Nathan's Message to David—David's Victories—David's Messengers ill-treated—Rabbah taken and spoiled—The Plague stayed—Preparation for the Temple—Solomon made King—The Order of Aaron's Sons—The Number of the Singers—The Division of the Porters—The Twelve Captains—David's Exhortation—David's Reign and Death.

A. M. 2889. The Second Book of *Chronicles* embraces:—Solomon's Offering—Solomon sends to Hiram—Building of the Temple—The Vessels of the Temple—Temple finished—Solomon's Blessing—His Sacrifice—Builds Cities—Queen of Sheba's Visit to Solomon—Rehoboam made King—Judah strengthened—Rehoboam's Reign and Death—Abijah's Victory over Rehoboam—Asa destroys Idolatry—His Covenant with God—His Death and Burial—Jehoshaphat's Good Reign—Micaiah's Prophecy—Jehoshaphat's Care for Justice—His Fast and Prayer—Jehoram's Wicked Reign—Ahaziah's Wicked Reign—Joash made King—Zechariah stoned—The Edomites overcome—Uriah's Leprosy—Jotham's Good Reign—Ahaz's Wicked Reign—Hezekiah's Good Reign—The Passover proclaimed—Provision for the Priests—Hezekiah's Death—Manasseh's Wicked Reign—Josiah's Good Reign—Josiah slain in Battle—Jerusalem destroyed.

Ezra.

A. M. 3468. The books of Ezra and Nehemiah were regarded by the Jews as one volume, and were divided by them into the first and second books of Ezra. The same division is recognised by the Greek and Latin Churches. Ezra is generally admitted to be the author of the book which bears his name. Every page of the book, indeed, proves that the writer of it was personally present at the transactions which he has recorded. The book harmonizes with the prophecies of Haggai and Zechariah. It evinces the paternal care of the Almighty over his chosen people, and consists of two parts—

1. A narrative of events from the return of the Jews,

under Zerubbabel, to the rebuilding of the temple, chapter first to the sixth.

2. The arrival of Ezra at Jerusalem, and the reformation made there by him, chapter seventh to the tenth.

The memory of Ezra has always been held in the highest veneration by the Jews.

SUMMARY OF SUBJECTS.

The Proclamation of Cyrus—The Return of the People from Babylon—The Erection of the Altar—The Decree of Artaxerxes—Tatnai's Letter to Darius—The Temple finished—Ezra's Journey to Jerusalem—Keeps a Fast—His Prayer—Ezra's Mourning.

Nehemiah.

A. M. 3558. This book was written by the person whose name it bears. Nehemiah was cup-bearer to Artaxerxes Longimanus. This book contains—

1. An account of Nehemiah's departure from Shushan with a royal commission to rebuild the walls of Jerusalem, and his arrival there, chapter first; second, 1–11.

2. An account of the building of the walls, notwithstanding the obstacles interposed by Sanballat, chapter second, 12–20; third to the seventh, 4.

3. The first reformation accomplished by Nehemiah, chapter seventh to the twelfth.

4. The second reformation, on his second return to Jerusalem, and his correction of the abuses which had crept in during his absence, chapter thirteenth.

His administration lasted about thirty-six years.

SUMMARY OF SUBJECTS.

The Book of Nehemiah contains:—His Lamentations for Jerusalem—Artaxerxes's Encouragement to Nehemiah—Names of the Builders—The Appointment of a Watch—Reformation of Usury—Sanballat's Practices—Hanani and Hananiah's Charge—The Reading of the Law—Solemn Fast appointed—Points of the Covenant—Persons dwelling at Jerusalem—The High-priest's Succession—Divers Abuses reformed—Nehemiah's

Prayer—He is sent to Jerusalem—Malice of Sanballat—Rebuilding of the Wall—Opposition of Sanballat—Precaution of Nehemiah—Plot of Sanballat—Completion of the Wall—Return of the Captives, and Register of their Families—The Joy of the People—Prayer of the Levites at the Solemn Fast—Sealing of the Covenant—Renewal of the Sacred Rites—Distribution of the People—Dedication of the Wall—Abuses rectified—Charge respecting the Sabbath—Dismissal of Strange Wives.

Esther.

A. M. 3485. This book is termed by the Jews the volume of Esther, because it chiefly consists in the relation of her history. The history contained in this book comes in between the sixth and seventh chapters of Ezra. It consists of two parts—

1. The promotion of Esther to the throne of Persia, and the essential service rendered to the king by Mordecai, in detecting a plot against his life, chapter first to the second.

2. The advancement of Haman—his designs against the Jews, and their frustration—and the advancement of Mordecai, chapter third to the tenth.

In our copies the book of Esther terminates with the third verse of the tenth chapter; but in the Greek and Latin there are ten more verses annexed, together with six additional chapters, which the Greek and Roman Churches consider canonical. As they are not extant in the Hebrew they are expunged from the sacred canon by Protestants, and are supposed to have been compiled by some Hellenistic Jew.

SUMMARY OF SUBJECTS.

Ahasuerus's Royal Feast—Esther made Queen—Haman despised by Mordecai—Mourning of the Jews—Esther obtains the King's Favour—Mordecai's Good Services—Haman is Hanged—Rejoicing of the Jews—Haman's Ten Sons hanged—Mordecai's Advancement.

CHAPTER II.

POETICAL BOOKS.

THE poetical books, denominated by the Jews the Hagiographa, are placed between the historical and prophetical books, without any reference to date. They are called *poetical*, because they are almost wholly composed in Hebrew verse.

Job.

A. M. 2484. This book has derived its title from the venerable patriarch whose name it bears. Some critics have doubted the existence of such a character as Job. That point, however, is satisfactorily proven by the prophet Ezekiel and the apostle James, both of whom mention him as a real character. The length of his life places him in patriarchal times, and some are of the opinion that he lived about one hundred and eighty-four years before the time of Abraham. It is in the form of a dramatic poem, and was, in all probability, written by Job, and transcribed by Moses, when he was an exile in Arabia. It has been quoted by almost every Hebrew writer from the age of Moses to that of Malachi. It may be divided into six parts—

1. Contains the exordium or narrative, written in prose, chapter first and second.

2. Comprises the first debate or dialogue of Job and his friends, chapter third to the fourteenth.

3. Includes the second series of debate or controversy, chapter fifteenth to the twenty-first.

4. Comprehends the third series of controversy, chapter twenty-second to the thirty-first.

5. Sums up the argument, chapter thirty-second to the thirty-seventh.

6. Jehovah determines the controversy. Job humbles

himself—is accepted—restored to health and prosperity, chapter thirty-eighth to the forty-third.

SUMMARY OF SUBJECTS.

An Account of Job's Losses and Temptations—Smitten with Boils—Curses the Day of his Birth—Eliphaz reproves him—Job wishes for Death—Excuses this Desire—Bildad showeth God's Justice—The Innocent often afflicted—Job expostulates with God—Zophar reproves Job—God's Omnipotency maintained—Job's Confidence in God—The Conditions of Man's Life—Eliphaz reproves Job—Job reproves his Friends—His Appeal to God—Bildad's Reproof—Job's Complaint—The Portion of the Wicked—The Destruction of the Wicked—Job accused of Divers Sins—God's Decree Immutable—Sin goeth often unpunished—Man cannot be justified before God—Job reproves Bildad—The Hypocrite without Hope—Wisdom is the Gift of God—Job bemoans himself—His Honour turned to Contempt—Professes his Integrity—Elihu reproves and reasons with Job—God cannot be Unjust—Comparison cannot be made with God—The Justice of God's Ways—God's Great Works—His Wisdom is Unsearchable—His Power in his Creatures—Job's Humility—God's Power in Creation—Job's Prosperity, Age, and Death.

Psalms.

This book is called, in Hebrew, the *book of hymns or praises*, because the praises of God constitute their chief subject, and as they were set to be sung not only with the voice, but also to be accompanied with instruments. The Septuagint designates them Βίβλος Ψαλμῶν, (*Biblos Psalmon,*) the *book of Psalms;* and this appellation is retained in our Bibles. They are generally termed the Psalms of David—that Hebrew monarch being their chief author. Many of them bear his name. We have no information when these divine poems were collected into a volume.

The book of Psalms being composed in Hebrew verse, must be studied according to the laws of Hebrew poetry. To enable one to enter into their force and meaning, it is necessary to attend to the following hints:—

1. Investigate the argument of each Psalm.

2. Examine the historical origin of the Psalm, or the circumstances which led to its composition.

3. Attend to the structure of the Psalms.

SUMMARY OF SUBJECTS.

The Happiness of the Godly—The Kingdom of Christ—The Security of God's Protection—Prayer for Audience—David's Profession of Faith—His Complaint in Sickness—The Destruction of the Wicked—God's Love to Man—God praised for his Judgments—The Outrage of the Wicked—God's Providence and Justice—David's Plea to God for Help—Boasts of the Divine Mercy—The Natural Man described—David's Hope of his Calling—A Citizen of Zion described—His Confidence—Praise to God—Prayer for Grace—The Church's Confidence in God—Thanksgiving for Victory—Complaint and Prayer—Confidence in God's Grace—God's Worship in the World—Confidence in Prayer—David resorteth unto God—His Love to God's Service—Blesseth God—Reasons for honouring God—Praise for Deliverance—Rejoicing in God's Mercy—The Blessed—God is to be praised—Who are blessed—Prayer for Safety—Excellency of God's Mercy—Persuasion to Patience—God moved to Compassion—The Brevity of Life—Obedience the Best Sacrifice—God's Care of the Poor—David's Zeal to serve God—His Prayer to be restored—The Church's Complaint to God—The Majesty of Christ's Kingdom—The Church's Confidence in God—The Kingdom of Christ—The Privileges of the Church—Worldly Prosperity contemned—God's Majesty in the Church—David's Prayer and Confession—His Confidence in God—The Natural Man described—David's Prayer for Salvation—His Complaint—His Promise of Praise—Description of the Wicked—Prayer for Deliverance—Comfort in Promises—Vows of Perpetual Service—No Trust in Worldly Things—Thirst for God—Complaint of Enemies—The Blessedness of God's Chosen—Exhortation to Praise—Prayer for God's Kingdom—Prayer at the Removing of the Ark—Complaint—Prayer for the Godly—For Perseverance—Prayer for Solomon—The Righteous sustained—Prayer for the Sanctuary—Rebuke of the Proud—God's Majesty in the Church—David's Combat with Diffidence—God's Wrath against Israel—Prayer for the Church—Exhortation to praise God—Reproof of the Judges—The Church's Enemies—Longing for the Sanctuary—Prayer for Mercies—Complaint of the Proud—Nature and Glory of the Church—David's Complaint—God praised for his Power—His Providence set forth—The State of the Godly—God Praised for his Great Works—The Majesty of Christ's Kingdom—The Danger of tempting God—Praise for God's Greatness—The Majesty of God—All Creatures exhorted to praise God—He is to be worshipped—To be praised cheerfully—David's Profession of Godliness—Mercies to be recorded—God blessed for his Constancy—Wonderful Providences—David's Confidence in God—Plague of Egypt—Israel's Rebellion—Complaint—The Kingdom of Christ—Happiness of the Godly—An Exhortation to Praise—The Vanity of Idols—Thankfulness—Praise for Mercy and Truth—Trust in God—Meditation, Prayer, and Praise—David's Prayer against Doeg—Safety of the Godly—Joy for the Church—Confidence in God—Prayer for the Godly—Church prays for Mercy—Virtue of God's Blessing—Fear of God—Haters of the Church cursed—Hope in God—Humility—Care for the Ark—Saints' Communion—Exhortation—Praise for Judgments—Manifold Mercies—Constancy of the Jews—Confidence in God—The Wicked defied—Prayer for Deliverance—For Sincerity—Comfort in Trouble—David's Complaint—Prayer for his Kingdom—Help to the Godly—Vows of Perpetual Praise—Praise for Providences—All Creatures should praise God—God praised for his Benefits—Praised upon Instruments.

Proverbs.

A. M. 3004. The book of Proverbs has always been ascribed to Solomon. The general opinion is that several persons made a collection of them; and that Hezekiah, Agur, Isaiah, and Ezra, were among the number. It is frequently quoted by the apostles. It may be divided into five parts, viz.:—

1. In the proem, or exordium, containing the first nine chapters, the teacher gives his pupil a series of admonitions, directions, and cautions, as well as excitements to the study of wisdom.

2. Extends from chapter tenth to the twenty-second, and consists of what may be strictly and properly called proverbs—namely, unconnected sentences, expressed with beauty and simplicity.

3. Reaches from chapter twenty-second, verse seventeen, to chapter twenty-fifth, inclusive. In this part the teacher drops the sententious style, and addresses his pupil as present.

4. The proverbs contained in this part are supposed to have been selected from some larger collection of Solomon, by the prophets whom he employed to restore the service and writings of the Jewish Church. This part extends from the twenty-fifth to the thirtieth chapter.

5. Comprises chapters thirtieth and thirty-first. The first are the instructions given by Agur, and the latter the precepts given to Lemuel by his mother, a Jewess, married to some neighbouring prince.

SUMMARY OF SUBJECTS.

The Use of the Proverbs—The Benefit of Wisdom—Exhortation to Sundry Duties—Persuasions to Sundry Duties—Mischiefs of Licentiousness—Seven Things hateful to God—Description of a Harlot—The Call of Wisdom—The Doctrine of Wisdom—Virtues and Vices contrasted—Observations about Kings—Sundry Maxims—Observations on Impiety—Of Public Government—Agur's Prayer—Lemuel's Lesson of Chastity.

Ecclesiastes.

A. M. 3027. The title of this book is derived from the Septuagint, and signifies *a preacher*, or one who harangues a public congregation. In Hebrew it is termed The Words of the Preacher. Although this book does not bear the name of Solomon, it is evident he was the author of it. Its design is to demonstrate the vanity of all earthly objects, and draw off men from their pursuit, as an *apparent* good, to the fear of God and communion with him as a *permanent* good. It consists of two parts, viz.:—

1. The vanity of all earthly conditions, occupations, and pleasures, chapter first to the sixth.

2. The nature, excellence, and beneficial effects of true religion, chapter sixth to the twelfth.

The conclusion, chapter twelfth.

SUMMARY OF SUBJECTS.

The Vanity of all Earthly Things—The Common End of Wisdom and Folly—A Time for All Things—The Good of Contentment—The Vanity of Riches—The Conclusion of Vanities—Remedies against Vanities—Kings are to be respected—Wisdom is better than Strength—Wisdom and Folly—Directions for Charity—The Preacher's Care to edify.

Song of Solomon.

A. M. 2990. This book has always been reputed to be the production of the Hebrew monarch. This poem was composed on the occasion of Solomon's marriage. All interpreters agree that it is a mystical poem, or allegory. It can only be explained by the aid of Oriental literature and manners.

SUMMARY OF SUBJECTS.

The Church's Love to Christ—Christ's Care of the Church—Christ the Church's Glory—The Graces of the Church—Christ's Love to his Church—The Church's Faith in Christ—Graces of the Church—The Calling of the Gentiles.

CHAPTER III.

PROPHETICAL BOOKS.

Isaiah.

A. M. 3224. THIS book is larger than all the twelve minor prophets put together. Isaiah was the son of Amoz, and discharged the prophetic office in the days of Uzziah, Jotham, Ahaz, and Hezekiah, kings of Judah. No prophet has so clearly predicted the circumstances relative to the advent, sufferings, atoning death, and resurrection of the Messiah, as the author of this book; and hence he is styled the evangelical prophet. The unfulfilled predictions of the ultimate triumph and extension of the Redeemer's kingdom, contained in this book, are unrivalled for the splendour of their imagery, and the beauty and sublimity of the language in which they are conveyed. This book may be divided into six parts, viz.:—

1. Contains a general description of the condition and state of the Jews in the several periods of their history, the promulgation and success of the gospel, and the coming of Messiah to judgment, chapter first to the fifth.

2. Comprises the predictions delivered in the reigns of Jotham and Ahaz, chapter sixth to the twelfth.

3. Contains various predictions against the Babylonians, Assyrians, Philistines, and other nations, with whom the

Jews had any intercourse, chapter thirteenth to the twenty-fourth.

4. Contains a prophecy of the great calamities which should fall upon the people of God, his merciful preservation of a remnant, and their restoration to their country, and their conversion to Christ, and the destruction of Antichrist, chapter twenty-fourth to the thirty-third.

5. Comprises the historical part of the prophecy of Isaiah, chapter thirty-sixth to the thirty-ninth.

6. Comprises a series of prophecies delivered, in all probability, towards the close of Hezekiah's reign, chapter fortieth to the sixty-sixth.

SUMMARY OF SUBJECTS.

The Complaint of Judah—Prophecy of Christ's Kingdom—Oppression of the Rulers—Christ's Kingdom a Sanctuary—God's Judgments for Sin—Isaiah's Vision of God's Glory—Christ promised—Israel and Judah threatened—The Church's Joy in Christ's Birth—God's Judgments upon Israel—Calling of the Gentiles—Thanksgiving for God's Mercies—Babylon threatened—Israel's Restoration—Lamentable State of Moab—Syria and Israel threatened—God's Care of his People—The Confusion of Egypt—Egypt and Ethiopia's Captivity—The Fall of Babylon—The Invasion of Jewry—Tyre's Miserable Overthrow—Judgments of God for Sin—Praise to God—God's Care of his Vineyard—Ephraim threatened—God's Judgment on Jerusalem—God's Mercies toward his Church—Desolation foreshown—Privileges of the Godly—Vindication of the Church—Blessings of the Gospel—Insult to Hezekiah by Rabshakeh—Hezekiah's Prayer—His Thanksgiving—Babylonian Captivity foretold—Promulgation of the Gospel—God's Mercies to his Church—Christ's Mission to the Gentiles—Comfort to the Church—The Vanity of Idols—Cyrus called—God's Judgment upon Babylon—The Intent of Prophecy—Christ sent to the Gentiles—Christ's Sufferings and Patience—The Certainty of God's Salvation—Christ's Free Redemption—The Humiliation of Christ—The Church's Enlargement—The Happy State of Believers—Exhortation to Holiness—God reproves the Jews—Hypocrisy reproved—The Covenant of the Redeemer—The Glory of the Church—The Office of Christ—God's Promises to his Church—Christ shows his Power to save—The Church's Prayer—The Calling of the Gentiles—The Growth of the Church.

Jeremiah.

A. M. 2375. The prophet Jeremiah was one of the sacerdotal race, being one of the priests that dwelt in the land of Benjamin, about three miles north of Jerusalem. He entered upon the prophetic office early in life, and prophesied about forty years. He followed the remnant of the Jews on retiring into Egypt. His prophecies are levelled against the crimes of his countrymen. His prophecies are not in the chronological order in which they were delivered. Chronologically arranged, they may be thus divided:—

1. Prophecies delivered in the reign of Josiah, chapter first to the twelfth, inclusive.
2. Prophecies delivered in the reign of Jehoiakim, chapters thirteenth, twentieth, twenty-second, twenty-third, thirty-fifth, thirty-sixth, forty-fifth, forty-eighth, and forty-ninth.
3. Prophecies delivered in the reign of Zedekiah, including chapters twenty-first, twenty-fourth, twenty-seventh, thirty-fourth, thirty-seventh, thirty-ninth, and forty-ninth.
4. Prophecies delivered under the government of Gedaliah, from the taking of Jerusalem to the retreat into Egypt, and prophecies delivered in that country, including chapters fortieth and forty-fourth.

SUMMARY OF SUBJECTS.

The Calling of Jeremiah—Israel spoiled for his Sins—God's Mercy to Judah—Israel called to Repentance—God's Judgments upon the Jews—Enemies sent against Judah—Jeremiah's Call for Repentance—The Calamities of the Jews—Jeremiah's Lamentation—The Vanity of Idols—God's Covenant proclaimed—The Prosperity of the Wicked—An Exhortation to Repentance—The Prophet's Prayer—Jeremiah's Complaint—The Utter Ruin of the Jews—The Captivity of Judah—The Type of the Potter—The Desolation of the Jews—Pashur smiteth Jeremiah—Nebuchadnezzar's War—The Judgment of Shallum—Restoration of God's People—The Type of Good and Bad Figs—Jeremiah's Reproof of the Jews—He is arraigned—Nebuchadnezzar's Conquests—Hananiah's Prophecy—Jeremiah's Letter—The Return of the Jews—The Restoration of Israel—The Imprisonment of Jeremiah—Christ, the Branch, promised—Zedekiah's Fate foretold—God blesses the Rechabites—Jeremiah's Prophecies—The Chaldeans' Siege raised—Jeremiah cast into a Dungeon—Jerusalem taken—Jeremiah set at Liberty—Ishmael killeth Gedaliah—Johanan's Promise—Jeremiah carried to Egypt—Judah's Desolation—Baruch comforted—Overthrow of Pharaoh's Army—Destruction of Philistines—Judgment of Moab—Restoration of Elam—Redemption of Israel—God's Judgments—Zedekiah's Wicked Reign.

Lamentations.

A. M. 3416. That Jeremiah was the author of these elegies, or lamentations, has never been doubted. This book contains five chapters, forming as many pathetic elegies. In the first four the prophet bewails the calamities of his country, and the fifth is an epilogue to the preceding ones.

SUMMARY OF SUBJECTS.

The Carrying away of King Jehoiakim, with Ten Thousand of the principal Hebrews—The Assault of Jerusalem—The Calamities undergone by the Prophet—The Overthrow of Jerusalem—The Carrying away of King Zedekiah, and the Slaughter of the Hebrews—The Wretched Condition of the People after the Destruction of the City.

Ezekiel.

A. M. 3499. Ezekiel was the son of Buzi, of the sacerdotal race, and one of the captives carried away to Babylon. The principal scene of his predictions was some place on the river Chebar, which flows into the Euphrates, about two hundred miles to the north of Babylon, where the prophet resided. He entered upon his prophetic office in the thirtieth year of his age, and continued in it about twenty years. His prophecies are chronologically arranged, and may be divided into four parts, viz.:—

1. His call to the prophetic office—his commission and instructions for executing it—chapters first, second, and third.

2. Denunciations against the Jewish people, chapters third and fourth to the twenty-fourth.

3. His prophecies against various neighbouring nations, enemies to the Jews, chapter twenty-fifth to the thirty-second.

4. Contains a series of exhortations and promises to the Jews of future deliverance, under Cyrus, and their final restoration and conversion to the Messiah, chapters thirty-third to the forty-sixth.

SUMMARY OF SUBJECTS.

Ezekiel's Vision—His Commission—Eating of the Roll—Type of the Siege—Type of Hair—Israel threatened—Israel's Desolation—Vision of Jealousy—The Marked preserved—Vision of Coals of Fire—The Presumption of the Priest—The Type of Removing—Lying Prophets—Idolaters exhorted—Rejection of Jerusalem—God's Love to Jerusalem—The Eagles and the Vine—Parable of Sour Grapes—Of the Lion's Whelps—Israel's Rebellions—Prophecy against Jerusalem—Jerusalem's Sins—Aholah and Aholibah—Jerusalem's Destruction—Ammonites threatened—The Fall of Tyrus—Tyrus's Rich Supply—Zidon threatened—The Judgment of Pharaoh—Desolation of Egypt—The Glory and Fall of Assyria—The Fall of Egypt—Ezekiel admonished—God's Care of his Flock—Judgment of Seir—Israel comforted—Vision of Dry Bones—The Malice of Gog—Description of the Temple—Ornaments of the Temple—The Priests' Chambers—Return of God's Glory—The Priests reproved—Division of the Land—Ordinances for the Princes—Vision of the Holy Waters—Portions of the Twelve Tribes.

Daniel.

A. M. 3399. Daniel was of royal birth, and, at an early age, was carried away a captive to Babylon. Having been instructed in the language and literature of the Chaldeans, he afterwards held a very distinguished office in the Babylonian empire. He was a contemporary with Ezekiel, and his extraordinary piety and wisdom were proverbial. He lived in great credit with the Babylonian monarchs, and his uncommon merit procured him the same regard from Darius and Cyrus, the first two sovereigns of Persia. His prophecy may be divided into two parts:—

1. Comprises the historical portion of this book. It contains a narrative of the circumstances which led to Daniel's elevation, chapter first to the sixth.

2. Comprises various prophecies and visions of things future, until the advent and death of the Messiah, and the ultimate conversion of the Jews and Gentiles to the faith of the gospel, chapter seventh to the twelfth.

This amazing series of prophecies extends through many successive ages, from the first establishment of the Persian empire, five hundred and thirty years before Christ, to the general resurrection.

SUMMARY OF SUBJECTS.

Daniel's Captivity—His Advancement—The Account of Shadrach, Meshach, and Abednego—Nebuchadnezzar's Pride and Fall—Belshazzar's Impious Feast—Daniel's Interpretation of the Mysterious Writing—He is invested with Power—Decree of Darius—Daniel in the Den of Lions—Vision of the Four Beasts—Interpretation—Vision of the Ram and He-goat—Gabriel's Interpretation—Confesses Israel's Sins—Comforted by an Angel—Overthrow of Persia—Israel's Deliverance.

Hosea.

A. M. 3219. Hosea was an Israelite, who lived in the kingdom of Samaria. His predictions are chiefly levelled against the Israelites, for their sins. His book contains fourteen chapters, and may be divided into five parts, viz.:—

1. Their idolatry is described, and they are exhorted to forsake it. Promises are introduced on the general conversion of the *twelve* tribes to Christianity, chapters first, second, and third.

2. A reproof of the bloodshed and idolatry of the Israelites, against which the inhabitants of Judah are exhorted to take warning, interspersed with promises of pardon, chapters fourth to the sixth.

3. The prophet's exhortations to repentance proving ineffectual, God complains of their obstinacy, and threatens them with captivity, chapters sixth, seventh, and eighth.

4. Captivity and dispersion further threatened. Return to their own country foretold. Further threatenings on account of idolatry, chapters ninth, tenth, eleventh, twelfth, and thirteenth.

5. Denunciation of punishment. Exhortation to repentance. Their restoration from idolatry, and their conversion to the gospel foretold, chapters thirteenth and fourteenth.

SUMMARY OF SUBJECTS.

Judgments for Whoredom—Idolatry of the People—Desolation of Israel—Judgment threatened—Israel a Treacherous People—Exhortation to Repentance—Reproof of Manifold Sins—Israel threatened—Captivity of Israel—Israel's Impiety—Ingratitude to God—Ephraim reproved-Ephraim's Glory vanished—Blessings promised.

Joel.

A. M. 3194. This prophet was a contemporary with Amos and Hosea. His book consists of three chapters, which may be divided into so many parts, viz.:—

1. An exhortation to the priests and people to repent, by reason of the famine brought upon them by the palmer-worm, in consequence of their sins. A denunciation of greater calamities, if they continued impenitent, chapter first.

2. An exhortation to keep a public and solemn fast, with a promise of removing the calamities of the people, and an effusion of the Holy Spirit, chapter second.

3. A prediction of their general conversion and return, with the destruction of their opponents and the glory of the Church, chapter third.

SUMMARY OF SUBJECTS.

God's Sundry Judgments—He exhorteth the People to mourn, and prescribes a Fast—Terribleness of God's Judgments—Exhortation to Repentance—The Prophet comforts Zion—Merciful Promises of Restoration—God known in Judgment—The Blessings of God upon his Church.

Amos.

A. M. 3214. This prophet was a native of Tekoa, a small town in the kingdom of Judah, about four leagues south of Jerusalem. His prophecy consists of three parts, viz.:—

1. The judgments of God denounced against the neighbouring nations, viz.: the Syrians, Philistines, Tyrians, Edomites, Ammonites, and Moabites, chapters first and second.

2. The divine judgments denounced against Judah and Israel, chapters second to ninth.

3. Consolatory promises to the Church, describing her restoration to the Messiah, chapter ninth.

SUMMARY OF SUBJECTS.

Judgments against Nations bordering upon Palestine—God's Wrath against Moab—Judah—Israel—Complains of their Ingratitude—Necessity of God's Judgments against Israel—Publication of it, with the Causes thereof—Israel reproved for Oppression, Idolatry, and Incorrigibleness—Lamentation for Israel—Exhortation to Repentance—God rejects their Hypocritical Service—Wantonness of Israel—Threatened with Desolation—The Judgments of Grasshoppers and Fire diverted by the Prayer of Amos—The rejection of Israel symbolized by a Wall and a Plumb-line—Amaziah's Complaint of Amos—Amos's Vindication—Amaziah's Judgment—The Propinquity of Israel's End shown by a Basket of Summer Fruit—Oppression reproved—A Famine of the Word threatened—The Certainty of the Desolation—Restoration of the Tabernacle of David.

Obadiah.

A. M. 3417. This prophet was contemporary with Jeremiah, one of whose predictions constitutes the greater part of this book. This prophecy may be divided into two parts, viz.:—

1. A denunciation of the country of Edom, for its pride and security, and for the cruel insults and enmity of the Edomites to the Jews, verse tenth to the sixteenth.

2. Consolatory promises. The restoration of the Jews, and their victory over their enemies, verse seventeenth to the twenty-first.

SUMMARY OF SUBJECTS.

Destruction of the Edomites, for their Pride and Carnal Security—Their Land made Desolate, because of their Refusal to let Israel pass through Idumea—The Total Extinction of the Edomites foretold—The Salvation and Victory of Jacob foretold, and the Judgment of Esau.

Jonah.

A. M. 3317. Jonah was a native of Gath Hepher, in Galilee. He is supposed to have prophesied to the ten tribes, under the reign of Joash. The design of the book is to show, by the very striking example of the Ninevites, the divine forbearance and long-suffering towards sinners who are spared on their sincere repentance. It consists of two parts, viz.:—

1. Jonah's mission to Nineveh, and his attempt to flee to Tarshish. The judgment which fell upon him, chapters first to the second.

2. His mission, and its happy result to the Ninevites, chapters third and fourth.

SUMMARY OF SUBJECTS.

Jonah sent to Nineveh—His Flight to Tarshish—Betrayed by a Tempest—Thrown into the Sea, and swallowed by a Fish—Prayer of Jonah—His Deliverance—Sent again to preach to the Ninevites—God averts his Wrath on their Repentance—Jonah is reproved for repining at God's Mercy in sparing the Ninevites.

Micah.

A. M. 3254. This prophet was a native of Morasthi, a small town in the southern part of the territory of Judah. He prophesied in the reigns of Jotham and Hezekiah, and was, consequently, contemporary with Isaiah, Joel, Hosea, and Amos. His book may be divided into three parts, viz.:—

1. The introduction, or title, chapter first.

2. Comprises the prophecies delivered in the reign of Jotham, in which the divine judgments are denounced against both Israel and Judah for their sins, chapter second.

3. Contains the predictions delivered in the reign of Hezekiah, chapters fourth, fifth, and seventh.

The fifth chapter contains a prediction of the place of the Messiah's nativity.

SUMMARY OF SUBJECTS.

Micah shows the Wrath of God against Idolatry—Exhortation to Mourning against Oppression—A Lamentation—A Reproof of Injustice and Idolatry—A Promise of Restoration to Jacob—The Cruelty of the Princes—Falsehood of the Prophets—Security of both—The Glory, Peace, Kingdom, and Victory of the Church—Birth of Christ, his Kingdom and Conquest—God's Controversy for Unkindness, Ignorance, Injustice, and Idolatry—Complaint of the Church, on Account of the Paucity of her Numbers, and the General Corruption—Confidence in God, not Man—She triumphs over her Enemies—God comforts her by Promises—Confounds her Enemies, and manifests his Mercies.

Nahum.

A. M. 3291. Nahum was a native of Elkosha, a village in Galilee, and lived between the Assyrian and Babylonian captivities. He denounced the final and inevitable doom of Nineveh, and the Assyrian empire, by the Chaldeans. His prophecy is one entire poem, opening with a sublime description of the justice and power of God, tempered with long-suffering, chapter first, 1–8. He foretells the destruction of the Assyrian empire, (9–12,) together with the deliverance of Hezekiah, (13–15.) The destruction of Nineveh is then predicted, with singular minuteness.

SUMMARY OF SUBJECTS.

The Majesty of God revealed in Goodness to his People, and Severity to his Enemies—The Fearful and Victorious Armies of God against Nineveh—The Awful Ruin of Nineveh for its Crimes.

Habakkuk.

A. M. 3378. This prophet exercised his office in the reign of Jehoiakim, and, consequently, was a contemporary with Jeremiah. His book consists of two parts, viz.:—

1. A dialogue between God and the prophet, in which

the Babylonish captivity is announced, with a promise of deliverance, and the ultimate destruction of the Babylonian empire, chapter first.

2. Contains the prayer or psalm of the prophet, in which he implores God to hasten the deliverance of his people, chapter second.

SUMMARY OF SUBJECTS.

The Vision of Habakkuk—Complaint of the Iniquity of the Land—Fearful Vengeance by the Chaldeans—Complains of the Agency by which the Land is desolated—The Prophet is taught to wait for an Answer by Faith—Judgment upon the Chaldeans for Insatiableness, Covetousness, Cruelty, Drunkenness, and Idolatry—Habakkuk trembles in view of God's Majesty—His Confidence in God.

Zephaniah.

A. M. 3374. This prophet was the son of Cushi, and discharged the prophetic office before Josiah had reformed the corruptions and abuses of his dominions. His prophecy may be divided into four parts, viz.:—

1. A denunciation against Judah for their idolatry, chapter first.

2. Repentance the only means to avert the divine judgments, chapter second.

3. Prophecies against the Philistines, Moabites, Ammonites, Ethiopia, and Nineveh, chapter second.

4. The captivity of the Jews, and their future restoration and ultimate prosperity, chapter third.

SUMMARY OF SUBJECTS.

God's Severe Judgments against Judah for Divers Sins—An Exhortation to Repentance—The Judgment of the Philistines—Of Moab, Ammon, Ethiopia, and Assyria—Reproof of Jerusalem for Divers Sins—An Exhortation to wait for the Restoration of Israel—Rejoicings for her Salvation by God.

Haggai.

A. M. 3484. This prophet was the first who declared the will of God to the Jews, after their captivity. He encouraged them in the work of rebuilding the temple. His book may be divided into three parts, viz.:—

1. A severe reproof for neglecting the rebuilding of the temple, chapter first.

2. Comforts the aged men by assuring them that the glory of the latter house should be greater than that of the former, chapter second.

3. Foretells the establishment of Messiah's kingdom, chapter second.

SUMMARY OF SUBJECTS.

Haggai reproves the People for neglecting the Building of God's House —Incites them to the Work—Promises God's Assistance—Encourages the People in their Work, by Promises of Greater Glory to the Second Temple than was in the First—Their Sins hindered the Work, shown by the Type of Holy and Unclean Things—God's Promise to Zerubbabel.

Zechariah.

A. M. 3484. This prophet was contemporary with Haggai. His book consists of two parts, viz.:—

1. The restoration of the temple, interspersed with Messianic predictions, chapters first to the sixth.

2. Comprises prophecies relating to more remote events, viz., the war of the Romans against the Jews, chapters seventh to the fourteenth.

SUMMARY OF SUBJECTS.

Exhorts to Repentance—The Vision of the Horses—Comfortable Promises made to Jerusalem, at the Prayer of the Angel—The Vision of the Four Horns and the Four Carpenters—Jerusalem measured—The Redemption of Zion—Promise of God's Presence—Restoration of the Church shown under the Type of Joshua—Christ promised under the Similitude of a Branch—The Good Success of Zerubbabel's Foundation shown by the Golden Candlestick—The two Anointed Ones foreshown by the Two

Olive-trees—The Curse of Thieves and Swearers shown by the Vision of the Flying Roll—The Final Destruction of Babylon shown by the Pressing of a Woman in an Ephah—Vision of the Four Chariots—The Temple and Kingdom of the Branch shown by the Crown of Joshua—Inquiry of the Captives in regard to Fasting—Sin the Cause of their Captivity—Restoration of Jerusalem—Encouragement to build by God's Favour shown—Good Works required, and Enlargement promised—Defence of the Church—Rejoicings for the Coming of Christ—Promised Victory—God, and not Idols, to be sought after—Restoration promised—The Destruction of Jerusalem—Howling of the Shepherds, and Spoiling of their Glory—The Staves of Beauty and Bands broken by the Rejection of Christ—The Type and Curse of a Foolish Shepherd—Jerusalem a Cup of Trembling to herself, and a Burdensome Stone to her Adversaries—The Victorious Restoration of Judah, and the Signal Interposition of God—Repentance of Jerusalem—Fountain of Purgation for Jerusalem from their Idolatry and False Prophecy—The Death of Christ, and the Trial of the Third Part—Jerusalem's Destroyers destroyed—Coming of Christ, and the Graces of his Kingdom—Plagues on Jerusalem's Enemies—Turning of the Remnant, and the Sanctification of their Spoil.

Malachi.

A. M. 3607. This prophet delivered his predictions while Nehemiah was governor of Judah—more particularly after his second coming from the Persian court. The people having relapsed into irreligion, the prophet was commissioned to reprove them, and also the priests. The book may be divided into two parts, viz.:—

1. Reproof to the Jews for want of reverence to God, their benefactor, and judgments denounced therefor, chapters first and second.

2. Foretells the coming of Christ and his harbinger, John, to purify the sons of Levi, chapters third and fourth.

SUMMARY OF SUBJECTS.

Malachi complains of Israel's Irreligion, Unkindness, and Profanity—Reproves the Priests for neglecting their Covenant with God—Reproves the People for Idolatry, Adultery, and Infidelity—The Messenger of Christ—The Majesty and Grace of Christ—Rebellion, Sacrilege, and Infidelity of the People—The Promise of Blessings to those that fear God and think of his name—God's Judgments on the Wicked, and his Blessings on the Good—Exhortation to the Study of the Law—The Coming of Elijah, and his Office.

CHAPTER IV.

HISTORICAL BOOKS OF THE NEW TESTAMENT.

Matthew.

A. M. 4000. MATTHEW, surnamed Levi, was the son of Alpheus, a native of Galilee. Before his conversion to Christianity he was a publican, or tax-gatherer, under the Romans, and collected the customs of all goods exported or imported at Capernaum, a maritime town on the Sea of Galilee, and also received the tribute paid by all passengers who went by water. While employed at the receipt of custom, Jesus called him to be a witness of his words and works—thus conferring upon him the honourable office of an apostle. After the ascension of the Saviour he continued at Jerusalem with the other apostles, and with them, on the day of Pentecost, was endued with the gift of the Holy Spirit. He was the first of all the evangelists who wrote. His Gospel was written in Judea, for the Jewish nation, and designed to confirm Jewish converts in the truth of Christianity. It consists of four parts, viz.:—

1. Treats of the infancy of Jesus Christ, chapters first and second.

2. Records the discourses and actions of John the Baptist and of Jesus Christ, preparatory to the commencement of the public ministry of the Saviour, chapters third and fourth.

3. Relates the discourses and actions of Christ in Galilee, by which he demonstrated that he was the Messiah, chapters fourth to the twentieth.

4. Contains the transactions relative to the passion and resurrection of Christ, chapters twentieth to the twenty-eighth.

SUMMARY OF SUBJECTS.

The Genealogy of Christ, from Abraham to Joseph—Conceived by the Holy Ghost, and born of the Virgin Mary, when she was espoused to Joseph—The Angel satisfies the Mind of Joseph, and interprets the Names of Christ—Wise Men from the East are directed to Christ by a Star—The Worship of the Magi—Their Offerings of Gold, Frankincense, and Myrrh—Joseph's Flight into Egypt with Jesus and his Mother—Slaughter of the Children by Herod—Herod's Death—Christ is brought back again into Galilee, to Nazareth—The Preaching of John—His Office, Life, and Baptism—He reprehends the Pharisees, and baptizes Christ in Jordan—Christ's Fast and Temptation in the Wilderness—Angels minister to him—Dwells in Capernaum—Begins to preach—Calls Peter and Andrew, James and John—Heals all Diseases—Sermon on the Mount—Declares who are blessed—Who are the Salt of the Earth, the Light of the World—Came to fulfil the Law—Its Nature—Exhortation to suffer Wrong, love Enemies, and labour for Perfection—Giving of Alms—Prayer—Forgiveness—Fasting—Teaches where to lay up our Treasure—Cannot serve God and Mammon—Exhortation to seek first the Kingdom of God—Reproves Rash Judgment—Things Holy should not be cast to Dogs—Exhortation to Prayer, and to enter the Strait Gate—Warns of False Prophets—Exhorts to be Doers of the Word, and not Hearers only—Good Foundation—Cleanses the Leper—Heals the Centurion's Servant, Peter's Mother-in-law, and many others—Shows how he is to be followed—Stills the Tempest on the Sea—Drives Devils out of two Men, and suffers them to enter the Swine—Cures the Palsy—Calls Matthew—Eats with Publicans and Sinners—Defends his Disciples for not Fasting—Cures the Bloody Issue—Raises the Daughter of Jaïrus to Life—Gives Sight to two Blind Men—Heals a Dumb Man possessed of Devils, and has Compassion on the Multitude—Sends out his Twelve Apostles, and gives them Power to work Miracles—Gives them their Charge, and promises a Blessing upon all who receive them—John sends his Disciples to Christ—Christ's Testimony concerning John—The Opinion of the People—The Unthankfulness and Impenitency of Chorazin, Bethsaida, and Capernaum—Gospel revealed to the Simple—The Burthened invited—Blindness of the Pharisees concerning the Sabbath reproved—The Dumb and Blind Man restored—Blasphemy against the Holy Ghost not forgiven—Reproves those who seek after a Sign, and shows who are his Brother, Sister, and Mother—The Parable of the Sower and the Seed, and its Exposition—The Parable of the Tares, Mustard-seed, Leaven, Hidden Treasure, Pearl, and Drag-net—Herod's Opinion of Christ—John beheaded—Jesus departs into a Desert-place, where he feeds Five Thousand with Five Loaves and Two Fishes—Walks on the Sea—Heals the Sick by the Touch of the Hem of his Garment—Reproves the Pharisees for transgressing the Commandments by Traditions—Heals the Daughter of the Syro-Phœnician Woman, and many others—Feeds Four Thousand with Seven Loaves and a few

Little Fishes—Pharisees require a Sign—Jesus warns his Disciples against the Hypocrisy of the Pharisees and Sadducees—The People's Opinion of Christ—Peter's Confession of him—Jesus foreshows his Death, and reproves Peter—Those who will follow him must bear the Cross—Transfiguration of Christ—Heals the Lunatic—Foretells his own Passion, and pays Tribute—Warns his Disciples to be Humble, Harmless, avoid Offences, and not despise Little Ones—Teaches how to deal with our Brethren when they offend us, and how often we must forgive them—Illustrates Forgiveness by a Parable—Heals the Sick—Answers the Pharisees concerning Divorce—Shows when Marriage is necessary—Receives Little Children—Instructs the Young Man how to attain Eternal Life, and how to be Perfect—Tells his Disciples how hard it is for a Rich Man to enter into the Kingdom of Heaven—Promises a Reward to all who forsake anything to follow him—Similitude of the Labourers in the Vineyard—Foretells his Passion by answering the Mother of Zebedee's Children—Teaches his Disciples to be Lowly, and restores to Sight two Blind Men—Rides in Triumph into Jerusalem—Drives the Buyers and Sellers out of the Temple—Curses the Fig-tree—Puts to Silence the Priests and Elders—Similitude of the Two Sons and the Husbandmen—Parable of the Marriage of the King's Son—The Calling of the Gentiles—The Punishment of him who had not on the Wedding Garment—Tribute paid to Cesar—Confutes the Sadducees concerning the Resurrection—Answers the Lawyer—Admonishes the People not to follow the Examples of the Scribes and Pharisees—The Disciples must beware of Ambition—Denounces Eight Woes against Hypocrisy and Blindness—Prophesies the Destruction of Jerusalem—Foretells the Destruction of the Temple—Preceding Calamities—Signs of his Coming to Judgment—Day and Hour unknown—Exhorts to Watchfulness—Parable of the Ten Virgins—Of the Talents—Description of the Last Judgment—Rulers conspire against Christ—The Woman anoints his Head—Judas sells his Lord—Christ eats the Passover—Institutes his Holy Supper—Prays in the Garden—Is betrayed by a Kiss—Carried to Caiaphas—Denied by Peter—Delivered bound to Pilate—Judas hangs himself—Pilate, admonished by his Wife, washes his Hands—Liberates Barabbas—Christ is crowned with Thorns, crucified, reviled, dies, is buried—His Sepulchre is sealed and guarded—His Resurrection is declared by an Angel to the Women—He himself appears to them—The Chief-priests bribe the Sentinels—Christ appears to his Disciples—He sends them to teach and baptize all Nations, and promises to be with them to the End of the World.

Mark.

A. M. 4030. The Hebrew name of this evangelist was John. He was the son of Mary, a pious woman who dwelt at Jerusalem, and at whose house the apostles and first Christians often assembled. He wrote his Gospel at Rome, between the years sixty and sixty-three. It may be divided into three parts, viz.:—

1. The transactions from the baptism of Christ to his entering on the more public part of his ministry, chapter first.

2. The discourses and actions of Jesus Christ to his going up to Jerusalem to the fourth and last Passover, chapters first to the tenth.

3. The passion, death, and resurrection of Christ, chapters eleventh to the fourteenth.

SUMMARY OF SUBJECTS.

The Office of John the Baptist—Baptism of Jesus—His Temptation His Preaching—Calls his Disciples—Heals one who had a Devil—Heals Peter's Wife's Mother, and many others—Cleanses a Leper—Heals one sick of the Palsy—Calls Matthew—Eats with Publicans and Sinners—Excuses his Disciples from Fasting, and for plucking Ears of Corn on the Sabbath—Heals the Withered Hand, and many other Infirmities—Rebukes the Unclean Spirits—Chooses his Twelve Apostles—Confutes the Pharisees' Blasphemy, and shows who are his Brother, and Sister, and Mother—Parable of the Sower, and its Exposition—Must communicate the Light of our Knowledge to others—The Parable of the Seed growing secretly—Parable of the Mustard-seed—Christ stills the Tempest—Delivers the possessed of a Legion of Devils—The Woman healed—Jaïrus's Daughter raised—Christ contemned of his Countrymen—Gives the Twelve Power over Unclean Spirits—Divers Opinions of Christ—John beheaded and buried—Apostles return from Preaching—Miracle of Five Loaves and Two Fishes—Christ walks on the Sea, and heals all who touch him—Pharisees find fault with the Disciples for eating with Unwashed Hands—They break the Commandments of God by their Traditions—Meat defileth no Man—Healing of the Syro-Phœnician's Daughter, and one that was Deaf and Dumb—Christ feeds the Multitude miraculously, and refuses a Sign to the Pharisees—Admonishes his Disciples to beware of the Leaven of the Pharisees—Restores Sight to the Blind—Acknowledges himself to be the Christ—Exhorts to Patience in Persecution—Is transfigured—Instructs his Disciples in regard to the coming of Elias—Casts out the Deaf and Dumb Spirit—Foretells his Death and Resurrection—Exhorts to Humility—Must not prohibit those who are not against us, nor give Offence to any—Disputes with the Pharisees concerning Divorce—Blesses Children—Rich Young Man instructed—Danger of Riches—Advantage of forsaking anything for Christ—Foretells his Death and Resurrection—The Two Ambitious Suitors—Bartimeus restored to Sight—Entry into Jerusalem—Fig-tree cursed—Purges the Temple—Exhortation to Steadfastness and Forgiveness of Injuries—Defends the Lawfulness of his Actions by the Witness of John—Parable of the Vineyard—Tribute to Cesar—Error of the Sadducees—Answers the Scribes—Refutes their Opinions of him—Warns against Ambition and Hypocrisy—Commends the Poor Widow—Foretells the Destruction of the Temple—Persecutions of the Gospel—Must be preached to all Nations—Calamities upon the Jews foretold—Manner of his coming to Judgment—The Hour unknown—To watch and pray the Duty of all—Conspiracy against Christ—Anointed by a Woman—Judas sells his Master for Money—Christ foretells his Betrayal—Passover eaten—Lord's Supper instituted—Predicts the Flight of his Disciples, and the Denial of Peter—Judas betrays him—Apprehended in the Garden—Falsely accused and impiously condemned—Shamefully abused—Denial of Peter—Bound and accused before Pilate—Murderer released, and Jesus delivered to be crucified—Crowned with Thorns—Spit on and mocked—Faints in bearing his Cross—Hanged between Two Thieves—Suffers the reproaches of the Jews, but confessed by the Centurion to be the Son of God—Honourably buried by Joseph—His Resurrection declared to Three Women—Appears to Mary Magdalene—To two others—To the Apostles, whom he sends to preach, and afterwards ascendeth to Heaven.

Luke.

A. M. 3999. Luke was descended from Gentile parents, and in youth had embraced Judaism, from which he was converted to Christianity. He was, for the most part, the companion of the Apostle Paul. His Gospel was written about the year sixty-three or sixty-four, for Gentile Christians. It may be divided into five parts, viz.:—

1. Contains a narrative of the birth of Christ, with the precedent, attending, and following circumstances, chapters first and second.

2. Comprises the particulars relative to our Saviour's infancy and youth, chapter second.

3. Includes the preaching of John, and the baptism of Christ, whose genealogy is annexed, chapter third.

4. Comprehends the discourses, miracles, and actions of Jesus Christ, during the whole of his ministry, chapter fourth to the ninth.

5. Begins with chapter ninth, and contains an account of our Saviour's last journey to Jerusalem; consequently, this part comprises everything relative to his passion, death, res-

urrection, and ascension to heaven, chapter tenth to the twenty-fourth.

SUMMARY OF SUBJECTS.

Preface to the Gospel—Conception of John and Christ—Prophecy of Elizabeth and Mary—Nativity and Circumcision of John—The Prophecy of Zacharias—The Roman Empire taxed—The Birth of Christ related to the Shepherds—Circumcision of Christ—Purification of the Virgin Mary—Simeon and Anna prophesy of Christ—Christ with the Doctors—Subject to his Parents—Preaching and Baptism of John—His Testimony of Christ—John imprisoned—Christ baptized—Age and Genealogy of Christ, from Joseph to Adam—Temptation and Fasting of Christ—Overcomes the Devil—Begins to preach—Cures one possessed of a Devil, Peter's Mother-in-law, and divers other Sick Persons—Devils acknowledge Christ—Preaches through the Cities—Teaches the People out of Peter's Ship—Miraculous Draught of Fishes—Cleanses the Leper—Prays in the Wilderness—Cures the Palsy—Calls Matthew—Eats with Sinners—Foretells the Fastings and Afflictions of his Disciples, after his Ascension—Parable of Worn Garments and Old Bottles—Reproves the Pharisees about the Sabbath, by Scripture, Reason, and Miracle—Chooses Twelve Apostles—Heals the Diseased—Preaches to his Disciples before the People—Blessings and Curses—Obedience of Faith—Constancy—Great Faith of the Centurion Gentile—Raises the Widow's Son at Nain—Answers John's Messengers—His Opinion of John—Denounces the Jews for their Unbelief—Mary Magdalene—Women minister to Christ—Parable of the Sower and the Candle—Declares who are his Mother and Brethren—Rebukes the Winds—Casts out a Legion of Devils—Is rejected of the Gadarenes—Heals the Woman, and raises Jaïrus's Daughter—Sends his Apostles to work Miracles and preach—Herod desires to see him—Feeds Five Thousand—Inquires what Opinion the World had of him—Foretells his Passion—Proposes a Pattern of Patience—Transfiguration—Cures the Lunatic—Commends Humility—Divers would follow him, on their own Conditions—Sends out Seventy Disciples to preach—Admonishes them wherein to rejoice—Thanks his Father for his Grace—Magnifies the Happy Estate of the Church—Instructs the Lawyer—Reprehends Martha, and commends Mary—Teaches Instant Prayer—Casts out a Dumb Devil—Rebukes the Blasphemy of the Pharisees—Shows who are blessed—Preaches to the People—Reprehends the outward show of Holiness in the Scribes and Pharisees—Preaches to his Disciples to avoid Hypocrisy and Fearfulness in publishing his Doctrine—Warns the People to beware of Covetousness, by the Parable of the Rich Farmer—Ready to give Alms—Christ's Ministers must see to their Charge—Look for Persecution—People must improve the Time of Grace—Fearful Thing to die without Reconciliation—Repentance preached upon the Punishment of the Galileans—The Fruitless Fig-tree may not stand—Christ heals the Crooked Woman—Shows the Powerful Working of his Word by the Parable of the Grain of Mustard-seed and the Leaven —Exhorts to enter in at the Strait Gate—Reproves Herod and Jerusalem —Heals the Dropsy on the Sabbath—Teaches Humility—Teaches to feast the Poor—Parable of the Great Supper—Must count the Cost in becoming Christians—Backsliders like Salt that hath lost its Savour—Parable of the Lost Sheep—The Piece of Silver—The Prodigal Son—The Unjust Steward—Hypocrisy of the Pharisees reproved—The Rich Man, and Lazarus the Beggar—Occasions of Offence to be avoided—One must forgive another—Power of Faith—Our Obligations to God—Christ heals Ten Lepers—The Coming of the Son of Man—The Unfortunate Widow—The Pharisee and Publican—Children brought to Christ—A Ruler that would follow Christ, but is hindered by his Riches—The Reward of those who would leave all for his Sake—Foretells his Death—Restores a Blind Man to Sight—Zaccheus, a Publican—The Ten Pieces of Money—Triumphant Entry into Jerusalem—Weeps over the City—Purges the Temple—Teaches in it daily—Rulers desire to destroy him—Declares his Authority by John's Baptism—Parable of the Vineyard—Tribute to Cesar—Sadducees convinced—Christ the Son of David—Warns his Disciples to beware of the Scribes—Commends the Poor Widow—Foretells the Destruction of the City and Temple—Signs before the Last Day—Exhortation to Watchfulness—Jews conspire against him—Judas prepared by the Devil to betray him—Passover—Holy Supper—Warning against Ambition—Promise to Peter—Prays in the Garden, and sweats Blood—Is betrayed—Heals Malchus's Ear—Denied of Peter Three Times—Shamefully abused—Confesses himself to be the Son of God—Accused before Pilate, and sent to Herod—Herod mocks him—Herod and Pilate make Friends—Barabbas loosed, and Christ sent to Crucifixion—He tells the Women that lament him of the Destruction of Jerusalem—Prays for his Enemies—Two Evil-doers crucified with him—His Death and Burial—His Resurrection declared by Two Angels—Appears himself to the Two Disciples, on the Way to Emmaüs—Appears to the Apostles—Gives them a Charge—Promises the Holy Ghost, and ascends to Heaven.

John.

A. M. 4033. Saint John, the evangelist and apostle, was the son of Zebedee. He was eminently the object of our Lord's regard and confidence, and was, on various occasions, admitted to free and intimate intercourse with him—so much so that he was characterized as that disciple whom Jesus loved. He wrote his Gospel about the year ninety-seven.

The general design of John, in common with the rest of

the evangelists, was to prove that Jesus was the Messiah, the Son of God. Besides this, there were two special motives that induced him to compose his Gospel. One was, to supply those important events in our Saviour's life which had been omitted by the other evangelists—the other was that he might refute the heresies of Cerinthus and the Nicolaitans, who had attempted to corrupt the Christian doctrine. Of the Nicolaitans nothing certain is known; but concerning Cerinthus we have the following:—He was a Jew, and had studied literature and philosophy at Alexandria. He attempted to construct a new system of religion, by combining the doctrines of Jesus Christ with the opinions and errors of the Jews and Gnostics. From the latter he borrowed their *pleroma*, or *fulness*—their *œons*, or *spirits*—their *demiurgus*, or *creator* of the visible world. He taught that the Most High God was utterly unknown before the appearance of Christ, and dwelt in a remote heaven called *pleroma*, with the chief spirits, or *œons*: that this Supreme God generated an *only-begotten son*, *Monogenes*, who again begat the *Word*, *Logos*, which was inferior to the first-born: that Christ was a still lower *œon*, though far superior to some others: that there were two higher *œons*, distinct from Christ,—one called *Zōe*, or *life*; and the other, *Phos*, or the *light*: that from the æons again proceeded inferior orders of spirits, particularly one, *Demiurgus*, who created this visible world out of eternal matter: that this Demiurgus was ignorant of the Supreme God, and much lower than the æons, which were wholly in-invisible: that he was, however, the peculiar God and protector of the Israelites, and sent Moses to them, whose laws were to be of perpetual obligation: that Jesus was a mere man, of the most illustrious sanctity and justice—the real son of Joseph and Mary: that the æon, Christ, descended upon him in the form of a dove, when he was baptized, revealed to him the unknown Father, and empowered him to work miracles: that the æon, *light*, entered John the Bapsist in the same manner, and, therefore, that John was, in some respects, preferable to Christ: that Jesus, after his union with Christ, opposed himself with vigour to the God of the Jews, at whose instigation he was seized and crucified by the Jews; and that, when Jesus was taken captive, and came to suffer, Christ ascended up on high, so that the man Jesus, alone, was subjected to the pains of an ignominious death: that Christ will again return, and, renewing his union with the man Jesus, will reign in Palestine one thousand years, during which time his disciples will enjoy the most exquisite sensual delights. John's Gospel is divided into three parts, viz.:—

1. Contains doctrines in opposition to those of Cerinthus, chapter first.

2. A proof of those doctrines, in an historical manner, chapters first to the twentieth.

3. Conclusion, or appendix, chapter twentieth to the twenty-first.

SUMMARY OF SUBJECTS.

The Divinity, Humanity, and Office of Jesus Christ—The Testimony of John—The Calling of Andrew, Peter, *et. al.*—Christ turns Water into Wine—Goes to Capernaum and Jerusalem—Cleanses the Temple—Foretells his Death and Resurrection—Many believe, because of his Miracles—Christ teaches Nicodemus the Necessity of Regeneration—The Great Love of God to the World—Condemnation for Unbelief—The Baptism, Witness, and Doctrine of John, concerning Christ—Christ talks with a Woman of Samaria—His Disciples marvel—Declares his Zeal for God's Glory—Many Samaritans believe on him—Goes to Galilee, and heals the Ruler's Son, at Capernaum—Cures a Man who had been diseased Thirty-eight Years—Jews cavil because he did it on the Sabbath—He answers, and presents Testimony of himself—Feeds Five Thousand—The People desire to make him a King—He walks on the Sea—Reproves the People—Declares himself the Bread of Life to True Believers—Many depart from him—Peter confesses him—Judas is a Devil—Jesus reproves the Ambition and Boldness of his Kinsman—Goes from Galilee to the Feast of Tabernacles—Teaches in the Temple—Opinions concerning him—Pharisees are Angry because he was not taken by their Officers—Nicodemus takes his Part—Christ delivers the Woman taken in Adultery—Proclaims himself the Light of the World—Answers the Jews who boasted of Abraham—Restores Sight to the Blind—The Pharisees are offended at it, and cast the Blind Man out of the Synagogue—Christ is the Door and the Good Shepherd—Proves by his Works that he is the Son of God

—Escapes the Jews, and goes beyond Jordan, where many believe on him—Raises Lazarus from the Dead—Many Jews believe—Chief-priests and Pharisees conspire against him—Prophecy of Caiaphas—Jesus hides himself—They inquire for him at the Passover—Excuses Mary for anointing his Feet—People flock to see Lazarus—Chief-priests consult to kill him—Triumphant Entry into Jerusalem—Greeks desire to see Jesus—He foretells his Death—Jews generally blinded—Many Rulers believe, but do not confess him—He washes his Disciples' Feet—Exhorts them to Humility and Charity—Foretells the Betrayal of Judas—Commands them to love one another, and warns Peter of his Denial—Comforts his Disciples with a Hope of Heaven—Professes himself the Way, the Truth, and the Life, and One with the Father—Asks for Love and Obedience—Promises the Holy Ghost—Leaves his Peace with them—Parable of the Vine—Comfort in the Hatred and Persecutions of the World—The Office of the Holy Ghost—Office of the Apostles—Comfort to the Disciples, in view of Persecution—Peace in the Lord, though in the World Tribulation—Christ prays to the Father to preserve the Apostles in Unity and Truth, and to glorify them, and all other Believers—Judas betrays him—The Officers fall to the Ground—Peter cuts off Malchus's Ear—Christ is taken—Peter denies him—Examined before Caiaphas—Before Pilate—His Kingdom—Barabbas loosed—Christ scourged, crowned with Thorns, and beaten—Pilate delivers him to be crucified—Lots cast for his Garments—Commends his Mother to John—He dies—Is pierced—Buried by Joseph and Nicodemus—Mary comes to the Sepulchre—Peter and John also—Jesus appears to Mary—Incredulity and Confession of Thomas—The Scripture sufficient to Salvation—Appears again to his Disciples, and is known by the Great Draught of Fishes—Dines with them, and gives Charge to Peter—Rebukes his Curiosity.

Acts of the Apostles.

A. M. 4033. This book is a postscript to the Gospels, and an introduction to the Epistles. It was written by Saint Luke, about the year sixty-three, and may be divided into three parts, viz.:—

1. Contains the rise and progress of the mother Church, at Jerusalem, from the time of our Saviour's Ascension to the first Jewish persecution, chapter first to the eighth.

2. The dispersion of the disciples, the propagation of Christianity among the Samaritans, the conversion of Saint Paul, and the foundation of a Christian Church at Antioch, chapter eighth to the twelfth.

3. The conversion of the more remote Gentiles, by Bar-

nabas and Paul, and his associates, chapter thirteenth to the twenty-eighth.

SUMMARY OF SUBJECTS.

Christ prepares his Apostles to behold his Ascension—Commands them to wait at Jerusalem for the Gift of the Holy Ghost—Warned by Two Angels to depart—Return and give themselves to Prayer—Day of Pentecost—Apostles filled with the Holy Ghost—Speak all Languages—Peter preaches—A Great Number converted and baptized—Apostles work Miracles—Church daily increases in Numbers—A Lame Man healed—Peter preaches—Exhorts to Repentance and Faith in the Lord Jesus, for the Remission of Sins—The Rulers offended at Peter's Sermon—Peter and John imprisoned, and commanded no more to teach in the Name of Jesus—Church resorts to Prayer—The Place moved where they were assembled—Ananias and Sapphira struck dead for Lying—The Apostles are again imprisoned, but are delivered by an Angel—Gamaliel's Intercession—Apostles are beaten, but they glorify God, and cease not Preaching—Provide for the Poor by the Appointment of Deacons—Stephen falsely accused of Blasphemy—Answers to the Accusation—He is stoned to Death—Prays for his Murderers, and commends his Soul to Jesus—Church in Samaria—Philip's Preaching—Simon the Sorcerer—Peter and John confirm the Church, by the Imposition of Hands, and the Gift of the Holy Ghost—Simon covets the Power of the Apostles—The Angel sends Philip to teach and baptize the Ethiopian Eunuch—Saul, on his Way to Damascus, is stricken to the Earth, and called to the Apostleship—Baptized by Ananias—Preaches Christ boldly—The Jews lie in wait to kill him—So, also, the Grecians—The Church having Rest, Peter heals Eneas of Palsy, and restores Tabitha to Life—Cornelius sends for Peter—Peter, in a Vision, is taught not to despise the Gentiles—He preaches Christ to Cornelius—The Holy Ghost falls on them, and they are baptized—Peter is accused for going to the Gentiles—Makes his Defence—Barnabas sent to confirm the Disciples at Phenice, Antioch, and Cyprus—The Disciples called Christians—They send Relief to Brethren in Judea, in the Time of Famine—Herod kills James, and imprisons Peter—In his Pride he is smitten of God, and dies—After his Death the Word of God prospers—Paul and Barnabas chosen to go to the Gentiles—Sergius Paulus, and Elymas the Sorcerer—Paul preaches at Antioch—The Gentiles believe, but the Jews gainsay and blaspheme—They turn to the Gentiles—Those ordaine to Life believed—Paul and Barnabas persecuted at Iconium—At Lystra Paul heals a Cripple—Paul is stoned—Pass through Divers Churches, confirming the Disciples, and return to Antioch—Great Dissension about Circumcision—The Apostles consult about it, and send their Decision to the Churches—Paul and Barnabas separate—Paul circumcises Timothy—Baptizes Lydia—Dispossesses the Damsel of the Evil Spirit—He and Silas are whipped and imprisoned—Prison

Doors are opened—Jailer is converted, and they are set at Liberty—Paul preaches at Thessalonica—Is sent to Berea, and preaches there—Goes to Athens—Preaches, and many are converted—Preaches at Corinth to the Gentiles—Encouraged in a Vision—Accused before Gallio—Passing from City to City, he strengthens the Disciples—Apollos preaches Christ—The Holy Ghost given by Paul's Hands—The Jews blaspheme his Doctrine, which is confirmed by Miracles—Jewish Exorcists—Conjuring Books burned—Demetrius's Opposition to Paul—Town-clerk interposes—Paul goes to Macedonia—Celebrates the Lord's Supper—Eutychus restored to Life—Paul at Miletus—Calls the Elders of the Church—Commits the Flock to them—Warns them of False Teachers—Commends them to God in Prayer—Goes to Jerusalem—Philip's Daughters—Paul is apprehended at Jerusalem—Permitted to speak for himself—Declares how he was converted—Clamour raised against him—Claims the Privilege of a Roman Citizen—While pleading his Cause, Ananias commands him to be smitten—Dissension among his Accusers—God encourages him—He is sent to Felix, the Governor—Tertullus accuses Paul—He answers for himself—Preaches Christ to the Governor and his Wife, and is left in Prison—The Jews accuse him before Festus—Answers, and appeals to Cesar—Before King Agrippa—Declares his Life and Wonderful Conversion—Ships for Rome—Foretells the Danger of the Voyage—Shipwrecked—All saved—Entertained by the Barbarians at Malta—A Viper fastens on his Hand—He heals many, and departs for Rome—Resides and preaches there Two Years.

CHAPTER V.

DOCTRINAL BOOKS.

Epistle to the Romans.

A. M. 4062. THIS epistle was written by the Apostle Paul, about the year fifty-eight. The design of the apostle in writing it was to comfort the converts at Rome, in the midst of their trials, and reconcile the differences among them, arising from the early prejudices of the Jewish and Gentile converts, in regard to certain rites.

It may be divided into four parts, viz.:—

1. The introduction, chapter first, 1–13.

2. The doctrinal part of the epistle, concerning justification, chapters first and second, to the eleventh.

3. Comprises the hortatory, or practical part, chapter twelfth to the fifteenth.

SUMMARY OF SUBJECTS.

Paul commends his Calling to the Romans—He shows that the Gospel is for the Justification of Men, through Faith—They that sin, though they condemn it in others, have no Excuse for themselves—Gentiles and Jews in like Condemnation—The Jews' Prerogative—The Law convinces them of Sin—No Flesh justified by the Law—Justification by Faith only—The Law not abolished—Abraham's Faith imputed to him for Righteousness—By Faith he received the Promise—Abraham the Father of all that believe—Our Faith imputed for Righteousness—Being justified by Faith, we have Peace with God—We are reconciled by the Death of Christ—Sin and Death came by Adam—Righteousness and Life by Jesus Christ—Grace more abundant than Sin—We may not live in Sin who are dead to it—Sin must not reign in us, for Death is the Result—No Law has Power over Man when he is dead—We are dead to the Law—The Law is not Sinful, but Holy, Just, and Good—Those who are in Christ, and live according to the Spirit, are Free from Condemnation—The Harm that comes of the Flesh, and the Good of the Spirit—Privilege of being God's Children—Nothing can sever us from the Love of God—Paul's Sorrow for the Jews—All the Seed of Abraham not the Children of Promise—The Calling of the Gentiles, and the Rejection of the Jews—The Reason why so few Jews embraced Righteousness by Faith—The Scriptures show the Difference between the Righteousness of the Law and that of Faith—Jews and Gentiles saved by Faith—Israel was not Ignorant of these Things—God has not cast off Israel—Some were elected, though the Rest were hardened—There is Hope of their Conversion—The Gentiles may not insult them—God's Judgments are Unsearchable—God's Mercies must move us to please him—None must think too highly of himself—Duties required of us—Revenge forbidden—Obedience to Rulers enjoined—Love is the Fulfilling of the Law—Gluttony, Drunkenness, and Works of Darkness, are out of Season in the Time of the Gospel—Men must not be condemned for Things indifferent—We must not give Offence—The Strong must bear the Weak—Must not please ourselves—Imitate Christ—Paul excuses his Writing, promises to see them, and asks their Prayers—Desires the Brethren to greet many—Advises them to take heed of those who cause Dissensions—Ends with Praise to God.

First Epistle to the Corinthians.

A. M. 4060. This epistle was written from Ephesus, in the year fifty-seven. The Corinthian Church consisted partly of Jews, and partly of Gentiles; and hence the apostle had to combat Jewish prejudices and heathen licentiousness. The peace of this Church was disturbed by the intrusion of false teachers. Strifes arose among the disciples, and parties were formed affecting the unity of the Church. The design of this epistle was to correct the errors and abuses which had crept in during his absence. It may be divided into three parts, viz.:—

1. The introduction, chapter first, 1–9.

2. A discussion of various particulars adapted to the state of the Corinthian Church, chapters first to the sixth, and fifteenth.

3. Conclusion, containing various exhortations and directions, chapter sixteenth.

SUMMARY OF SUBJECTS.

After his Salutation and Thanksgiving, he exhorts them to Unity, and reproves their Dissensions—The Wisdom of the Wise destroyed by the Foolishness of Preaching—Paul's Manner of Preaching the Gospel, and its Design—Strife and Division are Arguments of a Fleshly Mind—He that plants, and he that waters, Nothing—Ministers are God's Co-labourers—Christ the only Foundation—How to account of God's Ministers—Paul's Afflicted State—The Incestuous Person—The Old Leaven is to be purged out—Heinous Offenders to be shunned—Going to Law with Brethren—Unrighteous shut out of Heaven—Our Bodies Members of Christ—Temples of the Holy Ghost, and must not be defiled—Marriage a Remedy for Fornication—Every Man must be content with his Vocation—Virginity wherefore to be embraced—Reasons for marrying and not marrying—Abstinence from Meats offered to Idols—Must not abuse our Christian Liberty—Subject our Knowledge to Charity—Paul shows his Liberty, and how Ministers should live by the Gospel—Life compared to a Race—The Sacrament of the Jews—Punishments are Examples—Idolatry—Table of the Lord must not be perverted—Things indifferent—Reproof for Men appearing in Holy Assemblies with the Head covered, and Women with their Heads uncovered—Profaning the Lord's Supper with their Feasts—Exhortation—Spiritual Gifts are diverse, and to that End were diversely bestowed—Unity of the Members of the Body—The Excellence of Charity—Speaking, Praying, and Giving of Thanks, in an Unknown Tongue—Arguments in Proof of the Resurrection of the Dead—The Manner of the Resurrection—The Apostle commends Timothy—Salutation.

Second Epistle to the Corinthians.

A. M. 4061. This epistle was written from Philippi, in Macedonia, within a year after the preceding. It is vindicatory and commendatory, and consists of three parts, viz.:—

1. The introduction, chapter first, 1, 2.
2. The apologetic discourse, chapters second to the seventh, eighth, and ninth, and tenth to the thirteenth.
3. The conclusion, chapter thirteenth.

SUMMARY OF SUBJECTS.

Corinthians encouraged to put their Confidence in God—Paul's Excuse for visiting Corinth—Ministration of the Law and the Gospel—Tribulations of the Apostles—Doctrine of the General Judgment—Ministry of Reconciliation—Paul's Faithfulness in the Ministry—Exhortation to Purity of Life—Liberality of the Macedonians—Exhortation to Liberality—Titus and others commended—Paul vindicates his Person and Ministry—His Concern for the Corinthians—Character of False Apostles—Paul glories in his Affliction—His Fear for the Corinthians—Exhortation to Self-examination.

Epistle to the Galatians.

A. M. 4056. This epistle was written from Corinth, about the latter part of the year fifty-two. The design of the apostle in writing it was to assert his authority as a teacher, and the doctrines he taught in opposition to the erroneous teachings of others, and to confirm the Church in the principles of Christianity. It consists of three parts, viz.:—

1. The introduction, chapter first, 1–5.
2. The discussion of the subjects which occasioned the epistle, chapters first, second, third, fourth, fifth, and sixth.
3. Conclusion, consisting of a summary of the topics discussed, chapter sixth.

SUMMARY OF SUBJECTS.

Paul's Concern for their having left him and the Gospel—His Accusation against those who preach any other Gospel—Gives his Reasons for going to Jerusalem—His Conduct while there—The Foolishness of the Galatians—The Law not in Opposition to the Promises—Paul's Remembrance of the Galatians—Exhortation to abide in Christian Liberty—An Enumeration of the Fruits of the Spirit—Procedure against Offenders—Liberality to Teachers enjoined—Paul's Glorying in Christ.

Epistle to the Ephesians.

A. M. 4065. This epistle was written about the year sixty-one, and its design was to guard the converts at Ephesus against the heathen practices and customs of that rich and voluptuous city, and to urge them to walk in a manner becoming the gospel of Christ.

SUMMARY OF SUBJECTS.

Salutations—Doctrine of Election and Adoption a Great Mystery—Character and Conversion of the Ephesians—The Manner of Edifying the Church—Salvation of the Gentiles revealed—Exhortation to Unity of Spirit—Exhortation to Holiness, and to avoid all Bitterness and Wrath—Husbands commanded to love their Wives—Duty of Children to Parents, Servants to Masters, and Masters to Servants.

Epistle to the Philippians.

A. M. 4066. This epistle was written about the end of the year sixty-two. Its design was to confirm the Philippians in the faith of the gospel, and to guard them against Judaizing teachers, who preached Christ through envy and strife.

SUMMARY OF SUBJECTS.

Paul testifies his Gratitude to God, and his Love for his Philippian Brethren—His Exhortation to Love, Unity, Humility, and a Careful Walk in the Way of Salvation—His Earnestness in the Christian Course—An Exhortation to walk in his Steps—Commendation for their Liberality—His Confidence in the Providence of God—Commends the Philippians—Salutations.

Epistle to the Colossians.

A. M. 4066. This and the preceding epistle bear a strong resemblance. Its design is to show that all hope of man's redemption is founded on Christ our Redeemer, and to caution the Colossians against the insinuations of Judaizing teachers, philosophical conceits, and human traditions.

SUMMARY OF SUBJECTS.

Paul thanks God for their Faith—Prays for their Increase in Grace—Describes the Nature and Office of Christ—Shows how he preached Christ—Exhortation to Steadfastness—To beware of Philosophy and Vain Traditions—Worshipping of Angels, and Legal Ceremonies—Shows where Christ should be sought—Exhorts to Mortification—To put off the Old Man and put on Christ—Exhortation to Charity and Humility—Fervency in Prayer—Deportment towards those without—Salutes them, and wishes them all Prosperity.

First Epistle to the Thessalonians.

A. M. 4056. The first epistle to the Thessalonians was the first of all the apostles' writings. Its date is about the year fifty-two. It was written to confirm the faith of the Church, and animate its members to all holy conversation. It may be divided into four parts, viz.:—

1. The miracles wrought by the first preachers, in attestation of their divine commission, chapter first.
2. The truth of the gospel sustained by character, chapters second and third.
3. The gospel shown to be worthy of God, by the sanctity of its precepts, chapter fourth.
4. The resurrection of Christ from the dead establishes his claims as the Son of God and the Judge of the world, chapters fourth and fifth.

SUMMARY OF SUBJECTS.

Paul's Regard for them at All Times—His Belief in their Faith and Sincerity—The Manner in which the Gospel was brought and preached to them—Reasons of his Long Absence—His Great Regard for them—Exhortation to Holiness—Moderate their Sorrow for the Dead—The Coming of Christ to Judgment—Divers Precepts given—Greetings.

Second Epistle to the Thessalonians.

A. M. 4056. This epistle was written soon after the first, and its design was to rectify the mistake into which the Thessalonians had fallen, in supposing that the former epistle taught that the day of judgment was just at hand. It consists of five parts, viz.:—

1. The inscription, chapter first.
2. St. Paul's thanksgiving and prayer for them, chapter first.
3. The rectification of their mistake, and the man of sin, chapter second.
4. Various advices relative to Christian virtue, chapter third.
5. The conclusion, chapter third.

SUMMARY OF SUBJECTS.

Commendation for their Faith, Love, and Patience—Reasons for Comfort in Persecution—Steadfastness in the Truth—Apostasy predicted—Discovery of Antichrist—Exhorts and prays for them—His Confidence in them—Asks their Prayers in his Behalf—Gives Divers Precepts, especially to shun Idleness and Vain Company—Concludes with Prayer and Salutation.

First Epistle to Timothy.

A. M. 4069. This epistle was written about the year sixty-four. Its design was to instruct Timothy in the choice of proper officers in the Church, as well as in the exercise of a well-ordered ministry; as well as to caution him against the influence of false teachers, and urge him to zeal and fidelity in the sacred office. It consists of three parts, viz.:—

1. The introduction, chapter first, 1, 2.
2. Instructions to Timothy, chapter second to the sixth.
3. Conclusion, chapter sixth.

SUMMARY OF SUBJECTS.

Timothy is reminded of his Charge—The Right Use and End of the Law—Paul's Vocation—Hymeneus and Alexander—Prayer should be offered for All—The Dress of Women—Not permitted to teach—They shall be saved if they continue in the Faith—Qualifications of Bishops, Deacons, and their Wives—The Church and the Blessed Truth taught therein—Paul foretells a Departure from the Faith—Divers Precepts—Rules to be observed in Reproving—Widows—Elders—Timothy's Health—Some Men's Sins go before to Judgment—Duty of Servants—Gain of Godliness—Love of Money—Exhortation to flee Youthful Lusts, and follow after Charity—Contentment enjoined—Admonitions.

Second Epistle to Timothy.

A. M. 4069. The design of this epistle was to acquaint Timothy with the writer's circumstances, and request him to come to Rome. It contains a variety of advices relative to the Church, and to himself—exhorting him to steadfastness in the gospel.

SUMMARY OF SUBJECTS.

Paul's Love to Timothy—His Mother and Grandmother—Exhortation to stir up the Gift within him—Steadfastness in Faith and Doctrine recommended—Phygellus and Hermogenes—Onesiphorus—Exhorted to Fidelity, and to shun Babblings—Hymeneus and Philetus—The Sure Foundation of God—In what Manner he should behave—Informed of the Times to come—Paul describes to him the Enemies of the Truth—Exhibits his own Example, and commends the Holy Scriptures—Informs him of his Near Approach to Death—Desires him to come speedily, and bring Mark—Warns him of Alexander—Benediction.

Epistle to Titus.

A. M. 4069. Titus was left in Crete, to settle the Churches in the several cities on that island. The Epistle was written to assist him in this work. It consists of three parts, viz.:—

1. The inscription, chapter first.

2. Instruction concerning the ordination of elders, and directions in regard to advice to the respective ages and

sexes. Obedience to the civil magistrate, chapters second and third.

3. An invitation to visit the writer, &c., chapter third.

SUMMARY OF SUBJECTS.

Paul's Statement of his Character, his Hope, and his Office—His Address to Titus, and his Reason for leaving him at Crete—Qualifications of Elders and Bishops—False Teachers—Character of the Cretans—The Pure and the Impure—False Professors—Directions to Aged Men—Aged Women—Young Women—Relative to his own Conduct—To Servants—What the Gospel of the Grace of God teaches All Men—Glorious Prospect held out by it—Salvation from all Sin, and Final Glory—Directions concerning Teaching—Rejection of Obstinate Heretics—Appoints the Time of his Coming to him.

Epistle to Philemon.

A. M. 4066.

Philemon was a citizen of Colosse, and an opulent Christian. The design of this epistle is to recommend Onesimus, his former runaway slave, but now converted Christian, to his master, and induce him to receive and treat him as such.

SUMMARY OF SUBJECTS.

Paul rejoices to hear of the Faith and Love of Philemon—Desires him to receive Onesimus, his Slave, and treat him as a Brother—Salutations.

Epistle to the Hebrews.

A. M. 4067.

The Hebrews were Jewish Christians, resident in Palestine. This epistle was written about the year sixty-two. The design of the apostle in writing this letter was to show the deity of Jesus Christ, and the excellency of his gospel, when compared with the institutions of Moses; and to prevent the Hebrew converts from relapsing into those rites and ceremonies which were now abolished, and were totally insufficient to produce reconciliation with God. It was also designed to show the nature, efficacy, and triumph of faith, by which saints of all ages had been accepted of God. It consists of three parts, viz.:—

1. Demonstrates the divinity of Christ, by the declarations of Scripture, and his superiority over angels and men, chapters first to the ninth.

2. Comprises the application of the preceding arguments and proofs, chapters tenth to the thirteenth.

3. The conclusion, containing a prayer for the Hebrews, and apostolical salutations, chapter thirteenth.

SUMMARY OF SUBJECTS.

Christ preferred above Angels, both in Person and Office—Obedience to Christ—Took upon himself our Nature—More Worthy than Moses—We shall, in rejecting him, be more Guilty than the Jews—Christian Rest attained by Faith—The Power of God's Word—The Son of God, our High-priest, subject to Infirmities, but not to Sin—Boldness in approaching the Throne of Grace—Authority and Honour of our Saviour's Priesthood—Negligence in the Knowledge thereof reproved—Exhortation not to fall back from the Faith—Diligence and Faith in the Work of Salvation—God's Promise—Christ a Priest after the Order of Melchisedec—More Excellent than the Priests of Aaron's Order—Levitical Priesthood abolished—Description of the Rites and Sacrifices of the Law—The Sacrifice of Christ—The Sacrifice of Christ's Body—One Offering—Exhortation to hold fast the Faith, with Patience and Thanksgiving—Definition of Faith—Without Faith God cannot be pleased—Fruits of Faith—Exhortation to Constancy in Faith—New Testament above the Old—Admonitions to Charity, and Divers Other Graces—Obedience to Governors—Prayer for Ministers—The Conclusion—Salutation.

CHAPTER VI.

EPISTOLARY BOOKS.

Epistle of James.

A. M. 4065. JAMES was distinguished as one of the apostles of the circumcision, and, soon after the death of Stephen, was appointed president of the Christian Church at Jerusalem. On account of his distinguished piety, he was surnamed the Just. This epistle was written about the year sixty-one. The persons to whom it was addressed were Hebrew Christians, who were in danger of falling into those sins which abounded among the Jews at that time. It divides itself into three parts, without the introduction, viz.:—

1. Contains exhortations to patience, humility, and suitable dispositions to receive the word of God aright, chapter first.
2. Condemnation of various sinful practices and erroneous opinions in regard to the doctrine of justification, chapters second to the fifth.
3. Comprises various exhortations and cautions, chapters fifth to the seventh.

SUMMARY OF SUBJECTS.

Rejoicing under the Cross—Prayer for Wisdom from God in Trials—Not to impute our Weakness or Sins to God—Not to regard the Rich, and despise the Poor—Any One Breach of the Law involves Guilt—Faith without Works is dead—Rash Reproof condemned—Government of the Tongue—True Wisdom—Cause of Contention—How to overcome Lusts, and gain God's Favour—Warnings of God's Judgments—Patience—Prayer in Adversity—Labours for the Conversion of Sinners.

First Epistle of Peter.

A. M. 4064. Simon, surnamed Cephas, or Peter, was the son of Jonah. This epistle of the apostle Peter was, like that of James, addressed to Hebrew Christians, and designed to support them under their afflictions and persecutions. It may be divided into four parts, exclusive of the introduction, viz.:—

1. Contains an exhortation to the Jewish Christians to maintain steadfastly their faith unto the end, chapters first and second.

2. Comprises exhortations to a holy life, and a particular discharge of their relative duties, chapter third.

3. Contains an exhortation to patience and submission, by considering the example of Christ, chapters third and fourth.

4. Directions to ministers of the Churches, and conclusion, chapter fifth.

SUMMARY OF SUBJECTS.

The Apostle blesses God for the Hope of Immortality—The Salvation of Christ foretold—Exhortation against Uncharitableness—Privileges of Believers—Duty of Wives and Husbands—Exhortation to Unity—Suffering for Righteousness' Sake—Exhortation to cease from Sin, by the Example of Christ—The End of All Things—Exhortation to feed the Flock of Christ—The Younger to obey the Elder—Resistance of the Devil.

Second Epistle of Peter.

A. M. 4064. This epistle, like the other, was addressed to Hebrew Christians, under persecution from the Emperor Nero. It consists of three parts, viz.:—

1. The introduction, chapter first.

2. An exhortation to improve in Christian graces, chapter second.

3. The conclusion, chapter third.

SUMMARY OF SUBJECTS.

Peter salutes the Christians, and admonishes them of the Promises and Gifts of the Gospel—Foretells them of False Teachers—Their Impiety and Punishment—The Certainty of Christ's Coming to Judgment—Exhortation to Godliness—His Doctrine agrees with Paul—Sums up—Conclusion.

First Epistle of John.

A. M. 4073. This epistle was written about the year sixty-eight. Being written for the use of Christians in all countries, it is of interesting importance to mark its contents. It consists of six parts, viz.:—

1. Asserts the true divinity and humanity of Christ, and urges the union of faith and holiness of life, chapter first.
2. Shows that all have sinned, and explains the doctrine of Christ's propitiation, chapter second.
3. Asserts Jesus to be the same person with Christ, chapter second.
4. The privileges of true believers, chapter third.
5. Criteria by which to distinguish Antichrist, chapter fourth.
6. Shows the connexion between faith in Christ and victory over the world. Shows that a sinful life is inconsistent with Christianity.

SUMMARY OF SUBJECTS.

John declares what he had seen and heard of the Word of Life—To have Fellowship with God, he enjoins Holiness—Christ our Advocate and Propitiation—To know God aright is to keep his Commandments—Must beware of Seducers—The Love of God toward us declared—Obedience is keeping the Commandments, and loving one another—Spirits must be put to the test—Reasons for Brotherly Love—He that loves God loves his Children—True Faith—Believers have Eternal Life.

Second and Third Epistles of John.

A. M. 4089. The *second* epistle is addressed to an eminent Christian lady, whose name was *Electa*, who is commended for her care in giving her children a religious education.

The *third* is addressed to a converted Gentile, called Gaius. Its design is to commend his faith.

SUMMARY OF SUBJECTS.

John's Regard for a certain Pious Lady and her Children—He exhorts them to Perseverance in the Faith, and to beware of Seducers—Commends Gaius for his Piety and Hospitality—Censures Diotrephes, whose Evil Example is not to be followed.

Epistle of Jude.

A. M. 4069. There is a marked similarity between this epistle and the Second Epistle of Peter. It is addressed to all who had embraced the gospel, and its design is to guard them against false teachers, and induce them to contend earnestly for the faith.

SUMMARY OF SUBJECTS.

Exhortation to Earnestness in defence of the Faith—False Teachers who turned the Grace of God into Lasciviousness—Judgment of Fallen Angels—Doom of Sodom—Destruction of False Teachers—Their Character described—Exhortation to Prayer, and Faith, and Holiness—Dedication.

Revelation of St. John the Divine.

A. M. 4100. The revelations contained in this book were made to St. John while in exile on the Island of Patmos, in the Ægean Sea, toward the end of the Emperor Domitian's reign. It was published at Ephesus, about the year ninety-seven. The design of the book is twofold:—*First*, to communicate a knowledge of the then present state of the Church; and, *secondly*, a revelation of events which should transpire in the future, in relation to the Church, through all time. It consists of two principal divisions, viz.:—

1. Epistles to the seven Churches of proconsular Asia, which lay in the form of an amphitheatre, and were addressed according to their geographical positions, chapter first to the third.

2. Contains prophecies, some of which have been fulfilled, and others which time alone can expound, chapter fourth to the twelfth.

SUMMARY OF SUBJECTS.

John's Salutation to the Seven Churches—The Coming of Christ—His Glorious Power and Majesty—What is commanded to be written to the Churches—The Angel of the Church of Sardis is reproved, commanded to repent, and threatened—The Angel of the Church of Philadelphia is approved—The Angel of the Church of Laodicea rebuked—Christ stands at the Door and knocks—The Vision of the Throne of God in Heaven—The Four-and-Twenty Elders—The Four Beasts, full of Eyes—The Prostration of the Elders before the Throne—The Book sealed with Seven Seals—The Lamb slain praised by the Elders—The Opening of the Seals in Order—Prophecy of the End of the World—Servants of God sealed in their Foreheads—The Number of the Sealed—Their Robes washed in the Blood of the Lamb—Seven Angels with Seven Trumpets—Four of them sound their Trumpets—Plagues follow—A Star falleth from Heaven—The Pit opened—The First Woe passed—Four Angels, that were bound, loosed —An Angel with a Book open—Two Witnesses prophesy—They have Power to shut Heaven—The Beast fights against them and kills them—The Second Woe is past—A Woman, clothed with the Sun, in travail—The great Red Dragon ready to devour her Child—When she is delivered, she flies into the Wilderness—Michael and his Angels fight with the Dragon, and prevail—The Dragon, cast down, persecutes the Woman—The Dragon gives Power to a Beast which rises out of the Sea, having Seven Heads and Ten Horns—Another Beast comes out of the Earth—Men worship it, and receive its Mark—The Lamb on Mount Zion, with his Company—An Angel preaches the Gospel—The Fall of Babylon—The Harvest of the World, and putting in the Sickle—The Vintage and Wine-press of the Wrath of God—Seven Angels, with the Seven Last Plagues—Song of those who overcome the Beast—Seven Vials full of the Wrath of God—The Angels pour out their Vials full of Wrath—Plagues —Christ comes as a Thief—Blessed are they that watch—Woman arrayed in Purple and Scarlet—Interpretation of the Seven Heads and Ten Horns—The Victory of the Lamb—The Punishment of the Whore—Fall of Babylon—People of God commanded to leave her—Kings of the Earth, and others, lament her—The Saints of God rejoice in the Judgments of Babylon—God is praised in Heaven or judging the Great Whore and avenging the Blood of his Saints—The Marriage of the Lamb—The Angel will not be worshipped—Fowls called to the Slaughter—Satan bound for a Thousand Years—The First Resurrection—The Blessed that have Part in it—Satan let loose again—Gog and Magog—The Devil cast into the Lake of Fire and Brimstone—The Last and General Resurrection—A New Heaven and New Earth—The Heavenly Jerusalem—The Kings of the Earth bring their Riches to it—The River of the Water of Life—The Tree of Life—The Light of the City—The Angel will not be worshipped —Nothing may be added to the Word of God, or taken therefrom.

Part Eighth.

BIBLICAL CHRONOLOGY.

The science of Biblical chronology relates to the time in which the events recorded in the Bible transpired, and the order in which they occurred. As various efforts have been made, by the infidel world, to invalidate the chronology of the Bible, it may not be inappropriate, in this connexion, to allude to them, and show their utter fallacy. A great display of learning has been attempted by the enemies of Divine Revelation, and scarcely any department of science has been exempted from torture, in the vain attempt to falsify the sacred record.

The dynasties of China and India have been consulted, their records unrolled, and the names and lives of kings have been produced, many cycles before the accounts of Moses. The craters of extinct volcanoes have been explored, and their indurated *scoriæ* have been examined, to make them tell of ages anterior to the birth of man. Shafts have been sunk to the very foundations of the mountains, and the different strata of rocks, to the primeval formation, have been examined, to find a record, in their geological structure, contradicting the cosmogony of Moses. To these objections the attention of the reader is briefly directed, and, although this work is not designed as a defence of the Bible from the attacks of infidels, but as a help to the student in the investigation of its facts, prophecies, and mysteries, it may not be irrelevant to assist in dissipating the vapours which have been evoked from the stagnant sea of error, to obscure the landmarks bounding the coast of truth.

In regard to the antiquity of India, it has been claimed that astronomical tables were discovered that were formed at least three thousand five hundred years before Christ, and that they were but the mere fragments of an earlier and far more perfect science. It is known that the origin of astronomy in Persia and India has suffered the same fate that it has among all other ancient nations, being lost in the darkness of their early history. Laplace remarks:—"There is no reason to believe that these Indian tables can claim a high antiquity; besides, the conjunction of the planets which these tables describe, could not possibly have taken place." The monstrous claims in regard to the antiquity of China, in which the names of long lines of kings are displayed, and accounts of dynasties furnished, extending back millions of ages, is answered by Sir William Jones, one of the most distinguished Oriental scholars in the world, in the following language:—"On the most liberal construction, the existence of an established government in the East can be traced back no further than two thousand years before the Christian era—the age of Abraham—when there was an established dynasty in Egypt, and commerce and literature flourished in Phœnicia."

Equally absurd are the claims of Volney, in regard to the antiquity of Egypt. He has no hesitancy in placing the formation of the sacerdotal colleges in Egypt thirteen thousand three hundred years before the Christian era, and calling that early period the second èpoch of their history. Huge and half-formed colossal images, subterranean temples, together with the zodiacs found at Dendera and Esneh, which were supposed to represent the state of the heavens at the time in which the temples where they were found were erected, were appealed to as bearing a date vastly anterior to the chronology of the Bible. Through the labours of Champollion, in hierology, the mysterious and hitherto undecipherable characters found on the obelisks, in the pyramids, tombs, and temples of Egypt, were explained, and the language of hieroglyphics, long unknown, and whose meaning was supposed to have been forever lost, disclosed the fact that the zodiacs extended back no further than the time of Nero and Tiberius, as he read on one of them the name of Tiberius, and on the other that of Nero.

There is but one more subject upon which the enemies of the Bible depend to invalidate its chronology, and that is the science of geology. This science, like that of astronomy, and many others, is but yet in its infancy. System after system has risen, conflicting with each other on many important points. In 1806 there were no less than eighty computed theories, contradicting each other, and all opposed to the Scripture cosmogony; not one of which has stood to the present time. The geologist proves that the earth has existed through an indefinite series of ages, having only assumed its present form a few thousand years ago, when it became the habitation of man. He has shown, in the language of Harris, "that the mere shell of the earth indicates an unknown series of ages, in which creation followed creation, at mighty intervals; and though he cannot establish its chronology, it nevertheless has a history. The first step below the surface of the earth takes the geologist below the dust of Adam, and beyond the limits of recorded time. The nearest beds of the tertiary formation exhibit no traces whatever of human remains." In the language of the "*Pre-Adamite Earth*," "Let our graves be ever so shallow, we have to make them in the dust of a departed world. As we proceed downward, formation follows formation, composed chiefly of sand, clay, and lime, presenting a thickness of more than a thousand feet each. As we descend through these, we find ourselves on a road where the lapse of duration is marked—not by a succession of seasons and years, but by the slow excavation, by water, of deep valleys in rock marble—by the return of a continent to the bosom of an ocean, in which, ages before, it had been slowly formed—or by the departure of one world and the formation of another. If our first step took us below the line consecrated by human dust, but few steps more we will find that the fossil remains of all those forms of animal life with which we are most familiar, become more and more scarce, until their places are gradually supplied by strange and yet stranger forms, till, in the last fossiliferous formation of this division, traces of existing species become exceedingly rare, and extinct species everywhere predominate. The secondary rocks receive us into a new fossiliferous world, or into a new series of worlds. Taking the chalk formation as the first member of this series, we find a stratification upwards of one thousand feet thick. Who shall compute the tracks of time necessary for its slow sedimentary deposition? So vast is it, and so widely different, in its physical conditions, from those which follow, that only one trace of animal species now living is to be found in it. Crowded as it is with conchological remains, for example, not a shell of one of all the seven thousand existing species is discoverable. Types of organic life, before unknown, arrest our attention, and prepare us for still more surprising forms. The next system in order is the oolitic, with its many subdivisions, and its thickness of about half a mile discloses new proofs of the dateless antiquity of the earth. Enormous as this bed is, it evidently was formed by depositions from sea and river water, the operation of which was so gradual and tranquil that, in some places, the organic remains of the different strata resemble the shelves of a well-ordered cabinet. Here, too, the last trace of animal species, still living, has vanished. The last link is broken and gone. We have arrived at a time when the earth was in the possession of the monster animals, more appalling than ever was feigned by the poet's fancy; and these are their catacombs. After passing through a thousand feet of red sandstone and saliferous marls, our subterranean path brings us to the carboniferous system, or coal formations. These coal strata, many thousand feet thick, consist entirely of the spoils of successive ancient vegetable worlds. In the rank jungles and vegetable wildernesses which are here accumulated and compressed, we recognise no plant of any existing species. Here, too, we have passed below the last trace of reptile life. The speaking foot-prints impressed on the preceding rocks are absent here. There is no indication that these primeval forests ever echoed to the voice of birds. Between these strata, beds of limestone, of enormous thickness, are interposed, each proclaiming the prolonged existence and final extinction of a creation. These limestone beds are not so much the charnel-house of fossil animals as the remains of the animals themselves. The mountain masses of stone which now surround us, extending for miles in length and breadth, were once sentient existences—testaceous and coralline—living at the bottom of ancient seas and lakes. How countless the ages necessary for their accumulation, when the formation of only a few inches of strata required the life and death of many generations. In this region the mind is not merely carried back through immeasurable periods, but amidst the petrified remains of this succession of primeval forests, and extinct races of animals, piled up into sepulchral mountains, we seem to be encompassed by the thickest shadows of the valley of death.

"On quitting these stupendous monuments of death, we leave behind us the last vestige of land-plants, and pass down to the old red sandstone, the geological formation of which tells us of the flight of innumerable ages. Though many thousand feet in depth, it is obviously derived from the materials of more ancient rocks, fractured, decomposed, and slowly deposited in water. The gradual and quiet nature of the process, and, therefore, its immense duration, are evident from the numerous platforms of death which mark its formation, each crowded with organic structures, which lived and died where they are now seen, and which, consequently, must have perished by some destructive agency, too sudden to allow of their dispersion, and yet so subtle and quiet as to leave the place of their habitation undisturbed. Immeasurably far behind us we have left the fair face of the extant creation, while travelling into the night of ancient time; yet we feel that we are but standing upon the threshold of the next Silurian system, and, looking down to the foundations of the earth, we find that we have not descended half-way. On surveying the fossil structures in this region, we are struck with the total change in the petrified inhabitants of the sea, as compared with what was found in mountain limestone, implying the lapse of long periods of time. Below this we reach the Cambrian system, of equal thickness, and formed by the same slow process. In this region the gradual decrease of animal remains admonishes us that even the vast and dreary empire of death has its limits, and that we are on its very outskirts. There is a solitude greater than that of the boundless desert, and a dreariness more impressive than that which reigns in a world entombed. On leaving the slate-rocks of the Cambrian, and descending to those of the Cumbrian formation, the worlds of organic remains are past—a region is found older than death, because it is older than life itself. Passing down farther, through beds of mica schist, many thousand feet in depth, the great gneiss formation is reached, and stratification itself ceases.

"The succession of worlds through which we have passed, from the surface of the earth, only extends to the depth of ten miles. Below us are the granitic masses, unexplored by man, extending to a depth of nearly four thousand miles. Geology here stands in an immeasurable night of time, having for her days and years ages and cycles of ages."

In view of these facts, what becomes of the chronology of the Bible? The common idea is, that the divine historian makes the earth but about six thousand years old, while geology shows it to have an antiquity almost beyond the power of computation.

This, however, is not the true interpretation of the sacred record. It says:—"*In the beginning God created the heavens and the earth;*" but it nowhere fixes the *time* of that *beginning.* From the night that reigned over a succession of extinct worlds, Jehovah spake into existence the present order of things, at the time specified by Moses, and the records of geology attest the truthfulness of his statements. He tells us when Eden was planted and man created; and there are no traces indicating their existence beyond that period. Among all the fossil remains of the different orders of animals found in the various strata of worlds through which the geologist has passed, not one human bone has yet been found.

The great stand and starting point of the Bible is the creation of man, as an occupant of the beautiful world fitted up for his special residence.

The first verse of the Bible is but a distinct announcement of the fact that the material universe was primarily originated by God, out of elements not previously existing; and that the originating act was quite distinct from the acts included in the six natural days of the Adamic creation.

The Bible is thus found to be perfectly coincident with the teachings of geology, and the time of the facts and events which it records is accurate beyond all question.

It is thought proper, in the further discussion of this subject, to divide the facts and events of the Bible into distinct periods, or ages. Beginning at the *first year of the world*, as recorded in the Bible, all the principal events, in the order of time, shall be noted, embracing a period of four thousand one hundred years.

FIRST AGE.

YEAR.	EVENTS.	REMARKS.
A. M.		
1	Reduction of chaos to order—Planting of Eden—Creation of man—Fall of man—Promise of a Saviour.	In all the records of antiquity, for a period of 2000 years from the commencement of the creation of man, nothing can be found deserving the name of authentic history. The period alluded to is usually denominated the *Fabulous Age*. Astronomy first studied by Seth.
2	Birth of Cain and Abel.	
3	The earth first peopled after the expulsion from Paradise.	
129	The sacrifices of Cain and Abel—The murder of Abel—Banishment of Cain.	
130	The birth of Seth.	
235	The birth of Enos—Men begin to call on the name of the Lord.	
325	The birth of Cainan.	
395	Mahalaleel born.	
460	Jared born.	
622	Enoch born	The seventh man.
687	Methuselah born.	
874	Lamech born................................	The father of Noah. Attempts at navigation.
930	Death of Adam—First notice of idolatrous sacrifices....................................	Aged 930 years.
987	Enoch translated, having first predicted a future judgment.	Aged 365 years.
1042	Death of Seth	Aged 912 years.
1056	Noah born....................................	Speech of Lamech the oldest extant poetry.
1100	Mighty men introduce great violence and licentiousness..................................	Oannes teaches art and letters.
1535	Noah commanded to preach repentance and to build the ark 120 years before the flood......	Manufacture of musical instruments. Working of metals.
1556	Birth of Japheth.	
1558	Birth of Shem.	
1651	Lamech dies	The first man who died a natural death before his father.
1655	Death of Methuselah	Aged 969 years, the oldest man.
1656	The Deluge.	
1656	Waters subside—Noah comes out of the ark—Offers a burnt-offering—God makes a covenant with him—Rainbow....................	Plants a vineyard and becomes intoxicated with wine.
	SECOND AGE.	
1757	The earth divided among the sons of Noah....	Asshur.
1770	First foundation of the Assyrian monarchy laid by Nimrod.	
1771	Nineveh, the capital of Assyria, built.	
1772	Commencement of the building of the city of Babylon and the Tower of Babel...........	Languages confounded.
1816	Menes, supposed to be the Mizraim of the Bible, establishes the kingdom of Egypt.	
1886	Mizraim leads colonies into Egypt, and lays the foundation of a kingdom which lasts 1663 years.	
2006	Death of Noah..............................	Aged 950—lived 350 years after the flood.

SECOND AGE.

YEAR.	EVENTS.	REMARKS.
A. M.		
2008	Abram born.	
2036	Ninus is supposed to reign in Assyria. At his death, Semiramis, his queen, assumes the government and moves the seat of government from Nineveh to Babylon, which she greatly enlarges and improves.	
2079	Chedorlaomer subdues the kings of Sodom, Gomorrah, Admah, Zeboiim, and Bela, who serve him twelve years.	
	THIRD AGE.	
2083	Promise of the Messiah made to Abram—Commanded to enter upon the land of Canaan.	
2084	Famine in Canaan—Abram and family go into Egypt—Same year Abram and Lot return to Canaan—Separate—Lot goes to Sodom—Abram builds an altar in Hebron—Returns from the slaughter of the kings, and is blessed by Melchizedek.	
2107	God makes a covenant with Abram, and in token changes his name to Abraham—Circumcision instituted—Isaac promised—God reveals to Abraham the destruction of Sodom—Intercedes for Lot and his family—Sodom and the neighbouring cities destroyed.	Period of the Patriarchs.
2108	Isaac born.	
2133	The trial of Abraham on Mount Moriah.	
2167	Jacob and Esau born..........................	Expulsion of the shepherd kings from Egypt.
2183	Death of Abraham.	
2244	Jacob supplants Esau.	
2265	Jacob wrestles with an angel and is called Israel.......................................	Inachus, a Phœnician, is supposed to have founded the kingdom of Argos. He erects a temple to Apollo on Mount Lycaon.
2274	The age of Job..............................	Ogyges in Attica.
2275	Joseph sold by his brethren to Ishmaelites, who carry him into Egypt.	
2289	Interprets Pharaoh's dreams, and is made governor of Egypt—Seven years of plenty begin.	
2296	Commencement of the seven years of famine.	
2297	Jacob sends his sons to Egypt to buy corn—Joseph is made known to his brethren, and his father is sent for........................	Israelites settle in Goshen, a province of Lower Egypt.
2369	Death of Joseph.—Here the *book of Genesis* ends, containing the history of 2369 years.	
2427	Commencement of the bondage of the children of Israel.	
2431	Moses born—Becomes the adopted son of Pharaoh's daughter...........................	Scamander founds the city and kingdom of Troy.
2473	Moses flees to Midian, where he dwells forty years......................................	Cecrops founds Athens—Thebes built by Cadmus.

THIRD AGE.

YEAR.	EVENTS.	REMARKS.
A. M. 2513	God appears to Moses on Mount Horeb in a burning bush—Is sent to deliver the Israelites—The ten plagues of Egypt.	

FOURTH AGE.

YEAR.	EVENTS.	REMARKS.
2513	The Passover instituted—Same month, at midnight, 600,000 Israelites, exclusive of their children, take up their march for the Red Sea—The army is conducted by a pillar of cloud by day and a pillar of fire by night—The waters are divided—Egyptians drowned—The following month they reach the wilderness of Zin, between Elim and Sinai.	May 4th.
2514	Arrive at Sinai—God publishes his law on tables of stone—3,000 idolaters destroyed by the Levites—God passes by Moses, and shows him his glory—The tabernacle, ark of the covenant, altar, table of show-bread, priests' garments, holy ointment, candlestick, and other utensils and vessels belonging to the sacrifices, are finished in the desert at Sinai and brought to Moses.	
2515	The tabernacle is set up, and priests consecrated—Nadab and Abihu are struck dead by fire from heaven—God speaketh to Moses from the mercy-seat—The second passover is instituted—Spies sent to the land of Canaan.	
2516	Encampment at Kadesh-barnea.	
2533	Destruction of Korah, Dathan, and Abiram, with 250 of their associates, for mutiny—Destruction of 14,700 men for murmuring against Moses and Aaron—Aaron's rod buds—Laid up in the ark for a memorial.	
2552	After travelling nearly 40 years, the Israelites encamp in the wilderness of Zin—Death of Miriam—People murmur for water—Rock smitten—For speaking unadvisedly, Moses and Aaron are debarred admission to Canaan—Aaron dies on Mount Hor—Plague of fiery serpents—Brazen serpent erected—Encampment at Mount Pisgah—Sihon, king of the Amorites, slain—Og, king of Bashan, and all his people destroyed—Encampment at Moab—Balak sends for Balaam, a prophet in Mesopotamia, to come and curse Israel—Through the influence of the women of Moab and Midian, 24,000 men are hung, slain by plague, and killed by sword, in one day—The high-priesthood settled forever on the house of Phineas—Number of the Israelites 601,730, besides the Levites, whose number was 23,000—Land of Canaan divided among the tribes on this side of the river Jordan—The people commanded to set up great stones and engrave thereon the ten commandments—Moses writes the law, and delivers it to the priests and elders of the people to be kept—Same day writes his song, and teaches it to the people to be sung—Finishes the book of the law, and commands it to be kept in the ark—Blesses every tribe by way of prophecy, save the tribe of Levi—Ascends Mount Nebo—Beholds the Land of Promise, and dies—He	The five books of Moses written. Aged 123 years. Aged 120 years.

FOURTH AGE.

YEAR.	EVENTS.	REMARKS.
A. M.		
2552	is mourned for 30 days—Close of the Pentateuch, embracing a history of 2,552 years—Succeeded by Joshua—Israelites cross the Jordan on dry ground—	
2553	Twelve stones set up in the channel—Circumcision revived after having been omitted 40 years—Passover celebrated for the first time in Canaan—The Lord Jesus Christ appears to Joshua with a drawn sword in his hand as Captain of the hosts of his Father —Book of the law read in the ears of the people.	
2554	The rise of the Sabbatical years taken from the autumn of this.	
2559	The land divided in Canaan proper among the remaining tribes—The giants of the land destroyed.	
2560	The tabernacle set up at Shiloh....................	Remains for 328 years.
2561	Death of Joshua....................................	110 years old.
2591	The Israelites, for their idolatry and forgetfulness of God, are delivered into the hands of Chushan, king of Mesopotamia, who holds them in subjection 8 years.	
2599	Othniel defeats Chushan, and delivers the children of Israel from bondage—The land has rest for 40 years..	First dawn of poesy—Period of the Judges.
2661	On the death of Othniel, the people fall into sin, and are enslaved by Eglon, king of Moab, 18 years.	
2679	Ehud kills Eglon—Gathers the people, and slays 10,000 valiant men—The land rests 80 years.	
2691	On the death of Ehud, the people relapse again into sin, and are enslaved by Jabin, king of Canaan, for 20 years.	
2719	Deborah, Barak, and Jael, overcome and destroy Sisera, and deliver Israel—Again the land has rest 40 years.	
2752	Israelites sinning again, are enslaved by the Midian-	
2753	ites for a period of 7 years—Are delivered by Gideon	
2759	—He refuses the government but receives gold earrings, which, converting into an ephod, the people become idolaters—The land again has rest 40 years.	Argonautic Expedition.
2768	Death of Gideon—Idolatry of Israel.	
2769	Abimelech, wishing to obtain the kingdom which his father refused, slays 70 of his brothers.	
2771	Abimelech, having reigned 3 years over Israel, is conspired against—Flees, and is killed................	Theban war.
2794	Tola judges Israel 23 years.	
2798	Jair succeeds Tola, and judges Israel 22 years.	
2816	Israelites worship the gods of other nations, and are enslaved 18 years—Jephthah devotes his daughter, and judges Israel 6 years—He slays 42,000 Ephraimites for their insolence...........................	Troy destroyed by the Greeks.
2822	Ibzan succeeds Jephthah, and judges Israel 7 years.	
2829	Elon succeeds Ibzan.	
2840	Abdon succeeds Elon.	
2848	Eli, the high-priest, succeeds Abdon, and judges Israel 40 years—For the sin of the Israelites they are again enslaved for a period of 40 years............	In the mean time Eli dies.
2849	Samson is born at Zorah.	
2867	Samson slays 30 men of Askelon.	
2868	Destroys the vineyards and olive-gardens of the Philistines—Slays 1,000 Philistines.	
2887	Betrayed by his concubine—His eyes put out—Pulls down the temple of the god Dagon, slaying more at his death than in all his life.	

FOURTH AGE.

YEAR.	EVENTS.	REMARKS.
A. M. 2888	Israelites lose 4,000 men in one battle with the Philistines—They bring the ark of the Lord into the camp from Shiloh, which is taken, and 30,000 Israelites are slain—Eli falls from his seat at the dreadful intelligence and is killed—Philistines set the ark in the temple of their god Dagon—The image falls before it twice and is broken in pieces—Plagues follow wherever it is taken until they send it home—Upwards of 50,000 men are smitten.	Mariner's compass in use in China.
2908	Israelites repent at Mizpeh, and God delivers them.	
2909	Israelites require a king to be given them—Samuel anoints Saul, and he is proclaimed king.	
2918	David born.	
2941	God rejects Saul, and sends Samuel to anoint David.	
2943	David, having Saul twice in his power, refuses to hurt him.	
2948	David flees from Saul to Gath.	
2949	Saul consults the witch of Endor—In battle, Saul falls on his own sword, and dies by the hand of an Amalekite, whom David puts to death—Abner makes Saul's son king over part of Israel.	
2953	Abner joins David, but is treacherously murdered by Joab—David anointed king the third time.	
2954	David with all Israel marches to Jerusalem, and takes the fort of Zion—Calls it the city of David, and makes Jerusalem the seat of his kingdom, where he reigns 33 years.	
2956	The ark of the covenant brought from the house of Abinadab in Kirjath-jearim, and placed in Zion, 30,000 choice men attending it and singing the 68th Psalm.	
2957	David communicates to Nathan his desire to build a house for the Lord—It is answered, that not he, but Solomon should build it—David, by many wars with surrounding nations, extends his kingdom.	
2969	David is guilty of adultery and murder.	
2970	Repents, and composes the 51st Psalm.	
2971	David marries Bathsheba—Solomon born.	
2972	Amnon, David's eldest son, defiles his sister Tamar.	
2974	Absalom avenges his sister by killing Amnon, and flees to Syria.	
2977	Returns to Jerusalem, and after two years is reconciled to his father.	
2980	Absalom steals away the hearts of the people from his father David.	
2981	Engages in a rebellion against his father, and causes him to flee from Jerusalem—Ahithophel hangs himself—Absalom, having lost 20,000 men, in fleeing is caught in the bough of an oak, and is run through by Joab.	
2987	David, tempted by Satan, commands Joab to number the people—God sends a pestilence, during which 70,000 men die in one day—On David's repentance, the plague is stayed.	
2988	Rehoboam is born to Solomon.	
2989	Solomon anointed king—David dies.	
2990	Pharaoh, king of Egypt, gives his daughter in marriage to Solomon—God gives him wisdom, riches, and honour—Wisdom manifested in judging between two harlots.	

FIFTH AGE.

YEAR.	EVENTS.	REMARKS.
A. M.		
2992	Solomon lays the foundation of the temple.	
2999	Temple finished, having been seven and a half years in building.	
3000	Dedication of the temple celebrated with great magnificence....................................	Age of Homer and Hesiod.
3029	Solomon writes Ecclesiastes—Death of Solomon—Rehoboam made king—Revolt of ten tribes under Jeroboam, who become idolaters, and worship the golden calves set up by the king at Bethel and Dan.	
3030	Rehoboam becomes an idolater.	
3033	Shishak, king of Egypt, spoils Jerusalem and the temple.	
3046	Abijam, son of Rehoboam, succeeds his father.	
3047	Obtains a great victory over Jeroboam—Kills 500,000 men in one battle, and takes Bethel.	
3049	Asa succeeds his father Abijam.	
3050	Nadab succeeds his father Jeroboam in the kingdom of Israel.	
3051	Nadab is slain—The whole race of Jeroboam destroyed.	
3053	Asa destroys idolatry, and establishes a standing army. Zerah with an innumerable army invades Judah—Asa overcomes him, and makes a covenant with God.	
3074	Elah succeeds his father in the kingdom of Israel.	
3075	Zimri conspires against Elah, and kills him and reigns in his stead—Destroys the family of Baasha—The army makes Omri their king—Zimri sets fire to the palace, and perishes.	
3079	The people of Israel divided into two factions.	
3080	Omri removes the seat of his kingdom to Samaria.	
3086	Ahab succeeds his father in the kingdom of Israel—Does evil in the sight of the Lord.	
3090	Jehoshaphat succeeds his father Asa.	
3092	Destroys the groves and high places, and sends Levites to instruct the people in the law of the Lord.	
3103	Ben-hadad, king of Syria, lays seige to Samaria, but suffers great loss.	
3111	Ahab obtains Naboth's vineyard by fraud—Elijah denounces judgments against him.	
3113	Ahab makes his son Ahaziah an associate in the government of the kingdom—Jehoshaphat also associates with him his son Jehoram.	
3114	Ahab consults 400 false prophets—Is slain at Ramoth-gilead..	Dido founds Carthage.
3115	On the death of Ahab the Moabites revolt from the kingdom of Israel—Elijah destroys the men sent by Ahaziah to arrest him by fire from heaven—Jehoram succeeds his brother Ahaziah in the kingdom of Israel—Elijah is taken up to heaven in a chariot of fire and horses of fire.	Caranus founds the Macedonian kingdom.
3119	Jehoshaphat invests his son Jehoram with the throne—After the death of his father, he puts all his brethren to the sword—The Edomites revolt from the kingdom of Judah.	
3120	Jehoram, following the advice of his wicked wife, establishes idolatrous worship.........................	Lycurgus establishes his celebrated constitution.
3123	Ahaziah succeeds his father in the kingdom of Judah.	
3124	Jezebel cast out of the window, and eaten by dogs—Ahab's family destroyed—The priests of Baal slain—	

FIFTH AGE.

YEAR.	EVENTS.	REMARKS.
A. M. 3124	Jehu kills Ahaziah and 42 of his kinsmen—Athaliah, the daughter of Ahab, usurps the kingdom, and destroys the royal family, with the exception of Jehoash, an infant son.	
3130	Jehoash anointed king, and Athaliah slain.	
3147	Jehoash orders the repair of the temple—Jehoahaz succeeds his father, Jehu, in the kingdom of Israel.	
3163	Jehoash, the son of Jehoahaz, is taken into consortship in the kingdom of Israel.	
3164	Zechariah is stoned to death in the court of the house of the Lord, for reproving the people for idolatry. This was done at the command of king Jehoash, who is next year murdered in his bed and succeeded by his son Amaziah.	
3165	Jehoahaz dies, and is succeeded by his son Jehoash—Visits Elisha—Elisha dies, and a dead man is brought to life by being laid in the prophet's grave.	
3168	Jeroboam the Second taken into consortship with his father in the kingdom of Israel.	
3178	Jehoash overcomes Amaziah in battle, and takes him prisoner—Breaks down 400 cubits of the wall of Jerusalem—Spoils the temple and the king's palace, of vast treasure.	
3179	Jehoash dies—Jeroboam the Second reigns.	
3194	Amaziah is murdered at Lachish—Succeeded by his son Uzziah.	
3196	The thirteenth Jubilee held—Isaiah, Joel, Jonah, Hosea, and Amos lived at this time—Inhabitants of Nineveh, the capital of Assyria, repent at the preaching of Jonah.	
3220	Jeroboam dies—Kingdom falls into anarchy—An interregnum of eleven years and a half.............	First Olympiad, —an era from which the Greeks reckoned time.
3231	Zachariah begins his reign over Israel.	
3232	Shallum murders Zachariah, and reigns one month—Menahem kills Shallum—Unnatural murder of women in Tiphsah.	
3233	Menahem prevents the king of Assyria from invading his country by giving him 1,000 talents of silver.	
3243	Pekahiah succeeds his father Menahem.	
3245	Pekah, one of his captains, kills him in his own palace, and reigns in his stead.	
3246	Jotham succeeds his father, Uzziah, in the kingdom of Israel—He subdues the Ammonites—Under him and his two successors the prophets Micah, Hosea, and Nahum execute their office.	
3253	Ahaz succeeds his father, Jotham—*The promise of Immanuel*, to be born of a virgin—Ahaz forsakes God, his deliverer—120,000 of the men of Judah slain, and 200,000 carried into captivity.	The age of Amos.
3265	Hoshea, the son of Elah, murders Pekah, and usurps the kingdom—The state without any form of government.	The age of Hosea and Micah.
3276	Shalmaneser, king of Assyria, comes up against Hoshea, and makes him pay tribute.	
3278	Hezekiah succeeds his father, Ahaz, in the kingdom of Judah—Destroys idolatry—Celebrates a solemn passover.	

FIFTH AGE.

YEAR.	EVENTS.	REMARKS.
A. M. 3283	Shalmaneser besieges Samaria, destroys the kingdom of Israel, and carries the Israelites captive to his own country......................................	The kingdom of Israel stands divided from that of Judah 254 years.
3291	Sennacherib besieges Judah, but is appeased by a tribute—Hezekiah obtains a prolongation of his life —The sun goes ten degrees backward.	
3294	Sennacherib violates the treaty of peace—An angel of the Lord slays 185,000 of the Assyrian army—Sennacherib is slain by his own sons—Hezekiah dies.	
3306	Manasseh succeeds his father—Sets up idolatry—Carried away captive to Babylon—Repents, and is restored to his kingdom.............................	The age of Isaiah.
3348	Nebuchadnezzar, king of Assyria, sends Holofernes to Judea to besiege the country—At Bethulia his head is taken off by Judith, a woman of the tribe of Simeon..	The age of Nahum, Jonah, Joel, Habakkuk, and Obadiah.
3361	Amon succeeds his father Manasseh—An idolater as his father, but no penitent—Is murdered by his servants.	
3363	Josiah, a child eight years old, succeeds his father Amon —In his time lived Jeremiah and Zephaniah, prophets, and Huldah the prophetess..................	Zephaniah and Jeremiah.
3372	Commences a reformation in Judah and Jerusalem...	Ezekiel.
3378	Orders the repair of the temple—The book of the law found—Ordered to be read to all the people—Burns dead men's bones on the altar of Bethel, and celebrates a solemn passover.	
3392	War between the kings of Egypt and Assyria—Josiah engages in it and is slain in the valley of Megiddo—His death bewailed by public mourning—The Lamentations of Jeremiah composed in remembrance of his death—The people anoint Shallum, one of his sons, king—He is deposed by Pharaoh-necho, who places his elder brother, Eliakim, king over Judah and Jerusalem, and changes his name into Jehoiakim.	
3393	Uriah and Jeremiah prophesy against Jerusalem—The former is put to death—The latter is acquitted and set at liberty.....................................	Habakkuk.
3398	Nebuchadnezzar the Great made by his father, Nabopolassar, his associate in the kingdom of Assyria and Babylon—Jehoiakim is put in chains, and carried to Babylon—70 years captivity commenced—The choicest youth of the royal family educated in the language and science of the Chaldeans, for the service of the king.	
3400	Nabopolassar dies, and is succeeded by Nebuchadnezzar—Carries the vessels of the temple to Babylon—Places them in the temple of his god Belus.	
3402	Daniel recovers Nebuchadnezzar's dream, and interprets it—He and his companions are promoted.....	The age of Daniel.
3405	An army of Chaldeans, Syrians, Moabites, and Ammonites invade Judea, and carry away 3,023 captives —Jehoiakim is put to death, and left unburied at the gate of Jerusalem—Jehoiachin succeeds his father—Against him Nebuchadnezzar leads an army, besieging Jerusalem—Makes all prisoners—Takes all the treasure in the king's palace—Breaks all the	

FIFTH AGE.

YEAR.	EVENTS.	REMARKS.
A. M. 3405	vessels of gold and furniture which Solomon had made for the temple—Carries to Babylon the king, his mother, wives, courtiers, magistrates, and 10,000 able men out of Jerusalem, leaving none but the poorer sort—From the country he carries away 8,000 artificers—An epistle is sent from Jeremiah warning them to beware of the idolatry in Babylon.	Solon, the legislator of Athens and benefactor of the human race. Geographical maps and globes first invented.
3416	Nebuchadnezzar makes Zedekiah king of Judah—Jerusalem is again taken by Nebuchadnezzar—Zedekiah's eyes are put out, and he sent to Babylon—The temple and city are fired and reduced to ashes—Obadiah denounces judgments against Edom for taunting the people of God in their calamity—So also Jeremiah and Ezekiel.	
	SIXTH AGE.	
3435	Nebuchadnezzar deprived of his reason, and driven out from the society of men.	
3442	His reason and kingdom restored to him—Soon after dies—Evil-merodach succeeds him—Liberates Jehoiachin—Promotes him to honour.	
3449	Evil-merodach murdered, and succeeded by his son Belshazzar—Daniel has his vision of the four beasts, signifying the four great monarchies of the world.	
3451	Daniel's vision of the ram and he-goat, betokening the destruction of the Persian monarchy..........	Zoroaster, Confucius.
3456	Belshazzar's guilty feast—Mysterious characters on the wall—Interpreted by Daniel—Proclaimed President of the kingdom—The same night Belshazzar is slain—Babylon is taken by Cyrus—Given to the Medes and Persians—Cyrus makes Darius the Mede king, and reserving some palaces for himself, returns to Persia—Daniel's greatness excites envy—An unrighteous decree made—Cast into the den of lions—Receives no hurt—His enemies devoured by the lions.	
3467	Daniel's prophecy of the 70 weeks.	
3468	Cyrus becomes emperor of Persia and Media—His proclamation, liberating all the Jews, and sending them back to Jerusalem, with a command to immediately rebuild the temple—Restores all the holy vessels—42,360 return to their own land—Levites appointed to oversee the work—Samaritans disturb the Jews in their work—Artaxerxes forbids the Jews from going on with their work of rebuilding.	
3484	In the second year of the reign of Darius Hystaspis, Zerubbabel and Jeshua recommence the work—Prophecy of Haggai that the glory of the latter temple should exceed that of the former	The age of Haggai and Zechariah.
3485	Zechariah exhorts the Jews to repentance.	
3486	Ahasuerus puts away his wife Vashti, and marries Esther, the niece of Mordecai the Jew.	
3489	The temple completed—The dedication celebrated with great joy—Passover also celebrated.	
3494	Haman offended at Mordecai—Resolves to take vengeance on the whole nation—Obtains an edict for	

SIXTH AGE.

YEAR.	EVENTS.	REMARKS.
A. M. 3494	their indiscriminate slaughter—Mordecai, Esther, and all the Jews fast and pray—Ahasuerus hearing it read in the Chronicles that Mordecai had discovered a conspiracy to him, has him publicly honoured—Esther, at a public banquet, accuses Haman.	Roman republic.
3495	The gallows Haman had prepared for Mordecai he is hanged on himself..............................	Time of Ezra.
3537	Ezra, the priest, a man skilled in the law of Moses, obtains a large commission from Artaxerxes to settle the Jewish commonwealth and to reform the Church at Jerusalem—Ezra sets out with a great multitude of Jews from Babylon.	
3549	All who had taken strange wives are ordered by Ezra to send them back—Nehemiah, the governor of Judea, has permission to rebuild the walls......	The age of Malachi.
3552	He returns to Persia................................	Herodotus—Thucydides — Socrates.
3589	The twenty-first Jubilee, the last that the prophets of the Old Testament ever saw—Malachi's prophecy. *Here ends the chronology of the Old Testament, as obtained from its canonical books.*	
3669	Alexander the Great, king of Macedonia, passes out of Europe into Asia and invades Persia..............	Apocryphal period.
3671	Sanballat obtains leave from Alexander to build a temple on Mount Gerizim—Makes Manasses high-priest thereof—Alexander prevented from besieging Jerusalem by the reception he meets with from the high-priest and people all in white—Sacrifices in the temple—Bestows favours upon the Jews and natives.	
3673	The Persians are overcome—Darius slain—Alexander universal monarch of the world.	
3681	Alexander dies—His dominions divided among his generals: Asia, to Antigonus; Babylon, to Seleucus; the Hellespont, to Lysimachus; Macedon, to Cassander; Egypt, to Ptolemæus.	
3684	Ptolemæus makes himself master of Jerusalem by stratagem—Sends colonies of Jews into Egypt.	
3727	Ptolemæus Philadelphus, son of Ptolemæus Soter, being a great friend of learning, builds a most magnificent library at Alexandria—Demetrius Phalereus, to whom he had committed the work of selecting books from all countries, persuades him to employ 72 Jews to translate the Holy Scriptures out of the original Hebrew into the Greek tongue.	
3827	Heliodorus is struck down for invading the temple.	
3828	Seleucus is succeeded by Antiochus Epiphanes in the kingdom of Syria.	
3829	Jason obtains the office of high-priest by corrupting King Antiochus.	
3832	Menelaus obtains the priesthood by bribery and corruption.	
3834	Antiochus takes Jerusalem, pillages the temple, destroys 40,000 of the inhabitants, and sells many more—Endeavours to abolish the Jewish worship—Samaritans disown them in their adversity, and consecrate their temple on Mount Gerizim to Jupiter.	
3835	The kingdom of the Macedonians ends.	

SIXTH AGE.

YEAR.	EVENTS.	REMARKS.
A. M. 3837	King Antiochus commands all nations to embrace the worship of the Grecians on pain of death—Many Jews suffer martyrdom—Matthias, a priest, with his five sons, slays those who are sent to compel them to offer sacrifice to idols—They flee to the desert, are pursued, and, because they do not defend themselves on the Sabbath, are killed.	
3838	Matthias dies, and Judas Maccabeus takes his place, and delivers his country from abominations—Apollonius is slain by him, and his army discomfited—Seron, governor of Lower Syria, invades Judea—Judas slays 800 of his men, and puts the rest to flight.	
3839	He defeats a great army which Antiochus had sent into Judea—Lysias returns with greater power—Judas kills 5,000 of his men, and the rest retreat—He purifies the temple after it had been desolate three years, and builds a wall around Zion.	
3842	The judgments of God fall upon Antiochus—He dies, and his son, Eupator, reigns in his stead—Onias retires into Egypt, where Ptolemæus Philometer and Cleopatra, his wife, permit him to build a temple at Heliopolis, where they constitute him high-priest—Demetrius Soter escapes from Rome, comes to Syria—Puts to death Antiochus and Lysias, and is crowned king.	
3845	Demetrius sends Nicanor with a great army against Judas—Is slain—Demetrius sends another army of 20,000—Judas meets it with 800, and is slain—His brother, Jonathan, is chosen general in his stead—Jonathan enters into an alliance with the Romans—The first league ever known between the Romans and Jews.	
3846	Alcimus is struck dead for commanding the inner court of the temple to be pulled down............	Rome, the arbitress of nations from the Atlantic to the Euphrates.
3856	Demetrius is slain in battle by Alexander—Alexander Balas is married to Cleopatra.	
3858	The temple of Dagon burned by Demetrius Nicanor—Ptolemæus takes his daughter from Alexander, and marries her to Demetrius.	
3859	Ptolemæus dies—Jonathan besieges the citadel of Jerusalem.	
3860	Demetrius is vanquished, and Jonathan renews his league with the Romans.	
3861	Jonathan is decoyed to Ptolemais by Tryphon, where he is taken prisoner, and his men put to the sword—Jonathan put to death—Tryphon murders the young Antiochus, and puts the crown on his own head—The Romans and Lacedæmonians write their league on tables of brass.	
3862	Simon, the son of Jonathan, has the government and high-priesthood settled on him—Drives all idolaters out of the city of Zion.	
3865	Antiochus slain—Simon and his two sons barbarously murdered by Ptolemæus, the son of Abubus.	
3870	John Hyrcanus takes Shechem—Demolishes the temple on Mount Gerizim.	

SIXTH AGE.

YEAR.	EVENTS.	REMARKS.
A. M.		
3897	Judas, eldest son of Hyrcanus, succeeds his father in the government and high-priesthood—Sets a crown upon his head, and changes the state into a monarchy..	The first instance of the kind since the captivity.
3916	Anna, the prophetess, becoming a widow, remains in the temple, where she serves God day and night, by fasting and prayer, 84 years.	
3941	Jerusalem taken by Pompey, and the Jews made tributary to the Romans.............	Judea dependent upon the Romans.
3955	Herod, the son of Antipas, an Idumean, is made king of Judea.	
3966	Hillel, a descendant of David, lives in Jerusalem—His disciple, Jonathan, is the author of the Chaldee paraphrase.......................................	Herod takes possession of Jerusalem and Judea.
3977	Cæsar Augustus assumes the title of emperor—The republic is changed into a monarchy.	
3986	The angel Gabriel appears to Zachary, the priest, as he is offering incense in the temple.	
3999	The same angel sent to the Virgin Mary—The annunciation.	
4004	John the Baptist born six months before Christ.	
	SEVENTH AGE.	
	The advent of our Lord and Saviour. The eighth day after his nativity he is circumcised and named Jesus—The Magi bring presents—Joseph flees into Egypt—Herod commands the infants in Bethlehem to be slain—Herod dies, and Archelaus is made tetrarch by Cæsar—Christ is brought back from Egypt.	
4008	Our Lord goes with his parents to Jerusalem to attend the Passover—Disputes with the doctors—Augustus dies, and Tiberius succeeds him.	
4014	Josephus, called Caiaphas, is made high-priest of the Jews.	
4026	Pontius Pilate made procurator of Judea.	
4027	John the Baptist preaches and baptizes in the wilderness of Judea—Baptizes Christ in Jordan—Christ is tempted in the wilderness.	
4030	Christ returns to Galilee—Andrew, Peter, Philip, and Nathanael acknowledge him the Messiah—Marriage at Cana—The first passover of Christ's public ministry—Christ enters the temple and drives out the money changers—John cast into prison by Herod—Christ discovers himself to the woman of Samaria.	The first miracle.
4031	Christ goes through Galilee and teaches in the synagogues, working miracles—Matthew called to be a disciple—The second Passover held—Christ heals the impotent man at the pool of Bethesda—The twelve Apostles chosen—Sermon on the Mount.	
4032	The twelve sent out two by two to preach the gospel and heal the sick—John the Baptist is beheaded—Christ feeds 5,000 men, besides women and children, with the five loaves and two fishes—Refuses to be made king—The third Passover held—The transfiguration on the mount—Christ pays tribute to	

SEVENTH AGE.

YEAR.	EVENTS.	REMARKS.
A. M. 4032	Cæsar—The seventy disciples sent out two by two to preach and work miracles.	
4033	The disciples taught to pray—Lazarus raised from the dead—Caiaphas's prophecy concerning the death of Christ—Conversion of Zaccheus—Bartimeus restored to sight—Mary, the sister of Lazarus, anoints the feet of Jesus—The triumphal entry of Christ into Jerusalem—He curses the fig-tree—The fourth Passover celebrated—The sacrament of the Lord's Supper instituted—Christ washes the disciples' feet—Christ is betrayed by Judas—Next day condemned by Pilate and crucified—The third day (April 5th, A. D. 33,) he rises from the dead—Appears first to Mary Magdalene—Afterwards appears to his disciples, and dines with them—Promises to them the effusion of the Holy Ghost—Commissions them to teach and baptize all nations—Ascends from Mount Olivet to heaven—The day of Pentecost—Gift of tongues—3,000 converted—Peter and John cast into prison—Ananias and Sapphira struck dead.	
4034	Seven deacons ordained—Stephen stoned to death—Great persecution—Philip preaches in Samaria—Simon, the sorcerer, believes, and is baptized.	
4035	The Ethiopian converted and baptized—Saul is converted on his way to Damascus—Preaches the gospel.	
4038	A conspiracy against Saul—Receives instructions to leave Jerusalem—Goes to Tarsus, Cilicia, and Syria—Peter visits the Churches of Judea, Samaria, and Galilee—Cures Eneas, and restores Tabitha to life.	
4041	Cornelius instructed to send for Peter—He is converted and baptized—The disciples from Phenice and Cyprus come to Antioch—Send for Barnabas—He and Saul preach there a whole year—Disciples first called Christians.	
4044	Herod Agrippa beheads James—Imprisons Peter—He is smitten of God at Cesarea, and eaten of worms.	
4045	Barnabas and Saul start out and plant the Christian faith in Seleucia, Cyprus, and other places—Sergius Paulus—Elymas, the sorcerer, struck blind—Saul's name changed to Paul—They preach at Antioch and Iconium.	
4046	Persecuted, they fly to Lystra and Derbe, in Lycaonia—Are called gods: Barnabas, Jupiter; and Paul, Mercurius—Paul stoned and dragged out of Lystra as dead—Next day departs with Barnabas to Derbe—Timothy, a child, embraces the Christian faith.	
4052	Judaizing teachers introduce circumcision—Council held at Jerusalem to settle the matter—Decrees of the council sent to the Churches.	
4053	Paul and Barnabas, disagreeing, separate—Barnabas and Mark go into Cyprus, and Paul and Silas go into Syria and Cilicia—Paul takes Timothy from Derbe—His mother being a believing Jew, he causes him to be circumcised—He is admonished by a vision to go into Macedonia—Arrives at Philippi—Lydia converted—Paul and Silas imprisoned—Miraculously delivered—Philippian jailer converted.	
4054	They journey through Amphipolis and Apollonia—Come to Thessalonica—Go to Berea, and thence to	

SEVENTH AGE.

YEAR.	EVENTS.	REMARKS.
A. M.		
4054	Athens—Dionysius, the Areopagite, converted—Goes to Corinth—Meets Aquila and Priscilla, who had been banished from Rome—Remains here a year and six months—Writes to the Thessalonians.	
4055	Accused by the Jews, and brought before Gallio, proconsul of Achaia.	
4056	Leaves Corinth and goes to Ephesus—From thence to Jerusalem—Goes to Cesarea, Antioch, Galatia, and Phrygia.	
4057	Returns to Ephesus, and disputes daily in the school of Tyrannus.	
4058	Writes his epistle to the Galatians.	
4060	Demetrius, a silversmith, opposes him—A schism arises in the Church at Corinth—He writes his First Epistle to the Corinthians—Leaves Ephesus and goes to Macedonia—Writes his second letter—Goes to Corinth, and writes his letter to the Romans—Goes to Philippi, and from thence to Troas, where he restores Eutychus to life—Goes to Miletus—Goes to Jerusalem—Is apprehended and imprisoned in the castle—Claims the privilege of a Roman citizen—Pleads his cause before Ananias, high-priest—He is sent to Felix—Imprisoned at Cesarea.	
4062	Accused before Felix by Tertullus, the orator—Paul before Festus—Appeals to Cæsar—Paul makes his defence before King Agrippa.	
4063	Taken to Rome, a prisoner at large, where he preaches two years.	
4064	From Rome Paul writes to the Philippians, to Philemon, to the Colossians, and to the Ephesians.	
4065	He is set at liberty, and writes to the Hebrews—Preaches the gospel in the Isle of Crete.	
4066	Writes his letters to Timothy and Titus—Peter writes his letters—St. John and St. Jude write about this time.	
4067	St. Peter and St. Paul suffer martyrdom.	
4070	Jerusalem besieged, taken, sacked, and burned by Titus—1,100,000 Jews perish; 97,000 are taken prisoners	Herculaneum and Pompeii destroyed.
4096	St. John is banished to the Isle of Patmos by Domitian—Writes his Revelation—Returns to Ephesus, and, at the request of the Church, writes his Gospel.	

Here the events connected with Bible chronology end. Those of a collateral character might have been more copiously adduced, but what we have given are thought to be sufficient for all the purposes of the present work.

Part Ninth.

BIBLICAL GEOGRAPHY.

Under this head we propose to give the names of the principal countries of the Bible, embracing the mountains, seas, lakes, rivers, cities, towns, &c., &c. We shall present them in alphabetical order, and briefly notice whatever is remarkable as connected with the localities enumerated.

As most of the scenes of the Bible lie in Palestine, it may not be improper, in this place, to make some remarks in regard to the *climate* and *face of the country*.

The state of the atmosphere is different in different places, but it is not so changeable as in some parts of Europe. During the first part of the year, which is called the *harvest*, extending from the middle of April to the middle of June, the sky is serene, the atmosphere is warm—sometimes oppressively so—excepting in the valleys, or on the shores of the sea, where it is temperate. During the second part of the year, which is called *summer*, extending from the middle of June to the middle of August, the heat is intense, and the inhabitants sleep, in the night, under the open sky. The third season, from the middle of August to the middle of Octcber, is called the *hot season*, for then the heat has reached its greatest intensity; but it soon abates. From the time of harvest, or from the middle of April to the middle of September, there is neither rain nor thunder. Prov. xxvi, 1; 1 Sam. xii, 17. In the months of May, June, July, and August, not a cloud is to be seen, and the earth is only moistened with the dew, which is everywhere used as a symbol of the divine benevolence. Gen. xxvii, 28; xlix, 25; Deut. xxxii, 2; xxxiii, 13; Job xxix, 19; Micah v, 7. The fourth part of the year is called the *seed-time.* It extends from the middle of October to the middle of December. The autumnal rains begin in the latter part of October. The leaves fall in the latter part of November, and the snow in December. Some do without fire the whole winter. The fifth part of the year extends from the middle of December to the middle of February, which is called *the winter.* The snow soon melts away, and only remains on the mountains. As January departs, and February enters, the grain-fields flourish, and the trees put on their foliage. The sixth period is called the *cold season,* because, in the commencement of it, the weather is still cold, though it lasts but for a short time.

Palestine is a *mountainous* country. Two ranges, the one on the east and the other on the west of the Jordan, extend from Syria into Arabia, interrupted, however, in various places, by valleys. The principal mountains are Lebanon, Carmel, Tabor, Mountains of Israel, and the Mountains of Gilead.

Abana—A river in Syria, spoken of by Naaman the leper, when he was directed to wash away his leprosy in Jordan.

Abarim—A mountain in Palestine, on the summit of which Balak and Balaam had an interview, and the latter was entreated to curse the Israelites, who were encamped in the plain.

Abdon, or *Hebron*—A city of the Levites, in Palestine.

Abel—A town or province in Palestine, of which Lysanias was tetrarch.

Abel of the vineyards—in Palestine; the place where Jephthah smote the Ammonites.

Abel, Plain of.

Abel of *Beth-Maachah*—Palestine. Joab pursued Sheba to this place, who was afterwards slain.

Abel-Maim—Palestine. Taken by Benhadad, king of Syria.

Abel-Meholah—Palestine. Here the Midianites were routed by the Israelites, under Gideon.

Abel-Mizraim—Palestine. Here Joseph mourned seven days for Jacob his father.

Abel-Shittim—Palestine; an encampment of the Israelites, on the plains of Moab.

Aben-Bohan—Palestine; a boundary-stone between Benjamin and Judah.

Abez—Palestine; a boundary-town between Issachar and Manasseh.

Abila, or *Abel*—Palestine.

Abilene—Syria. Lysanias was tetrarch of this place.

Abimael—Persia.

Abumah—Palestine.

Accad—A city in Turkey, built by Nimrod.

Accaron, or *Ekron*—Palestine. The Canaanites were never expelled from this place.

Accho, or *St. Jean d'Acre*—Palestine. The Canaanites were never expelled from this city.

Aceldama—Palestine; a field purchased by Judas for the price of his Lord.

Achaia—Turkey. Here Paul was accused before Gallio.

Achmetha, or *Ecbatana*—Persia. Here the records were found, relating to the rebuilding of Jerusalem.

Achor—A valley in Palestine, where Achan was stoned by the children of Israel.

Achshaph—A Levitical city of Palestine.

Achzib—Palestine. The Canaanites were never expelled from this city.

Acrabbim—The southern boundary of Judea.

Adadah—Palestine.

Adam—Palestine. From this place to the Dead Sea the waters of the Jordan were dried up, during the passage of the Israelites.

Adamah—A fortified city of Palestine.

Adar—A boundary-town between Edom and Judah, in Palestine.

Adithaim—Palestine.

Admah—One of the cities of Palestine, in the valley of Siddim, destroyed by fire.

Adoraim—A city of Palestine, built by Rehoboam.

Adramyttium—Turkey.

Adria—The Mediterranean. Here Paul was shipwrecked

Adullam—Palestine. In a cave, near this city, David hid himself when pursued by Saul.

Adummim—Palestine.

Ænon, or *Enon*—The fountain of On, in Palestine, where John baptized.

Ahava—A river of Assyria. Here Ezra proclaimed a fast, previous to the return of the Israelites.

Ahlab—Palestine.

Ai, or *Hai*—Palestine. Taken and burned by Joshua.

Aiath—Palestine.

Aijalon—Palestine. Elon, one of the judges of Israel, was buried here.

Aijalon, or *Aiaja*—A city of the Levites, where the Philistines were subdued by Samuel.

Aijalon—A valley of Palestine, where the sun and moon stood still, at the command of Joshua.

Ain, or *Oin*—Palestine.

Ain, or *Ashan*—A Levitical city.

Ain—A valley.

Alemeth—A Levitical city.

Alexandria—A city of Egypt, from whence St. Paul sailed for Rome.

Allon—Palestine.

Allon-Bachuth—Palestine. Here Deborah, the nurse of Rebecca, was buried.

Almodad—Persia. A colony of Joktan, son of Shem.

Almon-Diblathaim—Palestine. A station of the Israelites.

Aloth, District of—A territory in Palestine, under the government of one of Solomon's purveyors.

Alush—An encampment of the Israelites, in Arabia.

Amalek—Arabia.

Amana, or *Anti-Lebanon*—On Mount Lebanon; celebrated for the growth of its cedars.

Ammah—A hill in Palestine, to which Joab and Abishai pursued Abner.

Ammon-Ham—Palestine.

Ammon-No—Egypt.

Amorites, Mount of—Turkey. The Canaanites were never expelled from this place.

Amphipolis—Turkey. Paul preached in this city.

Anab—Palestine. From this place Joshua cut off the Anakims.

Anaharath—A boundary-town between Issachar and Manasseh.

Ananiah—Palestine.

Anamim—Egypt; a colony of Mizraim.

Anathoth—A Levitical city in Palestine. Jeremiah had a possession here.

Anem—A Levitical city.

Antioch—Syria. Disciples first called Christians at this city. Here Paul and Barnabas separated. Here Paul was stoned, but afterwards recovered.

Antipatris—Syria. From here Paul was sent to Cesarea.

Antonia, Castle of—Syria. At this place Paul was confined, previously to being sent to Felix.

Aphek—Syria. The Canaanites were never expelled from this place.

Aphekah—Syria. Here the Philistines overcame the Israelites.

Aphek in Syria—Here the Syrians, and thirty-two kings, under Benhadad, were defeated by Ahab.

Apollonia—Syria. Paul visited this city, on his way to Thessalonica.

Appii-Forum—Italy. Here Paul was met by his brethren, on the way to Rome.

Arab—Syria. This place was given, by command of Jehovah, to Lot.

Arabah—Syria. A boundary-town of Benjamin.

Arabia—Through part of this country (Arabia Petræa,) the Israelites, under Moses, wandered for forty years.

Arad—Syria. A royal city, and one of the thirty-one kingdoms subdued by Joshua.

Aram, or *Padan Aram*—Mesopotamia. The country of Nahor, Abram, Jacob, &c.

Aram—Syria.

Ararat, or *Armenia*—Erivan.

Ararat, Mount—Armenia. On this mount the ark rested after the Deluge, and from thence the descendants of Noah peopled the earth.

Arba—Syria. The place of Abraham and Isaac's sojourning.

Arbah.

Arbel—Syria.

Archi—Syria. A boundary-town.

Areopolis—Syria.

Argob—Syria. This place was under the government of one of Solomon's purveyors.

Argob, *Regions of*—Syria. The cities of which were taken by the Israelites.

Ariel, *Jebus*, *Salem*—Palestine. Ancient capital of the East, and the birth-place of Solomon.

Arimathea—Palestine. The birth-place of Joseph the counsellor.

Arkites, *Country of the*—Syria. A colony of Canaan, a son of Ham.

Armageddon—Palestine; mountains and valley of.

Armenia, or *Ararat*—Erivan.

Arnon, *Fords of*—Palestine. These waters are said to have divided for the passage of the Israelites.

Arnon, *River*—Syria.

Aroer—Palestine. A city built by the children of Gad.

Aroer—Palestine. A city which David smote.

Arpad—Syria. A place of the grossest idolatry.

Arphaxad—Turkey.

Arvad—Syria. Celebrated for its shipping in the time of Solomon.

Aruboth—Turkey. Under the government of one of Solomon's purveyors.

Arumah—Palestine. The place where Abimelech dwelt.

Ashan—Palestine. A city of the Levites.

Ashdod, or *Azotus*—Palestine. A place of idol-worship. The Philistines placed the ark here, in the temple of Dagon. Here Philip was found, after the conversion of the eunuch.

Ashdoth-Pisgah—Palestine.

Asher—Palestine. A boundary of Manasseh.

Ashkenaz—Turkey.

Ashkenaz, Sea of, (Pontus Euxinus)—Turkey and Russia.

Ashtaroth—Palestine.

Ashteroth Karnaim—Palestine. Here Chedorlaomer smote the Rephaims, or giants.

Asia (Proper)—Turkey.

Asia Minor—Turkey.

Askelon or *Ashkelon*—Palestine. Taken from the Philistines by the tribe of Judah. Here Samson gave his marriage-feast, propounded his riddle, and smote thirty of the Philistines.

Asshur, or *Assyria*—Persia.

Assos—Turkey. A port of Asia Minor, in which the gospel was generally diffused.

Atad—Turkey. Here the Israelites mourned over the body of Jacob seven days.

Ataroth—Turkey. A boundary between Gad and Reuben.

Athens—Greece. Here Paul found an altar to the unknown God, and preached on Mars' Hill.

Ather—Syria.

Alroth—Palestine.

Attalia—Turkey. Paul and Barnabas here took ship for Antioch.

Ava—Persia. A place of captivity.

Aven—Turkey. Denounced by the prophet Amos.

Aven—Palestine. The Philistines sent the ark of the covenant to this place.

Aven, or *Beth-Shemesh*—Egypt. Pharaoh gave Asenath, a daughter of the high-priest of this place, to Joseph.

Avim—Palestine.

Azekah—Palestine. Here the Amorites were defeated by Joshua.

Azmon—Palestine. A boundary-town between Judah and Arabia.

Azza, or *Gaza*—Palestine. This was the capital of the country of the Philistines.

Baal, high places of—Palestine.

Baalah, or *Kirjath-jearim*—Palestine.

Baalah, *Mount*—Palestine.

Baal-Berith—Palestine.

Baal-Gad, Mountain and town of.

Baal-Hamon—Palestine. At this place Solomon had vineyards.

Baal-Hazor—Palestine. Here Absalom killed Amnon.

Baal-Meon—Palestine. A fenced city of Gad. A place of idolatry.

Baal-Peor—Palestine. Here Balaam came to curse Israel.

Baal-Perazim—Palestine. Here David smote the Philistines.

Baal-Shalisha—Palestine. The inhabitants of this place sent presents to Elisha, at Gilgal. South of this place stood Micah's house of idolatry.

Baal-Tamar—Palestine. Here the Israelites smote the Benjamites.

Baal-Zephon—Egypt. Opposite this place the Israelites pitched their tents, previous to passing through the Red Sea.

Babel, or *Babylon*—Turkey. Here the Lord confounded the language of the children of Noah during the building of the Tower of Babel.

Babylon, or *Babel.* The royal city of the kings of Assyria. The place of the captivity of the children of Israel.

Babylonia, or *Chaldea*—Turkey.

Baca, Valley of—Palestine. Celebrated for its mulberry-trees.

Bahurim—Palestine. At this place Shimei cursed David.

Bamoth—Palestine. An encampment of the Israelites.

Bashan—Palestine. Celebrated for its large oak-trees.

Bashan-Havoth. All the cities in this country were taken by Jair, the son of Manasseh.

Bashan, Hill of—Palestine.

Bealoth—Palestine. A boundary-town between Judah and Dan.

Beer, or *Beer-Elim*—Syria. Here the Israelites halted, and sang praises, after finding water.

Beer, or *Beeroth*—Palestine. Here Jotham, the son of Jerubbaal, secreted himself from his brother Abimelech, who sought to slay him.

Beer-lahai-roi—Palestine. Here an angel appeared unto Hagar, and promised her a son, who was called Ishmael.

Beersheba—Palestine. Here Abram planted a grove, and built an altar, after his covenant with Abimelech, king of Gerar, to whom he represented his wife as being his sister.

Beersheba, Wilderness of—Here the angel appeared unto Hagar, and pointed out a spring of water.

Bela, or *Zoar*—Arabia. One of the cities of the plain, from which Lot and his two daughters fled, previous to its destruction by fire.

Bene-Berak—Syria.

Bene-Jaakan—Arabia. A station of the Israelites.

Berachah, Valley of—Palestine. The place of thanksgiving of Jehoshaphat and his army, after they had defeated the Moabites in Seir.

Berea—Turkey. Here Paul and Silas preached.

Berotha—Turkey. David conquered this city, and found great treasures of brass.

Besor, River—Here David met with an Egyptian, who conducted him to the army of the Amalekites.

Besor, Desert of—Palestine.

Betah—Turkey.

Beten—Palestine.

Bethabara—Palestine. Here John baptized our Lord, and here the ark rested, while the Israelites passed the Jordan.

Bethanah—Palestine. A fenced city.

Bethany—Palestine. This was the abode of Lazarus and his sisters. Here Christ cursed the fig-tree.

Beth-Arabah—Palestine. A boundary-town.

Betharabel—Palestine. Denounced by the prophet Hosea.

Beth-Aven—Palestine. From this place Joshua sent spies to Ai, which city he afterwards subdued.

Beth-Aven, Wilderness of—Palestine. Near this place the children who derided Elisha were destroyed by two bears.

Beth-Barah—Palestine. Gideon took possession of the countries between this place and Jordan.

Beth-Car—Palestine. The Philistines were subdued by the Israelites at this place.

Beth-Dagon—Palestine. A boundary-town on the borders of Syria.

Bethel, or *Luz*—Palestine. Here Jacob dreamed that he saw a ladder, and set up his pillow of stone as a pillar of testimony.

Bethel, Mountains of—Palestine. At this place a great battle was fought, between the Israelites and Philistines.

Bethel, Wilderness of—Palestine.

Bethesda, Pool of—Miraculous waters. Here Christ healed a man who had been waiting thirty-eight years.

Beth-Jeshimoth—Palestine. An encampment of the Israelites.

Bethlehem-Ephratah—Palestine. *The birth-place of our Saviour.* Here David was crowned king by Samuel.

Beth-Maachah—Syria. This city was taken from the Israelites by Benhadad, king of Syria.

Bethmillo—Syria. Here Abimelech was made king.

Bethonnaba—Syria. A city of the priests. Here Abimelech, the priest, furnished bread, and the sword of Goliath, to David, when he was pursued by Saul.

Bethphage—Syria. From this place Christ made his triumphant entry into Jerusalem.

Beth-Rehob—Syria. A city of the Levites.

Bethsaida of Galilee. At this place Christ restored sight to a blind man.

Bethsaida, or *Chorazin*—Syria. Denounced by Christ on account of the unbelief of its inhabitants.

Bethshalisha—Syria. See *Baal-shalisha.*

Bethshan—Syria. A principal city of Decapolis. The bodies of Saul and his three sons were fastened to the walls of this city by the Philistines.

Bethshemesh. An idolatrous city of Egypt.

Bethshittah—Syria. The Midianites fled to this city when pursued by Gideon.

Bezek—Palestine. At this place the kingdom of Israel was confirmed to Saul.

Bezek. At this place Judah defeated the Canaananites and Perizzites.

Bezer, or *Bozrah, in the wilderness* of Palestine. A city of refuge, and a city of the Levites.

Bithynia—Turkey. Paul and Timotheus were prevented by the Spirit from visiting this country.

Boaz, Field of—Syria. Here Boaz first saw Ruth.

Boscath—Syria. The birth-place of Jedidah, Josiah's mother.

Bozez, Rock of—Syria. This rock formed a pass, and here Jonathan and his armour-bearer smote twenty Philistines. Afterwards the lot was cast between Saul and Jonathan. Near this place Samuel anointed Saul.

Bozrah. A capital city of Svria.

Buz—Turkey. A city in alliance with the princes of Edom.

Cabul—Palestine. Given by Solomon to Hiram king of Tyre for sixscore talents of gold.

Calah—Turkey. Built by Asshur.

Caleb—Palestine. Here Hezron, one of the judges of Israel, died.

Caleb's Land. Caleb's Field and Tomb.

Calneh—Turkey. A city built by Nimrod.

Calvary, Mount. This was the common place of execution in Judea. Here Christ was crucified.

Camon—Palestine. Jair, a judge of Israel, was buried here.

Cana of Galilee. Here the Saviour performed his first miracle by turning water into wine.

Canaan—Palestine. The scene of the principal events recorded in the Scriptures.

Capernaum—Palestine. The place where Christ commenced his public ministry.

Caphar-Sorek—Palestine. The residence of Delilah before she became the wife of Samson.

Caphtorim—Lower Egypt.

Cappadocia—Turkey. A country visited by Paul.

Carbon—Syria.

Carchemesh—Turkey. Besieged and taken by Nebuchadnezzar.

Caria—Turkey. The coast visited by Paul.

Caria, Sea of—Mediterranean. Sailed over by St. Paul.

Carmel—Palestine. Here Nabal had possessions, and Abigail his wife sent presents to David.

Carmel, Mount. On this mount Elijah was answered by fire from heaven.

Casiphia—Persia. The country from whence Ezra brought the Nethinims to Jerusalem.

Casiphia, Sea of—Persia. The Caspian Sea.

Cedron or *Kedron.* David, in fleeing from Absalom,

crossed this brook, and Christ crossed it to enter the garden where he was betrayed.

Cedron, Fields of. To this place the idolatrous images and vessels were taken from the temple at Jerusalem and destroyed by order of Josiah.

Cenchrea—Greece. The port where Paul performed his vow.

Cesarea Philippi—Palestine. Here our Saviour revealed himself to his disciples.

Cesarea. Here Peter preached the gospel to Cornelius and his household.

Chabor—Persia. A place of captivity under Tilgath-pilneser.

Chaldea or *Babylonia*—Turkey. This was the country where Daniel prophesied.

Charran—Turkey. Here Abraham sojourned and received the command to go to Canaan.

Chebar, River—Turkey. Here Ezekiel had his visions.

Chemosh—Palestine. A place of idol worship built by Solomon.

Cherith, Brook of—Palestine. Here Elijah was fed by the ravens.

Chezib—Palestine. The birth-place of Shelah.

Chimham—Palestine. The residence of Chimham.

Chios, Isle of—Levant. An island where St. Paul touched on his way to Miletus.

Chor-Ashan—Palestine. To the inhabitants of this city David sent the spoil which he had taken from the Amalekites.

Chun—Palestine. David took the shields of gold from the inhabitants of this place.

Cilicia—Turkey. A country visited by St. Paul, and the place of his nativity.

Cinnereth, Lake of Gennesareth—Palestine. On this sea and on the coasts thereof, Christ wrought many miracles. Here Peter walked on the water. Here also Christ stilled the tempest.

City of Palm-trees, or *Jericho*—Palestine. The Israelites were conquered at this place by Eglon, king of Moab, for their disobedience.

Clauda, Isle of—Mediterranean. An island under which Paul sailed with danger, on his way to Rome.

Corinth—Greece. Here Paul became acquainted with Aquila, and here he resolved to go to the Gentiles.

Cuth—Russia. A place of idol-worship.

Cyprus, Isle of—Mediterranean. The birth-place of Barnabas.

Cyrene—Barbary. The birth-place of Simon, who bore the cross of the Saviour.

Dalmanutha—Palestine. Visited by the Saviour after he had performed the miracle of the loaves and fishes.

Dalmatia—Turkey. Here Titus ministered the gospel.

Damascus—Syria. Near this place Abram defeated the armies under Chedorlaomer. Near this place Saul was miraculously converted.

Dan—Palestine, near the springs of Jordan.

Danneh—Palestine. A city in the mountains.

David, City of. The southern part of Jerusalem, which was built by David.

Dead Sea—Palestine. This was formerly the plain of Jordan, and the most fertile and beautiful valley in the world.

Debir—Palestine. A city taken by Joshua.

Decapolis—Palestine. A country which was visited by the Saviour.

Derbe—Turkey. Visited by Paul immediately after he was stoned.

Dothan—Palestine. Here Joseph was sold by his brethren to the Ishmaelites, and here the army which came to take Elisha was smitten with blindness.

Dumah—Palestine.

Dung Gate. An eastern gate of Jerusalem repaired by Nehemiah.

Dura, Plain of. Here Nebuchadnezzar set up his image, ninety feet high, for refusing to worship which, the three Hebrew children were cast into the furnace of fire and were preserved.

East Country—Media and Persia. The country from whence Abram came.

Ebal, Mount—Turkey. Here Moses pronounced twelve curses, and Joshua erected an altar for burnt-offerings.

Ebenezer, stone called—Palestine. Here the Israelites defeated the Philistines.

Eber—Persia. A colony of Arphaxad.

Ed—Syria. An altar erected by the Israelites in testimony of their vows to God.

Edar, Tower of—Persia. The tents of Israel were spread near this spot for a temporary residence. This tower is supposed to have been occupied by the shepherds at the time the angels announced the birth of Christ to them.

Eden, Garden of—Turkey. Its present location supposed to be on the banks of the Arab River, not far from the mouth of the Euphrates. Here God created Adam and Eve.

Edom—Arabia.

Eglaim—Arabia. Referred to by Ezekiel.

Eglon—Palestine.

Egypt, or *Land of Ham.* Here Moses was miraculously preserved from death in infancy, as also our Lord by the flight of Joseph and Mary. It was also the scene of Joseph's life.

Ekron—Syria. Here the ark rested on its way to Ashdod.

Elah, Valley of. Here David slew Goliath.

Elam or *Persia.*

Elam in Syria.

Elath—Arabia. A principal sea-port from whence Solomon brought gold from Ophir.

El-Bethel—Palestine. Jacob erected an altar here when he fled from Esau.

El-Elohe-Israel. An altar erected by Jacob in the Promised Land.

Elim—Palestine. An encampment of the Israelites where there were twelve wells and seventy palm-trees.

Elisha, Isles of—Levant. Celebrated for the production of blue and purple linen.

Elkosh—Palestine. The birth-place of Nahum the prophet.

Emmaüs—Palestine. A village near Jerusalem to which two of the disciples were journeying on the day of the resurrection when Christ appeared to them and talked with them.

Endor—Palestine. Here Saul invoked a witch to raise Samuel, who appeared and announced the destruction of his army and his own death with that of his sons next day.

En-Eglaim—Arabia.

Engedi—Palestine. Here David took refuge in a cave, and here he spared the life of Saul.

En-Hakkore—Palestine. Here Samson slew one thousand men with the jaw-bone of an ass.

Enon—Palestine. Here John baptized.

Enrogel—Jerusalem. Here Adonijah usurped the kingdom of David, and here he was slain by the order of Solomon.

Ephesus—Turkey. One of the seven Churches.

Ephraim, Mount. Here Joshua the son of Nun had an inheritance.

Ephraim, Wood of. Here Joab killed Absalom.

Ephraim or *Ephron*—Palestine. Here Jesus retired with his disciples after raising Lazarus.

Ephrath—Palestine. Near this city Rachel died and was buried.

Ephron, Field of—Palestine. In which was the cave where Abraham and Sarah were buried.

Erbonah—Arabia. A station of the Israelites.

Esek. A well dug by the servants of Isaac near Beersheba.

Eshcol—Palestine. From this place the spies sent by Moses brought grapes and pomegranates.

Eshtaol—Palestine. Samson was born and buried between this place and Zorah.

Etam, Rock of—Palestine. Here three thousand men of Judah assembled against Samson.

Etham. A part of the Desert of Arabia where the Israelites wandered forty years.

Ethiopia—Turkey.

Euphrates—Turkey. A principal river of Eden.

Ezel, Stone of—Palestine. Here David and Jonathan made a covenant together.

Ezion-Geber—Arabia. A port for Solomon's navy.

Fair Havens—Mediterranean. A port touched at by Paul on his voyage to Rome.

Fish-gate—Jerusalem. Rebuilt by the son of Hassenaah.

Fuller's Field—Palestine. Here Isaiah met Ahaz, and predicted that a virgin should conceive.

Gaash, Valley and Brooks of—Palestine. An inheritance of Joshua.

Gaash, Hill of. Here Joshua was buried.

Gadara—Palestine. Here Christ dispossessed of the evil spirits the man who dwelt among the tombs.

Galatia—Turkey. Here St. Paul preached the gospel and established a Church.

Gilead—Palestine. Jacob made a covenant with Laban at this place.

Galilee. One of the principal divisions of the Holy Land. The scene of the principal events in the life of Christ, and the place appointed by him previous to his death for an interview after his resurrection with his disciples.

Galilee, Sea of. A body of fresh water seventeen miles long and eight broad, abounding in fish.

Gath—Palestine. David fears Saul, feigns himself mad, and goes to the king of this place.

Gath-Hepher—Palestine. The birth-place of Jonah.

Gaza—Palestine. Samson carried away the gates of this city to the top of a hill.

Geba—Palestine. Here Jonathan smote the garrison of the Philistines.

Gebal—Arabia. A seaport of Syria.

Gennesaret—Palestine. The sick were healed here by touching the hem of Christ's garment.

Gerar—Palestine. The dwelling-place of Isaac during the famine. Here he denied his wife.

Gergesa—Palestine. Here Christ performed the miracle of the swine.

Gerizim, Mount—Palestine. Here Moses pronounced twelve blessings, Joshua wrote the law of Moses on stone, and Jotham delivered his parable of the trees.

Geshur—Palestine. Absalom fled to this place after killing his brother Amnon.

Gethsemane—Palestine. An occasional resort of Christ. The scene of his agony and the place of his betrayal.

Gezer—Palestine. The king of this city with the whole of his army was defeated by Joshua.

Gibeah—Palestine. At this place the Levite slew his concubine. Saul dwelt here, and seven of his sons were slain by the inhabitants.

Gibeon—Palestine. Five kings of the Amorites slain here by a hail-storm. During the battle the sun and moon stood still.

Giblum—Syria. The Giblites were employed by Solomon to prepare stones and timber for the temple.

Gidom—Palestine. The Benjamites were smitten by the children of Israel and pursued hither.

Gihon, River—Persia. The second river in Eden.

Gihon, Fountain of. Solomon was here anointed.

Gilboa, Mount. The scene of Saul's death—cursed.

Gilead—Palestine. The place where Joseph was sold.

Gilead, Ramoth. A city of refuge.

Gilgal This was the first place taken by Joshua west of

the Jordan. Here Samuel hewed Agag king of the Amalekites to pieces.

Giloh—Palestine. The birth-place of Ahithophel, the counsellor of David.

Goath, *Valley of*. Between Jerusalem and Mount Carmel, and declared to be holy unto the Lord forever.

Gog.—Russia. A colony of Japheth.

Golan—Palestine. A city of refuge.

Golgotha, or *Calvary*—Palestine.

Gomorrah—Palestine. One of the cities of the plain and destroyed by fire from heaven.

Goshen—Palestine. Here Joshua defeated the Canaanites.

Goshen—Egypt. Here Joseph received his brethren. This land was exempted from the plagues which were inflicted by the Almighty on other parts of Egypt.

Gozan—Persia. A place of captivity.

Great Sea—Mediterranean—Navigated by Paul.

Greece or *Achaia*.

Gur—Palestine. At this place Jehu smote Ahaziah, after which he fled to Megiddo and died.

Gur-Baal—Palestine. Uzziah smote the Arabians that dwelt in this place.

Habor—Persia. Pul and Tiglath carried the Reubenites, Gadites, and half tribe of Manasseh, captives to this place.

Halah—Russia. The Israelites were carried captive to this place.

Ham, *Land of*. Includes the whole of Africa, Arabia, and part of Persia.

Hamath. A kingdom of Syria.

Hamath—Palestine. Northern boundary.

Hammon-Gog—Palestine. Ezekiel prophesied that this should be the burial-place of Gog and his multitude.

Hapharim—Arabia. A station of the Israelites.

Haran—Mesopotamia. Terah, Abram and family, resided here.

Hareth, *Forest of*—Palestine. Here Saul commanded his

servants to slay the priests of the Lord. They refusing, Doeg the Edomite killed eighty-five of them.

Harod, Well of. Here the Midianites fell by the hand of Gideon—the stratagem of lamps and pitchers.

Harosheth—Palestine. Sisera's vast army was defeated here by Deborah and Barak. Jael slew him by driving a nail through his head.

Havilah—Turkey. A part of the land of Eden.

Hazerim—Arabia. The dwelling-place of the Avims.

Hazeroth—Arabia. A station of the Israelites. Here Miriam was struck with leprosy.

Hazor—Syria. The tent of Jael was near here.

Hebron—Palestine. A city of refuge. Here Sarah died. Here Joab killed Abner, and David wept over his grave.

Hebron, Vale of—Palestine. Here Joseph was thrown into the pit.

Helam—Palestine. At this place David conquered the Syrians.

Helbah—Palestine. The Canaanites were never expelled from this place.

Helbon—Syria. Celebrated for its wine and white-wood.

Helkath—Palestine. Here twelve valiant men of Ish-bosheth and David slew each other.

Hepher—Palestine. The king of this place was taken by Joshua.

Heres, Mount—Palestine. The Amorites kept possession of this place in despite of the Israelites.

Heshbon—Palestine. A city of the Amorites taken by Joshua. The fish-pool was here.

Hiddekel, River. One of the rivers of Paradise.

Hierapolis—Turkey.

Hill Country—Palestine. The city of Hebron was here.

Hinnom, Valley of—Palestine. Jeremiah declared that it should be called the Valley of Slaughter, because the Jewish parents offered children in sacrifice to Moloch in this place.

Hobah—Syria. At this place Abram gained a victory over Chedorlaomer and his allies.

Hor Mount, or *Seir*—Arabia. Here Aaron, after being stripped of his priestly robes by Moses, died and was buried.

Horeb—Arabia. Here God commanded Moses to strike the rock to supply the Israelites with water.

Hormah, or *Zephath*—Palestine. Here the Israelites were smitten by the Amalekites and Canaanites.

Hukok—Palestine. A Levitical city.

Hur—Palestine. Smitten by the Israelites under Moses.

Ibleam—Palestine. A city of the Levites.

Iconium—Anadolia. In the province of Lycaonia. Here St. Paul preached in the synagogue.

Idumea, or *Edom*—Arabia. The Greek name of Edom. This place was denounced by Isaiah. From this place a great multitude followed Christ.

Ijon, or *Ivon*—Palestine. A fenced city, smitten by Ben-hadad king of Syria.

Illyricum—Turkey. Here St. Paul preached the gospel.

India—Hindoostan. So named from the river Indus.

Ish-tob—Syria. Here the Syrians came to help the children of Ammon.

Isles of the Gentiles. Islands in the Mediterranean.

Jabbok, River—Palestine. Sihon king of the Amorites was defeated at this place.

Jabbok, Fords of—Palestine. At this place Jacob wrestled with the angel and called the place Peniel.

Jabesh-Gilead—Palestine. Here Saul destroyed the Ammonites and afterward became the first king of Israel. Here also the bodies of Saul and Jonathan were deposited.

Jabneh—Palestine. A strong city of the Philistines conquered by Uzziah.

Jacob's Well—Palestine. Here Christ conversed with the woman of Samaria.

Jahaz—Palestine. A city of the Levites. Sihon king of the Amorites was defeated here by Moses.

Japhet—Asia. So called from one of the sons of Noah who peopled the whole of Europe and part of Asia.

Japho, or *Joppa*—Palestine. The port at which materials were received for the building of the temple.

Jazer—Palestine. Taken by the Israelites under Moses.

Jehoshaphat, *Valley of*—Palestine. This place is called the King's Dale. Here Absalom set up a pillar. It was a favourite cemetery of the Jews.

Jehovah-jireh—Palestine. At this place Abraham was about to offer up Isaac as a burnt-offering, but the angel of the Lord prevented him.

Jehovah-Nissi—Arabia. Here Moses erected an altar and here Aaron and Hur held up his hands while he prayed.

Jehovah-Shalom—Palestine. Here the angel appeared to Gideon and brought fire out of the rock.

Jericho, or *City of Palm-trees*—Palestine. Here the spies of Joshua were hid by the harlot Rahab.

Jericho, *Plains of*—Palestine. On the arrival of the Israelites at this place the manna ceased and they ate of the fruit of the land of Canaan.

Jericho, *Waters of*—Palestine. The impurity of these waters was removed by Elisha.

Jeruel, *Wilderness of*—Palestine. Here the inhabitants of Jerusalem overcame the combined forces of Ammon, Moab, and Mount Seir.

Jerusalem, *Salem*, *Jebus*, or *Ariel*—Palestine. Supposed to have been founded by Melchizedek. It was afterward taken by the Jebusites who erected the fortress called Jebus, on Mount Zion. David expelled them, and built the city of David, and made it the seat of government. Here David died and was buried.

Jezreel—Palestine. Near this place was Naboth's vineyard.

Jezreel, *Valley* or *Plain of*—Palestine. Here the Spirit of the Lord descended upon Gideon, and he received a sign by which the fleece was wet or dry at his bidding.

Jogbehah—Syria. Here the army of Zebah and Zalmunna was overthrown by Gideon.

Joppa—Palestine. Here Jonah took ship for Tarshish. Here Peter restored Tabitha to life.

Jordan, Plains of—Palestine. This was chosen by Lot on his separation from Abraham.

Jordan, River. The principal river of Palestine—rises in Mount Lebanon and empties into the Dead Sea. Our Lord was baptized in its waters.

Judah, on Jordan—The bridge supposed to be Jacob's is near this place.

Judah, Mountain of—Palestine. Hebron, a city of refuge, stood on this mountain.

Judea—One of the grand divisions of Palestine in the time of *our Saviour*, and of which Herod was tetrarch.

Judea, Wilderness of—Palestine. It was to this place Jesus was led by the Spirit; here he fasted forty days, and was tempted by the devil.

Kadesh—Arabia. Here Miriam, the sister of Moses, died and was buried.

Kadesh-Barnea—Arabia. Here the Israelites encamped.

Kadesh-Meribah—Arabia. Here the rock gave water, and Moses offended the Lord.

Keilah—Palestine. Here David smote the Philistines, for robbing the threshing-floors of Keilah.

Kenath—Palestine. Taken from the Amorites by Nobah, who afterwards called it by his own name.

Kidron, or *Cedron*, *Brook of*—Palestine. Shimei was forbidden by Solomon to pass over this place, on pain of death.

Kidron, Fields of—Palestine. Here Hilkiah burned the images and vessels of idolatry, by order of Josiah.

Kir-Hareseth—Syria. Here the Moabites were deceived by the miraculous appearance of water. The king of Moab offered his eldest son as a burnt-offering.

Kirjathaim—Palestine. The Emims, in this place, were smitten by Chedorlaomer.

Kirjath-arba—Palestine. Here Sarah, the wife of Abraham, died.

Kirjath-huzoth—Syria. Here Balak brought Balaam, to curse the people of God.

Kirjath-jearim—Palestine. The ark of the Lord was brought from Abinadab's house, and Uzzah was struck dead for touching it.

Kishon, Brook—Palestine. Here the prophets of Baal were slain, by the order of Elijah.

Lachish—Palestine. Taken by Joshua, who smote Horam, king of Gezer, who came to defend it.

Laish—Palestine. Here the children of Dan robbed Micah of his idols, and took his priest with them.

Lasea—Mediterranean. St. Paul sailed under this place, in his voyage to Rome.

Laodicea—Turkey. Here St. Paul preached, and wrote his First Epistle to Timothy.

Lebanon, Mountains of—Syria. Celebrated for its cedars.

Lebanon, Valley of—Palestine. Joshua destroyed all the cities and inhabitants from Mount Halah unto this place.

Lebonah—Palestine. Near this place the Benjamites carried off the daughters of Shiloh.

Leshem—Palestine. Taken by the children of Dan, who called it Dan-Laish.

Lycaonia—Turkey. A province of the Roman Empire, in Asia, in the time of the apostles.

Lydda—Palestine. Here Peter cured Eneas of the palsy, after he had kept his bed eight years.

Lydia—Turkey. A province of the Roman Empire.

Lystra—Turkey. Here Paul healed a cripple.

Maacha—Palestine. Here David defeated the Ammonites.

Macedonia—Turkey. A province of Greece, visited by the Apostle Paul.

Machpelah, Cave of—Palestine. The burial-place of Abraham and his wife Sarah.

Madon—Palestine. The king of this place, with several others, was destroyed by Joshua, at the waters of Merom.

Magdala—Palestine. Christ took shipping and sailed to this place, after feeding five thousand miraculously.

Mahanaim—Palestine. So named by Jacob, after he met the angels.

Mahaneh-Dan—Palestine. The birth-place of Samson.

Mamre, Plain of—Palestine. Here Abraham entertained three angels, who revealed the destruction of Sodom. Here, also, he received the promise of a son.

Manasseh, on this side Jordan.

Marah—Arabia. Here Moses sweetened the waters, by throwing into them the branch of a tree.

Maralah—Palestine. Here Asa smote the Ethiopian, who came out against him with a great army. Here, also, the prophet Micah was born.

Mars' Hill—Turkey. Here was the court of the Areopagites, and here Paul preached to the Athenians.

Massah, Rock of—Arabia. So called by Moses, after he had smitten the rock, from whence water was obtained.

Mattanah—Palestine. Here the princes of the Israelites dug a well, by the direction of Moses, with staves.

Meah, Tower of—Palestine. Rebuilt by Eliashab, the high-priest.

Media—Persia. One of the countries of the Bible.

Megiddo—Palestine. One of the purveyorships of Solomon.

Melita—Malta. An island in the Mediterranean, where St. Paul was shipwrecked.

Memphis—Egypt. The residence of the kings of Egypt.

Merom, Waters of—Palestine. Here divers kings were overcome by Joshua.

Meroz—Palestine. The inhabitants cursed.

Michmash—Palestine. Here Samuel announced to Saul that his kingdom should not be continued to him.

Midian—Arabia. Moses fled to this place and married an Egyptian woman, named Zipporah.

Miletus—Turkey. Visited by Paul, on his way to Jerusalem.

Millo, House of. Built by Solomon, in the city of Jerusalem. Here the men of Shechem made Abimelech king.

Mitylene—Asia. Visited by Paul, on his way to Jerusalem.

Mizpeh—Palestine. Here Jephthah made his rash vow.

Mizpeh, of Moab—Palestine. David came to this place with the four hundred men who joined themselves to him at the cave of Adullam.

Mizpeh, or *Stone of*—Palestine. Set up by Samuel.

Mizraim—Egypt, or land of Ham.

Moab—Palestine. Taken by Sihon, king of the Amorites.

Moab, Plains of—Palestine. From thence Balak first sent for Balaam.

Moreh, Vale of. Abram passed through this place, on his way to Bethel.

Moriah, Land of—Palestine. The country to which Abraham was commanded to take his son, and offer him on a mountain, which was to be shown him.

Moriah, Mount. Palestine. Here was the threshing-floor of Ornan. Here the Lord accepted the sacrifice of David, and stayed the hand of the destroying angel. Here Solomon erected the temple.

Myra—Turkey. Visited by St. Paul.

Nahor, City of—Algezira. To this place Abraham sent his servant, to get a wife for his son Isaac.

Nain—Palestine. Near the gate of this city Christ raised the widow's son to life.

Nazareth—Palestine. This was the dwelling-place of our Saviour until he was thirty years of age. Here the Jews threatened to cast him from the brow of the hill.

Neapolis—Turkey. Visited by St. Paul.

Nebo, Mount—Palestine. From this mount Moses had a view of the promised land. Here he died.

Nicopolis—Turkey. From this place St. Paul wrote his Epistle to Titus.

Nimrod, Kingdom of—Turkey. The first kingdom on record; established by a son of Cush.

Nineveh—Turkey. A city built by Asshur. The inhabitants, repenting at the preaching of Jonah, were saved.

No—A celebrated city of Egypt.

Nob—Palestine. This city, and its priests, were destroyed by Saul.

Nod, Land of—Persia. Cain fled to this place, after the murder of his brother.

Og, Kingdom of—Palestine. Subdued by Joshua.

Olives, Mount of, or *Mount Olivet*—Palestine. From this place our Lord made his triumphant entry into Jerusalem.

Ophir—India. From this place Solomon obtained his gold.

Ophrah—Palestine. Here an angel appeared to Gideon.

Oreb, Rock of—Palestine. The rock on which two princes of the Midianites were slain, by order of Gideon.

Padan-Aram—Turkey. The country of Nahor, Abram, Isaac, and Jacob.

Palestine—Turkey. The name of the country formerly occupied by the Philistines; now the Holy Land.

Pamphylia—Turkey. Here Paul and Barnabas parted.

Paphos—Syria. Here Elymas, the sorcerer, was struck blind, at the word of Paul.

Paran, Wilderness of—Arabia. The dwelling-place of Ishmael.

Parvaim—Persia. From this place gold was carried for the ornaments of the temple.

Patara—Turkey. St. Paul touched here, on his way to Phœnicia.

Patmos, Isle of—Archipelago. Here the Apostle John was banished, and here he had his revelation, which closed the canon of Scripture.

Peor, Mount—Palestine. On this mount Balaam pronounced a blessing upon Israel.

Perea—Palestine. A province of the Roman Empire, in the time of Christ.

Perez-Uzzah—Palestine. So named from the judgment inflicted on Uzzah.

Perga—Turkey. Visited by St. Paul.

Pergamos—Turkey. One of the seven Churches of Asia.

Pethor—Turkey. The dwelling-place of Balaam.

Pharpar, River—A river in Syria.

Phœnicia—Palestine. Here Paul and Barnabas preached.

Phenice—Levant. A port in the island of Crete, where St. Paul encountered the Euroclydon, and was shipwrecked.

Philadelphia—Turkey. One of the seven Churches of Asia.

Philippi—Turkey. Visited by St. Paul, and from whence he wrote his epistles to the Corinthians.

Phrygia—Turkey. Visited by St. Paul.

Pirathon—Palestine. Here Abdon, one of the judges of Israel, died and was buried.

Pisgah, Mount. The highest peak of Mount Nebo, where Moses had a view of the promised land.

Pisidia—Turkey. Visited by St. Paul.

Pison, River—Persia. The first river of Paradise.

Pithom—Egypt. A city built by the Israelites, under their task-masters.

Plain, Sea of the—Palestine. The Dead Sea.

Pontus—Turkey.

Potter's Field—Palestine. The burial-place of strangers in Jerusalem.

Ptolemais—Palestine. The Canaanites were never expelled from this place. Here Paul sojourned, at the house of Philip.

Puteoli—Italy. St. Paul stopped here seven days, on his voyage to Rome.

Rabbah—Palestine. Besieged by Joab.

Rachel's Tomb—Palestine. A pillar was erected here over Rachel's grave by Jacob.

Rahab—Egypt.

Ramah or *Arimatheá.*

Ramah—Palestine. Between this place and Bethel the prophetess Deborah dwelt under a palm-tree.

Ramath-Lehi—Palestine. Here Samson slew one thousand Philistines.

Rameses—Egypt. A city built by the Israelites, in bondage.

Ramoth-Gilead—Palestine. A city of refuge. At the instigation of false prophets, Jehoshaphat and Ahab went up against this place, and the latter was slain.

Red Sea—Arabia. The children of Israel crossed this on dry ground. The Egyptians following them were drowned.

Rehob—Palestine. The spies sent by Joshua searched the land from the Wilderness of Zin to this place.

Rehob, Kingdom of—Syria. The inhabitants of this place were smitten by the Israelites under Joab.

Rehoboth—A city built by Asshur in Turkey.

Rehoboth, Well of—Palestine. A well dug by the herdmen of Isaac after their contention with the herdmen of Gerar.

Rephidim—Arabia. At this place the Israelites defeated the Amalekites.

Rhegium—Italy. Paul touched here on his way to Rome.

Rimmon, Rock of—Palestine. Here six hundred Benjamites hid themselves in caves for four months from the fury of the Israelites.

Rogelim—Syria. Barzillai came down from this place and went over the Jordan with David.

Rome—Italy. Here Paul dwelt two years, and here he wrote Epistles to the Galatians, Ephesians, Philippians, Colossians, Philemon, and the Second Epistle to Timothy.

Salamis—Syria. Here Paul preached in the synagogues.

Salcah—Palestine. A country of giants conquered by the Israelites under Moses.

Salem—Palestine. Here Jacob purchased a portion of land, pitched his tents and built an altar. Near this place John baptized.

Salmone—Candia. Passed by Paul, on his way to Rome.

Salt, Valley of—Syria. Here Amaziah slew ten thousand Edomites.

Samaria—Palestine. Built by Omri. Ahab was buried here.

Samaria, Hill of. Purchased by Omri, who built a city thereon.

Samaria, Pool of—Palestine. Here Naboth was stoned by a stratagem of Jezebel wife of Ahab, and here the dogs licked her blood.

Samos—Archipelago. Touched at by Paul.

Samothracia—Archipelago. Visited by Paul.

Sardis—Turkey. One of the seven Churches of Asia.

Sechu, Well of—Palestine. Saul sent to this place for Samuel and David. (1 Sam. xix, 22.)

Seir, Land of—Syria. To this place Jacob sent messengers to propitiate his brother Esau.

Seir, Mount—Palestine. Given to Esau for a possession.

Seirath—Palestine. Ehud fled here after killing Eglon.

Selah—Arabia. Here Amaziah slew those servants who had slain Joash, his father.

Seleucia—Syria. Paul and Barnabas came to this place immediately after they were sent to preach the gospel to the Gentiles.

Seneh, Rock of—Palestine. Seneh and Bozez are the two rocks forming the passes of Michmash where Jonathan miraculously defeated the Philistines.

Sheba—Arabia. The queen of this country having heard of Solomon's wisdom, came to prove him with hard questions.

Shebarim—Palestine. The Israelites were driven to this place by the men of Ai.

Shechem—Palestine. Here Joshua made a covenant with

the children of Israel and set up a great stone as a witness unto them. This was the last public act of his life.

Shem—Persia. Peopled by the descendants of Shem.

Shiloh—Palestine. The tabernacle was set up at this place.

Shinar, *Land of*—Turkey. Part of the kingdom of Nimrod.

Shittim, *Valley of*—Palestine. A place of captivity.

Shunem—Palestine. At this place Elisha and his servant were entertained by a woman who had a chamber built for him. The prophet promised her a son, whom he afterward restored to life.

Shushan—Persia. The winter residence of the Persian monarchs, and the place where Daniel prophesied.

Sidon—Palestine. Founded by the eldest son of Canaan.

Sihon, *Kingdom of*—Palestine. Conquered by the Israelites.

Sihor, or *Nile*. The great river of Egypt.

Siloam, *Pool of*—Palestine. A blind man washed in this pool and was restored to sight.

Siloam, *Tower of*—Palestine. Eighteen persons were killed by the falling of this tower.

Sin, *Wilderness of*—Arabia. At this place the Israelites murmured for bread, and manna and quails were given them.

Sinai, *Mount*—Arabia. The Lord descended in a cloud upon this mount and gave Moses the law of the Ten Commandments.

Sirah, *Well of*—Palestine. Joab sent messengers to this place after Abner.

Smyrna—Turkey. One of the seven Churches of Asia.

Sodom—Palestine. Here Lot dwelt and entertained the angels, who warned him to flee from it.

Sorek, *Valley of*—Palestine. At this place Samson abode with Delilah, and here she betrayed him.

Succoth—Egypt. Jacob built him a house and lived here for a time.

Syracuse—Naples. At this city Paul tarried three days on his way to Rome.

Tabbath—Palestine. Here the Midianites were defeated by Gideon.

Taberah—Arabia. The fire of the Lord burned here upon the Israelites for their complaining against him.

Tabor, Plain of—Here Saul's heart was changed and he was numbered among the prophets.

Tabor, Mount—Palestine. Here Barak and Deborah assembled ten thousand men against Sisera and defeated his host.

Tadmor in the Wilderness—Syria. A city built by Solomon.

Tarshish—Spain. The most celebrated port in the time of Solomon from whence ships traded to all the then known parts of the world.

Tarsus—Turkey. The birth-place of St. Paul.

Taverns, The Three—Italy. To this place the brethren came to meet Paul when he was on his way to Rome.

Tekoa, Wilderness of—Palestine. Here Jehoshaphat assembled his army previous to battle.

Telabib—Turkey. Here the spirit of prophecy was given to Ezekiel.

Telaim—Palestine. Saul was sent by Samuel to this place, to utterly destroy the Amalekites; but sparing Agag their king and the best of the cattle, he was rejected of the Lord.

Teman, Idumea, or *Edom.*

Thebez—Palestine. From a tower of this city a woman dropped a stone upon the head of Abimelech, after which he was slain at his own request by his armour-bearer.

Thessalonica—Turkey. Here St. Paul preached in the synagogue of the Jews.

Thyatira—Turkey. One of the seven Churches of Asia.

Tiberias, Sea of—Palestine. On the shores of this sea Christ wrought many miracles.

Timnath—Palestine. Here Samson chose his wife and killed a lion.

Timnath-Serah—Palestine. The inheritance of Joshua, and here he was buried.

Tiphsah—Turkey. This city was despoiled by Menahem, and wanton cruelty was inflicted upon the women.

Tirzah—Palestine. A royal city, and some time the seat of government.

Tabor—Palestine. The residence of Jephthah. Here Christ was transfigured.

Tophet—Palestine. Places of idol worship were erected here by the children of Judah.

Troas—Turkey. Here the brethren waited for Paul, and here he celebrated the Lord's supper with them.

Trogyllium—Turkey. Here Paul tarried on his way to Jerusalem.

Ulai—Persia. Here Daniel saw the vision of a ram with two horns.

Ur of the Chaldeans—Turkey. The primitive abode of Terah, Abram, Nahor, and Haran.

Uz, Land of—Syria. The country of Job, a wealthy prince of Arabia Petræa.

Valley-gate—Palestine. Uzziah built towers near this gate.

Vineyards, Plain of—Palestine. Near this place the daughter of Jephthah came to meet her father.

Water-gate—Palestine. Here the people gathered together and requested Ezra to bring out the Book of the Law of Moses, which he read distinctly, gave the sense, and caused them to understand its meaning.

Zair, or *Seir*—Syria. Here Joram smote the Edomites.

Zalmon, Mount—Palestine. Here Abimelech cut wood, with which he burned the tower of Shechem and one thousand men and women.

Zanoah—Syria. The inhabitants of this place repaired the valley-gate of Jerusalem together with the wall and dung-gates.

Zarephath—Palestine. To this place Elijah was commanded to go to a woman who would support him. Here he restored the meal and oil.

Zaretan—Palestine. Near this place the Israelites crossed the Red Sea. Hiram king of Tyre caused the immense brass pillars for Solomon's Temple to be cast between this place and Succoth.

Zeboiim—Palestine. A city of the plain destroyed by fire from heaven.

Zeboiim, Vale of—Palestine. At this place the Israelites were obliged to go down to the Philistines to sharpen their axes, coulters, and mattocks.

Zelah—Palestine. Here was the sepulchre of Kish, in which the bones of Saul and Jonathan were finally deposited.

Zelzah—Palestine. Rachel's sepulchre was near this place. Here also Saul was anointed by Samuel.

Zephathah—Palestine. Here Asa king of Israel overcame the vast army of the Ethiopians under Zerah, which consisted of one million soldiers and three hundred chariots.

Zereda—Arabia. The birth-place of Jeroboam.

Ziklag—Palestine. A city given by Achish king of Gath to David.

Zion—Palestine. Taken by David from the Jebusites.

Ziph; Wilderness of—David fled from Saul to this place, and Jonathan comforted him.

Zoar—Palestine. A city in the vale of Siddim, to which Lot retired by the permission of the Lord previous to the destruction of Sodom.

Zobah—Syria. Saul made war against this country.

Zoheleth, Stone of—Palestine. Here Adonijah conspired against David and usurped the kingdom.

Zophim, Field of—Palestine. One of the three places where Balak caused seven altars to be erected, and brought Balaam to curse Israel.

INDEX.

Compendium of Methodism.

A Compendium of Methodism: embracing the History and Present Condition of its various Branches in all Countries; with a Defense of its Doctrinal, Governmental, and Prudential Peculiarities. By Rev. James Porter, D.D. Revised edition.

12mo., pp. 501. Price.. $1 00

This work has received universal favor. The facts that our bishops have put it in the course of study for local preachers, and that it has been translated into the German and Scandinavian languages, commend it to the confidence of all Methodists. Its peculiar advantages are, 1. That it gives a connected history of Methodism from the beginning in all countries, and in all its denominations. 2. That it shows our doctrinal agreements and disagreements with other sects. 3. That it exhibits the different systems of church government in the world, and the relative merits of each. 4. That it explains and defends all our prudential means of grace and other peculiarities as no other book does. It is a WHOLE LIBRARY in one volume, and is a *labor*-saving as well as a *money*-saving production. Its importance to preachers and others is indicated by the following testimonials:

It is, in fact, a digest of Methodism. The arrangement and execution of the several parts are admirable. The style is a model of perspicuity, ease, and vigor; and in point of condensation, the volume is literally crowded with important matter. We have hardly seen as great compactness without confusion, or an equal number of pages from which so few could be eliminated without detriment. But what is far more important than the mode of composition is the spirit which pervades the work. The author writes with that candid discrimination so essential to the proper discussion of the topics which he handles.—*Ed. of North. Adv.*

This work is a valuable acquisition to our Church literature. It embodies much important information, arranged in a natural and convenient form, and affords a good general outline of Methodism. It is a work of much merit. I do cheerfully commend it, as a whole, to the favorable consideration of our friends and the public generally.—T. Morris, *Bishop of M. E. Church.*

I like the book much. It will do good. Our people and friends ought to read and study it thoroughly. It furnishes a satisfactory answer to the petty objections urged against the Methodists by a set of ecclesiastical croakers with which we are everywhere beset. One gentleman, whom I let have a copy, after reading it carefully, remarked, "It is the book needed; I would not take *twenty dollars* for my copy if I could not obtain another."—Rev. Justin Spaulding.

I have just finished the reading of this book, and I wish to express my decided approbation of it. *It should be a family book*, a Sunday-school book, and I would add especially, *a text-book for all candidates for the ministry.*—J. T. Peck, D.D.

The work throughout is *not* a criticism on Methodist usages, but a statement and defense of them. As such, we trust it will meet with the wide circulation it deserves, both in and out of the Church.—*Methodist Quarterly Review.*

We have examined the book, and most cordially recommend our friends, one and all, to procure it immediately. No Methodist can study it without profit, and gratitude to the great Head of the Church for the wisdom imparted to those who have been the instruments employed in constructing the rules and regulations under which the operations of this most successful branch of the Church are conducted.—*Editor of the Christian Guardian, Toronto.*

It is precisely the volume needed to instruct our people in the peculiarities of our system. The *special* character of Methodism is here developed in such a manner as to show that it is specially excellent, and worthy of *special* zeal and *special* sacrifices. It is very systematically arranged, and therefore convenient for reference on any given point. To the Methodist, especially the "official" Methodist, this book is fitted to be a complete manual; and to all others who would understand what Methodism precisely is, as a whole, or in any specific respect, we commend Dr. Porter's work as an ACKNOWLEDGED AUTHORITY.—A. Stevens, LL.D.

The Life and Times of Bishop Hedding.

Life and Times of Rev. Elijah Hedding, D. D., late Senior Bishop of the Methodist Episcopal Church. By Rev. D. W. CLARK, D. D. With an Introduction, by Rev. Bishop E. S. JANES. Pp. 686. Price, large 12mo., $1 50; 8vo., $2 00.

A memoir of the Rev. Dr. Hedding, late senior bishop of the Methodist Church, has been prepared by the Rev. Dr. Clark, which is published in a handsome volume. It professes to portray the life and times of this venerable man, and involves almost the entire history of this denomination, at least for some thirty years past. In the controversies and vicissitudes of the denomination during this period, Bishop Hedding took always a prominent part, giving the characteristic form and policy to the issue. He was evidently a man of great energy and power, and possessed those personal qualities which make fast friends and gave him a preponderating influence in the Church of which he was so long bishop. The religious traits of his character were prominent as well as peculiar. The memoir is composed with great beauty of style and affectionateness of feeling: and altogether it will be regarded by the denomination as a welcome and instructive work.—*New-York Evangelist.*

We have received a copy of this work, which presents, mechanically, an elegant appearance. We have not yet found time for its perusal, but when we do, we shall speak more minutely of it. The name of Bishop Hedding lingers in the memory of the Church like the fragrance of a rose after its beauty hath departed, and is cherished with a filial fondness, while that of the talented author is a surety that his onerous but honorable task is well performed. This book must have a large and ready sale.—*North-Western Christian Advocate.*

Life of Rev. Robert Newton.

The Life of Rev. Robert Newton, D. D., by THOMAS JACKSON, embellished with a fine portrait. 12mo., pp. 427. Price, $1 00.

This volume is destined to have a great run. Although it has been published in London but a few weeks, *sixteen thousand* copies have already been sold.

Temporal Power of the Pope.

The Temporal Power of the Pope: containing the Speech of the Hon Joseph R. Chandler, delivered in the House of Representatives of the United States, January 11, 1855. With Nine Letters, stating the prevailing Roman Catholic Theory in the Language of Papal Writers. By JOHN M'CLINTOCK, D. D. 12mo., pp. 154. Price, 45 cents.

A series of letters to the Hon. J. R. Chandler, stating the prevailing Roman Catholic theory in the language of papal writers, forms the substance of this volume. They were prepared in reference to the speech of Mr. Chandler, delivered at the last session of Congress, and from the position and character of the writer, as well as from his mode of treating the subject, are eminently deserving of public attention.—*N. Y. Tribune.*

Carlton & Phillips, No. 200 Mulberry-street, New-York, have just issued a neat duodecimo volume of one hundred and fifty-four pages, with the foregoing title. It needs not that we say the work is a most timely and masterly production.—*Western Christian Advocate.*

www.ingramcontent.com/pod-product-compliance
Lightning Source LLC
LaVergne TN
LVHW020057110826
845151LV00001B/2

* 9 7 8 1 4 2 5 5 4 5 2 3 9 *